CHAUCER STUDIES XII

CHAUCER AND THE EARLY WRITINGS OF BOCCACCIO

CHAUCER AND THE
EARLY WRITINGS OF BOCCACCIO

DAVID WALLACE

D. S. BREWER

First published 1985 by D. S. Brewer
an imprint of Boydell & Brewer Ltd
PO Box 9, Woodbridge, Suffolk IP12 3DF
and 51, Washington Avenue, Dover, New Hampshire, 03820, U.S.A.

British Library Cataloguing in Publication Data

Wallace, David
    Chaucer and the early writings of Boccaccio.—
    (Chaucer studies; 12)
    1. Chaucer, Geoffrey—Sources 2. Boccaccio,
    Giovanni—Influence—Chaucer
    I. Title   II. Series
    821'.1   PR1912.B6

    ISBN 0-85991-186-1

Photoset in Great Britain by
Rowland Phototypesetting Ltd, Bury St Edmunds, Suffolk
and printed by St Edmundsbury Press,
Bury St Edmunds, Suffolk

For
The Master, Fellows,
Students and Visiting Scholars
of
St Edmund's House, Cambridge

Contents

PREFACE

The study of Chaucer and Boccaccio turns up many fascinating questions. What is it about Boccaccio's early writings that Chaucer finds so congenial? Why does he never mention Boccaccio by name? Why, if he held Dante and Petrarch in such high regard, does he not try to become more like them and less like Boccaccio? How good was his Italian? What mental image did he form of Boccaccio, as poet, scholar and human being, during his visit to Florence in 1373? Such questions are certainly intriguing, and I shall attempt to answer some of them in the course of this book. But they remain secondary to the book's chief subject, which is Chaucer's development as a European poet fashioning extended narrative from the limited resources of his native vernacular. This development may best be viewed along the axis of the Chaucer-Boccaccio relationship: for this relationship promises unique access both to Chaucer's most strenuous and localised efforts at *makinge* and to his most lofty and generalised aspirations for an English *poesye*. It is vital that these two aspects, the local and the general, be viewed within a single framework. Chaucer has assumed immense historical importance as the originating father-figure of a national tradition; and Chaucer himself, one feels, would have been well pleased at being thus rehabilitated within his own House of Fame. But in elevating Chaucer to the statuesque status befitting 'the father of English poetry', we tend to overlook and underestimate the uncertainty, flux and experimentation which attended his writing. Artistic uncertainties are, admittedly, often voiced at the surface of Chaucer's fictional world; but do they relate to genuine, experienced uncertainties, or are they just part of the fiction? Boccaccio's early writings offer us unique opportunities to look beneath the surface of Chaucerian narrative.

This book crosses many inter-disciplinary boundaries. I have found it necessary to give some account of the cultural formation of each poet; to consider not only Italian and English traditions of narrative, but also their common French ancestry; and to consider popular as well as illustrious traditions (and the trafficking conducted between them). The list of European and North American scholars to whom I am indebted is, consequently, rather long. I would like to thank a number of them here whilst absolving them for any blame for what follows. My interest in the European Middle Ages was first aroused by some excellent teachers at the University of York: A. C. Charity, N. R. Havely, David Lawton, Derek Pearsall and the late Elizabeth Salter. This book owes most, however, to the learning, versatility, tolerance and skill of my three Cambridge supervisors: Derek Brewer, Robin Kirkpatrick and A. C. Spearing. The book's final form has benefited from much good advice offered by my Ph.D. examiners, Piero Boitani and Jill Mann. I would also like to thank the following scholars for their criticisms, encouragement and friendship: Thomas Cable, Janet Coleman, Tim Cribb, Philip Damon, Derek Dowson, Deborah Ellis, Jennifer Fellows, Kenelm Foster O.P., Helen Houghton, H. R. Jauss, Andrew King, Alastair Minnis, James I. Wimsatt and Nicolette Zeeman. Especial thanks to Rita Copeland for eroding my unreasonable resistance to new developments in the study of medieval rhetoric, in translation studies and in literary theory, medieval and modern; and thanks for much else besides. Some of the arguments advanced in this book were given late public airings at a number of meetings and conferences: Syracuse University Humanities Doctoral Program, Spring Lecture Series (March 1984); American Association for Italian Studies, Bloomington (April 1984); The Medieval Institute, Kalamazoo (May 1984); New Chaucer Society, York (August 1984). Many thanks to all those who talked things over with me on these occasions; you have helped me write a better book.

All foreign primary sources quoted in the text are accompanied by my own translations (except in parts of chapters V and VI, where Chaucer proves himself to have been a better translator than I could ever hope to be). Secondary sources in the text have generally been translated, although certain key phrases or passages of the original are often reported in the notes. All references to the writings of Chaucer follow *The Works of Geoffrey Chaucer*, edited by F. N. Robinson, second edition (Oxford UP, London, 1966). All references to Latin texts follow the editions of The Loeb Classical Library unless otherwise indicated.

I warmly appreciate the interest taken in this book by new friends and future colleagues at Stanford University and at The University of Texas at Austin. The book is dedicated to the memory of six happy and fruitful years at St Edmund's House, Cambridge.

David Wallace
St Edmund's House, Cambridge
September 1984

ABBREVIATIONS

Books and Periodicals
ASI   Archivio storico italiano
ASNSP   Annali della R. Scuola normale superiore di Pisa
CCS   Companion to Chaucer Studies
CID   The Cambridge Italian Dictionary
CNeo   Cultura neolatina
CR   The Chaucer Review
DELI   Dizionario enciclopedico della letteratura italiana
ED   Enciclopedia Dantesca
GDLI   Grande Dizionario della Lingua Italiana
GSLI   Giornale storico della letteratura italiana
IMU   Italia medioevale e umanistica
LI   Lettere Italiane
M&H   Medievalia et Humanistica
MED   Middle English Dictionary
MLN   Modern Language Notes
MP   Modern Philology
OED   The Oxford English Dictionary
PMLA   Publications of the Modern Language Association of America
S&A   Sources and Analogues of Chaucer's Canterbury Tales
SP   Studies in Philology
SsB   Studi sul Boccaccio

Works by Chaucer
Anel   Anelida and Arcite
BD   The Book of the Duchess
CT   The Canterbury Tales
FranklT   The Franklin's Tale
HF   The House of Fame
KnT   The Knight's Tale
LGW   The Legend of Good Women
MerchT   The Merchant's Tale

xi

PF	The Parliament of Fowls
Rom	The Romaunt of the Rose
Sq Tl	The Squire's Tale
T&C	Troilus and Criseyde
WBT	The Wife of Bath's Tale

Works by Boccaccio

AV	Amorosa Visione
CD	Caccia di Diana
CN	Comedia delle ninfe fiorentine
Dec	Decameron
Fc	Filocolo
Fs	Filostrato
NF	Ninfale fiesolano
Tes	Teseida

Works by Other Authors

DVE	De Vulgari Eloquentia
Inf	Inferno
JRB	Le Jugement dou Roy de Behaingne
Met	Metamorphoses
Par	Paradiso
Purg	Purgatorio
RF	Remede de Fortune
RR	Le Roman de la Rose
VN	Vita Nuova

English Romances

A	Athelston
A&A	Amis and Amiloun
F&B	Floris and Blauncheflur
Gam	Gamelyn
KH	King Horn
SL	Sir Launfal
SO	Sir Orfeo

Cantari

BB	Brito di Brettagna
BG	Il Bel Gherardino
CFB	Cantare di Fiorio e Biancifiore
DdV	La donna del Vergiù
F-e-F	Febus-el-Forte
Gib	Gibello
L	Storia di Liombruno
PT	Cantare di Pirramo e di Tisbe
SCS	Storia del calonaco di Siena
Sp.	Spagna
UIMT	Ultime imprese e morte di Tristano

Other Abbreviations

EETS	Early English Text Society
ES	Extra Series
GB	Giovanni Boccaccio
ME	Middle English
NS	New Series
OE	Old English
OF	Old French
OS	Original Series
OUP	Oxford University Press
Sd'I	Scrittori d'Italia

Introduction

Chaucer made more use of Boccaccio's early vernacular writings than of any other group of texts in any language. His most obvious and extensive debt is, of course, to the *Filostrato*. By juxtaposing the *Filostrato* with *Troilus and Criseyde* we may observe Chaucer's engagement in the line-by-line business of *makinge*. Chaucer's employment of other early Boccaccian texts is more troublesome to evaluate, or even describe, but its contribution to his poetic achievement is no less significant. The *Teseida* furnished a wealth of iconographic details for a wide range of Chaucerian narratives and a source for Chaucer's Knight.[1] The *Filocolo* suggested how an unpretentious tale of love and separation might support the weight of serious philosophical concerns; and how such an opus might be aligned with the *Commedia* and the *Roman de la Rose*. The *Filocolo*'s fourth Book, which provided a source for Chaucer's Franklin, juxtaposes an assembly of fowls with a parliament of courtiers and considers the situation of pagan lovers at the threshold of Christian enlightenment. The *Amorosa Visione*, like *The House of Fame*, attempts to accommodate the influence of Dante within the French-derived framework of a love vision. The *Ninfale Fiesolano*, like *Sir Thopas*, pays an affectionate, personal tribute to a popular, native tradition of stanzaic romance.

The subject of Chaucer and Boccaccio's early writings extends, then, from the minutest particulars of translation practice to the largest, most abstract questions of cultural enterprise. No subject offers better opportunities for the historicising of Chaucer as a European author. But although it seems full of promise, the subject has, over the years, proved to be a source of considerable critical frustration, and even (incredibly) of tedium. Towards the end of a lengthy chapter entitled 'The Relations of *Troilus and Criseyde* to *Filocolo*', for example, Karl Young admits that the 'dry comparison of details' conducted by his study has amounted to an 'arid and soulless process'.[2] Hubertis M. Cummings prefaces his 'investigation of the Chaucer-Boccaccio problem' by casting himself in 'the role of quasi-iconoclast'; having investigated (in pseudo-forensic fashion) various claims for Chaucer's usage of Boccaccian texts he arrives at conclusions which are 'almost unvaryingly negative'.[3]

The positivistic method of quantifying Chaucer's indebtedness to Boccaccio

I

by matching details of plot, imagery and characterisation had evidently exhausted its energies by 1916. The method enjoys a swansong, however, in the monumental study of Sanford B. Meech, who identifies himself at the outset as a disciple of Young.[4] But the real way forward to a better understanding of the Chaucer-Boccaccio relationship was pointed out by C. S. Lewis in his splendid pioneering effort of 1932, 'What Chaucer Really Did to *Il Filostrato*'.[5] The essay begins with a plea for historical understanding: if critical studies ignore 'the historical position and affinities of a book . . . they may leave us with a preposterous picture of the author as that abstraction, a *pure* individual, bound to no time or place'.[6] Lewis proceeds to deliver a fine account of Chaucer as 'an "Historial" poet contributing to the story of Troy'; as 'a pupil of the rhetoricians'; as 'a poet of *doctryne* and *sentence*'; and, finally, as 'the poet of courtly love'.[7] But Lewis does not extend his plea for historical understanding to consideration of the *Filostrato*. Virtually no space is dedicated to discovering the intentions and literary affiliations of this supposedly 'renaissance' poem.

Lewis' essay has been highly and deservedly influential: critical thinking over the last half-century has explored all the paths that Lewis signposted so clearly. But Chaucerians have still not troubled to learn much about Boccaccian texts before proceeding to deduce what Chaucer 'did' to them. Italian scholarship has been virtually ignored. Meech makes his ignorance a matter of policy:

> As for scholarship devoted to Boccaccio other than as a source for Chaucer, I shall draw upon it hardly at all. Since I approach the *Filostrato* and other works of his contributory to the *Troilus* as materials for Chaucer's transforming art, and not as the transformations, as they laudably are, of antecedent literature and of the Italian's personal experience, I need not be concerned with their particular sources, the general literary background of their author, his life before the courtship of Maria d'Aquino, nor even, very much, with this to him most momentous affair.[8]

The folly of this policy lies in equating the quality of our ignorance with the presumed ignorance of Chaucer himself. Any account of 'Chaucer's transforming art' must be preceded by some consideration of the literary and historical 'formation' of the text that Chaucer is engaged with, particularly when the text in question is the work of a near-contemporary vernacular author. In studying Boccaccio's early writings and the peculiar complex of Latin, French and Italian influences within which they took shape we come to appreciate why they proved quite so congenial to Chaucer. We also come to appreciate that the quality of literary and linguistic discernment that Chaucer brought to bear on these texts was extraordinarily high: Chaucer understood before he 'transformed'. The need for a broad-based assessment of Boccaccio's early writings is made especially urgent by past neglect and by the current realisation that Chaucer 'must have viewed the development of his own poetry' in a context which was 'essentially European, not narrowly insular'.[9] The feasibility of making such an assessment has been much enhanced in recent years by the remarkable revival of Boccaccian studies which was spearheaded by the publication (some three years before the appearance of Meech's *Design*) of Branca's *Boccaccio medievale*.[10] Branca's book upholds the promise of its polemical title by enabling us to appreciate that the foundations of Boccaccio's art are thoroughly medieval in character.

This book applies Lewis' plea for historical understanding to both sides of the Chaucer-Boccaccio relationship in order to situate the two writers within a common European framework. It makes extensive use of Italian scholarship, believing that the more we understand about Boccaccio's early writings the better sense we may make of Chaucer's reactions to them. The first four chapters devote considerable space to establishing 'the historical position and affinities' of Boccaccio's early writings. They introduce many of the complex questions of artistic enterprise that made the Italians such compelling reading for Chaucer. Chapters Five and Six pursue these questions through a detailed examination of Chaucer's appraisal, translation and augmentation of the *Filostrato* in *Troilus and Criseyde*. The final chapter summarises the attitudes that Chaucer and Boccaccio maintained towards popular and illustrious traditions of vernacular narrative and suggests that the two writers—despite irreconcilable differences in education, social sensibility and temperament—have more in common than Chaucer cared to admit or C. S. Lewis cared to imagine.

CHAPTER 1

Accommodating Dante: the Amorosa Visione and The House of Fame

When Chaucer travelled to Florence on a trade mission in the spring of 1373 he probably heard Boccaccio spoken of as Dante's most distinguished disciple.[1] As early as 1350 Boccaccio had been commissioned to present Dante's daughter Beatrice, a nun at Ravenna, with ten gold florins on behalf of the Florentine merchant Compagnia di Or San Michele.[2] Between 1350 and 1372 Boccaccio had written three versions of his biographical *Trattatello in laude di Dante*.[3] And on 23 October 1373 he gave the first of his celebrated Dante lectures at the Florentine church of Santo Stefano di Badia.[4] The public petition seeking these lectures (approved by a majority of 167 votes on 9 August) was submitted to the Florentine civic authorities in June 1373, just one month after Chaucer's return to England. Boccaccio was the obvious choice as lecturer.[5] It seems reasonable to suppose that discussion of this project would have been current in literary, civic and mercantile circles (the lectures were to cater for a broad, mixed audience) during Chaucer's stay at Florence. These first *lecturae Dantis* were, unfortunately, cut short by Boccaccio's terminal illness. Following his death on 21 December 1375, Boccaccio was mourned by his fellow poet, *novellatore* and sometime merchant Franco Sacchetti as one who had offered, as an alternative to the harsh, money-grubbing 'mechanical arts' of mercantile Florence, the arts of poetry, scholarship and literary criticism.[6] Boccaccio's death may well bring about the death of Dante studies:

> Come deggio sperar che surga Dante
> che già chi 'l sappia legger non si trova?
> E Giovanni ch'è morto ne fe' scola.   (91–3)

> How am I to hope that Dante might thrive
> since one who knows how to read him cannot now be found?
> And Giovanni, who is dead, schooled us in reading.

In 1373, then Boccaccio was looked to and spoken of as a distinguished champion of Florentine culture. But although he always took pride in his

5

Florentine citizenship, Boccaccio spent his formative years not at Florence but at Naples. The Boccaccian works that Chaucer made most use of date from this early, Neapolitan period: the *Filostrato* (1335); the *Filocolo* (1336–8); and the *Teseida* (1339–41).[7] Born in 1313, Boccaccio left Florence for Naples in 1327 and did not return until the winter of 1340–1. Two years later he wrote the *Amorosa Visione*, a poem which struggles to acclimatise itself to a radical change of culture.[8] It is the *Amorosa Visione* which records Boccaccio's 'first unconditional, whole-hearted adhesion to the civilisation of Tuscany and of Dante'.[9] Composed in *terza rima*, the verse form of the *Commedia*, the *Visione* stages a scene of tribute to Dante and vigorously upbraids the Florentine citizenry for its failure to uphold the great poet's fame:

> 'Viva la fama tua, e ben saputa,
> gloria de' Fiorentin, da' quali ingrati
> fu la tua vita assai mal conosciuta!'   (VI (A), 13–15)

> 'Let your fame live, and be well-known,
> O glory of the Florentines; by Florentine ingrates
> the recognition accorded to your life was miserably small!'

In 1373, then, the *Visione* was a Florentine poem in season. And as a poem which celebrates the fame of Dante (whilst attempting to contain Dante's influence within a French-derived, love vision framework) it would have been of urgent, topical interest to Chaucer. The *Visione* is certainly a problem poem: for four centuries, its editors and critics have been baffled, frustrated and embarrassed by its shortcomings.[10] But such shortcomings (if such they are) prove instructive when compared to those encountered within Chaucer's most problematical poem, *The House of Fame*. Chaucer follows Boccaccio in attempting to accommodate the influence of Dante within a French-derived, dream poem format. And he follows Boccaccio in producing a poem that has traditionally been taken to express a crisis in his development.[11] Perhaps this 'crisis' might be diagnosed as the after-effects of his first full exposure to 'the civilisation of Tuscany and of Dante'; as literary culture-shock.

It was long ago suggested that Chaucer's *House of Fame* borrows from Boccaccio's *Amorosa Visione*.[12] Various efforts have been made to prove or disprove this suggestion: but no definite conclusions can be reached either way because too many uncertainties envelop the texts of Boccaccio's poem.[13] And considered in isolation, such suggestions are of limited interest: they may not tell us much about the enterprise of either writer. But if such comparisons are preceded by some evaluation of the traditions which inform each poem—that is, if each poem is first established within its own context—they may prove more illuminating. And since the *Visione* might be regarded as a *summa* of Boccaccio's complex Neapolitan education, such an account will help contextualise Chaucer's usage of those Neapolitan works that he found so congenial.

It is important to recognise, at the outset, that Chaucer's primary debt (and primary commitment) was to his own vernacular tradition. His decision to write in English was by no means obvious or inevitable: Gower, after all, wrote extensively in Latin and French as well as in English. Chaucer could not commit himself to writing English narrative without committing himself, to some extent, to the forms of narrative that English made available. He certainly looked abroad, from the first, for literary models that might augment the resources of his chosen vernacular. But he never borrowed from foreign texts just to patch holes in the fabric of English narrative. Such texts were not simply *added to* English, they were *absorbed into* a growing body of language: chewed over, broken down, digested, atomised and reconstituted. Chaucer, like the pioneering poets of Italy, laboured to transform his native language from within by feeding it from without. Continental poets inspired and enabled Chaucer to write poetry in English.

It was the English metrical romances that provided the first foundations of Chaucer's narrative style.[14] In opening Book II of *The House of Fame*, Chaucer prefaces a catalogue of six classical and Biblical dreamers and imitations of Boccaccio and Dante with a call to attention reminiscent of *Havelock*'s abrupt beginning[15]:

> Now herkeneth, every maner man . . . (509)
>
> Herkneth to me, gode men . . . (1)

The couplet introducing Dido's lament for Eneas brings together a stock romance gesture and a double exclamation reminiscent of Orfeo's lament for Dam Heurodis[16]:

> She gan to wringe hir hondes two.
> 'Allas!' quod she, 'what me ys woo!' (299–300)
>
> 'Allas', quaþ he, 'now me is wo!' (331)

Only through the complex quality of its syntax[17] does Dido's first lament (300–10) surpass that of Orfeo (331–42). *Sir Orfeo* appears to have exerted a long and fruitful influence on Chaucer's imagination.[18] In toiling upward to the 'castel' (1161, 1185) in which Fame is to be found Chaucer seems to be following as much in the footsteps of the English romance hero as in the *orme* ('footsteps') of Boccaccio and Dante:

> Amidde þe lond a castel he seiʒe
> Riche and real and wonder heiʒe.
> Al þe ut-mast wal
> Was clere and schine as cristal.
> An hundred tours þer were about,
> Degiselich and bataild stout.
> Þe butras com out of þe diche
> Of rede gold y-arched riche.
> Þe vousour was avowed al
> Of ich maner divers aumal.
> Wiþ-in þer wer wide wones
> Al of precious stones;
> Þe werst piler on to biholde
> Was al of burnist gold . . .
> . . . .

7

No man may telle, no þenche in þouȝt,
Þe riche werk þat þer was wrouȝt . . .

. . . .
Orfeo knokkeþ atte gate . . .

. . . .
'Parfay!' quaþ he, 'icham a minstrel, lo!'

(355–68; 373–4; 379; 382)

Chaucer follows the poet of *Sir Orfeo* in exploiting the quick movement of short couplets to accumulate a wealth of fabulous detail. The outer wall of the castle in *Sir Orfeo* is translucent ('clere') and shines like crystal; Chaucer improves upon this (and lends didactic weight to his narrative) by having his castle built upon a 'roche of yse' (1130) which 'shoon ful more clere' than 'alum de glas' (1124–5). Chaucer shares the romancer's fascination with architectural details[19] in describing the exterior of his castle (1181–94); his interior is similarly resplendent with 'gold' and 'the fynest stones' (1342–53). Both poets throw up an edifice that is distinctively gothic in character[20]; both proclaim its magnificence with an inexpressibility topos. (Chaucer's extraordinarily lengthy topos (1167–80) incorporates the romancer's rhyming of 'þouȝt' with 'wrouȝt' (1173–4).) Sir Orfeo identifies himself as a minstrel at the castle gate; the first human figures espied by Chaucer at the castle are 'mynstralles' (1197) and the first sound heard is that of 'Orpheus' playing (1201–3). Orfeo's harping captivates the inhabitants of the castle, who lie down at his feet (439–41); lesser harpers sit beneath Orpheus and gape upward in admiration (1209–11). Orfeo is brusquely requested to give an account of himself; Chaucer is similarly interrogated:

Þe king answerd, 'What man artow
Þat art hider y-comen now?'   (421–2)

And seyde, 'Frend, what is thy name?
Artow come hider to han fame?'   (1871–2)

Chaucer and Orfeo give similarly modest accounts of themselves and their art (1873–82; 429–34). Chaucer's modesty in *The House of Fame* is commendable: but having surveyed the limited capabilities of his native vernacular Chaucer must have realised that he had much to be modest about when approaching French, Italian and Latin authors. Such a realisation becomes a vital element of *The House of Fame*, a work which meditates most energetically upon 'the relation of poetry to the traditions which form its material'.[21]

Chaucer, we have noted, elected to expand the capabilities of English narrative by imitating the illustrious example of foreign texts. His first models were French: his translation of a portion of the *Roman de la Rose* may well have marked the launching of his poetic career.[22] In *The Book of the Duchess*, composed some time after the death of Blanche of Lancaster in 1368,[23] Chaucer chose to work within the conventional bounds of the *dits amoreux*, a poetic tradition that had developed from Guillaume de Lorris to Guillaume de Machaut.[24] In creating a poetic dream world in which a noble patron is seen to bring comfort and consolation to himself, Chaucer extended this tradition by imitating and improving upon the example of Machaut.[25] During the years

8

preceding the composition of the *Duchess* – years in which Machaut's great admirer and imitator, Froissart, was resident at the English court –[26] Chaucer must have been a diligent student of French verse. It has even been suggested that Chaucer began his poetic career by writing in French.[27] This, however, seems unlikely: for although the *Duchess* sometimes speaks with a practised French accent, it often falls back into what C. S. Lewis has termed 'the old, bad manner'[28]: the language of the English romances.

The House of Fame, composed some time after Chaucer's return from Italy in 1373, contains less systematic imitation of French material than does *The Book of the Duchess*: but W. O. Sypherd's claim that the poem is 'directly inspired by the Old French love-vision literature'[29] remains perfectly valid. The chief defect of Sypherd's useful book lies in its occasional attempts to drive a wedge between French and Italian literatures and the influence that they exerted on Chaucer.[30] Before considering Chaucer's engagements with Italian texts we may pause to acknowledge something that Chaucer and Italian writers before Petrarch would doubtless have conceded: 'the priority, the breadth, and the centrality of French literature in the Middle Ages'.[31] *Le Roman de la Rose* was of seminal importance for Italian as well as for English writers. D. J. Fansler (writing in the same period as Sypherd) implicitly accepted this in proposing that some influence from the *Rose* 'descended to Chaucer indirectly through Boccaccio and Dante, and Machault, Froissart and Deschamps'.[32]

But although *The House of Fame* is recognisably a descendant of *The Book of the Duchess*, it contains much that is new and differs from its predecessor 'in tone, intention and plan'.[33] Much of this new content and orientation attests to Chaucer's growing interest in the authors of classical antiquity. This interest was doubtless nurtured by Chaucer's first visit to Florence and by his first encounter with the writings of Dante: for Chaucer exhibits an interest not only in the *auctores* per se but also in their relationship to him as a vernacular poet. Such a relationship is established in the opening canto of the *Commedia* by Dante's acclamation of Vergil[34]:

> 'O de li altri poeti onore e lume,
> vagliami 'l lungo studio e 'l grande amore
> che m'ha fatto cercar lo tuo volume.
> Tu se' lo mio maestro e 'l mio autore,
> tu se' solo colui da cu' io tolsi
> lo bello stilo che m'ha fatto onore.'   (Inf I, 82–87)

> 'O honour and light of other poets
> may the long study and great love
> that has made me search your volume help me now!
> You are my master and my author,
> you alone are he from whom I took
> the beautiful style that has brought me honour.'

Dante's last two lines here look back to *De Vulgari Eloquentia* II, iv, 1–3 where it is proposed that vernacular eloquence may be attained by following the stylistic example of the great Latin poets ('poete magni').[35] We are offered a dramatic image of this process later in the *Commedia* as Dante follows after Vergil and Statius:

9

Elli givan dinanzi, e io soletto
di retro, e ascoltava i lor sermoni,
ch'a poetar mi davano intelletto.   (Purg XXII, 127–9)

They walked in front, and I walked alone
behind, and I listened to their disquisitions
which, in making poetry, gave me understanding.

When Chaucer 'follows after' Vergil in the first book of *The House of Fame* he produces what might be seen as a wryly ironic commentary on Dante's prescription for the achievement of vernacular eloquence. Chaucer's translation (or deformation) of the *Aeneid* begins as a tolerably close literal rendering (143–48), contracts to become a paraphrase (149–238) and then concentrates on the romance of Dido and Aeneas (239–382). Following a series of exempla derived from the *Heroides* (388–426), the paraphrase is continued (427–65) and then summarily concluded with a romancer's formula (466–7). Chaucer inserts his claim for poetic originality (311–14) just before Dido's lengthy *compleynt* (315–60); her second lament proves to be just as wooden and melodramatic as her first (300–10). The downhill progress which characterises this translation is evident elsewhere in the poem. Book III degenerates into repetitiveness and final silence; the 'Invocation' to Apollo with which it opens begins as a studied imitation of *Paradiso* I, 13–27 and ends in humorous self-deflation and with a blunt imperative (1091–1109).

Dante evidently succeeds Machaut as Chaucer's poetic mentor in *The House of Fame*. Attempts have been made to set Chaucer's poem against the *Commedia* in a systematic way[36]: but a more straightforward and telling comparison—one that Chaucer himself undoubtedly made—is yielded by juxtaposing the quick, nervous movement of Chaucer's octosyllabic couplets against the measured gravity of Dante's tercets. By the time Chaucer travelled to Italy in 1372, Tuscan had established itself still more securely as a *vulgaris illustris*[37]: viewed in such a context, Chaucer's poem presents itself as a rueful reflection on the state of an inchoate poetic vernacular. Its language cannot stand comparison with Dante's poetry. But its language, form and content do present instructive parallels with one of the *Commedia's* forebears: Brunetto Latini's *Tesoretto*. Dante encounters Brunetto among the sodomites of *Inferno* XV. He honours his sometime teacher as one who taught ' "how man makes himself immortal" '.[38]

The *Tesoretto*, which dates from the period of Brunetto's political exile in France (1260–6), draws its fundamental inspiration from the *Roman de la Rose* of Guillaume de Lorris.[39] It is written in couplets of seven-syllable lines, *settenari a rima baciata*. Brunetto is obviously frustrated by the limitations imposed by his metre; he complains aloud on several occasions and obviously yearns for the less restrictive medium of prose.[40] The encyclopaedic ambitions that strain the poem were more fully realised in the *Trésor*, a work in French prose with which the *Tesoretto* is closely associated.[41] Such ambitions are comparable to those worked out in the second part of the *Rose*, and Brunetto's employment of Boethius and Alanus de Insulis,[42] his urbane manner and his (occasionally) sarcastic wit[43] are often reminiscent of Jean de Meun: indeed, Brunetto has strong claims to be considered as a continuator of the *Rose* since his work predates Jean's extension of Guillaume's poem.

The narrative action of the *Tesoretto* begins when the author (returning from an embassy to Spain on behalf of the Florentine 'Comune') learns, from an itinerant scholar, of the Guelf defeat at Montaperti (114–162). Turning to another path, he loses himself in a forest before coming to the domain of Nature (163–282). Having instructed Brunetto in the wonders of Creation (283–1124), Nature points him down a path leading to Philosophy and her sisters (the other liberal arts) and the four Virtues; he may also come across Fortune, Barratry and the God of Love (1125–82). Armed with a banner that Nature has given him, Brunetto comes to a fine plain where he discovers many great, wise and famous men surrounding their Empress, Virtue (1183–1244). He explores the habitations of the queenly daughters of Vertute (1245–1356), and then accompanies a handsome knight who receives instruction in the knightly virtues (1357–2170). Finally, he goes on his way seeking Fortune and Love (2171–80). In May, he comes to a fair, flowered meadow, the Kingdom of Love (2181–2218). Among allegorical figures representing various aspects of Love, Brunetto falls under Love's spell (2219–2351); he makes this circumstance an excuse for the defects of his writings (2352–56). Ovid, who stands nearby, gives him sufficient ingenuity to escape the Kingdom (2357–95); Brunetto decides to repent and confess his sins (2396–2426).[44] At Montpellier, he confesses to a friar; he urges his close friend[45] to do likewise, encouraging him with an exposition of the seven deadly sins (2427–2876). Having renounced his desire to find Fortune, Brunetto returns to the forest; one morning he finds himself at the peak of Olympus (2877–99). From here he surveys the world (2900–10). He meets Ptolemy, who is about to grant his request for an account of the four elements when the poem breaks off, at line 2944.

Brunetto's poem exhibits obvious correspondences with many of the *dits amoreux* inspired by Guillaume's *Rose*, and points of correspondence with Chaucer's dream poems, particularly *The House of Fame*. The insatiable appetite for 'tydynges' (the word occurs some twenty-two times, singular and plural) which animates the narrator of Chaucer's second dream poem is matched by the ceaseless hunger for knowledge which drives the *Tesoretto*'s narrator forwards:

> E io, ch'ognora atendo
> di saper veritate
> de le cose trovate,
> pregai per cortesia
> che sostasser la via
> per dirmi il convenente
> de luogo e de la gente.   (2230–6)

> And I, who am always eager
> to know the truth
> of things encountered,
> asked if they, through courtesy,
> might delay their journey
> to tell me what I needed to know
> about the place and the people.

Here Brunetto, freshly arrived in the Kingdom of Love, stops four boys ('quattro fanti') to seek his bearings; like other narrators before and after him, he fails to realise that he is most vulnerable when most inquisitive.[46] Brunetto, like Chaucer, appears uncomfortable when cast in the role of lover: his references to personal involvement are brief and vague; he employs the wit of Ovid not to advance himself in love but to extricate himself from it (2343–6; 2390–3); he appears relieved to return to God and the saints (2400–3) and to offer up 'questo mio libretto' and all his other works to clerical scrutiny and correction,

> per far l'opera piana
> co la fede cristiana. (2413–4)

> to square the work
> with the Christian faith.

It is not, perhaps, surprising that the *Tesoretto* and *The House of Fame* should have so much in common: for both Chaucer and Brunetto stand near the beginnings of their native poetic traditions. Both writers attempt to expand the limited capabilities of their native vernacular by employing a French-inspired narrative framework to contain their particular sentimental, speculative and scientific interests. Both apply themselves to the task armed with a considerable knowledge of Latin learning, in which Boethius, Macrobius and Alanus de Insulis figure prominently; and both are intimately familiar with the rhetorical arts.[47] Both poets, in employing verse forms resembling Guillaume's octosyllabic couplets, find their chosen medium restrictive. Both poems end incomplete, at a point high above the earth, at a moment when the poet-narrator is about to receive illumination from a man of great authority.

The *Tesoretto*, which remained influential throughout the thirteenth century, represents the first phase of the process in which the example of the *Rose* was assimilated into Italian verse.[48] This process was continued by the *Detto d'Amore* and *Il Fiore*, two liberal reworkings of the complete *Rose* which date from the late thirteenth century.[49] The *Intelligenza*, an allegorical and didactic poem dating from the same period, makes use of the *Rose* and of other French writings in a still more free-handed way. The poem consists of three-hundred-and-nine stanzas of *nona rima*, nine-line stanzas of eleven-syllable lines rhyming ababababccb.[50] The poem's centrepiece consists of an extended description (stanzas 70–288) of the carvings and paintings ('l'intagli e le pinture', 70,7) which adorn the palace in which the poet's lady dwells. This description begins—after a cursory mention of the wheel of Fortune (70,8–9)—by depicting the God of Love and the famous lovers that he leads in chains ('le tenne in sua catena', 73,5). The diction is full of Gallicisms, owes something to the *stil nuovo* and perches precariously between courtly and popular registers:

> E non fallío chi fu lo 'ntagliadore
> e la bella Analida e'l buon Ivano;
> èvi intagliato Fiore e Blanzifiore,
> e la bell'Isaotta Blanzesmano,
> sí com'ella morío per fin amore,
> cotanto amò Lancialotto sovrano;
> èvi la nobile donna del Lago,
> quella di Maloalto col cuor vago,
> e Palamides cavalier pagano. (75)

And he who was the sculptor did not omit
the beautiful Anelida and the good Yvain;
Floire and Blancheflor are sculpted there,
and the fair Isolde of the White Hands—
how she died through *fin amors*,
so much did she love the peerless Lancelot—
the noble Lady of the Lake is there,
she of Maloalto with the yearning heart
and the pagan knight Palamides.

The poem opens with a joyful springtime scene (1–2) in which the narrator is struck to the heart by a ray from Love ('dal fin Amore', 3,7); it concludes with the formal unravelling of the allegory (299–309). The carvings and painted figures represent the beautiful memories ('belle rimembranze') from which these poetic records ('queste ricordanze') are made (303,1–4). The lady represents intelligence, and her palace the human soul that she inhabits:

l'amorosa Madonna Intelligenza,
che fa nell'alma la sua residenza,
che co la sua bieltá m'ha 'nnamorato.   (299,7–9)

the amorous Lady Intelligence,
who makes her home in the soul,
who, with her beauty, has made me enamoured.

Boccaccio's *Amorosa Visione* is recognisably a descendant both of the *Intelligenza* and of Brunetto's pioneering effort. Frequently echoing the *Tesoretto*,[51] the *Visione* continues and extends its basic artistic enterprise: French narrative models are adapted to Italian conditions and asked to support considerable didactic and erudite interests. The sheer weight of these interests cripples the effectiveness of Boccaccio's poem: the *Visione* is one of his least successful compositions. Yet it represents a vital crux both in Boccaccio's development and in the development of Italian verse: looking back to Brunetto's *Tesoretto*, it looks forwards to Petrarch's *Trionfi*.[52] Girolamo Claricio, the first sixteenth-century editor of the 'B' text, clearly regarded the *Visione* as being imitative of Petrarch: he promised his readers 'cinque Triomphi quasi al modo petrarchesco'[53] and on his title-page announced 'five Triumphs (Triumphi), namely the Triumph of Wisdom (Sapientia), of Fame (Gloria), of Riches (Ricchezza), of Love (Amore) and of Fortune (Fortuna)'.[54] However, it is now accepted that the *Visione* predates Petrarch's *Trionfi*: not only did it bring Petrarch inspiration, it also appears to have directed his attention to the *Roman de la Rose*, a work for which he exhibited pronounced distaste.[55] The five 'triumphs' of which Claricio speaks are frescoes, discovered within the confines of a noble castle. The dreamer, goaded on by his didactic female guide, observes them with varying degrees of fascination and indifference; he is evidently relieved to pass from the castle into a delightful garden, the *locus amoenus*, where he discovers companies of ladies (some dancing in a ring), Venus and Cupid and, finally, his beloved. An educated fourteenth-century reader (such as Chaucer) would have perceived the poem's fundamental French affiliations.

13

The episodic structure of the *Visione* presents parallels with a number of the *dits amoreux* which followed the *Rose*: for example, the *Fablel dou Dieu d'Amours* and *De Venus la Deese d'Amor*, two closely-related thirteenth-century compositions, feature descriptions of a Palace of Love in scenes held together by the presence of a perambulatory narrator.[56] The vision framework employed in Boccaccio's poem is featured in the *Fablel*, in Machaut's *Dit dou Vergier*, in Froissart's *Paradys d'Amours* and in several other poems, although it is by no means a standard feature of the French (and certainly not of the Italian) tradition.[57] The *Visione*'s headstrong, faintly comical narrator would not seem much out of place in a Machaut poem. The lady that guides him seems, like Esperence in Machaut's *Remede de Fortune*, to be simply 'a kindly supernatural female being rather than an embodiment of an abstract power'[58]; and yet both guides have firm didactic intentions.[59] Even the verse form of the *Visione* has a partial parallel in Machaut: the *Jugement dou Roy de Behaingne* employs a four-line stanza in which the first three lines have ten syllables and the fourth four; this, combined with the interlocking pattern of the poem's rhyme scheme (aaab—bbbc—cccd . . .) yields an effect which is closer to the movement of the *Visione*'s tercets than it is to that of the octosyllabic couplets which are the norm of the French tradition.

Froissart's *Paradys d'Amours* (the chief source of the dream frame of Chaucer's *Duchess*)[60] contains passages that bristle with erudition. The narrator and his female guides come across a *carole* in which some twenty-nine celebrated lovers from Latin antiquity and medieval romance are mixed together (974–995). The narrator's *lay* which follows this includes references to Pygmalion, Orpheus, Tantalus, Actaeon and his dog Melampus (1123–43); to Narcissus, Tristan, Jason and to four other lovers (1151–3). Boccaccio takes greater care in classifying his heroes and heroines: his tenth canto, for example, is chiefly dedicated to illustrious Romans, and his eleventh to figures from French romance. But he too often relies upon the heavy impact of a catalogue: the first fourteen tercets of canto XI (A) feature eighteen French knights, plus Guinivere and Isolde. Boccaccio's detailed knowledge of French romances attests to their great popularity in fourteenth-century Italy: but it also represents an unofficial aspect of his upbringing and education at Angevin Naples.

Boccaccio's earliest surviving composition, *La Caccia di Diana*, has much in common with the *dits amoreux*; *Olympia*—the fourteenth part of the *Bucolicum carmen*, an opus which was not completed until Boccaccio's final years —features a dog which recalls the animal guides of the French tradition.[61] In his discussion of this tradition, Sypherd has cause to refer to the *Amorosa Visione* on nine occasions: his final reference invites us to compare the description of the God of Love and his entourage in the *Visione* with that in a variety of *dits*. Given such correspondences, it is not surprising that the *Visione* proved popular in France.[62]

The *Amorosa Visione* has been hailed as 'the most Dantesque of Boccaccio's early writings'.[63] The most obvious Dantean feature of the poem is, of course, its verse form. The impoverished poetry of the *Visione* suggests that Boccaccio was not comfortable when working within the confines of *terza rima*: he characteristically struggles against the strait-jacket of the Dantean verse form in order to follow the more headlong impulse of the natural prose writer. He pursues long sequences of subordinate clauses across line-endings and occasionally drops into a narrative rhythm reminiscent of the *ottave* employed in earlier works.[64] The *Visione*'s diction sometimes recalls that of the popular narrative tradition known as the *cantare* from which Boccaccio inherited his *ottava*: Guinivere is compared to a 'stella mattutina'; Paris contrives to bring Helen 'in sua balia'.[65] Boccaccio's usage of courtly terminology here and elsewhere lacks the precision and control one would expect from an aristocratic author.[66] But Boccaccio was not an aristocrat; nor was he schooled in an aristocratic household. His usage of *terza rima* might possibly be taken to express certain aristocratic pretensions: but such pretensions were shared by a number of popular fourteenth-century writers who chose to employ the Dantean verse form.[67]

Brunetto Latini had discovered emperors, kings, great lords and 'mastri di sci̇enze' who 'dittavan sentenze' in the company of Virtue (*Tesoretto* 1229–32); Boccaccio discovers Dante as the central figure in the triumph of Wisdom, surrounded by the great authors of antiquity (A&B, IV, 7–VI, 33). Placing Dante among distinguished classical authors is an appropriate compliment, one that Dante was pleased to pay himself in *Inferno* IV, 70–147. It reminds us that Dante's prescription for the attainment of vernacular eloquence envisages intimate acquaintance with the *auctores*, 'quos amica sollicitudo nos visitare invitat'.[68]

Boccaccio follows Dante in bringing the heroes and iconographies of the ancient world into vernacular verse: but whereas classical matter in the *Commedia* subserves the needs of the narrative, in the *Visione* it threatens to overwhelm it. Each of Boccaccio's five *triumphs* is illustrated by figures culled from classical texts. Some figures are imaginatively treated, but imaginative movement within the poem is often clogged by their sheer weight of numbers. Boccaccio's engagement with classical learning was decisively intensified during his last years at Naples.[69] This engagement is recorded in the erudite (and sometimes extremely lengthy) glosses which surround the *Teseida*.[70] This encircling flood of erudition breaks into the poetic bounds of the *Visione*: the poem is swamped with learning.

The ambitious congestion of the *Amorosa Visione* expresses a crisis in Boccaccio's development which, in certain ways, compares with that experienced by Chaucer in his densely-peopled *House of Fame*. Both poets seem unable to control and synthesise the wealth of literary resources (vernacular and Latin; popular and illustrious) at their disposal. Working within a dream vision framework derived from the tradition of the *Rose*, they struggle to come to terms with the example of Dante and with their relationship as vernacular poets to the *auctores*. Both poets have derived from Dante a heightened sense of the importance of vernacular eloquence: but this has infected them with certain qualities of artistic self-consciousness which are quite foreign to Dante. There are moments in the *Commedia* at which Dante draws attention to his specific task as poet. But such moments—for example, the invocations to the Muses [71]—are of characteristically brief duration and are perfectly integrated into the fabric of the poem. In Boccaccio's early writings, such moments are made to *stand out*: Dantean examples are habitually imitated, inflated and moved to more obviously prominent contexts.[72] A similarly self-conscious 'poeticising' process is evidently at work in *The House of Fame*.[73] Chaucer is not yet managing to convince himself that an English *makere* can write as if he were an English poet. *The House of Fame*, then, measures the distance between the practice of English *makinge* and the prospect of English poetry.

To such parallels in artistic enterprise observable between the *Amorosa Visione* and *The House of Fame* may be added parallels in content and in narrative development. It is hardly surprising, given the encyclopaedic inclusiveness of the *Visione*, that the two works should have so much in common: but some figures accorded extensive individual treatment in Boccaccio's poem seem particularly reminiscent of Chaucerian creations and preoccupations. Both authors (in poems which question the nature of poetic enterprise) are fascinated by the figure of Orpheus, the most magical (and suspect) of artificers.[74] Boccaccio's Orfeo makes a brief first appearance among ancient thinkers in the *triumph* of Wisdom (A&B, IV, 70) before being discovered among celebrated lovers in canto XXIII (A&B, 4–30):

> Orfeo dico, che col suo ingegno
> fece le misere ombre riposare
> con la dolcezza del cavato legno.   (XXIII (A), 7–9)

> I speak of Orfeo, who through his genius
> made the miserable shadows rest
> with the sweetness of the hollowed-out stick.

Orfeo entrances nature ('made the miserable shadows rest') with his ingenious art ('ingegno'): but he does so by employing a rudimentary natural instrument (a 'hollowed-out stick'). Similar contemplation of the paradoxical relations of nature to artifice is occasioned by Chaucer's presentation of the same mythical figure. Lesser musicians 'gape' upon Orpheus and his peers

> And countrefete hem as an ape,
> Or as craft countrefeteth kynde.   (1212–3)

Art ('craft') imitates nature ('kynde'): but Orpheus, we were told earlier, plays 'ful craftely' (1203). Art surpasses art imitating nature.

The figure which dominates Boccaccio's imagination in the *triumph* of Love in which Orfeo appears is Dido: Boccaccio devotes the greater part of a canto to narrating her history and her relationship with 'Enea' (A&B, XXVIII, 1–63) and a further eighteen tercets to her two laments and her death (A&B, XXVIII, 64–XXIX, 30). Like Chaucer, Boccaccio mixes memories of Vergil (*Aeneid* I, IV) and Ovid (*Heroides* VII) with personal improvisation; like Chaucer he draws upon a typically medieval strain of legalistic imagery.[75] Such imagery is maintained in the briefer report each writer offers of the infidelity of Demophon (Demofonte) to Phillis (Fillis).[76] Chaucer continues his theme of male infidelity by listing ten lovers (397–404; all of these are featured in the *Visione*) and then concludes it with the example of Theseus and Adriane (405–26; AV A&B XXII, 4–24). Chaucer (and Boccaccio) tell how Theseus (Teseo) betrayed Adriane (Adriana) by boarding ship with her sister Phedra (Fedra). In describing the abandonment of Ariadne both writers again derive their report from the direct speech of Ovid's *Heroides*[77]:

nunc quoque non oculis, sed, qua potes, adspice mente
haerentem scopulo, quem vaga pulsat aqua. (X, 135–6)

'Just look at me now—you may look with your mind, if not
with your eyes—clinging to a rock, beaten by restless water.'

He lefte hir slepynge in an ile
Desert allone, ryght in the se . . . (416–17)

e lui chiamava piangendo e soletta
sopr'un diserto scoglio in mezzo mare: (XXII (A), 17–18)

and she called him, weeping and alone
on a deserted rock amidst the sea.

When the Chaucerian dreamer wanders out of the temple of glass in order to
discover his whereabouts (480) he comes to a point equivalent to that at which
the narrative action of Boccaccio's poem begins. A series of correspondences
between the English and Italian narratives may now be observed.

Both dreamers, fearful and alone, find themselves in a deserted place
(482–91; A&B, I, 22–5). Chaucer finds himself in 'a large feld' which 'nas but
of sond' and discovers 'no maner creature . . . me to rede or wisse'; Boccaccio
sees himself running aimlessly, fearfully alone, across uninhabited shores.[78]
Each dreamer then gratefully perceives the arrival of a celestial and golden
guide (494–508; I, 26–42). Chaucer, raising his 'eyen to the hevene', sees an
eagle 'faste be the sonne'. He then spends seven lines describing the golden
effulgence of this extraordinary bird: it shines with a brightness never before
seen,

But yf the heven had ywonne
Al newe of gold another sonne . . .   (505–6)

Boccaccio is joined by a beautiful woman. Raising his eyes ('s'alzò . . .
l'occhio mio') he sees that her blond head is surmounted by a crown that is
more brilliant than the sun ('più che 'l sole/fulgida'): she carries a fair golden
globe ('bel pomo d'oro') in her left hand.

In opening Book II, Chaucer appeals to Venus ('Cipris'), the Muses and
'Thought' to assist him in telling of his 'avisyon' (518–28). Boccaccio opens the
second canto of his Visione with an invocation which is similarly indebted to
Dante (II, 1–18). Like Chaucer, he appeals to Venus ('Citerea'); and like
Chaucer, he strives to concentrate the powers of his 'engyn' ('ingegno'):

non sofferir che fugga, o Citerea,
a me lo 'ngegno all'opera presente,
ma più sottile e più in me ne crea.   (II (A), 4–6)

Do not allow ingenuity, O Citerea
to escape me in this present work,
but kindle it within me, more subtle and more abundant.

Each dreamer is led upward by his guide (Boccaccio scales a series
of stairways) towards the place in which the lady Fame is to be found. The

eagle reassures Chaucer and insists that all this 'is for thy lore and for thy prow' (579: compare AV, I, 31–33); he then informs him that the vision has been granted as a reward for long and fruitless service to 'Cupido' (605–71). In opening his poem, Boccaccio had announced his desire to narrate ('narrare')

> quel che Cupido graziosamente
>   in vision li piacque di mostrare
> all'alma mia . . .   (I (A), 3–5)

> that which Cupido graciously
>   pleased to show in a vision
> to my soul . . .

Love and 'Love's folk' (645) are the chief interests of these dreamers: they do their best to ignore the more serious, didactic intentions of their guides. Chaucer turns a deaf ear to much of the eagle's instruction. Boccaccio, encouraged by two boys, actually stages a rebellion and goes off to explore on his own; his guide follows exasperatedly behind.[79] Each dreamer is attracted towards the place in which Fame has her dwelling, Chaucer by the sound that issues from it and Boccaccio by the light; each eagerly questions his guide about this place (1054–65; II, 70–75).

The narrative action of the final Book of the English poem begins as Chaucer climbs upward 'with alle payne' (1118). He comes to the foot of 'a castel that stood on high' (1161); climbing again, he comes to the 'castel' (1176) itself, describes its fabulous architecture (1181–94) and then encounters two groups of artists (1201–81). Chaucer emphasises that these two groups are clearly separated (1214–15): the first is centred on Orpheus (1201–13); the second comprises an extraordinary mixture of lesser musicians, magicians, tricksters and illusionists (1216–81). Moving on, Chaucer discovers the splendidly-crafted, golden 'castel-yate' (1294) and enters the castle.

Boccaccio, climbing upwards, finds himself at the foot of a noble castle ('a piè d'un nobile castello', I, 59). Having followed his guide into the castle, he breaks away from her and enters a hall ('gran sala', IV, 9) whose rich and fabulous architecture excites a comparison with the work of Giotto (IV, 16–18). Moving to the centre of the hall, he discovers two groups of famous figures depicted on one of the walls; standing to the left and right of Wisdom, they represent the Trivium and Quadrivium respectively (IV, 25–V, 88). Having identified these figures (IV, 40–V, 84) and paid his tribute to Dante (V, 79–VI, 33) Boccaccio moves on to discover Fame.

On entering 'Fames halle' (1357), Chaucer immediately encounters what might well be described as a *triumph* of riches (1307–40); he realises that the throng consists of the

> . . . pursevantes and heraudes,
>   That crien ryche folkes laudes . . .   (1321–2)

Chaucer describes the extravagant gold-plated and bejewelled decoration of the hall (1341–55), slipping in a sly aside on his own impoverished state (1348–9). In the *Visione*, the triumph of Fame is followed by that of Riches

(XII, 55–XIV, 84): this features a huge mountain of gold, silver and precious stones (XII, 58–60) and a meditation by Boccaccio on his own impecunious state (XIV, 55–84).

In describing Fame,[80] Chaucer and Boccaccio emphasise her imperial estate, her universal governance, her uniqueness and her association with riches; each account (1360–1406; VI, 41–75) is concluded with an acclamation.

Having contemplated Fame, Boccaccio presents a number of figures from pre-Christian history, beginning with Giano, a mythical founder of the Italian race:

> Turbato nell'aspetto e di furore
> pien seguiva Saturno . . .   (VII (A), 4–5)

> Troubled in expression and full
> of fury, he followed Saturn . . .

He then presents two descendants of Saturn, and two figures from ancient Jewish history (7–12). He features Dardanus (Dardano, 16–24), progenitor of the Trojans and thereby of the Italians; the remainder of the canto is largely given over to other ancient and mythical rulers, to Trojan heroes (58–75) and to figures associated with Alexander the Great (76–88). His next canto is chiefly dedicated to characters connected with Troy and Thebes, although it opens with three Old Testament paragons (Solomon, Sampson and Absalom) and features Hercules (VIII, 34–36).

Chaucer, having observed the way in which Fame upholds the renown of Alexander and Hercules (1407–14), presents a figure standing upon a pillar

> That was of led and yren fyn,
> Hym of secte saturnyn,
> The Ebrayk Josephus, the olde,
> That of Jewes gestes tolde . . .   (1431–4)

Chaucer explains (in an aside reminiscent of a *Teseida* gloss) why this Jewish historian (and his seven peers) should be standing upon such a pillar: lead and iron, we are told, are associated with Saturn and Mars respectively (1441–50). He then moves from Jewish to Theban and Trojan matter, beginning with the 'Tholosan that highte Stace' (1460; Boccaccio commemorates 'Stazio di Tolosa' in V, 34).[81] Chaucer proceeds to list a number of writers associated with the matter of Troy (1464–72); he ends with Geoffrey of Monmouth ('Englyssh Gaufride') who, for an English audience, provides a link between Trojan and native histories.

Chaucer next sees four illustrious Latin writers: these are all featured in the *Visione*'s fifth canto.[82] Vergil (1481–5; V, 7–16) and Ovid (1486–92; V, 25–27) are accompanied by

> The grete poete, daun Lucan,
> And on hys shuldres bar up than,
> As high as that y myghte see,
> The fame of Julius and Pompe.   (1499–1502)

19

A' quai Lucan seguitava, ne' cui
atti parea ch'ancora la battaglia
di Cesare narrasse e di colui,
    Magno Pompeo chiamato . . .   (V (A), 19–22)

After these followed Lucan, by whose
movements it seemed as if he still might be
narrating the battle of Caesar and of him
    called Pompey the Great . . .

Chaucer briefly notes the presence of 'clerkes/That writen of Romes myghty
werkes' (1503–4), tells of Claudian (1507–12) and ends by noting (but refusing
to identify) a rabble of 'hem that writen olde gestes' (1514–19). Boccaccio's
writers include a number of Roman historiographers (V, 55–63), 'Claudiano'
(50) and many others that he does not recognise (65–66).

Chaucer is distracted from his contemplation of these writers by the arrival
of a host of petitioners to Fame (1520–37): some of these have their wishes
granted by the 'noble quene' and some are disappointed (1538–41). Similarly,
the people who approach Boccaccio's 'sovrana donna' (VI, 66) are variously
delighted ('lieto') or offended ('offeso') by their lot (VI, 82–85). Chaucer
proceeds to expand his account of how Fame dispenses her favours in what is
arguably the dullest (and certainly the most repetitive) section of his poem
(1549–1867). Few parallels with the content and narrative development of the
Visione are discernible from this point onwards.

Chaucer's presentation of Fame is characterised by an ambiguity of attitude
and presentation that is absent from Boccaccio's account. He gazes upon the
'noble quene' and at the 'nobley, honour, and rychesse' in which she sits with
evident approval (1407–16): yet he had earlier described her as a freakish
creature of uncertain dimensions, whose dwelling is built upon a 'feble
fundament' (1132) with 'walles of berile' (1288) that shine brighter than glass
and distort true appearances (1289–91); the hall itself is of varying size
(1493–6). The petitioners to Fame are said to be equally deserving (1544–5):
but they are

                . . . dyversly served;
      Ryght as her suster, dame Fortune,
      Ys wont to serven in comune.   (1546–8)

Robinson comments on this supposed sisterly relationship:

There seems to be no definite authority for the statement that Fame and
Fortune are sisters, but the frequent association of the two, and the
obvious derivation of much of Chaucer's description of Fame from the
accounts of Fortune, make it natural for him to invent the relationship (if
he did).[83]

Whereas Chaucer elects to unite the characteristics of Fame and Fortune
within a single creature, Boccaccio presents two distinct figures: but he implies
that these figures are closely related by discovering 'Fortuna' in a hall ('sala',
XXXI, 3) which, he tells us, resembles that in which 'Gloria' had been found

(XXXI, 4–6). The figures in this last *triumph* are expressly contrasted with the happy and well-dressed figures that have gone before (XXXI, 7–12). 'Fortuna' is evidently envisaged as the negation of 'Gloria': repulsive in appearance, she is deaf to all appeals and blind in her actions (XXXI, 16–24). Her movements are capricious and unpredictable:

> e legge non avea né fermo patto
> negli atti suoi volubili e incostanti . . .
>
> (XXXI (A), 25–26)

> and she had no law nor firm compact
> in her fickle and inconsistent actions . . .

This unhappy vision excites a passionate personal statement from Boccaccio the dreamer (XXXI, 50–63). His guide smiles and asks:

> . . . 'Allora e' tu se' di coloro
> ch'alle mondane cose hanno 'l disire?'
>
> (XXXI (A), 65–66)

> . . . 'So then, are you one of those
> who have the desire for worldly things?'

Chaucer the dreamer, we have noted, mounts a defence of his own integrity on being asked

> 'Artow come hider to han fame?'   (1872)

The Boethian and Vergilian texts that Chaucer draws upon in describing Fame were employed by Boccaccio for his figure of Fortune. By presenting Fame and Fortune as distinct but related figures, Boccaccio wins a momentary[84] autonomy for Fame and bathes her in a positive light, a light which proves particularly attractive to poets. Chaucer maintains a humorously ambiguous attitude towards the possibility of Fame for himself: discovered within Fame's hall, he denies having come in search of personal fame; in his 'Invocations', he both draws attention to and pokes fun at himself seen in the guise of poet. His presentation of Fame is continuously ambiguous: she is by turns attractive and repulsive, noble and primitive. Her positive claims are allowed little autonomy. Perhaps this indicates that Chaucer is a less audacious (and more typically medieval) writer than Boccaccio; perhaps Chaucer recognises that serious claims to Fame cannot yet be upheld by his native vernacular.

The difficulties experienced in writing *The House of Fame* and the *Amorosa Visione* spurred Chaucer and Boccaccio to reconsider their means and intentions as vernacular authors. A number of Chaucer's minor poems are evidently experimental in nature: *Anelida and Arcite* may have been written as a meditated response to the 'narrative débâcle'[85] of *The House of Fame*. The *Anelida*, having failed to find the right balance between narrative and lyric components, ends incomplete[86]: but it sees Chaucer taking the crucial step of extending his line and employing stanzas. The poem begins with a somewhat stiff-jointed imitation of stanzas from Boccaccio's *Teseida* and makes liberal use of Dante. Other influences encountered at Florence (such as the nine-line stanzas of the *Intelligenza*) may also have played their part in shaping this poem which, nevertheless, upholds Chaucer's allegiance to Machaut.[87]

Boccaccio came to realise that his passion for Latin learning could not be fully accommodated within the confines of vernacular fiction. This realisation—which may well have formed as Boccaccio struggled with the *Visione*—ensured that the narrative of the *Decameron* could develop without encumbrance. Latin learning was saved for the Latin works.

CHAPTER 2

Cultural Formations: Naples and London

At the time of Chaucer's visit to Florence in 1373 the elderly Boccaccio was honoured as Dante's chief disciple and as the preeminent champion of Florentine letters. But the Boccaccian vernacular writings that Chaucer made such generous use of belong to a different time and place. The *Filostrato*, *Filocolo* and *Teseida* were composed over thirty years earlier at Naples, a city which then boasted a complex of social, cultural and literary influences that no other European city could rival. It was in developing within this complex that the young Boccaccio became a literary innovator of extraordinary (and perhaps unparalleled)[1] versatility. This chapter offers a detailed profile of Boccaccio's cultural formation.[2] It then considers the youthful *Caccia di Diana* (1333–4), the only extended narrative from Boccaccio's Neapolitan period that Chaucer appears not to have known.[3] In putting Boccaccio (as first-person narrator) among contemporary aristocrats, this poem of love and hunting has much in common with Chaucer's earliest effort, *The Book of the Duchess*. The complex of Latin, French and native vernacular voices and of courtly and mercantile cultures within which the English poet grew to maturity suggests that Chaucer's London had much in common with Boccaccio's Naples. But the practised competence of Chaucer's manoeuvring within the aristocratic ambit of the *Duchess* finds no parallel in the *Caccia* or in any other Boccaccian text. Chaucer himself must have become increasingly aware of this discrepancy as he pondered over Boccaccio's texts, a discrepancy which was to have important consequences for the making of *Troilus and Criseyde*.

Boccaccio's Naples represents a unique and highly vulnerable pocket of cultural survival. In 1327, when the adolescent Boccaccio moved to join his father in the Florentine merchant colony at Naples, the city was threatened from the north by the Emperor Ludwig of Bavaria and from the south by Frederick of Aragon, who was in Sicily; in the winter of 1340–1, when Boccaccio returned to Florence, the Bardi banking company (for which his father worked) was in dire financial difficulties and King Robert's long reign was drawing to a close.[4] The achievements of this remarkable monarch were wasted and dissipated under his successor, Giovanna I (1343–82). Giovanna was deposed, imprisoned and assassinated in the summer of 1382; Carlo III, who succeeded her, was murdered in 1386. At the time of Chaucer the Kingdom of Naples was helplessly engulfed in domestic and international brigandage.[5] Such problems were a serious threat even during the reign of Robert: his legislative acts show him granting special powers to his justiciars in order to combat a rising tide of outrageous crimes such as forcible abduction, arson, murder, piracy, and even attempted regicide.[6]

Boccaccio himself perceived fundamental differences between Florentine and Neapolitan cultures:[7] Florence is commended for its democratic government and its endeavours to curb 'the fickle ostentation of the great'; Naples is celebrated for the aristocratic ideals it upholds in being 'joyful, peace-loving, abounding in good things, magnificent, and subject to a single king'.[8] Giorgio Padoan has persuasively associated such differing social ideals with differing modes of writing.[9] In fourteenth-century Florence, Padoan argues, an extraordinary interest in 'realistic annotation' ('l'annotazione realistica') finds expression in a remarkable abundance of diaries, chronicles and other writings which concentrate upon the minutiae of civic life ('fatti della vita cittadina'). This interest, which is most active among the merchant class, exerts a discernible influence on Boccaccio's Florentine writings and makes a powerful contribution to the *Decameron*. Boccaccio's Neapolitan works seem, by comparison, to be enveloped by a more gracious and unworldly atmosphere, an ambience suggestive of the spell of French romance.[10] Throughout his life, Boccaccio was undoubtedly beguiled by the romantic allure of Angevin Naples, the city of his youth. He made abortive attempts to re-establish himself there in 1355, in 1362 and in 1370;[11] his last attempt was made as an infirm and embittered old man.

The realistic strain that is so splendidly developed in Boccaccio's Florentine compositions is not, however, entirely absent from his Neapolitan writings. For Boccaccio grew to maturity not as a Neapolitan, but as a Florentine living at Naples, a distinction he draws himself in an indignant letter written to Francesco Nelli after the squalid conclusion of his visit to Naples in 1362[12]:

> Perhaps you are unaware, friend, that from boyhood to maturity I lived at Naples among noble youths of suitable age who, however noble, were never ashamed to enter my house or to pay me a visit. They saw me . . . living in style (assai dilicatamente vivere), just as we Florentines are accustomed to live . . .

Earlier in the letter Boccaccio claims that he was, from the first, familiar with the ways of 'cortigiani':

> From my boyhood on I was acquainted with the customs of courtiers and with their way of life.

Boccaccio does not represent himself as one who actively courted the attentions of young Neapolitan nobles: he suggests, rather, that they met him on his own ground, 'in casa mia'. Boccaccio's father occupied a position of considerable importance in the city; in April 1328 he became chief representative of the Florentine Bardi company at Naples.[13] Boccaccio spent some four years at Naples as an apprentice merchant or 'discepolo' of the Bardi before abandoning this in favour of studying canon law (and in favour of improving his Latin and of frequenting the Neapolitan Studio).[14] Boccaccio, whose stepmother boasted ties with the family of Dante's Beatrice, remained proudly conscious of his Florentine identity at all points of his Neapolitan career.

Literary activity flourished at all levels of society at Naples, forming what might be figured as a pyramid of influences for the young Boccaccio. King Robert stood at the apex of this pyramid: following his return from six years of residence at Avignon (1318–24), he made consistent attempts to encourage Latin learning. Robert was himself a prolific composer of sermons, *collationes*, theological tractates and addresses for special occasions.[15] His erudition was unexceptional and thoroughly medieval in character[16]: but he made exceptional efforts to promote the production of books, to extend his excellent library[17] and to attract prominent scholars to his Kingdom. The Genoese astrologer and astronomer Andalò dal Negro moved to Naples and remained in the city until his death in 1334.[18] Paolino da Venezia, a Franciscan diplomat, took up residence at the episcopal seat of Pozzuoli in 1326 and was active at the Angevin court until his death in 1344. He produced several large volumes of universal history which provided useful historical, geographical and mythological material for more gifted talents to exploit.[19] The gifted Paolo da Perugia pursued his scholarly career at Naples from 1324 until his death in 1348. Working within the medieval encyclopaedic tradition, he made certain intelligent innovations that class him as a worthy prehumanist: in his glosses to Horace's *Ars poetica*, for example, he established the principle of commenting on a classical author by quoting the work of other classical poets rather than the opinions of schoolmen and theologians.[20] When, in later years, Boccaccio began work on his *Genealogia deorum gentilium*[21] he sought to borrow a copy of Paolo's *Collationes*, a miscellany of varied erudition and mythology; he discovered, to his chagrin, that Paolo's widow had destroyed the manuscript. The chapter of the *Genealogia* which recounts this incident (XV, vi) pays tribute to other distinguished scholars encountered at Naples; the work as a whole has been aptly described as 'a real Neapolitan ice'.[22] *Filocolo* V, 8,16–27 pictures the young Boccaccio in the very process of absorbing such encyclopaedic learning. In this autobiographical interlude, Boccaccio (speaking as the metamorphosed Idalogo) tells of the delight with which he attended to the learned discourse of '"Calmeta pastore solennissimo"' (V, 8,16). Calmeta—who tells of the sun, moon, planets and stars—has been identified as Paolo da Perugia and (more commonly) as Andalò dal Negro.[23] Whatever his identity, the chapter stands as a sincere tribute to the scholars at Naples who inspired Boccaccio '"to follow Pallas"' (V, 8,27).

The scholar who exerted the most decisive influence on Boccaccio's early development arrived at Naples late in 1338 and remained there until his death in 1342. This was Dionigi da Borgo San Sepolcro, an Austin friar whose literary output included commentaries on Vergil, Seneca and Ovid, on three works of Aristotle and on the letters of St Paul. Dionigi completed his commentary on Valerius Maximus whilst at Naples; perhaps it was this which first attracted Boccaccio's interest.[24] Dionigi facilitated Boccaccio's access to a yet more brilliant cultural world[25]: he arrived from Avignon, fortified with the good wishes of Petrarch conveyed in two letters, *Metrice* I, iv and *Familiares* IV, 2. Petrarch obviously intended his metrical letter to smooth his friend's path into court society at Naples: he begins by seeking to seduce Dionigi into sharing the delights of Valchiusa, but cleverly defeats himself by implying that Valchiusa's chief boast lies in the fact that it was once frequented by 'magnum . . . Robertum' (58).[26] Boccaccio borrowed this letter from the friar and copied it into his first 'zibaldone' or literary scrapbook (fol. 74r);[27] this and other letters and poems kindled his admiration for Petrarch and fired his own ambitions as a composer of Latin epistles. Boccaccio's first four prose epistles date from 1339[28]; the second contains a fulsome tribute to Petrarch's talents which is lavishly embroidered with classical instances. All four epistles appear in the *Zibaldone Laurenziano* (51r–52r; 65r–65v). The exact order of transcription for the folios in this manuscript is uncertain,[29] but the late predominance of Petrarch seems obvious enough: following his first appearance in folio 73r, six of the manuscript's last twelve entries are dedicated to his work.

Zibaldone Laurenziano XXIX-8 comprises three groups of fascicles; the third of these is clearly in Boccaccio's hand. The first group (fols 2–25) contains two works by Andalò dal Negro, *Tractatus spere materialis* and an incomplete *Tractatus teorice planetarum*. The second group (fols 26–45) forms a modest, thoroughly medieval anthology: works represented include the *Liber de dictis antiquorum* employed by Dante and Boccaccio, the *Sibyllinorum verborum interpretatio* attributed to Bede, the *Chronica de origine civitatis*, much esteemed by the early Florentine chroniclers, and the highly influential *Epistola Alexandri ad Aristotelem*.[30] The third group (fols 46–77) reflects the heightening of Boccaccio's interest in classical writings by recording readings in Cicero (54r-55v), Livy (59v) and Statius (59v). The Petrarchan material is immediately preceded by a fine selection of letters and eclogues written and received by Dante (62v–63r, 67v–72v). Religious interests are represented by the beginning of the *Liber Sacrificiorum* attributed to Ivo, bishop of Chartres (46r) and by some verses of Thomas Aquinas (52r–52v). The writing is not uniformly serious: there are satirical verses against prelates (63v–64v) and Goliard verses favouring wine and disfavouring women (60v). Selections from Jerome's *Contra Jovinianum* and Walter Map's *Dissuasiones Valerii ad Rufinum ne ducat uxorem* (52v–54r) supply further anti-feminist material. These last two texts were much exploited by Boccaccio and Chaucer in composing their particular contributions to the anti-feminist tradition, the *Corbaccio* and the *Wife of Bath's Prologue*.

The scripts of the first two groups of fascicles in this manuscript are not identical, but they share certain characteristics which unite them against the third group. Di Benedetto suggests that all three might be the work of Boccaccio, who may have suffered a 'crisi grafica' in encountering the clear, simple style of Petrarch's hand.[31] This remains hypothetical: but Di Benedetto is right in proposing that the contents of the *Zibaldone Laurenziano* exactly reflect 'the succession of the cultural interests of Boccaccio, who was Andalò's pupil before becoming the resolute and faithful servant of the Muses and the attentive reader of classical and postclassical texts'.[32] The growth and development continued when Boccaccio returned to Florence and frequented the *cenacolo* that grouped itself around Sennuccio del Bene, a literary circle which took an especial interest in Petrarch.[33] Here the first *Zibaldone* was completed and the second begun.[34] Boccaccio was doubtless disappointed to miss the three-day public examination of Petrarch conducted by Robert in March 1341, an event which marks the apogee of classical culture at Angevin Naples.[35]

Petrarch (unlike Dante) held King Robert in high regard[36]: but Petrarch was dismayed to discover the appetite for jousting which prevailed at the Angevin court.[37] Petrarch held chivalry and similar French affectations in contempt.[38] He also disliked the *Roman de la Rose*: in presenting a copy of 'brevis iste libellus' to the Mantuan Guido Gonzaga, he took the opportunity of composing a metrical letter upholding the superiority of Latin culture.[39] Certain details of the *Trionfi* suggest, however, that Petrarch (prompted, perhaps, by Boccaccio) did not wholly escape the *Rose*'s influence.[40] In fact Petrarch, like Boccaccio, grew to maturity in a culture which favoured French influences; and he did not leave the environs of Avignon for good until 1353, when he was almost fifty. Some of Petrarch's finest discoveries were made on French soil: this was not (as Petrarch supposed) a happy accident, but the consequence of past labours by French classicists.[41]

Although Robert neglected the French vernacular in his passionate pursuit of Latin learning, French culture was firmly rooted at the Angevin capital. When Robert's grandfather Charles d'Anjou came to Naples (having defeated the Swabian Manfred in 1266) he discovered an aristocracy which was, following the Norman occupation, predisposed to regard French as the authentic language of court culture. The Angevin conquest was followed by a comprehensive drafting in of French and Provençal talents to fill the top religious and secular posts. Even in the early years of Robert's reign court circles remained the 'absolute dominion of French and, to a lesser extent, of Provençal culture'.[42]

Carlo I (1266–85) was a passionate littérateur. He exchanged *coblas* and set both his own verse and the verse of fellow poets to music. He judged *jeux-partis*, and once participated in one of these poetic duels against Perrin d'Angicourt. The Mantuan Sordello and other troubadors followed him to Naples; Adam de la Halle entered his service there around 1283. Jean de Meun, whom Charles had befriended and patronised while still in France, commended Charles and his adopted city in his continuation of the *Roman de la Rose*.[43] Carlo II (1285–1309) was a less brilliant figure, but French literature consolidated its position during his reign as the native nobility pursued their desire to be included within the ambit of French culture. Their aspirations are recorded in the work of two translators who were active at Naples during the last years of Carlo II and the first years of Robert's reign.[44] The first of these translated an important historiographical corpus from Latin into French; this corpus includes Isidore of Seville's *Cronaca* and the *Historia Langobardorum* of Paulus Diaconus, a text which Boccaccio employed to brilliant effect at the opening of the *Decameron*.[45] In his prologue, the translator explains that a certain 'monseignor conte de Militrée' commissioned his work 'pour ce qu'il set lire et entendre la lengue fransoize et s'en delitte' and intends it 'especialment pour sa delectation et pour la delectation de ses amis'. The translator's client has not been identified: but he is clearly not French, given his eagerness to advertise his knowledge of French and his pursuit of French culture. The quality of the translation indicates that the translator was not French either; nor was the second translator, who confesses in his prologue 'que ce fu trop grant presumption d'emprendre si haute chose a translater'. The 'haute chose' of which he speaks is Seneca's *Ad Lucilium Epistolae Morales*; its translation into French was undertaken at the request of 'misire Bartholomy Singuilerfe de Naples', a prominent member of a well-known family of the Neapolitan nobility. In spite of the translator's reservations, his work enjoyed a rapid and broad diffusion in Italy and elsewhere; it survives in five manuscripts.

Robert's championing of Latin learning did not weaken the links of the Neapolitan Angevins with France. When he returned from Avignon in 1324 Robert was accompanied by Marie de Valois, sister of the future Philip VI.[46] Marie's marriage to Robert's son Carlo in October 1323 formed but one strand in a dense web of Franco-Neapolitan alliances.[47] Talented Neapolitans continued to pursue careers across French and Italian territories during the reigns of Carlo II and of Robert.[48] In his *Filocolo* Boccaccio lays claim to French and Italian parentage by presenting himself as the fruit of a pastoral liason between the Tuscan shepherd Eucomos and Gannai, daughter of Franconarcos, King of France (V, 8,1–14).

Boccaccio's early writings attest to a fondness for French romance; all four Neapolitan works are substantially indebted to examples furnished by French literature.[49] It has been suggested that Boccaccio derived *ottava rima*, the verse form of the *Filostrato* and *Teseida*, from French court lyrics.[50] This seems unlikely: but it is quite possible that French models helped Boccaccio to realise the lyric possibilities of his *ottave* in much the same way that they undoubtedly helped Chaucer.[51] The single *ottava* which appears in the *Filocolo* as an epitaph to Biancifiore's mother (I, 43,3) has been hailed as the earliest example of an *ottava siciliana*; its verse form is similar to that employed by numerous French and Provençal poets, including Carlo I.[52] In later years Boccaccio, having come under the influence of Petrarch, adopted a somewhat disdainful attitude towards French romance.[53] But he remained mindful of the power and prestige of French culture: his *Trattatello in laude di Dante* pictures Dante conquering the Parisian theological schools in a disputation *de quodlibet*.[54]

The complexity of the Florentine response at Naples to the prestigious force of French and Latin cultures may be gauged from the attitudes of Boccaccio's friend Niccola Acciaiuoli. Acciaiuoli's origins, like Boccaccio's, were illegitimate; he shared Boccaccio's mercantile background and may have shared his early education in Florence at the school of Giovanni da Strada.[55] Acciaiuoli joined the Florentine colony at Naples in 1331, rose rapidly to assume the highest executive positions within the Angevin dynasty and remained intimately connected with the fortunes of the Kingdom until his death in 1365. His concern for literature was lively but always 'adapted ("en fonction") . . . to the needs of his government and his personal glory'.[56] His spectacular career and conservative cultural preferences find suggestive parallels in the life of Richard Lyons, who rose from obscure and illegitimate origins to become one of the most powerful merchants and financiers in England.[57]

Acciaiuoli held Latin culture in high (ostentatious) regard. He instituted an 'Accademia' at Sulmona: this seems to have had no literary programme or unifying principle beyond that of promoting the cult of Petrarch.[58] (It was the Latin learning of the laureate poet that was revered; his vernacular verse was practically neglected). Acciaiuoli repeatedly announced his desire to be free from the burden of worldly riches so that he could concentrate on tracing his family origins back through the Trojans to the Phrygian gods.[59] Perhaps he would have claimed the Trojan hero of Boccaccio's *Filostrato* as a blood relative.

Acciaiuoli combined such high esteem for classical antiquity with an emotional attachment to French culture. He exploited this attachment in 1352

28

by founding the 'Ordre du Saint-Esprit au Droit Désir', an institution modelled on the 'Ordre de l'Etoile' founded by Jean le Bon in 1351. The statutes of the Neapolitan Order were written in French and followed the French example in points of detail.[60] But Acciaiuoli had succumbed to the charm of chivalry much earlier than this: in 1335 he accepted a knighthood; in his will (dated 28 September 1338) he recorded his wish to be depicted on his tombstone in knight's arms.[61] This will is a revealing document: Acciaiuoli is strongly mindful of his personal merits, yet conscious of having exploited the resources of his merchant *compagnia* to further his career. He is full of self-justification but will not risk dying in debt:

> . . . ma comeche si sia, io lascia a la compagnia fiorini cinquecento d'oro per chiareza e isgravamento della mia anima.

> . . . but in any case, I bequeath five hundred gold florins to the company for the lightening and disburdening of my soul.

This blend of chivalry and superstition recalls that of the late thirteenth-century collection of tales known as the *Novellino*[62], in which death in financial debt is punished in the afterlife: such punishment is suffered even by Charlemagne (XVII-A) and by Henry III of England, the pattern of *cortesia* (XVIII, 98–109). And, as Henry's father remarks,

> Non piaccia a Dio che l'anima di così
> valente uomo stea in pregione per moneta.   (XVIII, 112–3)

> It is not pleasing to God that the soul of so worthy
> a man should be stuck in prison on account of money.

Acciaiuoli's impulse to surround money matters with ceremony and chivalric refinement is typical of the Italian merchant class.[63] The *Novellino* promised this class 'flowers' (that is, 'gems') 'of speech, of beautiful courtesies and of beautiful responses and of beautiful gallantries, of beautiful gift-giving and of beautiful loves'.[64] Boccaccio's *Decameron* is full of such 'fiori'; his work proved popular with a mercantile readership long before it won acceptance in aristocratic circles.[65]

Reading and writing, language and literature were held in the highest regard in merchant circles:

> And you need to know how to deal with book-keeping and with records, and how to write and reply to letters: which are not minor or fruitless skills, especially that of knowing how to write letters. For of all the great friends that we have, language is the greatest of all, when a man knows how to use it well; and the opposite holds true when a man does not know how to use it.

This advice is given in a short fourteenth-century piece written for the instruction of novices in the merchant trade; many longer tracts date from this period.[66] They share this emphasis upon language as a working instrument;

language brings the merchant *compagnia* into existence, holds it together and guarantees its continuance. Boccaccio was schooled in this attitude to language when, as a *discepolo* of the Bardi, he learned 'to weigh and weigh up (pesare e soppesare) money and letters and men in order scrupulously to draw the various parties into agreement'.[67] The writing of contracts called for a language of high precision which would attempt to foresee every problem of detail that might arise. A contract would typically begin with statements of profit-sharing, percentages and liabilities and then proceed to the most minute consideration of details, down to the division of cooking utensils, bedding and stable equipment at the dissolution of the *società*.[68]

The functional, realistic tenor of language in the letters and contracts of merchants was occasionally relieved by brief flowerings of pious language, or by a Biblical quotation.[69] It was important that the *discepolo* should learn to penetrate such extravagances in order to perceive true intentions. His 'discrezione' should help him to get behind the author's rhetoric:

> Discretion teaches that you must give credence not to the text of any piece of writing, but to the intention. And do not say: this authority or this teaching says such and such; but ask yourself what the author's intention was when he wrote this.[70]

The merchant *compagnia* valued loyalty and group-consciousness; a *compagno* derived his name from the medieval Latin *companio, companionis*, 'one who eats of the same bread'.[71] Outsiders could not easily penetrate the group; if admitted, their allegiance was often secured with marriage bonds. In the *Filocolo*'s garden parliament (which provided a source for Chaucer's Franklin) as in *compagnia* contracts, prescriptions for success are often veiled in gracious language: here, for example, both speakers speculate that material and spiritual ('gloria nell'animo'; 'pro d'anima') benefits will be secured by following a practical course of action:

> La detta compagnia noi Toro di Berto e Francesco di Marco sopradetti ordiniamo, e così promette ciascuno di noi tenere fermo la detta compagnia come detto è di sopra per tre anni prossimi che debbono venire; e da indi innanzi Iddio ci conceda grazia di lungamente mantenere compagnia insieme con pro d'anima e di corpo con accrescimento di persona e d'avere.

> We, the above mentioned Toro di Berto and Francesco di Marco, bring the said company into being, and in so doing each one of us promises to keep the said company in existence as stated above for the next three years; and from now on may God grant us grace to keep company together for a long time for the benefit of soul and body, with increase of personal status and of possessions.

> 'Tanto di bene seguirà a chi maggiore donna di sé amerà, che egli s'ingegnerà, per piacerle, belli costumi avere, di nobili uomini compagnia, ornato e dolce parlare, ardito alle 'mprese e splendido di vestire. E se l'acquisterà, più gloria nell'animo n'avrà . . .'

> 'Much good will accrue to him who loves a woman superior to himself, for in order to please her he will endeavour to maintain good manners, to

30

keep company with noble men, will be sophisticated and sweet in speech, ardent in his exploits and splendid in his style of dress. And if he acquires that love he will enjoy greater glory in his heart . . .'[72]

Florentine merchants did occasionally avail themselves of poetic forms. Dino Compagni included a 'Moral canzone on interest' in his *Cronaca* and even addressed a poem to Guido Cavalcanti lamenting that the great poet had not been a merchant, for he would then have been a paragon of *cortesia*.[73] Giovanni Frescobaldi composed some verses for intending travellers to England. His lines conclude, predictably enough, by stressing the importance of keeping within the familiar group:

> con tua nazione unirti t'appartiene,
> e far per tempo ben serrar le porte.[74]

> it befits you to stick with your countrymen,
> and make sure that the doors are locked early and well.

The Florentines at Naples could take considerable pride in their native vernacular: Neapolitan was, by comparison, a crude instrument. Dante's *Commedia* proved popular with Florentines and Neapolitans alike in popular quarters; it was drawn upon for sermons and was further promoted by the arrival of Graziolo dei Bambaglioli, composer of an early commentary on the *Inferno*, in 1334.[75] He was preceded, in 1330, by the Tuscan poet acclaimed by Dante as the finest Italian love lyricist and praised by Petrarch more highly than any other poet of his generation.[76] This was Cino da Pistoia, who taught civil law at the Neapolitan Studio while Boccaccio was a student of canon law there; courses were not rigidly separated in this period.[77] Boccaccio was able to copy a letter from Dante to Cino into his *Zibaldone Laurenziano* (fol 63r) which subsequently provided a model for his earliest epistles. He also gained access to at least one of Cino's *canzoni* which had a very limited diffusion outside Tuscan literary circles.[78] Boccaccio's knowledge of such rare texts suggests that he enjoyed direct and confidential contacts with Cino.

Cino's achievement, great in bulk if not in originality, represents a final outworking of the themes of the *stil nuovo*. In his verse the movement seems to have spent its vital energies and sacrificed its intellectual edge for a melodious, less astringent lyricism.[79] Cino makes much use of symbols and images conventionally associated with romance: ruby rings and Saracen carbuncles (CLVII, 1–7), thorns and flowers (LXXVIII, 5–8; CLXIV, 20–1; CXXIII, 9–13; CXIX, 9–11) adorn his verse, and he depicts himself as a devoted student of Andreas Capellanus (CLVI, 12–14). Cino associates the 'bianco fiore' with his beloved's eyes (CXX, 10–12); the *Filocolo*'s hero associates a 'bianco fiore' surrounded by thorns with the desperate plight of Biancifiore (III, 2,2–5). Boccaccio's management of this imagery is mechanical and inept; he ends by expounding its symbolic significance in flat-footed fashion. Boccaccio treats the *stil nuovo* as a convenient fund of poetic motifs; like Cino, he warms more readily to the charms of romance and *amour cortois*.

Robert offered Cino no recognition of his merits as a vernacular poet. In fact, Robert summoned Cino to the Studio not in his own name but in the name of the people of Naples; the visit was charged at their expense.[80] Cino, plagued by professional jealousies, stayed for less than two years at Naples.[81] He vented his frustration at the treatment accorded him there in a sharply-satirical canzone (CLXV). Cino condemns the Neapolitans for their want of courtesy and for their enviousness (CLXV, 25–7). In his most subtle and pointed criticism he reveals his fierce pride in being a poet of the Tuscan vernacular: the Neapolitans are likened to apes, who are 'senza lingua/la qual distingua'.[82]

Robert's aloofness is partly explicable by Cino's politics which, being Ghibelline, had at times made him a passionate opponent of the Angevin monarch, particularly at the time of Henry VII's expedition. Dante's politics allied him with Cino and against Robert: given the *Commedia*'s unflattering account of the Angevins it is not surprising that it was apparently ignored at the Neapolitan court.[83] Much of the political verse written about Neapolitan affairs was composed and voiced abroad by Tuscans.[84] Given such attitudes it is fanciful to assume that Boccaccio would have been welcome at the Neapolitan court as a poet of the Florentine vernacular. When Niccola Acciaiuoli rose to high and influential office at Naples he offered Boccaccio no encouragement or patronage.

Two documents from 1335 bear witness to Robert's deep distaste for the practice and influence of popular verse. One announces prosecution against the notary Jacobello Fusco, who had been courting a certain Neapolitan wife by standing under her window, 'singing (and getting others to sing) morning-songs and urging her to break her marriage vows':[85] the king proposes to act rigidly, 'per exemplum ceteri discant' ('so that others might learn by example'). In a statute earlier in the year Robert had denounced the behaviour of young men, which he saw as absurdly mannered, influenced by some strange new fashion,

> . . . ut in eis sit modus incertus, ritus varius, cultus diversus, et gestus ridicula distorsione spectandus . . .

> . . . so that they behave unstably, in various ways and in diverse manners, adopting visibly absurd poses . . .[86]

Robert might well have been observing the strange behaviour of the young heroes of the *Filostrato* and *Teseida*. These two works could not have pleased Robert the Wise: they draw inspiration from the *cantare*, a Tuscan tradition of popular narrative composed and performed by street-singers or *canterini*.[87]

The second Italian vernacular at Naples, forming the broad popular base of our literary pyramid, was Neapolitan. The considerable tradition of Neapolitan historiography and chronicle did not flourish until the second half of the fourteenth century: but popular forms enjoyed a continuous development, multiplying in a stream of *cantilene, strambotti, villanelle, canzonette*, religious songs and versions of French fabliau.[88] Boccaccio owes much to this teeming literary undercurrent; he temporarily immerses himself in it in a delightful letter signed 'IANNETTO DI PARISSE DALLA RUOCCIA'.[89] Writing in Neapolitan dialect, he pictures himself enduring the hard and thankless life (as a student of canon law) of 'abbot Jo. Boccaccio . . . and he does nothing by day nor by night except write!'[90] This humorous, burlesque piece spans the whole social and literary world of Angevin Naples: it offers a view of the top, seen from the bottom, penned by Boccaccio at a point somewhere near the centre. Having congratulated a friend on becoming the father of an unlooked-for baby boy, Boccaccio exclaims

O biro Dio, ca nd'apisse aputo uno madama la reina nuostra! Ah! co' festa ca nde faceramo tutti per l'amore suoio!

O heavens above, if only our queen had had a baby girl! Aaaah! What a party we'd all make for the love of her!

This Neapolitan letter, obviously enough, was never intended for court consumption: it dates from 1339–40, when Robert's queen, Sancia, was way beyond child-bearing age.[91]

Boccaccio's first major composition, the *Caccia di Diana*, gives early notice of his ability to digest a rich diversity of literary influences. The poem echoes a long Latin debate tradition in staging a conflict of allegiances between Venus and Diana; it reveals points of correspondence with French *tournoiments des dames* and owes something to the *cacce*, a flexible Italian genre of uncertain origin which, in various verse forms, presents scenes of fighting, fishing and hunting.[92] The poem, in eighteen cantos of *terza rima*, pays homage to Dante by repeating the final promise of the *Vita nuova* in both its opening and its closing canto.[93] This naive pledge of discipleship is supplemented by various opportunistic borrowings: the little cloud upon which Venus rides recalls the 'nuvoletta' which bears up Beatrice, and the landscape which Venus inhabits recalls the Dantean *paradiso terrestre*.[94] Such a landscape (one in which a Chaucerian narrator would feel quite at home) is evoked in the *Caccia*'s opening tercets[95]:

> Nel tempo adorno che l'erbette nove
> rivestono ogni prato e l'aere chiaro
> ride per la dolcezza che 'l ciel move,
>   sol pensando mi stava che riparo
> potessi fare ai colpi che forando
> mi gian d'amor il cuor con duolo amaro . . .   (I, 1–6)

> In the beautiful season, when the new-grown grass
> covers every meadow again and the clear air
> laughs at the sweetness that stirs the heavens,
>   I stood alone wondering what refuge
> I might find against the blows with which love
> was piercing my heart with bitter sorrow . . .

The cheerful rejuvenescence of the spring season in the first tercet contrasts with the sad state of the speaker in the second. The third tercet intrudes a voice that distracts the speaker from self-contemplation; the fourth calls into being the poem's main subject, the assembly of ladies. From this point on the narrator seems content simply to report what he sees and hears. This narrator's strategy—of alleviating the pangs of unfulfilled love by focussing his attention elsewhere—is one thankfully employed by the narrator of Chaucer's early dream poems.[96] Despite obvious similarities with the assembly of ladies in the *Prologue* to *The Legend of Good Women*, the *Caccia* more closely resembles *The Book of the Duchess*: in each poem, scenes of hunting—passively observed by a love-struck narrator—serve to prelude the emergence of the poem's chief character. Written in the early 1330s, the *Caccia* parallels a number of closely-contemporary French hunting poems, such as Jehan Acart de Hesdin's *Prise amoreuse* and (especially) Raimon Vidal's *Chasse aux médisants*.[97]

Boccaccio, like Chaucer and his French contemporaries, attaches great importance to the social group, the *brigata* or *compaignye*. In the *Caccia*'s hunting scenes, great emphasis is laid upon the interdependence of the huntresses: they hunt in groups, cooperating within their group to catch their prey, or responding collectively to assist others in danger or difficulties. One exceptional figure confirms the rule of collectivity: Zizzola d'Anna arrives late, having avoided the assemblies of ladies (I, IX–X). Significantly, she has been an unsuccessful huntress, having wounded many animals but captured none (XVI, 25–30). Her belated appearance is as curious as that of Chaucer's Canon in *The Canterbury Tales*; both late arrivals serve to strengthen the unity of the social group and to accentuate the value of sociability. Wilful privacy, much prized by Petrarch, is not found admirable in Boccaccio's vernacular writings: self-isolation symptomatises a sickness of spirit.[98] The self-seclusion of Troiolo and Troilus is to be seen as a malady; estrangement from society forms part of their tragedy.

Boccaccio's high regard for sociability and group-awareness doubtless owes as much to his formative experience within the merchant *compagnia* as it does to any experience of court circles. Although the *Caccia* features ladies of the Neapolitan nobility it cannot be regarded as a court poem. The way in which these women are portrayed suggests that they were names rather than acquaintances to the young Boccaccio. In canto X, a group of ladies is sighted, described and then abandoned as the narrator spots a 'more pleasing group' ('più piacente schiera', X, 9). Five noble families might take offence from such a crude comparison; but all ladies are put in the shade by the presence of Boccaccio's own (unnamed) lady,

> che tutte l'altre accresce e rinvigora.   (I, 48)
>
> who magnifies and reinvigorates all the rest.

Boccaccio ennobles his secret love by associating her with the noblest of the women, Zizzola Barrile; and even Zizzola, daughter of a great and powerful Neapolitan family, appears content to follow in the footsteps of Boccaccio's lady.[99] All this suggests that Boccaccio is writing from a position outside the court and does not expect his poem to penetrate court circles. His Tuscan verse (peppered with gems from Dante) would not have won public recognition at the Angevin court. His control of courtly diction is insecure: in asserting that each follower of Venus is 'fresco come un giglio' he sounds like a *canterino*.[100]

Boccaccio's self-presentation as narrator is, compared with that of Chaucer in *The Book of the Duchess*, remarkably uneven. In opening the poem he fails to establish himself firmly or memorably but quickly recedes into semi-anonymous reportage. He does not significantly draw attention to himself until the beginning of canto IX: but in this canto he firmly occupies the central point from which all is observed; he links the groups of huntresses seen wandering through the landscape, and he prepares us for the dramatic encounters between them. The narrator's prominence here is reflected by the frequent appearance of the first-person pronoun 'io'. 'Io' is quite often employed in the following canto, but is most remarkably evident in canto XI. Between lines 24 and 41 of this canto there are no fewer than eleven first-person verbs, strengthened by six usages of 'io'. But this remarkable intensity is isolated and of brief duration: not one first-person verb appears in the rest of the canto. For this short period, then, the drama of the poem centres not in events but in the narrator's perception of them.[101] Following this canto, the narrator becomes less prominent: but in the final canto he re-emerges most decisively.

'Io' is the first word of Boccaccio's last canto. 'Io' dominates the opening tercets as the main verb phrase is not reached until the eighth line; and this phrase (the resonant Dantean 'mi ritrovai') keeps our attention focussed on the narrator. We learn (for the first time) that the narrator has been a stag ('cervio'): but he now finds himself offered up to his lady as a man, 'umana e razionale' (XVIII, 10–12). The narrator, having praised his lady (13–36) and led prayers of thanks to Amor (37–48) calls a halt to his narrating and promises to praise his lady better in future works (49–58). The personal pronoun, once again, bears much weight:

> Il più parlare omai qui non *mi* piace . . .   (XVIII, 49)
>
> It does not please me to speak further here . . .

This artless and uneven insistence on the narrator's viewpoint makes it difficult to imagine the reception of the *Caccia* at any court. As Dante acknowledges in beginning his *Convivio*, first-person narration, which the rhetoricians find difficult to condone, should not be undertaken lightly.[102] In *The Book of the Duchess*, Chaucer takes pains to deflect attention away from his first-person narrator. The Chaucerian 'I' is happy to report events, but the burden of interpreting them or of connecting one event with the next is shifted to the Black Knight—the authoritative surrogate of the poem's aristocratic patron—or onto the reader. The Boccaccian 'Io', however, observes no such decorum. As Boccaccio wrote his first long poem to please himself it is only appropriate that he himself should emerge as the protagonist in the poem's final canto. In spite of its sprinkling of noble names, then, the *Caccia* cannot be regarded as a court poem; and neither can any of Boccaccio's other Neapolitan works.

Gervase Mathew's influential picture of Boccaccio as a 'court entertainer' performing before Robert the Wise is undoubtedly misleading.[103] And in recent years, Mathew's portrait of Chaucer as a court poet enjoying royal patronage has come to seem similarly unsatisfactory.[104] Derek Pearsall, for one, has invited us 'to look beyond the entourage of king and nobility for Chaucer's audience'.[105] Pearsall is not attempting to locate Chaucer's audience beyond the boundaries of the court, but rather to point out how ill-defined and unexamined such boundaries are. Indeed, the term 'court' itself is becoming as problematic for modern critics as it was for Walter Map: 'I am in the court, and speak of the court, and know not—God alone knoweth—what the court is'.[106] No detailed account of the complex metropolitan milieu in which Chaucer grew to maturity, worked and composed can be offered here. We may, however, measure certain aspects of Chaucer's cultural formation at London against that of Boccaccio at Naples.

As a cultural figurehead, Richard II could not have inspired the kind of admiration in Chaucer that Robert commanded in Boccaccio. Indeed, Chaucer seems to have pinned what slender hopes he had for official recognition as a poet not on Richard but on his queen, Anne of Bohemia.[107] Anne's father, Charles IV (1346–78), offered intelligent encouragement to artists and scholars and, in 1348, founded the Caroline University at Prague.[108] Charles ranks with Robert as an artistic patron of European stature: perhaps Chaucer hoped to receive a sympathetic hearing from his daughter. It is more likely however, that Chaucer's more learned and abstruse interests were developed in the company of fellow members of the king's household: men such as Henry Scogan, Sir Peter Bukton and Sir Philip de la Vache.[109] It is also possible that something of the classical scholarship that reached Boccaccio at Naples from Avignon reached Chaucer at London from the same source, borne by the many English civil lawyers and notaries who worked at the papal *curia*.[110]

French culture was rooted as deeply at London as it was at Naples: poetry and music in England and France enjoyed a 'constant interchange and cross-influence'.[111] Philippa of Hainault, following her marriage to Edward III in 1328, became patron to a number of Walloon men-of-letters; and French culture at London was further enriched by the French nobles imprisoned in England after the battles of Crécy (1346) and Poitiers (1356).[112] Some idea of the sheer volume and diversity of French lyric models available to Chaucer is provided by the University of Pennsylvania MS French 15, a collection of 310 mid-fourteenth-century French court lyrics. This remarkable anthology, possibly compiled by Chaucer's correspondent Oton de Granson, contains a 'balade' by Philippe de Vitry that makes clear reference to the Dantean figure of Minos. This raises the intriguing possibility that Chaucer might first have heard of Dante through French lyricists at London.[113] The tenacity of French culture at London certainly seems to have been under-estimated: the familiar thesis that French was becoming 'an accomplishment rather than a habit' by the 1360s may stand in need of revision.[114] It certainly continued to flourish in England and Italy as a *lingua franca* of international trade.[115]

At London as at Naples, then, court culture was still predominantly Latin and French;[116] and it is no more obvious that Chaucer's English would have pleased Richard II than that Boccaccio's Florentine would have pleased Robert the Wise. Indeed, to both monarchs the vernacular voice may have sounded uncomfortably close to the language of the street and of common trade. Petrarch, in asserting (once again) the superiority of Latin culture, had objected to Dante's 'popular' style on these grounds, a style acclaimed by 'the applause and gruff, approbatory murmurings of fullers, inn-keepers and wool-workers'.[117] The voices of such a working world certainly played an important part in Chaucer's formative experience. The son of a wine merchant, Chaucer was probably brought up in the Vintry, a low-lying district on the north bank of the Thames.[118] From this vantage point Chaucer was well placed to hear and observe the confusion of tongues and of social estates effected by mercantile London: apprentice merchants found their way to the metropolis 'speaking every English dialect' and representing 'almost every social group in the kingdom, paupers and nobility excepted'.[119]

The generous range of social and literary influences made available by Boccaccio's Naples does, then, find some correspondence in Chaucer's London. But such similarities should not tempt us to yoke the two poets together under the title 'bourgeois'.[120] It is true, as Scaglione points out, that both writers 'grew up within the milieu of the contemporary mercantile groups'.[121] But their formative experiences differ in one crucial respect. When Boccaccio was about fourteen years of age he moved into a merchant colony to train as an apprentice merchant: when Chaucer was about the same age he moved out of a merchant milieu to train as a page under the Countess of Ulster. So whereas the teenage Boccaccio had learned the rudiments of trade, Chaucer was learning those 'symbolic acts of service'[122] which regulated the life of an aristocratic household. By Christmas 1357 Chaucer was far from the Vintry, decking himself out in new holiday clothes in preparation for '[festu]m Nativitatis' and for the New Year visit of John of Gaunt.[123] Chaucer later transferred to the household of Edward III, was an esquire of the king's chamber by 1372 and remained in royal service for the rest of his life.

It must again be emphasised that court and mercantile worlds were not mutually exclusive: indeed, it is vital to grasp the full extent of their mutual penetration.[124] Boccaccio caught frequent glimpses of court life; Chaucer maintained contact with his family origins and later returned, as a civil servant, to work in a merchant milieu. Nevertheless, our brief comparison of their earliest extended narratives, the *Caccia* and the *Duchess*, has already suggested that some difference of outlook divides Chaucer from Boccaccio; and this difference will assert itself more vividly as we come to compare the *Filostrato* and the *Troilus*. This difference is as subtle and as difficult to define as it is fundamental. A definition might be approached by considering Du Boulay's struggles with the applicability to Chaucer of another elusive concept, that of 'gentleman': 'he [Chaucer] was a gentleman because he had a courtly upbringing and worked, behaved and wrote like one'.[125] In the same pragmatic spirit, this elusive but palpable difference between the two writers might be formulated as follows: Chaucer convinces us of his ability to generate and sustain a discourse fit for an aristocratic milieu; Boccaccio does not.

Chaucer must have recognised that he had much in common with Boccaccio: but in reading Boccaccio's early writings, he became increasingly aware of this difference in discourse. The conditions attending Chaucer's reading of Boccaccio can only have enhanced this awareness. Between 1374 and 1386 Chaucer was controller of wool-customs at London, a period in which 'the Italian merchant community was an integral part of his working world'.[126] In the 1370s, the decade in which Chaucer paid two visits to Italy, over one hundred Italian merchants are recorded at London. Chaucer must also have done business with members of the Bardi company for which Boccaccio and his father had worked.[127] Perhaps he learned something about Boccaccio through such contacts. But more importantly and more certainly, Chaucer would have become thoroughly familiar with the Italian merchant mentality, recognising that it had much in common with its English counterpart: the same hankering after the trappings of aristocracy (denounced so vigorously by the Dominican Bromyard); the same mixture of rational calculation and irrational, sentimental, family-centred traditions; the same fascination with the language, traditions and general mystique of the court.[128] And, turning to the *Filostrato*, Chaucer would have discovered the same mentality at work: a vision of the courtly life constructed by an enthusiastic outsider from his own fancy and from popular, oral-derived forms. As we shall see in chapter V, Chaucer's assessment of the *Filostrato* was remarkably acute and well-informed. This was due, in no small part, to the fact that the conditions of Chaucer's reading had much in common with the conditions of Boccaccio's writing. Chaucer was able to avail himself not only of a text of the *Filostrato*, but also of a context in which to read, comprehend and interpret it.

CHAPTER 3

Organising an opus: the Filocolo, the Troilus and The Canterbury Tales

Boccaccio must rate as one of the most wayward law students of all time. He was willing, as we have seen, to lay aside legal matters to compose a humorous, self-parodying piece in the local dialect, the *Epistola napoletana*, depicting himself as one who 'does nothing by day nor by night except write'. Boccaccio certainly did a lot of writing in this period (the late 1330s): but much if not most of it was dedicated not to canon law but to the composition of a monumentally lengthy version of the much-loved Floris and Blancheflor story. Boccaccio's prose *Filocolo* tells of the infant love of Florio and Biancifiore at the pagan court of King Felice, of the king's various attempts to frustrate this love and of Biancifiore's abduction by merchants. Florio embarks on a long, leisurely-paced and eventful journey in search of Biancifiore; discovering her at Alexandria, he accompanies her to Rome (where they are converted to Christianity) and then escorts her back to the court of Felice, where he succeeds his father as king and Christian governor.[1] The *Filocolo* occupies an important place in Italian literary history: in paving the way for the *Decameron*, it lays the foundations for almost five hundred years of Italian prose.[2] English scholars familiar with the *Filocolo* have agreed that Chaucer was probably acquainted with the work, but have failed to see what he could have learned from a text which (in their opinion) is so insufferably prolix and dull.[3]

Traditional source study, with its painstaking accumulation of textual parallels, cannot hope to tell us much about the influence of an Italian prose work on an English poet. But it may prove profitable to enquire what larger, more abstract concepts and ideas Chaucer might have derived from such a text. We can compare the organisation of Boccaccio's opus with the ways in which such complex, large-scale undertakings such as *Troilus and Criseyde* and *The Canterbury Tales* are organised. By organisation I mean those ways in which a narrative is framed, is mediated through an authorial *persona*, is set in motion, regulated, paced and concluded. More specifically, we might compare the attitudes maintained by each writer towards his source materials (distinguishing real sources from imaginary ones); we might compare the relationships that they envisage between their own artistic enterprise, the enterprise of the *auctores* and that of their fellow vernacular poets. We might compare their uses of allegory and their counterbalancing of lyric and narrative components, of antiquity and modernity, of paganism and Christianity, of *ernest* and *game, sentence* and *solas*, and so on.

This chapter, then, begins by examining the sources which provide the raw materials of the *Filocolo*: the French romances of *Floire et Blancheflor*, their Italian *cantare* derivatives and the classical texts which lend weight to Boccaccio's opus. We next consider the attitudes Boccaccio adopts towards his sources, particularly the posture he assumes of translating an ancient text into the vernacular. Such a combination of sources and such professed attitudes will be compared with those of Chaucer in *Troilus and Criseyde*. Comparison will then be made of the ways in which the *Filocolo* and the *Troilus* align themselves with the tradition of extended vernacular narrative conjoining the *Roman de la Rose* and the *Commedia*. Viewed in the long perspective of this tradition, Chaucer's *Troilus* differentiates itself as a *tragedye*, a frustrated pilgrimage. But the *Troilus* ends with the promise of a *comedye* to come: this chapter concludes by considering ways in which the organisation of the *Filocolo* may have contributed to Chaucer's conception of his greatest opus, *The Canterbury Tales*. The next chapter offers a detailed examination of the *Filocolo*'s fourth Book and its implications for Chaucer.

Following its first literary formulation in the later twelfth century,[4] the story of Floris and Blancheflor became highly popular and widely diffused. The author of *Flamenca* mentions *Floire et Blancheflor* as one of the works most read and enjoyed in female circles; the romance is commemorated in several French and Provençal songs; and Blancheflor is placed among the most celebrated heroines by both Andreas Capellanus and the author of the *Intelligenza*.[5] The French romance survives in two versions: version I, formerly referred to as the 'version aristocratique' and now called the 'roman idyllique', has come down to us in one fragmentary and three complete copies; version II, formerly known as the 'version populaire' and now termed the 'roman d'aventures', survives in a single manuscript.[6] It has been commonly accepted that the first version travelled north and the second south, each generating a series of translations and imitations in many countries over hundreds of years.[7] The English *Floris and Blancheflour*, dating from the mid-thirteenth century, represents a translation of version I, 'abrégé avec sécheresse'.[8] The Italian *cantare* narratives date from the earlier fourteenth to the later fifteenth centuries[9] and represent free renderings of version II. Many uncertainties and confusions (some caused by defective editing) have enveloped this literary nexus; the *Filocolo*'s position within this nexus remains difficult to define.[10] Helpful suggestions concerning the relationship of the *Filocolo* to its sources are, however, provided by Boccaccio himself in his first chapter.

This extraordinary opening chapter—which alerts us to the fact that the youthful Boccaccio was fired with the most complex, grandiose ambitions in composing this huge opus—falls into two parts: a dynastic history of the Neapolitan Angevins (I, 1,1–16), followed by an account of how the *Filocolo* came to be commissioned (I, 1,17–30).

Boccaccio's dynastic history is dominated not (as one would expect of an aspiring court poet) by Robert the Wise, but by his grandfather Charles d'Anjou. Boccaccio's account opens by tracing a transition from ancient to recent history, in which the Swabian Manfred is presented as the last defiant descendant of the Trojan remnant; as such, he arouses the wrath of Juno who, in Boccaccio's ingenious allegory, represents the Church (I, 1,1–3). She urges the Pope to destroy Manfred; the Pope calls upon Charles, who triumphs with divine approbation and lives long enough to found a dynasty before rendering his soul to God (I, 1,3–14). As we have noted,[11] the figure of Charles d'Anjou dominates a lengthy passage of Jean de Meun's continuation of *Le Roman de la Rose* (6601–6710). Jean's account of Charles' heroic exploits forms part of the discourse of Reason (4199–7154): it opens by announcing a transition from tales of ancient history ('d'ancienes estoires', 6602) to reports of modern battles (6601–6) and proceeds directly to condemn Manfred, slain by Charles (6607–18). Jean, like Boccaccio after him, confers divine approval upon Charles' dynastic and imperial ambitions: Charles becomes King of Sicily 'par devine porveance' (6612); his political enemies are regarded as a rebellious faction

> 'qui de Dieu s'iere departie
> et la bataille avoit emprise
> contre la fai de Seinte Iglise . . .'   (6676–8)

> 'who had departed from God
> and had undertaken the battle
> against the faith of Holy Church . . .'

Jean concludes his account by emphasising Charles' imperial power and authority and by telling an anecdote of his youthful prowess; he ends thus:

> 'Mes ne veill or de li plus dire,
> car, qui ses fez vodroit retrere,
> un grant livre en convendroit fere.'   (6708–10)

> 'But I don't want to say more of him now,
> for whoever wished to recount his exploits
> would have to make a large book about them.'

The *Filocolo* is, by any standards, a '"grant livre"': it may be that in prefacing his opus with an *apologia* for the Angevin empire—which concentrates upon the heroic Charles and the hapless Manfred—Boccaccio is making some claim for himself as a historical continuator of Jean de Meun. (In concluding his *Teseida*, Boccaccio clearly stakes a claim for himself as the Italian poet of arms (XII, 84), a position advertised as vacant in *De Vulgari Eloquentia* II, ii, 10). The *Filocolo*'s recall of the passage from the *Rose* seems consciously and deliberately made, and made primarily for literary effect: for had Boccaccio wished to win favour at court he would surely have paid a fuller and more fitting tribute to the current Angevin monarch. In fact, Robert's only significant act in this chapter is to sire an illegitimate daughter whose parentage he does not publicly recognise (I, 1,15).

Boccaccio's tribute to Charles contains a claim that has no counterpart in the *Rose*: that Charles is a lineal descendant of Charlemagne (I, 1,5). Version I of the French romance proposes that Blancheflor is the grandmother of Charlemagne (I, 8–12). If these two proposals are brought together Charles appears as a lineal descendant of Floire and Blancheflor. This would explain the appropriateness of Boccaccio's dynastic preface to the story that follows it.[12] Version I of *Floire et Blancheflor* further informs us that Floire, following his conversion, inherited the kingdoms of Bulgaria and Hungary by right of family connections (I, 25–32). This was an area of Europe in which the Angevins maintained a long and steady interest, an interest which Charles himself formalised shortly after the defeat of Manfred by signing a double marriage treaty with Hungary.[13]

Boccaccio continues his opening chapter by relating how, in the Neapolitan church of St Laurence on a certain Easter Saturday, he was smitten with love for Maria, natural daughter of King Robert (I, 1,17–22; this *innamoramento* has much in common with that of *Filostrato* I, 17–39). He goes on to describe how, a few days later, he finds himself in another church, this time at the convent of the Holy Archangel at Baiano. He discovers his lady there, engaged in playful and lively conversation with several of the nuns; he and his companion (or companions: 'alcuno compagno') are cordially ('domesti-camente') received into this group and its conversation (I, 1,23). Passing from topic to topic ('d'un ragionamento in un altro') they come finally to speak 'del valoroso giovane Florio, figliuolo di Felice, grandissimo re di Spagna, recitando i suoi casi con amorose parole' (I, 1,24). Maria laments the fact that no poet has troubled to uphold the fame of Florio and Biancifiore:

> 'Certo grande ingiuria riceve la memoria degli amorosi giovani . . . a non essere con debita ricordanza la loro fama essaltata da' versi d'alcun poeta, ma lasciata solamente ne' fabulosi parlari degli ignoranti.' (I, 1,25)

> 'Memory of the amorous youths is certainly suffering great injury . . . in that their fame has not, with due remembrance, been raised up by the verses of any poet, but has been left entirely to the extravagant utterances of the ignorant.'

Turning to Boccaccio, Maria requests him—by the love he bears her—to compose '"a little book speaking the vernacular"'.[14] Boccaccio makes a gracious speech of acceptance (I, 1,28).

From this account of the *Filocolo*'s inception it seems reasonable to deduce that Boccaccio was familiar with at least two versions of his source story: the first would have possessed distinguished literary qualities (making it precious and familiar to a gathering which includes nuns and a king's daughter); the second, that of the '"ignoranti"', would probably have formed part of the repertoire of the popular Italian street-singers, the *canterini*.

The *Cantare di Fiorio e Biancifiore* which appears in a manuscript copied (probably by a Tuscan merchant) in the 1340s is the most ancient of all securely-dateable *cantari*.[15] Boccaccio had already made use of the style and verse form of the *canterini* in composing his *Filostrato*; the *Filocolo* bears clear signs of *cantare* influence and contains one scene which has counterparts in the *cantare* but not in the French romances: the attempted seduction of Florio. The *cantare* girls offer a straightforward sexual invitation:

Ciascuna li mostrava 'l suo bel petto,
bianco e prezïoso, e le mamelle;
e dicean: 'Fiorio, or ne predi diletto,
di noi che siam sí fresche damiselle.'   (59,1–4)

Each one showed him her beautiful chest,
white and precious, and her breasts;
and they said: 'Fiorio, now take pleasure in this,
in us, for we are such fresh little ladies.'

Such cheerful sensuality is common in the *cantare* tradition. Boccaccio's
seductresses are similarly provocative: they are dressed

. . . di sottilissimi vestimenti, i quali dalla cintura in su strettissimi
mostravano la forma delle belle menne, le quali come due ritondi pomi
pingevano in fuori il resistente vestimento . . .   (III, 11,6)

. . . in the very thinnest of garments which, stretched very tightly from
the waist up, revealed the form of their beautiful breasts which, like two
well-rounded apples, pushed forward the resisting garment . . .

The *cantare* narrative certainly effects a cultural and literary debasement of
its French original. The *canterino* begins with a customary appeal for attention
before wheeling his narrative elements into action with unceremonious rap-
idity: a Roman knight, he tells us in his second stanza, promises to make a
pilgrimage to St James at Compostella if his wife ('quella rose fresca e
tenerella') becomes pregnant. His wish is soon granted:

Dentro in Roma si fè la promissione,
stando nel Palazzo de la Milizia:
la donna ingravidò quella stagione,
e tutta gente n'avea gran letizia: (3,1–4)

The promise he made at Rome
standing in the Palace of Knights:
the woman got pregnant at that time,
and everybody was very happy about it.

The Roman pilgrims set out for Spain in the fourth stanza; the Saracens set
out to meet them in the fifth stanza, and battle ensues in stanza six as the
canterino exploits the fortunate rhyming of 'cani' ('dogs'), 'pagani' and 'cristiani'. The French poets apply the term 'cortois' to the Saracen King (I, 132;
II, 27), but no such allowance is made by the *canterino*. Boccaccio's King
Felice, first encountered whilst engaged in the courteous pursuit of hunting (I,
10,1), takes a noble, altruistic interest in the safety of his people (I, 13, 8–10):
but in the heat of battle he is termed 'crudele' (I, 26,32). As this battle is about
to break out Boccaccio steps into his narrative to apostrophise his hero (and
whip up dramatic tension) in a manner typical of the *canterini*; similar

interventions[16] (and other aspects of *cantare* technique) recur throughout the *Filocolo*.

Maria commissions Boccaccio not to imagine a new love story, but to restore an ancient story that has suffered neglect and literary depreciation. Comparison of the two French romances makes it clear that the process of artistic devaluation that Maria alerts us to was well under way long before the *canterini* got to work. The original 'roman idyllique' survives within the second version, but only 'sous une form dénaturée'.[17] Textual resemblances between the two versions are remarkably few in number[18]: Reinhold seems to have been right in proposing that the later poet worked from a hazy recollection of the earlier poem, adding half a dozen spectacular scenes of the type to be expected of a 'roman d'aventures'.[19] Many of the fine literary effects of the earlier version are coarsened or forgotten in its derivative; its awareness of classical antiquity[20]—an awareness which Boccaccio would much have admired—is sadly absent.

The qualities which have encouraged critics to describe version I of *Floire et Blancheflor* as a 'roman idyllique' are evident early on in the evocation of the love which grows between the two infants. A single process governs and unites the learning of letters and the learning of love:

> Ensemble lisent et aprennent,
> De la joie d'amor contendent.   (I, 233–4)

> Together they read and learn,
> they aspire to the joy of love.

The infants of the 'roman idyllique' apply themselves eagerly to works in which they may learn of love, and take especial delight in the teachings of Ovid (I, 223–234); the infants of the *Filocolo* feed upon 'il santo libro d'Ovidio' (I, 45,6) in similar fashion. But the lengthy (I, 223–268; I, 45,3–II, 4,2) and delightful accounts of this loving and learning process in the 'roman idyllique' and the *Filocolo* find no equivalent in the later French romance. The love that springs up between the two infants is baldly stated in a single couplet of version II (239–40); the theme of education—which for Boccaccio and the first French poet provides a channel for the intelligent discovery of love—is introduced as a means of breaking the attachment between the two infants; the King sends Floire to school

> Por dessevrer icel amor
> Que il avoit a Blancheflor . . .   (II, 267–8)

> To loosen the bonds of that love
> that he had for Blancheflor . . .

The reciprocal relation of love to learning forms one of the major preoccupations of Boccaccio's early writings: it underlies the conception and progress of the *Comedia delle ninfe* and the *Amorosa Visione* and surfaces in the remarkable authorial address which opens the *Decameron*'s fourth *giornata*. The *enfance* which opens the 'roman idyllique' would doubtless have won Boccaccio's admiration and may well have inspired him to expand his own account of the early life of Florio and Biancifiore.

Further examination of the opening of version I reveals (as well as an unexpected reference to 'Naples . . . la cité bele')[21] a remarkable correspondence with the design of the *Filocolo*. The French poet opens his romance with a lively bid to capture the interest of lovers (I, 1–6) followed by a brief dynastic history (I, 7–32). The promise of this initial advertisement of the poem's double interest—in love and in history—is confirmed as the poet sets his story in motion. One day, he tells us, he entered a room, seeking female company. He discovers two sisters; one speaks to the other of a love

> Qui fu ja entre deus enfanz,
> Bien a passé plus de sept[22] anz,
> Més a un clerc dire l'oït,
> Qui l'avoit leü en escrit.
> El conmença avenaument,
> Einsi dit el conmencement: (I, 51–6)

> That there once was between two infants,
> (More than seven years have passed since then),
> But she had heard it from a clerk
> Who had read it from a written source.
> In gracious fashion she began,
> The tale got under way like this:

The story begins without further formalities. With this mise-en-scène the French poet cleverly implies that his story will charm female company, but ('Més', I, 53) that it is possessed of genuine historical backbone in the shape of a written clerical record. A similar assurance that the narrative is both delightful and historically authoritative is offered by Boccaccio's *Filocolo*. As we have noted, discussion of the 'amorosi giovani' Florio and Biancifiore first arises when Boccaccio joins a group of ladies in amicable conversation; Boccaccio later reveals that his account of their history has depended upon a written clerical testimony (V, 96,3; V, 97,10). The double assurance offered by the French poet in opening his poem finds its equivalent in the *Filocolo*'s final chapter as Boccaccio instructs his opus:

> . . . a coloro che con benivola intenzione ti riguardano, ingegnati di piacere . . . Tu se' di tal donna suggetto che le tue forze non deono esser piccole. E a' contradicenti le tue piacevoli cose, dà la lunga fatica di Ilario per veridico testimonio . . .   (V, 97,9–10)

> . . . do your best to please those who look upon you with kindly intentions . . . You are subject to such a woman that your powers cannot be small. And to those who speak against your pleasurable aspects, point to the long labour of Ilario as trustworthy testimony . . .

It seems, then, that the version of *Floire et Blancheflor* with which Boccaccio was familiar bore a greater resemblance to the surviving 'roman idyllique' manuscripts than to the unique 'roman d'aventures'. This proposal cuts across the lines traditionally drawn to indicate the dissemination of the French romance north and south: but as we have seen Boccaccio lived in an extraordinary milieu at Angevin Naples.

Margaret Pelan is puzzled by the fact that the 'roman idyllique' fails to develop some of the themes initially outlined: we hear nothing of Floire's conversion to Christianity (3006–9) until the narrative is virtually complete, and nothing at all of Floire's Christian government of Bulgaria and Hungary.[23] The *Filocolo* fulfils such undeveloped potential: Florio's conversion to Christianity and his actions as a Christian governor are the chief concerns of its final two Books. The way in which Boccaccio extends his secular romance into the domain of Christian piety recalls the procedure of *Guy of Warwick*. Guy, like Florio, energetically undertakes numerous adventures in attempting to win his beloved: but once the lady has been won he turns his thoughts to God and becomes a Christian adventurer.[24]

Both *Guy of Warwick* and a translation of version I of *Floire et Blancheflor* appear in the celebrated Auchinleck manuscript, a volume with which Chaucer may well have been familiar.[25] Chaucer's reading of such romances must, to some extent, have primed him for his encounter with the *Filocolo*: but the *Filocolo*'s extraordinary incorporation of classical material must have taken him by surprise. This free-handed incorporative process is spectacularly evident from the first as Boccaccio presses classical myth into the service of Christian history. The expulsion of Lucifer from heaven is merged with the story of the victorious struggle of Jove and Vulcan against the rebellious Giants; Adam is figured as Prometheus and Lucifer as Pluto (I, 3,1–9). Boccaccio's allegorising is often ingenious but sometimes messily complex: busily marshalling the assistance of Neptune, Eolus and Mars (supported by nymphs, fauns and satires) against Manfred, Juno feels bound to explain that the Trojan remnant was not destroyed on first entering Italy because it had first to establish the line of popes (I, 1,6–8). There is nothing proto-humanist about Boccaccio's employment of classical material here: his naive enthusiasm recalls the more flamboyant attempts of the English classicising friars.[26]

Boccaccio's persistent attempts to clothe Christian history in pagan myth owe much to the works of Ovid and something to Vergil.[27] The two poets are commemorated in the *Filocolo*'s final chapter as Boccaccio pays thoughtful tribute to five great authors: Vergil, Lucan, Statius, Ovid and Dante (V, 97,4–6).

Boccaccio begins his tribute by reminding his 'little . . . book' ('piccolo . . . libretto', V, 97,1) that, being the work of a 'humble youth' ('umile giovane'), it cannot rise to great heights:

> . . . e però agli eccellenti ingegni e alle robuste menti lascia i gran versi di Virgilio. (V, 97,4)

> . . . and so leave the great verses of Vergil to those of excellent intellect and of powerful mind.

Vergil's 'great verses' are to be revered from a distance and left to stronger minds: this admonition captures Boccaccio's attitude towards the *Aeneid* with admirable candour. The *Filocolo* acknowledges Vergil as the loftiest of poets ('altissimo poeta', IV, 14,2; 'somma poeta', V, 75,4): his verse is, consequently, 'orecchiata da lontano'.[28] Florio, like Aeneas before him, discovers love, journeys in pursuit of truth and founds a civilisation: but it is, inevitably, Dante's Vergil that exerts most influence on Boccaccio.

Boccaccio honours Lucan and Statius as poets of war:

'E quelli [versi][29] del valoroso Lucano, ne' quali le fiere arme di Marte si cantano, lasciali agli armigeri cavalieri insieme con quelli del tolosano Stazio.' (V, 97,5)

'And those [verses] of the worthy Lucan, in which the fierce arms of Mars are sung, leave them to warlike knights, along with those verses of Statius from Toulouse.'

In describing the battle between Christians and pagans in the *Filocolo*'s first Book Boccaccio makes considerable use of Lucan's *De bello civili*; in portraying its sad and gruesome aftermath in I, 32 he adheres remarkably closely to Lucan's account of Pharsalia.[30] Boccaccio also draws upon Statius for such scenes: by the time the *Filocolo* was complete Boccaccio had almost certainly embarked upon a careful reading of the *Thebaid* in preparation for his own epic of war, the *Teseida*.[31] Boccaccio's reverence for this poet was, of course, encouraged by the vital role accorded to Statius in the *Commedia*.

In *De Vulgari* Dante limits his approval of Ovid to 'Ovidium Metamorfoseos' (II, vi, 7); in the *Inferno* he makes a conscious and determined attempt to surpass Ovid in the art of metamorphosis (XXV, 97–102). The *Filocolo* is full of metamorphoses: in fact, the entire opus may be considered as a mighty attempt by the young author to metamorphose himself into a book and so fulfil his desire to be embraced by his lady.[32] Boccaccio draws inspiration from the Ovidian accounts of Arethusa (*Metamorphoses* V, 632–8) and Byblis (IX, 655–665) in describing the transformation of the grief-stricken Fileno, Florio's unsuccessful rival, into a fountain (IV, 3,9–11); and he triumphantly reverses the Ovidian process with Fileno's extraordinary demetamorphosis (V, 37,2–6). This remarkable spectacle—of a regenerate Fileno rising up out of the waters—clearly prefigures the general conversion and baptism of the company which occurs at the end of this Book; it is immediately preceded by a speech of forgiveness which recalls the words of St Paul.[33]

Ovid supplies Boccaccio with models of inward (spiritual) as well as outward (physical) transformation; the *Filocolo* is aligned with the Ovidian works which teach the art of love:

E chi con molta efficacia ama, il sermontino Ovidio seguiti, delle cui opere tu se' confortatore. (V, 97,5)

And let him who would make love to great effect follow Ovid from Sulmona, of whose works you are an ally.

It might seem odd to discover such an injunction at the end of a work which witnesses a general conversion to Christianity: but in its abiding concern with love, the work of Ovid performs a vital function for Boccaccio in smoothing the path from paganism to orthodoxy. In the first Book of the *Filocolo* the pagan King Felice decrees that Florio and Biancifiore should receive an education; this will repair the defects of nature (I, 45,2). The first text to be studied by the two infants is 'il santo libro d'Ovidio' (I, 45,6). Again, it may seem odd to describe the *Ars Amatoria* as 'the holy book of Ovid': but although the adjective 'santo' was later employed ironically by Boccaccio,[34] its application here seems perfectly serious. In II, 8,4 we learn that Florio, through his Ovidian 'santi studii', has become 'dirozzato' ('civilised, cultivated'); in III, 33,9–10 Fileno apostrophises 'Sulmona, secluded fatherland of the most noble poet Ovid'[35] and passes through the city with the reverence of a pilgrim ('reverente per lo mezzo di quella trapassò'); and at a crucial moment of personal trial, Filocolo (alias Florio)[36] draws upon the resources of his earlier education in recalling the teaching of Ovid:

> Filocolo, così incalciato, e più ognora dubitando, per avventura si ricordò d'un verso già da lui letto in Ovidio, ove i paurosi dispregia dicendo: 'La fortuna aiuta gli audaci, e i timidi caccia via . . .' (IV, 101,8)

> Filocolo, being pressed in this way, and becoming more desperate by the minute, happened to remember a verse that he had once read in Ovid, where Ovid rebukes the timorous, saying: 'Fortune favours the brave and chases the timid away . . .'

Inspired by the force of this precept, Florio strengthens his resolve to continue his struggle for the recovery of his beloved, Biancifiore. For Boccaccio in the *Filocolo*, Ovid is a teacher worthy of great respect: his writings, along with those of Vergil, represent the highest wisdom of the pagan world.[37]

Boccaccio shared Dante's simultaneous loves for the literatures of Christianity and of paganism.[38] He evidently admired the way in which the *Commedia* integrates the sages, gods and incubi of the ancient world into a coherently-presented Christian universe even though, in his *Filocolo* or elsewhere, he could not himself achieve such coherence and consistency. From the broadest concepts of design to the finest details of language, the *Commedia* exerts a powerful influence over the *Filocolo*. Although Boccaccio's romance is composed in five Books, the tripartite structure of the *Commedia* certainly helps shape its development and the progress of its protagonist: Florio starts out at the court of a pagan King (who is misled by the devil, I, 9,1–11,3); he travels over a vast terrain in the hope of being reunited with his beloved and then joins her at the highest peak of worldly happiness;[39] finally, in her company, he attains to the fullness of Christian revelation and learns the responsibilities incumbent upon a Christian governor.[40] The geography of the world that Florio traverses is ordered in a manner reminiscent of the *Commedia*;[41] and, as in the *Commedia*, the people who inhabit this world are seen to be subject to the laws of 'God's politics'.[42] Florio is guided on his travels by his teacher Ascalion; their relationship recalls that of Dante and Vergil.[43] The power of Dante's poetic example makes itself felt even when the context argues against it: in exhorting his companions to join him on his great voyage, Florio echoes Dante's Ulysses.[44]

Boccaccio's *Filocolo* respects Dante's prescription for the attainment of vernacular eloquence by imitating or 'following after' the style of the great Latin masters.[45] Dedicated to the development of an illustrious vernacular, Boccaccio (in completing the *apologia* of V, 97,10) recognises that its standing in the face of the *auctores* is precarious:

> . . . e, nel cospetto di tutti, del tuo volgar parlare ti sia scusa il ricevuto comandamento, che 'l tuo principio palesa.

48

. . . and, in the presence of everyone, let the command received (which your opening chapter discloses) be your excuse for your vernacular speech.

Dante follows after four great Latin poets; Boccaccio follows after Dante in the humble hope that he may assume sixth place in this poetic confraternity, a tradition of poetic enterprise which connects Latin antiquity to the Christian present:

> Né ti sia cura di volere essere dove i misurati versi del fiorentino Dante si cantino, il quale tu sì come piccolo servidore molto dei reverente seguire. (V, 97,6)

> Nor should you concern yourself with wishing to be where the measured verses of the Florentine Dante are sung; Dante, whom you must follow with the great reverence of a little servant.

In his excellent summary of past approaches to *Troilus and Criseyde* John P. McCall observes that two schools of thought have developed on Chaucer's transformation of his source story.[46] The first has flourished under the tutelage of C. S. Lewis, who 'has claimed that Chaucer's rendering of *Il Filostrato* was most influenced by medieval rhetoric and French romance, especially by the *Roman de la Rose*'.[47] Adherents to the second school 'have found it possible to move in a very different direction and have concluded that Chaucer has "Trojanized" his story and consciously made it more classical and pagan'.[48] McCall sensibly concludes that both views merit consideration:

> Since there is evidence for both views, many critics have concluded that Chaucer purposefully created two perspectives, medieval and ancient, for a double effect: the medievalization of the poem in various ways creates what Morton W. Bloomfield has called 'the strong reality and, in a sense, [the] nearness of the past' (p. 17); and the Trojan and pagan allusions create a sense of historical distance which reinforces the 'pastness' of the story. Whether such perspectives are at odds, or on different levels of reality, or finally in some way congruent has long been a central issue in the interpretation of the *Troilus*.[49]

The *Filostrato* provided Chaucer with an excellent story-line but had little to teach him as an opus. Boccaccio was little more than twenty when he wrote the *Filostrato*: his interest in classical antiquity and in his own status as a vernacular author had barely awakened. But the richness, abundance and diversity of the source material absorbed into the *Filocolo* and the complex attitudes assumed by Boccaccio in managing it provide illuminating parallels with the enterprise of Chaucer's *Troilus*. In fashioning a romance of epic proportions containing a world that is at once pagan and medieval Boccaccio explores the twin perspectives subsequently developed within *Troilus and Criseyde*.

Chaucer begins his *Troilus* by situating himself among lovers and by proposing to tell a tale of love which is, in such company, deserving of sympathetic attention (I, 1–56). Following two hints (I, 133,159) we are informed (as the first *Canticus Troili* is introduced) that Chaucer is translating:

49

And of his song naught only the sentence,
As writ myn auctour called Lollius,
But pleinly, save oure tonges difference,
I dar wel seyn, in al that Troilus
Seyde in his song, loo! every word right thus
As I shal seyn; and whoso list it here,
Loo, next this vers he may it fynden here.   (I, 393–9)

In opening Book II Chaucer insists three times that he is intent upon following his *auctour*; references to this *auctour* are, however, most numerous in the latter half of the final Book as Chaucer attempts to disengage himself from pagan fictions and to assume a position of impeccable religious orthodoxy.[50]

Boccaccio, we have noted, also begins his opus in the service of Love's servants. But he too subsequently informs us that he is translating: he follows the 'true testimony' of Ilario, the priest who received Florio and company into the Christian religion.[51] Both Ilario and Lollius are (almost certainly) imaginary. But their supposed existence allows each poet to take up a particular authorial posture: by affirming that his work incorporates the historical witness of an *auctour*, each suggests that his modern vernacular narrative is supported by a backbone of ancient authority.[52]

Chaucer was not (in the *Troilus* or elsewhere) much interested in pressing claims for the originality of his material: the medieval rhetoricians attached little importance to originality.[53] But Chaucer is, in the *Troilus*, eager to picture himself in the process of translating. At the very climax of his story-telling Chaucer turns from his protagonists to spend two stanzas discussing his translation practice with his imaginary audience (III, 1324–37); and in the stanza quoted above (I, 393–9) he promises to bring the words (not just the bare 'sentence') of his *auctour* vividly into the present. Boccaccio likewise makes no claims for originality in his choice of material in the *Filocolo*: he sets out not to invent a new story but to restore an ancient legend that has suffered neglect; the challenge to the ' "poeta" ' (I, 1,25) lies in this task of restoration, a task which will exercise his ingenuity to the full. The definition of poetry established in the *Filocolo* is essentially that which guided Chaucer throughout his career: 'poetry is a process of manipulating language so that the wisdom evolved in the past will become available, applicable, and operative in the present'.[54] The interrelations of present, past and future contained by this definition are brilliantly captured by Chaucer's three successive usages of the verb *seyn* in the stanza just quoted above (I, 396–8).

Chaucer's sense of himself as a vernacular author upholding and extending past poetic enterprise was first, we have noted, tentatively developed within *The House of Fame*. In this early poem Chaucer could only eye the great *auctores* in passing: but by the time he has reached the end of the *Troilus* he feels confident enough to align his work with theirs. Like Boccaccio at the end of the *Filocolo*, he claims—with characteristic modesty—sixth place in a company of six poets:

Go, litel bok, go, litel myn tragedye,
Ther God thi makere yet, er that he dye,
So sende myght to make in som comedye!

But litel book, no makyng thow n'envie,
But subgit be to alle poesye;
And kis the steppes, where as thow seest pace
Virgile, Ovide, Omer, Lucan, and Stace.   (V, 1786–92)

The five *auctores* commemorated here are those who were (quite literally) put on pedestals in *The House of Fame*.[55] For Chaucer, as for most medieval writers, Homer ('Omer') was little more than a name to be venerated: but Chaucer certainly revered the writings as well as the reputations of the four Latin authors named in V, 1792. Chaucer was acquainted with Lucan's *Pharsalia* although he does not appear to have made much use of it; and he certainly held the *Thebaid* of Statius in high regard.[56] Chaucer adopted Dante's example in 'following after' Vergil.[57] But Ovid is the *auctour* that he turns to most frequently: 'the appeal of Ovid was greater than that of any other single writer who contributed to his literary development.'[58] Like Boccaccio, Chaucer 'appears to have been most intimately acquainted with the *Metamorphoses*, the *Ars Amatoria*, the *Heroides* and the *Fasti*, in that order': and Chaucer, 'like other medieval humanists, recognized Ovid's worth as an ethical philosopher'.[59] It is, perhaps, in their especial fondness for Ovid that the sensibilities and temperaments of Chaucer and Boccaccio draw closest together.

The exercise of assembling and comparing the sum total of borrowings made by Chaucer and Boccaccio from ancient Latin poets might prove instructive;[60] it is certainly instructive to compare the attitudes they assume in aligning themselves with the *auctores*. The *Filocolo*'s commemoration of great authors is, we have noted, followed by an acknowledgement of the precarious status of vernacular composition (V, 97,10); in the *Troilus* an equivalent acknowledgement follows immediately:

And for ther is so gret diversite
In Englissh and in writyng of oure tonge,
So prey I God that non myswrite the,
Ne the mysmetre for defaute of tonge.
And red wherso thow be, or elles songe,
That thow be understonde, God I biseche!   (V, 1793–8)

It is evident from the *Roman de la Rose* and the *Commedia* that Jean de Meun and Dante also gave much thought to the relationship of the vernacular author to his Latin forebears.

Before his assembled *baronage*, at a point close to the centre of the *Rose*, the God of Love remembers poets who have served his cause: he laments Tibullus at some length (10477–91) and then, more briefly, Gallus, Catullus and Ovid (10492–5). He then treats of 'Guillaume de Lorriz', who is to begin the *Rose* (10496–534), and of 'Johans Chopinel' (Jean de Meun, the author of this passage) who will complete it (10535–644):

'car quant Guillaumes cessera,
Jehans le continuera . . .'   (10557–8)

'for when Guillaume shall cease,
Jean will continue it . . .'

51

Poetic activity conjoins past, present and future in a single cause. Jean's meditation here is indebted to an Ovidian text, *Amores* III, ix, which begins with the same god ('puer Veneris', III, ix, 7) lamenting the same poet, Tibullus (1–16). Orpheus and Linus, legendary but mortal poets of the past, are recalled (19–24), together with Homer, who also sank down into the black underworld at death:

> hunc quoque summa dies nigro submersit Averno.
>
> (III, ix, 27)
>
> a final day submerged him, too, in black Avernus.

Only the work of poets endures (28–32); all else perishes, and death has now claimed Tibullus (33–46), although his life was spared for a while (47–58). And yet, if anything survives after death, Tibullus will dwell in the vale of Elysium (59–60); Catullus—his brows wreathed with ivy—will come to greet him with his companion Calvus and, perhaps, with Gallus (61–64). If the spirit survives, Tibullus has increased the number of the blessed ('pios', 65–66).

At first sight it appears that only the earlier lines lamenting Tibullus have influenced the French poet: but Jean evidently took his references to other Latin poets from the latter part of the *Amores* passage, substituting Ovid for Calvus. Jean apparently recognised that the Latin poem—with its vision of past, present and future—shared his concern with the continuity of poetic enterprise. In composing his elegy, Ovid had occupied the present and surveyed past and future: in writing the *Rose*, Jean assumes Ovid's position and pushes the Latin poet back, with his near contemporaries, into the past. As Ovid was to Tibullus, so Jean is now to Guillaume: for both writers, the death of a near contemporary is both a cause for lament and a call to continue a poetic tradition.

Dante shares Jean's confidence in the ability of the vernacular poet to continue the enterprise of the 'regulatos . . . poetas'.[61] In *Inferno* IV, 90 Dante encounters Ovid, who occupies third place in the 'bella scola' of Vergil. The 'sire' of this school is Homer. In *Amores* III, ix Ovid had lamented that Homer had sunk down to 'black Avernus' at death: but he had later argued that great poets will, possibly, be waiting to greet their peers after death, in Elysium. *Inferno* IV upholds all this: Homer and Ovid after him have descended to Avernus and in doing so attained to Elysium, the most exalted terrain that they could conceive of. It is characteristic of Dante that he should allow the great pagans of antiquity the fullest realisation of their personal vision: a vision which, of course, stops short of Christian revelation.

Dante may well have been directed to the Ovidian text by his reading of Jean de Meun; he certainly appears to have been impressed by the passage of the *Rose* in which Jean accords himself sixth place in a confraternity which unites the enterprise of ancient and modern poets. The poets of *Inferno* IV assemble ('adunar') to accord Dante a similar honour in welcoming him as 'sixth among such intellects':

> Così vid' i' adunar la bella scola
> di quel segnor de l'altissimo canto
> che sovra li altri com' aquila vola.
> Da ch'ebber ragionato insieme alquanto,

volsersi a me con salutevol cenno,
e 'l mio maestro sorrise di tanto;
    e più d'onore ancora assai me fenno,
ch'e' sì mi fecer de la loro schiera,
sì ch'io fui sesto tra cotanto senno.   (IV, 94–102)

So I saw the assembling of the fair school
of that lord of the most lofty song
that soars above the others like an eagle.
    When they had conferred together for a while
they turnèd towards me with a sign of greeting,
and at this my master smiled;
    and they paid me yet greater honour still,
for they made me a member of their own company,
so that I was sixth among such intellects.

When Chaucer accords himself sixth place in a series of six poets he is, then, following precedents established by Jean de Meun, Dante and Boccaccio. Not one of these four vernacular poets chooses the same five companions[62]: but each nevertheless expresses allegiance to a common conception of poetic continuity in his elaboration of this shared *topos*. It is interesting to note, however, that certain features of the *Troilus* stanza place it closer to the *Filocolo* passage than to either of the others: its positioning at the end of the work; its form as a *congedo* or *envoy* addressed from the author to his opus; and the modesty of its appeal, which urges the work to recognise its own limitations.[63] Its first line recalls the opening phrase of Boccaccio's final chapter ('O piccolo mio libretto'); and Boccaccio's willing deference to wise or wiser men ('più savi') who may wish to amend his work in the light of 'their clear judgement' ('il loro diritto giudicio', V, 97,8) is paralleled by Chaucer's deference to 'moral Gower' and 'philosophical Strode' who, similarly, may wish to correct the work, 'ther nede is' (V, 1856–9).

It seems, then, that Chaucer wished to align his masterpiece of extended narrative, *Troilus and Criseyde*, with the tradition of extended vernacular narrative which grows out of the *Roman de la Rose* and includes the *Commedia* and the *Filocolo*. It is, I believe, possible to speak of such a tradition, although some critics have refused to countenance any rapprochement between the *Rose* and Dante's divine poem.[64] In fact, one of the best-qualified of medieval commentators believed that the *Commedia* issued from Dante's reading of the *Rose*. Laurent de Premierfait, the first French translator of Boccaccio, proposed that Dante

. . . advisa que ou livre de la Rose est souffisammant descript le paradis des bons et l'enfer des mauvais en langaige francois, voult en langaige florentin, soubz aultre manier de verys rimoiez, contrefaire au vif le beau livre de la Rose, en ensuyant tel ordre comme fist le divin poete Virgile ou sixiesme livre que l'en nomme Eneide.[65]

. . . having perceived that the paradise of the good and the hell of the evil is adequately described in the book of the Rose, wished to employ a different system of rhymed verse in the Florentine language to imitate closely the fair book of the Rose, following such order as is observed by the divine poet Vergil in the sixth book of the work called *Aeneid*.

Premierfait, like Christine de Pisan in the celebrated fifteenth-century Quarrel of the *Rose*,[66] associates the *Rose* and the *Commedia* in terms of their content, a content which reflects the learnedness of the two authors. Such learnedness is employed in the service of a universal theme which encompasses heaven and hell and their attendant pleasures and pains.[67] Medieval readers did not (before the very end of the fourteenth century) doubt the seriousness of Jean's engagement with such universals: his work apparently enjoyed approval in morally conservative circles.[68] Guillaume Deguileville's *Pèlerinage de la vie humaine* is, we are told, the fruit of a diligent reading of the *Rose*.[69] The author of *Cleanness* (the severest of orthodox moralists) draws from a speech expounded by 'Clopyngnel in þe compas of his clene *Rose*'.[70] Chaucer, in repenting of his 'translacions and enditynges of worldly vanitees',[71] does not renounce his translation of the *Rose*; in the *Prologue* to *The Legend of Good Women* the God of Love upbraids Chaucer for having made this translation:

> 'Thow mayst it nat denye,
> For in pleyn text, it nedeth nat to glose,
> Thow hast translated the Romauns of the Rose,
> That is an heresye ageyns my lawe,
> And makest wise folk fro me withdrawe . . .'   (G, 253–7)

The author of *Il Fiore* also expected 'wise folk' to shun the God of Love: his Amore demands that Amante should abandon belief in the evangelists and worship him, '"for I am your god"'.[72] The wisdom of the *Fiore*'s protagonist is, however, open to question: in LXXXII, 12–14 Amore compliments Durante on his obdurate resistance to Reason; and towards the end of the poem Durante finds occasion for rueful reflection on his own foolishness. His language here recalls the proverbial terseness of the *Troilus*' narrator:

> Ma spesso falla ciò che 'l folle crede.
> Così avenne al buon di Ser Durante.   (CCII, 13–14)

> But that which the fool believes in often fails.
> To such an end came the happiness of Ser Durante.

> But alday faileth thing that fooles wenden.   (I, 217)

This sense of the frailty of the individual poet (coupled with a confidence in the endurance of poetry) is a constant feature of the narrative tradition which stems from the *Rose*. It is, of course, integral to the *Rose* itself; and it forms part of Ovid's reflections in *Amores* III, ix, the elegy that did so much to stimulate Jean's thinking on poetic continuity. Ovid revels in the power of his poetic individuality; some claim, he notes, that poets are especially favoured by the gods, or even that they partake of divinity (17–18): but such claims are frustrated by mortality (19–20); poems survive, but not poets (28). This uneasy (but wryly humorous) assessment of the individual poet's significance is adopted by Jean de Meun and bequeathed to the poets that follow after him. The French poet's realisation of his 'poetic I'[73] draws strength from his awareness of a tradition that links him with Ovid and his peers: but this same 'I' is constantly subject to the erosion and self-deflation that is consonant with the ironic tenor of his writing.

The enigmatic, self-ironising authorial persona of *Il Fiore*, Ser Durante, has been subjected to the most searching critical appraisal.[74] Durante's work, which forms only a part of a greater French inheritance that made the *Commedia* possible, exerts a definite influence within Dante's poem.[75] It is even possible that Durante and Dante are one.[76] So Chaucer and Dante might have begun their poetic careers in identical fashion: as translators of the *Roman de la Rose*. It is evident, however, that the *Fiore* poet, in condensing the French poem to less than one sixth of its original length, had quite different intentions from the diligent literalists responsible for the English *Romaunt*. Durante concentrates chiefly on generating a lively narrative: Nature and Genius find no place in his poem, and the doctrinal matter is much reduced. Interest is focussed upon Amante's conquest of the rose, with occasional relief provided by three major episodes: the *ars amandi* instructions of Amico, La Vechia's teaching of Bellacoglienza[77] and the chicanery of Falsenbiante. The *Fiore* poet handles material from the entire *Rose* with remarkable ease and assurance: he doubtless benefitted from efforts made by earlier writers who had attempted to adapt the example of the *Rose* to Italian conditions. (Chaucer, we have noted, starts from scratch: his earliest efforts invite comparison with the *Tesoretto*). But Durante evidently struggled to find the right balance between lyric and narrative impulses: his solution (a continuous sequence of two hundred and thirty-two sonnets) is not entirely satisfactory. Such a struggle is characteristic of all the works in this extended narrative tradition (including the *Filocolo*, which strings together four hundred and fifty-nine segments of prose, and the *Commedia* itself); its resolution in *Troilus and Criseyde* is one of Chaucer's most brilliant achievements. Such achievements, remarkable in themselves, appear the more remarkable when considered within this European context. For we may observe Chaucer, in the span of a single English lifetime, addressing those problems in extended narrative that had engaged Italian writers over five generations: Brunetto; Durante; Dante; Boccaccio; Petrarch.

When viewed from English perspectives, *Troilus and Criseyde* seems to stand in glorious, not to say precocious, isolation. But when viewed from the European perspective that Chaucer points us to in concluding his opus, the *Troilus* is seen to stand in a clear line of descent. This European tradition supplies the appropriate context for the examination of Chaucer's reworking of the *Filostrato*, the subject of our fifth and sixth chapters. We will conclude this chapter (and prepare for the next) by considering one theme common to these European extended narratives: pilgrimage.

The obscene climax of the *Rose* comes as the lover, equipped with the sack and staff of a pilgrim (21317–397), approaches and penetrates the shrine of his beloved. But in addition to this profane parody of pilgrimage, the *Rose* contains a genuine movement towards religious enlightenment: we pass from the 'garden of pleasure' ('vergier de deduiz') to the 'fair park' ('biau park'), domain of the 'leaping white lamb' ('li blans agnelez saillanz', 20226). These two terrains are explicitly contrasted later in the poem in a lengthy speech by Genius (20237–629): they differ as does truth from fable ('voir a fable', 20258).

In his journey of discovery the *Tesoretto*'s narrator becomes beguiled with worldly vanities and ensnared in secular love: but he finally repents of his errors and makes a good, orthodox end. The *Fiore* retraces the profane pilgrimage of the *Rose* and reaches the same erotic climax: in this limited sense it is aptly described as 'a short *commedia*'.[78] Dante's *Commedia* also follows the outward action of the *Rose*: described in bare outline, the plots of the two poems are remarkably similar.[79] The *Commedia* also imitates the authentic religious movement of the French poem in its progression from the 'paradiso terrestre' (the 'earthly paradise' in which Beatrice, the beloved, is first encountered) to the domain of the 'blessed Lamb'[80] and the final vision of God. This movement is likened to that of pilgrimage: at the beginning of the *Paradiso* Beatrice gazes at the sun 'like a pilgrim who wishes to return home' (I, 51); and towards the end Dante gazes around like a pilgrim who has reached his goal:

> E quasi peregrin che si ricrea
> nel tempio del suo voto riguardando . . .   (XXXI, 43–4)

> And like a pilgrim who renews himself
> by gazing around the temple he had vowed to reach . . .

The *Filocolo*, as we shall see, makes imaginative use of the iconography of the *Commedia* and the *Rose* in observing the passage of its protagonists from pagan to Christian observance. This spiritual migration is encompassed by the framework of an actual pilgrimage. Having set out for Compostella, Quinto Lelio Africano and company are massacred by Saracens (I, 5–26). Lelio's wife survives long enough to give birth to Biancifiore, who is successively the object of Florio's amatory pilgrimage and his partner in completing the Christian pilgrimage with which the story opened. Following their conversion, Florio and Biancifiore discover the site of the massacre, gather up the bones of the Christian warriors and transport them to Rome (V, 88–91).

The *Filocolo*, like its predecessors in this extended narrative tradition, is a comedy. So too, for the duration of its first three Books, is the *Troilus*.[81] Its hero moves 'Fro wo to wele' (I, 4), and in Book III his amatory pilgrimage (his conquest of the Rose) achieves completion. The love of Troilus for Criseyde appears to mesh with universal order. The unhappy confusion of the early *Canticus* ('Al stereless withinne a boot am I', I, 416) is dispersed: God, Troilus proclaims, has willed that Criseyde should be his 'steere' (III, 1290–2). The final couplet of Chaucer's central Book (III, 1819–20) establishes a point of equilibrium and rest for Troilus equivalent to that enjoyed by Florio following his union with Biancifiore (IV, 122,3). But whereas the pilgrimage of the pagan Florio is extended into the domain of Christian revelation, the pagan Troilus falls 'out of joie' (I, 4): he loses both his faith in Criseyde and his faith in God. As the *Filocolo* draws to a close, author and hero are united in the Christian faith. But at the ending of *Troilus and Criseyde*, author and hero are painfully divided by an unbridgeable gulf. Chaucer ends on orthodox ground only by wrenching himself away from the world of his fiction.

The falling-off of Troilus moves Chaucer's narrative in a direction opposite to that of the *Rose*, the *Commedia* and the *Filocolo*: their common movement towards the happy fulfilment of pilgrimage—a movement that the *Troilus* initially complies with—is tragically frustrated. Chaucer's awkwardness and discomfiture in his last two Books is unmistakeable: he is working against the grain of an illustrious tradition. At the very moment in which he declares his 'tragedye' complete, however, Chaucer offers the promise of a 'comeyde' to come (V, 1786–8): this, of course, is *The Canterbury Tales*. Chaucer's celebrated pilgrimage moves in the same direction as its illustrious forebears. Its general design is, from first to last, remarkably similar to that of Boccaccio's *Filocolo*.

As we have seen, the *Filocolo* issues from the activity of a *brigata* which is governed by the poet's beloved, Maria. Within its all-encompassing pilgrimage framework it contains an abundant variety of characters, incidents and poetic styles. When its hero (speaking as a Christian governor in V, 59,1) declares that '"i nuovi accidenti nuove generazioni di parlari adducono"' ('"new events bring forth new forms of language"') he supplies a fitting epigraph for the tireless experimentation of the entire opus.

In opening his *Canterbury Tales*, Chaucer early establishes his poetic credentials by the sustained brilliance of his *General Prologue*'s opening period. Having set his scene with such dazzling precision, he describes his own appearance on it with studied casualness:

> Bifil that in that seson on a day . . .   (I, 19)

This compares with the casual formula employed by Boccaccio as he brings himself into the *Filocolo*'s action ('Avvenne che un giorno . . .', I, 1,17), a formula which is repeated as Boccaccio describes how he came (by chance) to join the *brigata*:

> . . . avvenne che un giorno, non so come,
> la fortuna mi balestrò in un santo tempio . . .   (I, 1,23)

> . . . it happened that one day, I don't know how,
> fortune catapulted me into a holy temple . . .

The Chaucerian equivalent of a *brigata* is a *compaignye*; the meeting of the pilgrims in 'The Tabard' is similarly fortuitous:

> . . . a compaignye,
> Of sondry folk, by aventure yfalle
> In felaweshipe . . .   (I, 24–6)

It might seem improbable to compare 'The Tabard' with the 'holy temple' in which Boccaccio finds himself: but both are convivial places in which religious and secular motivations are subtly combined; both gatherings have a holiday atmosphere about them; and both scenes see a mixture of the three social estates.[82]

Like Boccaccio, Chaucer tells of his amicable reception into the social group; in both works, the social bond is sealed by conversation (I, 1,23; I, 30–32). Chaucer goes on to tell how his opus, *The Canterbury Tales*, is called into being by the figure that the *compaignye* is to recognise as its 'governour' (I, 813) for the duration of its existence. The tales are to be told by the various members of the company; Chaucer draws attention to his specific responsibility as poet-reporter (I, 725–46). His pilgrimage then gets under way.

Chaucer and Boccaccio's common choice of a pilgrimage framework allows them a generous range of imaginative movement and emphasis. Their travellers are (more or less) mindful that their journeying has a serious end in prospect: but considerable pleasure lies in the travelling, much of it through story-telling. Given this constant assurance that their pilgrims are moving, moment by moment, towards a religious goal, Chaucer and Boccaccio are able to exercise their skills as secular poets with considerable freedom. Yet they evidently did not assume that the pilgrimage context could provide unqualified license for their pleasure-giving activities. In the course of their pilgrimage, the two poets exploit every colour of rhetoric and trick of art at their disposal; approaching its termination, however, they lay aside all this to point us towards a further journey,

> '. . . thilke parfit glorious pilgrymage
> That highte Jerusalem celestial.' (X, 50–51)

Each poet elects to round off his opus with a sermon in plain prose based on the seven deadly sins. Renunciation is the theme both of the *Parson's Tale* and of the deathbed sermon of Florio's father, King Felice (V, 92,3–24). Renunciation is expressed in the form as well as in the content of each discourse: the fluid and leisurely style of the earlier writing, characteristically coloured by extravagant astrological references and instances from the pagan world, yields to a drab, monotonous discourse which concentrates solely and systematically on the *unum necessarium* of Christian salvation. The brittle shell of poetic language falls away, revealing the hard kernel of Christian truth which (the poets might argue) has been the essence of their discourse all along.[83]

In the opinion of Boncompagno da Signa (the celebrated and influential teacher of the *ars dictaminis*), composition in prose was taken to warrant truthfulness, since 'tota scriptura trahit originem a prosa'.[84] Many Italians (such as Rusticiano da Pisa, Marco Polo's amanuensis) translated French romances into Italian prose in the apparent belief that prose invested their narratives with qualities suggestive of historical veracity.[85] Similarly, Boccaccio's choice of a prose medium for his adaptation of a French verse romance may have been intended to buttress his (spurious) claim that the *Filocolo* follows the ancient, 'truthful testimony' ('veridico testimonio', V, 97,10) of the priest Ilario. This late claim is, however, preceded by an illuminating account of Boccaccio's practice as a poet of secular love. In *Filocolo* V, 8 Florio, Biancifiore and company come across Idalogo, a young man who has suffered metamorphosis into a pine tree. Gradually, the reader comes to realise that this complex persona represents the voice of Boccaccio himself. Idalogo tells how, under the rule of Amore, he resolved to pursue his beloved and to employ *parole ornate*:

> 'Entrato in questo proponimento e uscito dell'usato cammino, abandonate le imprese cose, cominciai a disiderare, sotto la nuova signoria, di sapere quanto l'ornate parole avessero forza di muovere i cuori umani: e seguendo la silvestra fagiana, con pietoso stile quelle lungamente usai . . .' (V, 8,36)

> 'Having entered into this commitment, and having wandered from the well-trodden path and abandoned those things that I was supposed to be

doing, I began (under the influence of the new regime) to be desirous of knowing the extent to which embellished words might be empowered to move human hearts: and I employed such words in piteous style for a long time in pursuing the woodland hen pheasant . . .'[86]

Quaglio glosses 'l'ornate parole' as 'the value of love poetry, the power of rhymed love verses'.[87] This explains what the phrase stands for in its immediate context: but the remainder of the sentence in which it appears supplies its own gloss, which (with its reference to 'the power to move human hearts') brings out the rhetorical associations of the phrase. Such associations recall a passage of Brunetto Latini's *Rettorica* in which we are informed that 'rhetoric is that body of knowledge through which we learn how to speak and compose ornately'.[88] Elsewhere Brunetto warns that the gift of 'la lingua adorna', 'the embellishing tongue', may be put to bad use.[89] Beatrice requests Vergil to assist Dante by employing his 'parola ornata': but Jason deceives Hypsipyle by exercising the same talent.[90] *Parole ornate* are to be judged good or bad according to the uses to which they are put. Such ambiguity makes Chaucer's Franklin nervous and confused[91]: he declares his ignorance of and distaste for '"Colours of rethoryk"' (preferring '"swiche colours as growen in the mede"') before proceeding to employ rhetorical figures to brilliant effect. However, Chaucer's Parson (like Boccaccio's dying King) takes no chances and makes no concessions[92] with his '"myrie tale in prose"' (X, 46). And Chaucer himself follows the Parson's example; he employs plain prose to repent of his personal abuses of rhetorical art in composing 'the tales of Caunterbury, thilke that sownen into synne' (X, 1085).

The narrators of the *Filocolo* and *The Canterbury Tales*, like the protagonists of the *Rose* and *Commedia*, are fallible. Their opinions and poetic procedures lie open to scrutiny and correction. The lengthy, autobiographical discourse of *Filocolo* V, 8 closes with a crushing condemnation of women ('"le femine"') and with a muted criticism of divine wisdom:

> 'Esse, schiera sanza freno, secondo che la corrotta volontà le muta, così si muovono: per la qual cosa, se licito mi fosse, con voce piena d'ira verso gl'iddii crucciato mi volgerei, biasimandogli perché l'uomo, sopra tutte le loro creature nobile, accompagnarono di sì contraria cosa all sua virtù.' (V, 8,47)

> 'Women, an unbridled mob, move according to the fickle promptings of their corrupted will: and because of this, were it permissible, I would turn in torment towards the gods with a voice full of wrath, reproaching them for coupling man, the most noble of all their creatures, with a thing so contrary to his virtue.'

Biancifiore's reaction is dramatic and resolute: the tirade has hardly ('appena') come to an end before she rises to her feet, approaches the speaker and challenges his generalisation:

> 'O Idalogo, che colpa hanno le buone, e di diritta fede servatrici, se a te una malvagia, per tua simplicità, nocque non osservando la promessa?' (V, 9,1)

59

'O Idalogo, what can the guilt of good, faithfully-serving women be if one wicked woman, taking advantage of your ingenuousness, offended by not keeping a promise?'

In questioning Idalogo's right to generalise from a single example, Biancifiore insists upon her right as an individual not to be swept away in a universal condemnation of her sex, a condemnation which was, of course, a commonplace among medieval authors. Her protest is the more dramatic and effective because Idalogo represents Boccaccio himself: the character protests against her author. This is analogous to the protest of the Host against Chaucer and his '"rym dogerel"' (VII, 925). It also recalls the Wife of Bath's dramatic reaction to her clerical husband's readings from anti-feminist literature. Idalogo (like Jankyn and the pilgrim Chaucer) has the grace (or sense) to accept castigation and to stand corrected (V, 9,5–6).

It is most unlikely that Chaucer brought a manuscript of the voluminous *Filocolo* back to England, or that he read one right through whilst in Italy: had he done so he would have had practically no time for anything else. But Chaucer seems to have been impressed by the ways in which Boccaccio organised his opus: this organisation is deducible from a reading of the opening and concluding chapters and from some exploratory reading of chapters in between. The *Filocolo*, like the earlier European extended narratives with which it aligns itself, is concerned with pilgrimage. In those earlier works, however, the idea of pilgrimage is developed only as an incidental metaphor: in the *Filocolo* it is expanded to become the all-encompassing narrative framework of one long, historical pilgrimage. Chaucer improves upon Boccaccio's example: in extending between the Tabard and Jerusalem, the pilgrimage of *The Canterbury Tales* retains the force of metaphor; but to this it adds the vivid, immediate force of an actual event, a contemporary pilgrimage.[93] Boccaccio's complex manoeuvres within the *Filocolo*'s pilgrimage framework foreshadow the complex and various strategies devised by Chaucer as pilgrim and poet within his great *comedye*.

The *Filocolo*'s successful pilgrimage from secular, pagan love to religious orthodoxy also offers illuminating insights into the frustrated pilgrimage of *Troilus and Criseyde*. The combination of French, Latin and popular native source material assembled by the Italian work compares with that absorbed into the *Troilus*; and the way in which such material is organised yields remarkable parallels. The design of the *Filocolo* presented Chaucer with a model for his *Troilus* on the grandest scale in demonstrating how a French-derived romance might be transformed to become an extended narrative in the tradition of the *Rose* and the *Commedia*. It demonstrated much else besides: for example, how especial qualities of pathos might be realised by placing an intensely personal and inwardly-focused *planctus* beneath a mighty superstructure of mythological and astrological reference. Such lessons could not be learned from the slight *Filostrato*.

CHAPTER 4

Pagans at the Threshold of Enlightenment

Metaphors of travelling and pilgrimage exerted a steady, shaping influence on late medieval patterns of thought. It seems almost inevitable that when Petrarch came to organise his *Familiares* he should have figured this collection of letters as a journey from youth to maturity.[1] The sequence of the Petrarchan *Trionfi* enacts a pilgrimage from *cupiditas* to *aeternitas*; and the *Canzoniere* similarly (if less schematically) explores the emotional and intellectual terrain between Laura, the beloved, and Mary, Queen of Heaven.[2] This uncertain, intermediate space between earthly and heavenly love and between pagan and Christian observance exercised the imagination of the very greatest of four-teenth-century poets: Dante, Boccaccio, Petrarch, Langland[3] and Chaucer. Alastair Minnis has ably demonstrated how late medieval scholarly and theological speculation on the status of pagans informs Chaucer's poetic approaches to paganism.[4] Here such poetic approaches will be considered within the European tradition of extended narrative outlined in the previous chapter. Taking points of departure from the fourth Book of the *Filocolo*, we will observe Chaucer and Boccaccio exploiting the resources of the *Commedia* and the *Rose* in portraying pagans at the threshold of enlightenment.

Filocolo IV effects a radical extension of its French romance source. It sees Boccaccio opening up a generous, imaginative space in which to explore the status of his pagan hero, Florio, as he comes closer to his beloved and, in doing so, comes closer to Christian revelation. Boccaccio's intentions here are very different from those of the English romancer who effected the pious extension of *Guy of Warwick*. Guy complains that his pursuit of Felice, his beloved, has led him away from divine favour[5]: but Florio receives intimations of divine love in the very process of pursuing Biancifiore; pagan and Christian love are mysteriously contiguous. The first part of *Filocolo* IV centres on the activities of a party of friends or *brigata* which debates 'questions of love' ('questioni d'amore') in a garden near Naples: the source most active here is the *Commedia*, particularly those cantos describing the earthly paradise. This area of the *Filocolo* may have helped inspire Chaucer's *Parliament of Fowls* as well as providing a source for *The Franklin's Tale*. The second half of the Book tells how Florio penetrates the tower at Alexandria and consummates his love: the dominant influence here (the portion of the *Filocolo* in which Young noted the most numerous parallels with the *Troilus*)[6] is the *Rose*.[7]

Filocolo IV opens by describing the long and tortuous journey that brings Florio and company to Certaldo (Boccaccio's birthplace). Here the travellers come across an ancient temple, whose strange gods ('non conosciuti e strani iddii') Florio resolves to honour, since the fates ('i fati') have led him there. Sacrificing a bull, he apologises to these gods for the manner of his religious observance, which they might think strange; he beseeches them to consider his purity and good faith ('"mia purita e . . . buona fede"') as he has need of their help in reaching his goal as a young pilgrim of love:

> 'Io giovane d'anni e di senno, oltre al dovere innamorato, pellegrinan-do cerco d'adempiere il mio disio, al quale sanza il vostro aiuto conosco impossibile di pervenire . . .' (IV, 1,10)

> 'I, young in years and in wisdom, enamoured beyond due measure, seek by pilgrim-like journeying to fulfil my desire which, without your assistance, I know I cannot possibly attain . . .'

A voice answers him, commending his piety, offering him practical advice and predicting his ultimate success; it also foretells the poetic activity of Boccaccio himself:

> 'Onora questo luogo, però che quinci ancora si partirà colui che i tuoi accidenti con memorevoli versi farà manifesti agli ignoranti, e 'l suo nome sarà pieno di grazia'. (IV, 1,13)

> 'Honour this place, for there will depart from here he who, through memorable verses, will make your fortunes known to the ignorant, and his name will be full of grace'.

Boccaccio employs Dantean ingenuity in honouring himself and his name, Giovanni (John): but he follows Jean de Meun's example in situating his prophecy very close to the midpoint of the work.[8]

Outside the temple, Florio attempts to drink from a beautiful fountain that has caught his eye, but is surprised by a voice speaking out of the waters; this belongs to Fileno, his rival in love, who has been metamorphosed into a fountain of tears. The ensuing colloquy between Florio and Fileno borrows details from metamorphosic scenes in Ovid and Dante; the whole scene (IV, 2,1–5,1)—in which a young lover encounters a close image of himself as he bends over a 'clear fountain'—may have drawn inspiration from Guillaume's delicate elaboration of the myth of Narcissus.[9]

Florio's companions remark upon the dangers of entering the '"wrestling-school of Love"' ('"palestra d'Amore"'); those who lead '"a virtuous life without Love"' are indeed blessed (5,2): but Florio rejects this (5,4). Following the teaching of the strange god ('strano iddio', 6,1) they set out, and having suffered the terrors of a tempest they are eventually washed up at Naples (9,3); throughout all this, Ascalion continues to play the guiding and assuring role of Dante's Vergil.[10] Unfavourable weather forces Florio—like the hero of *Il Fiore* before him—to spend the winter inactively, in sighing and com-plaint.[11] He upbraids Eolus, protesting his innocence (and reminding us of the complex dynastic dimensions of the work established in its opening chapter):

> 'Apri gli occhi, e conosci ch'io non sono Enea, il gran nemico della santa Giunone: io sono un giovane che amo . . .' (IV, 11,10)

> 'Open your eyes, and recognise that I am not Aeneas, the great enemy of holy Juno: I am a young man in love . . .'

But the impatient lover is forced to await the arrival of spring; this comes with a splendid flourish of *parole ornate* which, in its syntactic complexity, its employment of astrological imagery, its celebration of natural regeneration, its emphasis that such a time is propitious for pilgrimage and its final recognition of the local facts of the narrative action invites comparison with the opening period of *The Canterbury Tales*:

> Ma essendo già Titan ricevuto nelle braccia di Castore e di Polluce, e la terra rivestita d'ornatissimi vestimenti, e ogni ramo nascoso dalle sue frondi, e gli uccelli, stati taciti nel noioso tempo, con dolci note riverberavano l'aere, e il cielo, che già ridendo a Filocolo il disiderato cammino promettea con ferma fede, avvenne che Filocolo una mattina, pieno di malinconia e tutto turbato nel viso, si levò dal notturno riposo. (IV, 12,1)

> But Titan being already received into the arms of Castor and of Pollux, and the earth decked out again in the most ornate clothes, and every branch hidden by its leaves; and the birds (having kept silent during the irksome season) were making the air reverberate with sweet notes; and as the heaven, now laughing, was promising Filocolo in firm faith the journey he longed for, it happened one morning that Filocolo got up from his nightly slumber full of melancholy and with a deeply-disturbed expression.

Florio gives an account of his strange vision ('"nuova visione"', 12,3): he seemed to have been on Mount Falerno (near Naples), upon which was a fair meadow decked with delightful plants and flowers. From here he seemed able to survey the whole universe (13,1). Whilst surveying the many regions, he saw a merlin ('"smeriglione"') fly up from the hill of Certaldo; circling in the sky, it then swooped down upon a beautiful hen pheasant ('"una fagiana bellissima"') which had risen up from a place near the birthplace of Ovid. The merlin caught his quarry on the meadow, close to Florio, fixing her firmly in his claws (13,2). Then he saw an owl ('"quello uccello che a guardia dell'armata Minerva si pone"') and a very black blackbird ('"uno nerissimo merlo"') fly up and follow the female bird, and then sit on the meadow in sight of her and her captor. Then from Sicily, he saw a dove ('"il semplice uccello, in compagnia di Citerea posto"') arise and take her place on the meadow, together with a cuckoo ('"cuculo"', 13,3). They were joined by a handsome sparrowhawk ('"uno sparviere bellissimo"') and a kestrel ('"gheppo"') from Paris, followed by a gyrfalcon ('"girfalco"'), a '"moscardo"',[12] a golden oriole ('"rigogolo"') and a crane ('"grua"') from Provence, who arranged themselves around the '"fagiana"' (13,4). A tiercel ('"terzuolo"') arrived from

Florence, followed by a swallow ("'la misera reina, ancora de' suoi popoli nimica'", a reference to Procne) from the neighbourhood of Certaldo. A swan ("'il padre d'Elena'") came from close by Marmorina, and a vulture ("'avoltoio'") from near Naples (13,5).

Florio marvelled to himself ("'in me medesimo mi maravigliava'") at this assembly ("'adunazione'") of birds; many more arrive from the Neapolitan shoreline. Occasionally employing classical allusions, Florio describes the arrival of a kite ("'nibbio'"), a falcon ("'falcone'"), an owl ("'gufo'"), a magpie, a jay ("'ghiandaia'"), a cock, a peacock, a calandra lark ("'calandra'"), a pigeon ("'picchio'"), a heron ("'aghirone'"), a nightingale, a hoopoe, an Indian parrot ("'indiano pappagallo'") and a hawfinch ("'frisone'"); all these birds formed a circle around the captive female (13,6). Here again the narrator wondered at this spectacle, regarding it with expectant attention:

'Io maravigliandomi incominciai ad attendere che questi volessero fare.' (IV, 13,7)

'Marvelling at this, I settled myself to await what these would do.'

As he watched, the birds proceeded to mount a violent and sustained attack on the hen pheasant and the merlin; he was tempted to assist the merlin in his defence of the female bird, but restrained himself from doing so. And so he waited, and then saw a great mastiff ("'un gran mastino'") rise up from the mountains near Pompeii, run in among the birds and bite off the head of the "'fagiana'" before snatching away the rest of her body. At this the merlin, crying, was somehow ("'non so come'") transformed into a turtle-dove ("'tortola'"); it flew up into a barren tree close by and grieved, almost in a human fashion (13,7-8). The sky clouded over darkly, it rained and thundered abominably, as if a new chaos had come; and all this downpour seemed to fall upon the "'fagiana'" (13,9-10). Following this vision, Florio concludes, he had others that he cannot recall; on awaking, he was still moved with compassion for the poor bird (13,11).

Ascalion declares that nobody will ever know the significance of Florio's dream, and that dreams are by nature strange and inscrutable (14,1). He proposes that the company should take a walk and consider its coming voyage. This they do, heading 'towards that region where the revered ashes of the most lofty poet Maro [Vergil] are laid to rest' (14,2). They have not gone far before they hear the sounds of young men and women in 'graziosa festa' ('gracious festivity') issuing from a garden. The sound of various instruments and of near-angelic voices enters their hearts 'con dolce diletto' ('with sweet delight'). Florio is content to stay awhile, as the song's sweetness assuages the 'malin-conia' ('melancholy') of his recent vision (14,3). He and his companions accept a gracious invitation to enter the garden and join the *brigata*'s festive activity (14,4-7).

Just two paragraphs separate Florio's reflection on his disturbing avine dream from his apprehension of the joyful human revellers. Each of these two gatherings is centred on a female figure: in fact, these two figures represent the same woman under different symbolic disguises.[13] It has been noted that the activity of Boccaccio's youthful *brigata* is generally analogous to that of Chaucer's birds in *The Parliament of Fowls*.[14] It may be that in reading this area of the *Filocolo* Chaucer hit upon the idea of fusing a dream vision of an assembly of birds (governed by a beautiful and authoritative female figure) with a parliament of courtiers. The *Filocolo*'s juxtaposition of painful *sentence* and joyful *solas* finds its equivalent in the *Parliament* as the narrator moves from the temple of Venus to the garden of Nature. The violence which grips the Italian birds threatens to break out in the English parliament; in both narratives, the unsettling effects of such unruliness are finally smoothed away by harmonious song.[15] It should be noted that violence erupts only during the latter part of Florio's vision and comes as a surprise to the narrator, who was full of anticipative wonderment.[16] Up to that point, the leisurely introduction of some thirty varieties of bird had been conducted in a cheerful spirit, in keeping with a joyful evocation of the spring season shortly before, in which 'the birds, who had kept silent during the vexatious season, made the air reverberate with sweet notes'.[17]

Quaglio sarcastically dismisses attempts made by the 'critica positivistica' to unravel the meaning of Florio's dream.[18] The dream's strange mixture of Christian symbols and autobiographical allusions certainly defies exhaustive interpretation. Such a mixture was, apparently, learned from Dante: the 'great mastiff' recalls the 'greyhound' prophesised in *Inferno* I, 101–111 which is to hunt down the she-wolf and drive her back to hell; the tree bare of foliage recalls the denuded tree in the vision of disasters in *Purgatorio* XXXII (109–114). The violent, bestial energies of these Dantean scenes (which, in spite of their animal imagery, are charged with a sharp sense of authorial involvement) reverberate through the latter part of Boccaccio's vision. This vision, like the '"obscure narration"' ('"narrazion buia"') at the close of the *Purgatorio*, may have been deliberately designed as a '"hard enigma"' ('"enigma forte"').[19] Ascalion leads the pagans by virtue of his wisdom and experience: but like Vergil (who, we have noted, is expressly recalled in IV, 14,2 as the pilgrims approach the garden's perimeter) he cannot make sense of symbols associated with Christian revelation.[20] His failure to interpret Florio's dream suggests that the vision's import lies beyond the bounds of pagan understanding.

Dante's arrival at the earthly paradise (like that of Florio at the Neapolitan garden) is prefaced by a premonitory dream (XXVII, 91–113). Within the Dantean *paradiso terrestre* we witness a passage of authority from Vergil to Beatrice; the *Filocolo* enacts a similar transition, from Ascalion to Fiammetta. Correspondences between Beatrice and Fiammetta are readily apparent. Ascalion maintains that he has never, in report or experience, encountered a woman of such worthiness ('"valore"') as Fiammetta; he crowns her with laurel as queen of the *brigata* (IV, 18,1–7). When Beatrice appears in *Purgatorio* XXX her bearing is queenly (70), she is crowned with olive (31,68) and clothed in the colour of living flame ('fiamma viva', 33); she excites the memory of an ancient flame in Dante ('"antica fiamma"', 48).

The later cantos of the *Purgatorio* bring together pagan, secular and religious experiences of love: in his premonitory dream, Dante refers to 'Citerea' (XXVII, 95); on encountering Dante, Beatrice berates him with the passion of an injured lover (XXX, 73–5); at the end of the *cantica* the compassion of Beatrice is compared with that of 'Maria' at the cross (XXXIII, 4–6). This remarkable range of reference is matched by the *Filocolo*'s garden episode: approaching Naples, Florio refers to '"santa Venus"' and her birthplace

(8,12); within the garden, the enraptured Caleon focusses our attention on Fiammetta with the intense gaze of a lover (43,1–4); and Caleon himself explains that Fiammetta is more commonly called by the name of Maria, '"through whom that wound, that the prevarication of our first mother opened, closed"'.[21] Boccaccio's reading of the *Commedia* evidently fortified his awareness of continuities linking pagan and Christian experiences of love. But he must also have sensed discontinuities: Caleon's oblique reference to Mary can have meant nothing to the pagan Florio and his companions. These simultaneous senses are delicately balanced in the episode which forms— structurally, thematically and dramatically—the centrepiece of the *Filocolo*'s garden parliament.[22]

On being asked to continue the sequence of *questioni d'amore* in the aristocratic circle, the Neapolitan nobleman Caleon fails to respond because he is absorbed in contemplating the beauty of Fiammetta. He notices how light reflected from a fountain strikes her face, bathing the whole company in a roseate glow (43,1–2). He sings a *ballata* praising her beauty in which Love (Amore) speaks as a spirit that has descended from the third heaven:

> '"Io son del terzo ciel cosa gentile . . ."'   (IV, 43,10)

> '"I am a noble being from the third heaven . . ."'

The third heaven is, in Dante's cosmology, that of Venus, whose angelic Order has for its special object of contemplation '"the supreme and most fervent love of the Holy Spirit"'.[23] Boccaccio's *ballata* assumes a religious tone in its final line as the spirit acknowledges Fiammetta as '"'true queen of my kingdoms'"'.[24] For Boccaccio, the significance of Venus is twofold: one half of this 'double' figure upholds Christian mores, the other offends against them.[25] The doubleness of Venus brings together pagan and Christian ideals within a single figure; it follows that the power of Venus revealed to Florio through Fiammetta is at once familiar and strange. Florio has long served Venus as a deity favouring his pilgrimage to sexual fulfilment, but has remained ignorant of the Christian Venus which has been influencing his pilgrimage to truth.

Having completed his song, Caleon alerts the company to the way in which Fiammetta's eyes sparkle like morning stars ('"come matutine stelle"', 43,14),[26] illuminating the whole gathering. Florio and his companions marvel at hearing this and, turning their eyes to the queen, 'saw that which, to hear speak of, had seemed impossible to them' (43,15). On arriving at the garden, Florio had identified himself as a 'pilgrim of love' (16,9): but this manifestation of love amazes him, passing beyond the bounds of his previous experience, for in gazing upon the 'splendour' ('splendore', 43,2) of Fiammetta's countenance, Florio is witnessing the reflection of divine truth. When Dante meets the eyes of Beatrice in *Purgatorio* XXXI he exclaims at the 'splendour of living, eternal light' ('isplendor di viva luce etterna', 139) that is unveiled to him. The term 'splendore' is generally used by Dante for reflected light, particularly in describing 'that light which God is'.[27]

In the subsequent debate between Fiammetta and Caleon, Florio learns something of the relationship between the love that he has pursued and the love that Fiammetta reflects. Caleon advances the claims of '"love for pleasure"' ('"amore per diletto"'), clearly believing the forces of pre-Christian literature to be aligned with his cause: he employs a battery of classical exempla in demonstrating the power of Amore, and claims that this God inspired Vergil, Ovid to achieve ' "eternal fame in holy verses" ' (45,3–8). Fiammetta insists upon the absolute superiority of ' "honest love" ' (' "amore onesto" '), by which ' "we merit becoming eternal possessors of the heavenly kingdoms" ' (44,5).

It is generally accepted that the fourth narrative in the *Filocolo's questioni d'amore* sequence furnished a source for Chaucer's *Franklin's Tale*.[28] The context in which Chaucer discovered this narrative has an important bearing on our appreciation of his *Tale*.[29] Boccaccio's narrative forms part of the deliberations of a *brigata* which has brought together Christians (recognisable as fourteenth-century courtiers) and pagans sharing an interest in Love.[30] The world of this *brigata*, like that of Chaucer's *Tale* (and of the *Troilus*, a poem with which *The Franklin's Tale* is habitually associated) is curiously suspended between Christian and pagan terms of reference. Its central episode gives rise to a debate concerning the relative merits of 'love for pleasure' and 'honest love', a debate which is absorbed into the dramatic action of *The Franklin's Tale*.

Several of the *Filocolo* story's broadest thematic oppositions survive within Chaucer's *Tale*: contrasts between the seasons of January and May and between the *loci* of garden and temple are fundamental to the structure of both narratives.[31] Each writer skilfully adapts an Ovidian exemplum in comparing changes in the physical world—the gradual erosion of stone—with gradual changes in the human intelligence.[32] In presenting scenes of magical transformation, both writers stress the importance of lunar motion, although their narratives develop in different directions from this common point of departure. The divergences here, in the common attempt to create a suggestively magical atmosphere, are characteristic: Boccaccio offers a lengthy and exotic *imitatio* of a *Metamorphoses* passage, whereas Chaucer (author of *A Treatise on the Astrolabe*) dazzles with a virtuoso display of technical vocabulary.[33] The most radical differences between the two narratives stem from Chaucer's decision to bring his female protagonist to prominence. The brilliant stroke of connecting Dorigen's anxiety about her husband with the task she sets her aspiring lover brings an extra dimension of psychological complexity to Chaucer's *Tale*: in the *Filocolo* the wife's request is nothing more than a ' "sottile malizia" ' (a ' "subtle piece of malice" ', IV, 31,6). Dorigen's large speculations on the nature of divine will (akin to those of Troilus)[34] lead us away from the more straightforward concerns of the *Filocolo* story, and still further from the interests of the *Decameron* analogue.[35] But such speculations form an essential part of *Filocolo* IV, the Book in which the closest analogue to *The Franklin's Tale* is contained. The question with which Chaucer's Franklin concludes his *Tale* (' "Which was the moste fre, as thynketh yow?" ') expects no answer: but it does recognise the story's origin as a *questione d'amore*.

Having left the *brigata*, Florio meditates upon the 'quistioni' (finding them relevant to his own sufferings) and upon the beauty of Fiammetta (which sharpens the pain of his separation from Biancifiore, IV, 73,1). A few days later, alone in a garden, he has a vision. Employing symbolism from the final cantos of the *Purgatorio*—colourfully supported by stil nuovist imagery—this vision serves to clarify the uncertain implications of the preceding chapters by representing Florio's future union with Biancifiore in the Christian religion.[36] It is clear, then, that the *Filocolo's* most celebrated sequence of chapters owes

67

much to—or even grows out of—the Dantean *paradiso terrestre*, an area of the *Commedia* with which Chaucer was well acquainted.[37] Similarly framed between two visions, each terrain witnesses a transition between ancient and Christian wisdom which is presided over by a female figure who excites comparisons with both Venus and the Virgin Mary. Stories of secular and pagan love abound in both gardens[38]: yet both cause illustrious pagan guides (Vergil and Ascalion) to fall silent with amazement in the face of Christian revelation. When Beatrice commissions Dante to record the outrageous images of the later vision she sits encircled by seven ladies (XXXII, 94–105): perhaps, in Boccaccio's eyes, she resembled the queen of a *brigata* and set in motion an imaginative process that found first expression in *Filocolo* IV and full realisation in the *Decameron*.

But another gathering of nobles might simultaneously have stirred Boccaccio's imagination. When the narrator of Guillaume's *Rose* arrives in the garden of Deduiz (a place he describes as a 'paradis terrestre', 634) he is welcomed into a circle of lovers by another queenly (1242) lady, Cortoisie (782–5). The gracious charm of Guillaume's writing radiates qualities that Boccaccio strove to capture from his youthful *Caccia* onwards: but in presenting his own *brigate* Boccaccio reveals a mentality which comes closer to that of the sharp-tongued Jean de Meun. The pattern of debate in the *Filocolo* assembly is based upon scholastic dialogue procedure; this often encourages a sharpness of verbal definition that is reminiscent of the *Rose*'s continuator. Words are sometimes razor-edged, and are sometimes employed to support an outrageous cause, such as when Pasiphae's seduction of the Cretan bull is cited as the supreme '"example of shyness"' ('"essemplo di temenza"', IV, 42,6).

It is, however, in the second half of *Filocolo* IV that the influence of the *Rose* is most apparent. When plucked unwillingly from his vision by solicitous friends, Florio heads directly for his ship, sets sail in search of his beloved, and eventually discovers her to be imprisoned in a tower at Alexandria (IV, 74,21–86,4). The rest of Book IV tells of his attempts to penetrate this stronghold and to consummate his love: given such a situation, it is not surprising that the influence of the latter part of the *Rose* should make itself felt. But Florio's union with Biancifiore represents more than a straightforward sexual conquest: the Neapolitan *brigata*'s central debate between 'love for pleasure' and 'honest love' remains powerfully active within Florio's mind. Florio's mental oscillation between erotic and religious forms of reference parallels that of Chaucer's pagan hero in *Troilus* Book III.

Having infiltrated the tower of the *Rose*, the French narrator draws back the curtain ('la courtine', 21569) which conceals the goal of his pilgrimage; he then explores the secret parts of the 'ymage' he has exposed (21571–21586). Having penetrated the tower of Alexandria, Florio draws back the curtains ('le cortine', 118,5) surrounding the bed upon which the naked Biancifiore sleeps; he then explores the 'segrete parti' of her body, experiencing sensations that send him beyond all limits of pleasure and delight:

> Egli distende le mani per le segrete parti . . . e toccando perviene infino a quel luogo ove ogni dolcezza si richiude: e così toccando le dilicate parti, tanto diletto prende, che gli pare trapassare di letizia le regioni degl'iddii . . . (IV, 118,6)

He spread his hands through her secret parts . . . and came, by touching, as far as that place where every sweetness is enclosed: and in so touching her delicate parts he experienced such delight that he seemed, through sheer joy, to pass through the regions of the gods . . .

Such paradisiac sensations are experienced by Troilus as he explores the naked body of his beloved:

> Hire armes smale, hire streghte bak and softe,
> Hire sydes longe, flesshly, smothe, and white
> He gan to stroke, and good thrift bad ful ofte
> Hire snowisshe throte, hire brestes rounde and lite:
> Thus in this hevene he gan hym to delite . . . (III, 1247–51)

Before falling asleep, Biancifiore had caressed a little belt ('cintoletta', 115,1) that Florio once gave her, and had called upon '"santa Venere"', praying that she might wake to find Florio in her arms (117,5–7). Florio lies between her arms (118,1): but she remains dormant, unresponsive to his embraces for a worrying length of time (118,2–7). When she finally wakes, the joyful effect is comparable to that of the metamorphosis in Jean de Meun's Pygmalion story. (Pygmalion had also presented his lady with a belt ('un si tres riche ceint', 20953) and had also prayed to '"seinte Venus"', 21056). When Biancifiore awakes Florio ceases his erotic exploration, declaring that he has laboured so long and hard not

'. . . per acquistare amica, ma per acquistare inseparabile sposa, la quale tu mi sarai. E fermamente, avanti che altro fra noi sia, col tuo medesimo anello ti sposerò, alla qual cosa Imineo e la santa Giunone e Venere, nostra dea, siano presenti.' (IV, 120,3)

'. . . to acquire a lover, but to acquire an inseparable spouse, which you will be to me. And assuredly, before anything else passes between us, I will marry you with your own ring; and may Hymen and holy Juno and Venus, our goddess, be present at this.'

Pygmalion is similarly concerned to establish a permanent, mutually binding contract: speaking as a loyal spouse, he invokes the presence of Hymen and Juno ('"li vrai dieu des noces"', 20990) in wedding his beloved:

> Anelez d'or es duiz li boute,
> et dist con fins leaus espous:
> 'Bele douce, ci vos espous
> et deviegn vostres, et vos moie.
> Hymeneüs et Juno m'oie,
> qu'il veillent a noz noces estre.' (20982–7)

He put gold rings on her fingers
and said, like a fine, loyal spouse:
'Fair sweet one, I here take you to wife
and become yours, and you mine.
May Hymen and Juno hear me,
and may they wish to be at our wedding.'

Troilus follows Florio in turning from erotic exploration to studied invocation of the gods. This turn from sensual abandon to reasoned discourse is impressively resolute: at III, 1253 Troilus is so transported by the joy of sexual exploration that 'he hardly knew what to do'; at III, 1254 he has recovered the power of reasoned utterance through an exercise of will that might have impressed Robert Holcot, if not Archbishop Bradwardine[39]:

> And therwithal a thousand tyme hire kiste,
> That what to don, for joie unnethe he wiste.

> Than seyde he thus, 'O Love, O Charite!
> Thi moder ek, Citherea the swete,
> After thiself next heried be she,
> Venus mene I, the wel-willy planete!
> And next that, Imeneus, I the grete;
> For nevere man was to yow goddes holde
> As I, which ye han brought fro cares colde.' (III, 1252–60)

Through their reading of the 'poete Marcian', Chaucer and his Merchant were aware that 'Ymeneus . . . god of wedding is'.[40] This particular god intertwines pagan and Christian traditions of literature and devotion in a manner that is richly suggestive for the *Filocolo* and the *Troilus*.[41] Such intertwining (a notable feature of the *Troilus*) is carried further in the *Filocolo* as Boccaccio's lovers formalise their '"indissolubile matrimonio"' (121,2). They pledge themselves to each other kneeling before a statue of mysterious origin and of complex symbolic significance: a sighted Cupid. The pupils in the eyes of this deity (which, we are reminded, is usually depicted as blind) are carbuncles, which keep the room as brightly illuminated as if it were flooded with daylight.[42] The marriage of Florio and Biancifiore is evidently modelled on that of Pygmalion to his statue[43]; Boccaccio probably realised the dramatic and symbolic potential of the mythical, self-luminous gems in reading a celebrated passage of the *Rose* which occurs shortly before the Pygmalion story. This describes the Christian earthly paradise, the 'biau parc' which is illuminated by '"uns carboncles merveillables"' (20498) situated at the centre of '"la fonteine de vie"' (20491).[44] In a lengthy passage (20495–560), Jean expatiates upon the beauty and virtue of the stone which, in his hands, is evidently a Trinitarian symbol; like Boccaccio (and like Augustine and Alanus de Insulis)[45] he emphasises its sun-like power to banish darkness through its '"resplendeur"' (20526–9). In setting his carbuncles in the eyes of Cupid, Boccaccio is again attempting to unite pagan and Christian iconographies within a single figure: he wishes us to regard the union of his lovers as signifying something more than the culmination of *fine amour* and something less than Christian marriage. So it is that Florio's petitions to this Cupid are answered, at his marriage, by the appearance of an unlikely trinity: Venus ('Citerea'); Hymen, crowned with olive (the tree which overhangs the 'fountain of life' in the *Rose*, and brings forth 'the fruit of salvation')[46]; and Diana, singing 'santi versi' (122,2).[47]

Troilus' invocation to the trinity of III, 1254–60 begins with a two-fold appeal to Cupid that audaciously juxtaposes secular and religious terms of reference: the employment of the synonyms '"Love"' and '"Charite"' both parallels Boccaccio's conception of a duplex Cupid and continues the inter-penetration of pagan and Christian perspectives that is a recurrent feature of Chaucer's third Book. This process is evident from the first as Chaucer (like Caleon in IV, 43) combines Christian cosmology and classical iconography in addressing Venus:

> O blisful light, of which the bemes clere
> Adorneth al the thridde heven faire!   (III, 1–2)

The first six stanzas of Book III celebrate the beneficient influence of Venus on her fellow gods, on the natural world and on human society. A little later in Book III a pagan deity is addressed in terms traditionally associated with the Christian God:

> 'Immortal god,' quod he, 'that mayst nought deyen,
> Cupid I mene . . .'   (III, 185–6)

The same god is later characterised as a source of grace (III, 461). In III, 718–21 Troilus urges Venus to recall her love for Adonis and to pray to her father for grace. This petition (which recalls references made by Boccaccio and Dante to Venus' love for Adonis)[48] echoes Chaucer's appeal to Venus in III, 39–42, an appeal which resembles a prayer to the Virgin. This last appeal may well derive inspiration from *Paradiso* XXXIII, 16[49]; this canto of the *Paradiso* certainly inspires the stanza which follows Troilus' trinitarian appeal:

> 'Benigne Love, thow holy bond of thynges,
> Whoso wol grace, and list the nought honouren,
> Lo, his desir wol fle withouten wynges.
> For noldestow of bownte hem socouren
> That serven best and most alwey labouren,
> Yet were al lost, that dar I wel seyn certes,
> But if thi grace passed oure desertes.'   (III, 1261–7)

Troilus begins this stanza by addressing Love in terms adapted from St Bernard's appeal to the Virgin[50]; he ends it (and begins the next) by adumbrat-ing Christian doctrine on merit, grace, election and salvation.[51] Bernard declares that Dante has risen to his present eminence from the deepest pit of the universe (XXXII, 22–23); Troilus claims to have been raised from a death-like region to the pinnacle[52] of human happiness:

> 'And for thow me, that leest koude disserve
> Of hem that noumbred ben unto thi grace,
> Hast holpen, ther I likly was to sterve,
> And me bistowed in so heigh a place
> That thilke boundes may no blisse pace . . .'
>
> (III, 1268–72)

Such a place is an earthly paradise: the hero, through his devoted pursuit of love, has come to the very threshold of revealed truth. Troilus subsequently declares that he feels '"a newe qualitee"'; Pandarus ascribes this to his experience of '"hevene blisse"' (III, 1654–9). The fame of Troilus following this spiritual transformation is said to ring 'unto the yate of hevene' (1725). The final words of Troilus in this Book form a hymn of praise to '"Love"' (1744–71). These four stanzas (modelled, with the possible assistance of the glossator Nicholas Trevet[53], on the eighth *metrum* of *De Consolatione* II) exclude the pagan deities featured in the opening stanzas of Book III and conform more closely to a Christian *weltanschauung*; in his final stanza Troilus believes himself capable of discerning the purposes of '"God, that auctour is of kynde"' (1765). But it is Chaucer himself who has the last word in Book III. In his penultimate stanza he turns our attention back to Venus and Cupid. The departure of these deities heralds the end of Troilus' happiness in love, his exile from the earthly paradise and the extinction of his hope (or dream) of salvation. Book IV is to trace Troilus' reversion to the rigid fatalism characteristic of an unregenerate pagan world.[54] Chaucer's curt farewell to Venus and Cupid at the end of Book III predicts the brusque, precipitate, slightly hysterical tone employed to sever author and audience from the pagan world at the end of Book V[55]:

> I kan namore, but syn that ye wol wende,
> Ye heried ben for ay withouten ende!   (III, 1812–3)

In commenting on the English *Floris and Blancheflour* George Kane identifies the essential power of the legend's appeal:

> Despite its artistic shortcomings the romance conveys the strong attraction of this beautiful, amoral fantasy of love opposed by no considerations other than the physical obstacles which separate lovers.[56]

The *Filostrato* might be described as 'a beautiful, amoral fantasy of love': but not the *Filocolo*, whose hero develops a moral sense in the very process of pursuing love by adhering faithfully to the highest wisdom available within the pagan world. Such faithful perseverance leads him to the very threshold of Christian revelation. Chaucer's Troilus, similarly faithful, is similarly raised to a state of heavenly bliss. Here he feels able to associate his love for his lady with the love that orders the universe; he too has come to a place where enlightenment seems imminent. Chaucer and Boccaccio do not seek to fuse or integrate the beliefs and practices of Christian and pagan worlds; nor do they, like Jean de Meun, juxtapose them for an effect that is preponderantly ironic: they seek, rather, to explore the uncertain space between them. (It was to further such an exploration, C. S. Lewis suggests, that Chaucer turned to Boethius).[57] Their depiction of such a space encourages us to admire the high moral integrity of pagan protagonists in their simultaneous pursuit of love and truth. And such admiration for the 'shadowy perfection'[58] of the pagans, shared by theologians and poets alike, brings us into contact with one of the more generous aspects of late medieval thought.

CHAPTER 5

The Filostrato: its Literary Affiliations and its Suitability as a Chaucerian Source

Certain continuities are evident as we move from the *Filocolo* to the *Filostrato*. Colourful indications of Boccaccio's individuality as a natural prose writer appear not only within the *Filostrato*'s prose *Proemio* but also within the main body of the poem itself: complex constructions often wind through entire, heavily-enjambed *ottave*. In addition to such formal and stylistic continuities we may observe large areas of overlapping content: more such areas exist between the *Filostrato* and the *Filocolo* than between any other pair of Boccaccian works.[1] (This fact has certainly complicated the business of untangling Chaucer's indebtedness to each of them). But, of course, vital differences separate these two works. The *Filostrato* represents an earlier phase of Boccaccio's development and receives its chief narrative impetus from the lower levels of literary inspiration that were available at Naples. Although Boccaccio treats of a classical subject he makes little use of classical texts: his fascination with pagan antiquity—so impressively developed in the *Filocolo*— is barely awakening. And yet Chaucer chose to employ this relatively un-sophisticated poem as the source of his great *tragedye*.

In this chapter we will first consider the *Filostrato*'s fundamental affiliations with popular narrative, devoting considerable space to the *cantare* tradition which provided Boccaccio with a verse form, a descriptive language and a basic narrative technique. This tradition has much in common with that of the English romances which, I have argued above (and will argue again below), provided the backbone of Chaucer's narrative style: we will consider ways in which the *Filostrato*'s appropriations from and development of popular narra-tive proved congenial to Chaucer. We will note how these popular traditions, like their illustrious counterparts discussed in the last four chapters, develop through protracted engagement with prestigious French precedents. Finally, having considered the various ways in which the *Filostrato* proved suitable as a Chaucerian source, we will venture to estimate how, in general terms, Chaucer might have assessed the Italian poem. In chapter VI we will scrutinise the quality of Chaucer's close engagements with the *Filostrato* and discover how—when working with and away from his Italian source—the English poet establishes and maintains his characteristic double identity as romancer and *auctour*.

To English readers, the *Filostrato* has assumed a momentous importance in isolating and developing the story of Troilus and thereby preparing the way for Chaucer, Henryson and Shakespeare. Viewed from the long perspective of this British tradition, the relation of Boccaccio to his sources has seemed relatively straightforward: 'out of Benoît and Guido came Boccaccio's *Il Filostrato*.'[2] But whereas Chaucer had a copy of the *Filostrato* on his desk in composing his *Troilus*, it is not obvious that Boccaccio made systematic use of Benoît, Guido or of any author.[3] So we are left with the task of assessing what elements Boccaccio might have taken from the formidable range of materials on the Trojan legend that Naples had to offer: local and universal chronicles, scholastic compilations, Latin poems and encyclopaedic works as well as French romances and Italian translations all deserve consideration.

Happily, such a task has been capably performed by Maria Gozzi.[4] Following a brief summary of the Trojan material available to Boccaccio at Naples, she conducts a rigorously organised comparative study of the *Filostrato* and six Trojan romances.[5] She finds that no single text may be identified as Boccaccio's source; this accords with her earlier observation that 'in design, in tone and even in size the *Filostrato* is a work that is very different from medieval narratives ("storie") of Troy'.[6] The *Historia Troiana* yields the most promising points of comparison with the *Filostrato*, but each of the six texts has something particular in common with it. It appears, then, that Boccaccio read widely in Trojan matters, appropriating details not to create a consistent, historical account but to serve his own, highly individual purposes. Gozzi concludes by questioning the relevance of treating the *Filostrato* in terms of its modifications of such 'sources'.[7] The Trojan material simply seems to have served Boccaccio as a pretext for the exploration of his own literary interests; he was not touched by the reverential respect with which Chaucer and other mature medieval poets approached the matter of Troy.[8]

It is clear, then, that the *Filostrato* cannot be satisfactorily evaluated or appreciated simply by comparing it with other Trojan narratives. Attempts to specify alternative sources of inspiration have met with limited success. But difficulties in this regard, particularly those experienced by Silber and Marletta, are themselves instructive. Silber investigates the claims of distinguished philologists (Savj-Lopez and Wilkins) that the *Filostrato* imitates passages from two Petrarchan sonnets: he dismisses the first of these claims by pointing to commonplaces in Provençal and Italian poetry, and the second by referring to seven instances in Ovid.[9] Marletta sets out to consider the possible influence exerted by a certain *serenata* on the *Filostrato*; having shown that Boccaccio's stanzas contain numerous popular commonplaces, he concludes that influence was almost certainly exerted in the opposite direction.[10] Such investigations certainly suggest that the *Filostrato* cannot easily be aligned either with the *poesia d'arte* or with the *poesia popolare*: it occupies a place somewhere between the two and draws upon both traditions. Popular proverbs and colloquialisms share stanzas with phrases and similes from Dante and Vergil; popular lore merges with the teachings of Ovid and Andreas Capellanus. Four stanzas of Cino da Pistoia's most celebrated canzone are swallowed wholesale into the poem;[11] echoes of the schoolroom are heard as Troiolo answers Cassandra 'like a good pupil of the scholastics'[12] (VII, 89–101).

In his lengthy speech (or lecture) to his sister Cassandra, Troiolo advances the claims of nobility of spirit above those of noble blood; this represents

Boccaccio's first imitation of Dante's *Convivio*.[13] Its appropriateness to the seventh 'Parte' of the *Filostrato* is questionable, considering the sadly ignoble behaviour of Criseyde at this point. Boccaccio might consciously have been seeking out an ironic effect here: but it seems more likely that he simply seized the opportunity to bring a favourite Dantean argument into his opus. The *Filostrato* is full of such opportunism: the most egregious example occurs in the penultimate 'Parte', in which the youthful author exhorts his peers to restrain their carnal appetites. The hollow tones of this admonition soon modulate into a garrulous discussion of the characteristics of young women. Chaucer, in his equivalent stanza, imitates Boccaccio's first two lines quite closely; but his tone then darkens to express an unmistakeably authentic religious seriousness.[14]

The *Filostrato*'s cheerful jumbling of popular and learned registers indicates that its youthful author has not yet attained to the discrimination and restraint characteristic of the mature Chaucer (if not the Chaucer of *The House of Fame*). An interesting commentary on Boccaccio's work is offered by a canzone appearing at the end of a *Filostrato* manuscript copied in 1397.[15] This canzone, formed on the Petrarchan model, is crammed to bursting with commonplace images and topoi, scraps of Latin learning, phrases culled from Dante and Petrarch and excessive adjectives. It amplifies an argument employed by Pandaro to wear down Criseida's resistance to Troiolo: that time flees and nobody loves an old woman. The opportunism and eclecticism of the canzone's author does not produce a good poem, but it does suggest that he has been inspired by the spirit of the *Filostrato*. Boccaccio's heroine had rapidly capitulated to Pandaro's argument ("'Oh me . . . tu di' vero'", II, 55,1); the *canzonista* might have been envisaging something similar. Chaucer's Pandarus also takes up this argument, embroidering it with great subtlety (II, 393–406). But there is never, of course, any question of Chaucer's Criseyde yielding to such a hoary old commonplace.

The *Filostrato*'s position between the *poesia popolare* and the *poesia d'arte* is not affected by its employment of the hendecasyllabic line. Boccaccio may have been impressed by Dante's demonstration of the capabilities of this medium, but he learned little from Dante's prosody: Chaucer learned much more.[16] Boccaccio's employment of hendecasyllables (and, in the *Caccia*, of a Dantean verse form) does not automatically entitle him to be regarded as an illustrious poet. In fact, a number of aristocratic poets of this period (including Iacopo Alighieri) elected to turn their backs on Dante's example by employing seven or nine-syllable lines reminiscent of those in Brunetto's *Tesoretto*.[17] *Terza rima* was, however, enthusiastically employed by more popular writers, such as the Florentine town-crier and *canterino* Antonio Pucci.[18] The straightforward, unabashed manner in which Pucci and others appropriated the Dantean verse form for their own parochial concerns reflects a remarkably pragmatic attitude towards poetic form. Pucci cheerfully employs *terzine* in describing his favourite Florentine piazza.[19] In one sonnet, he offers a recipe for a sauce; in another, he complains against a poultry-dealer who has sold him an aged hen.[20] Boccaccio's earliest verse reveals a similarly pragmatic (even, perhaps, irreverent) attitude towards poetic form. Each Book of the *Teseida* is prefaced by a sonnet outlining its contents; the whole is preceded by a sonnet summarising the entire action of its twelve Books. The syntax of these sonnets generally observes the 8+6 division suggested by the rhyme scheme: this divide is, however, bridged completely (by enjambement) in the sonnet containing the 'argomento generale'. The sonnet preceding Book XII has fifteen lines. These sonnets hardly merit consideration as verse: they stand like jam-jars into which content has been poured.[21] Boccaccio's youthful opportunism clearly extends down to his prosody: unlike Chaucer, he seems to regard metrical and stanzaic form as something to be boldly exploited (and energetically fought against) rather than quietly and respectfully observed.

Hendecasyllables were employed by the tradition of narrative that supplied Boccaccio with a stanzaic model for his *Filostrato*: the *cantare*.[22] These narratives occupied an intermediate cultural position in bringing the images, themes and values of the aristocratic world to the populace, a function performed in England by most of the metrical romances. Some understanding of the *cantare* tradition will help us to appreciate the *Filostrato* better and bring us closer to Chaucer's understanding of Boccaccio's poem. Vittore Branca's pioneering study of 1936 usefully alerts us to the various ways in which Boccaccio draws from the *canterini*. But Branca's assessment of this indebtedness is misleading. Maintaining that an unbridgeable gulf divides the work of a true artist from that of lesser spirits, he insists that the *canterini* exerted an essentially negative influence on Boccaccio.[23] Branca's cultural premises, developed out of Benedetto Croce's *Poesia popolare e poesia d'arte* (Bari, 1933), impede our appreciation of the lively manner in which the *Filostrato* benefits from its contacts with both popular and illustrious Italian writings.[24] As Piero Boitani passed over the question of the *cantare* influence on Boccaccio and its implications for Chaucer, we must consider the work of the *canterini* at some length.[25]

Most of the problems encountered in editing, classifying and assessing the *cantari* are similar in kind to those surrounding the study of the Middle English romances. These problems begin with definitions of the subject: the ensemble of works to be considered as *cantari* or romances contains a bewildering variety of subject matter, narrative length and literary quality. Dieter Mehl concludes that 'it is practically impossible to generalize about the romances because there is so little they all have in common'.[26] But although it is true, as Mehl observes, that the customary classification of the English romances under three headings (or *matières*) established in twelfth-century France is of little use,[27] it is also true, as Derek Pearsall observes, that 'the corpus of Middle English romance, from the period of its great flourishing between 1280 and 1380, gives the strongest impression of homogeneity'.[28] Italian scholars are, on the face of it, more fortunate in defining their subject: a classification in terms of content is provided by an extraordinary poem known as the *Cantare dei cantari*;[29] and whereas the English romances exhibit a considerable variety of metrical and stanzaic forms, the *cantare* stanza is invariably composed of eight hendecasyllabic lines rhyming ababababcc.[30] However, attempts to define the *cantari* more narrowly run into difficulties. The form and content of the *cantare* has much in common with that of the *strambotto* or *rispetto*;[31] a sequence of *rispetti* may constitute a *serenata* which, in form at least, might be regarded as a short lyric *cantare*.[32] Branca has insisted that to be termed a *cantare*, a work must have been intended for piazza recitation: but Branca himself admits that certain works—such as the *Orlando* in sixty-one *cantari*—are far too long to have served this purpose.[33] But in spite of such embarrassments, it is possible to speak of a *cantare* corpus corresponding to that of the English romances. It is unified by a very similar 'grammar' of conventions, and yields a similar impression of homogeneity. In fact, everything that Pearsall says here about the English romance could be translated to fit the Italian *cantare*:

> This homogeneity is most evident in the observance of a wide range of formal and literary conventions, what we might call the 'grammar' of romance. The same plot-patterns, the same situations, the same phrases, recur insistently from romance to romance, providing much of their popular strength. The reason for this close stereotyping, however, is to be found in the social context of Middle English romance, which is overwhelmingly popular and non-courtly.[34]

Such a social context also accounts for the poor rate of manuscript survival in both traditions: we work with remnants salvaged from 'the almost total shipwreck of an output more widespread and intense than can now be imagined'.[35] It is virtually impossible to ascertain when a given work first appeared,[36] although it is at least evident that both traditions, in their most vigorous phase of development, are distinctively fourteenth-century phenomena.[37] Few works from either tradition survive in more than three manuscripts, and those that do often exhibit extravagant variations from text to text: Pearsall remarks that 'it is questionable . . . whether we can talk about an English romance of *Beves* or whether there are not as many romances of *Beves* as there are texts'; and Jennifer Fellows feels bound to study the same romance 'not as a static literary phenomenon but as a protean creature . . .'.[38] Such variations within a single manuscript tradition often make distinctions be-tween author and copyist difficult to maintain: copyists evidently felt them-selves more or less free to elaborate and embroider the matter they were working on.[39] Such freedom in part corresponds to a freedom from the more exacting standards expected of copyists of religious writings; it also suggests familiarity with (or even participation in) those traditions of oral performance which precede and surround such popular texts.[40]

Distinctions between writers and performers in the *cantare* and romance traditions are, through poverty of evidence, difficult to observe.[41] It is reasonable to suppose that some authors publicly recited their own texts, while some simply prepared material for others to read or perform. Similarly, it is difficult to assess the faithfulness with which the surviving texts perpetuate the oral traditions preceding them.[42] But rather than seeking to delimit the activities of writer and performer—an exercise which does little to enhance our understanding of the surviving texts—it is more illuminating to consider their affinities. Baugh's imaginative recreation of a minstrel's performance could almost be taken to describe the process of penning a *cantare* or romance: the performer or writer

> . . . may drop out a couplet or a stanza, may substitute a familiar rime-tag or formula without even being aware of it, may alter a particular passage through equally unconscious contamination with a similar inci-dent in some other romance which he is accustomed to recite [or copy], may insert at times a couplet or a whole passage if it is part of his general stock of conventional descriptions and incidents, commonplace lines and phrases . . . The important thing for him is to keep going.[43]

For some writers, such as the fourteenth-century copyist of the Egerton *Floris and Blauncheflur*, the effort to keep going is obviously as taxing (but as all-important) as it was for any minstrel. The relevance of narrative detail sometimes takes a distant second place to the exigencies of rhyme:

> At þe ʒate is a ʒateward;
> He is not a coward.
> He is wonder proude withalle,
> Euery day he goþ in ryche palle.[44]

Reading fourteenth-century romance and *cantare* texts, we continually encounter narrative conventions and descriptive formulae that have passed on to parchment from oral tradition.[45] Branca regards such surviving elements as being essentially redundant, obstacles to true literary creativity[46]: but, artfully employed, they have a creative function; in reviewing and comparing the 'grammars' of *cantare* and romance, we shall encounter many features that Boccaccio and Chaucer were happy to make use of. In dwelling upon such features we come to appreciate that the *Filostrato* and the *Troilus* are more deeply innested within medieval traditions of oral performance than modern habits of silent, asocial, rapid reading encourage us to perceive.[47] And we come to realise that what the modern reader may find redundant the medieval reader or listener might have found indispensable.

Canterini and romance writers employed similar devices in maintaining narrative continuity, in ensuring domination of their auditors' attention and (in the more sophisticated compositions) in creating a friendly rapport with their audience. Such devices appear from the moment that the narrative is first set in motion:

> Litheth, and lesteneth · and herkeneth aright,
> And ʒe schulle here a talkyng · of a doughty knight . . .
> (Gamelyn, 1–2)[48]

> O buona gente, io vi voglio pregare
> che lo mio detto sia bene ascoltato,
> ed io vi voglio dire e raccontare
> de l'incominzamento com'è stato.
> Per cortesia deggiatemi ascoltare,
> e per questo intenda chi è inamorato,
> come fu nato Fiorio e Biancifiore:
> e' furon nati insieme in grande amore.
> (Cantare di Fiorio e Biancifiore, 1,1–8)

> O good people, I'd like to ask you
> that my tale be listened to well,
> for I want to tell you and to recount
> how things stood at the beginning.
> For courtesy, you must hear me tell,
> (especially you who are love-struck),
> how Fiorio and Biancifiore were born:
> they were born at the same time in great love.

Many works contain comparable appeals for attention and advertisements of subject matter: but few begin quite so abruptly. Writers in both traditions felt it appropriate[49] to begin with some kind of religious invocation before turning to their audience:

> Ihesu Cryste, yn Trynyté,
> Oonly God and persons thre,
> > Graunt vs wele to spede,
> And gyf vs grace so to do
> That we may come þy blys vnto,
> > On rode as thou can blede!
> Leue lordys, y schall you telle
> Of a tale . . . (*The Earl of Toulouse*, 1–8)[50]

> I' priego Cristo padre onnipotente,
> che per li peccator volle morire,
> che mi conceda grazia nella mente
> ch'i' possa chiara mia volontà dire.
> E priego voi, signori e buona gente,
> che con effetto mi deggiate udire,
> ch'io vi dirò d'una canzon . . . (*Brito di Brettagna*, 1–7)[51]

> I pray to Christ, father omnipotent,
> who chose to die for sinners,
> that he might grant me grace in my mind
> so that I might speak my intentions clearly.
> And I pray to you, gentlemen and good people,
> that you will give me a fair hearing,
> for I'll tell you a story . . .

It should be noted that the appeal Pucci makes here for divine assistance in realising his artistic intention is not an unusual feature of *cantare* invocations.[52] Some *canterini* exhibit considerable artistic self-consciousness in beginning their narratives: one reveals his relative inexperience (*Bel Gherardino* I, 2,1–2), another his experience (*Storia del calonaco di Siena*, 1,3–4)[53] as an author. Such self-consciousness rarely affects writers of the English romances: but they had no illustrious native tradition, and no Dante, to influence their sense of self-importance. Considering *The House of Fame*, we noted that Chaucer was also afflicted with artistic self-consciousness following his first encounter with Dante's writings.[54]

The piety expressed by such religious openings continues through each *cantare* and romance and typically provides a brief religious formula to round the work off:

> þus com Sir Orfeo out of his care;
> God graunt ous alle wele to fare! Amen.
>
> > (*Sir Orfeo*, 603–4)

> con altre terre, delle qual si tace.
> Al vostro onore Iddio ci ponga in pace.
> > (*Cantare della guerra degli otto santi*, 41,7–8)[55]

with other territories, not mentioned here.
Here's to you; God leave you in peace.

Such piety, doubtless sincere, was also functional. The opening prayer captured the public's attention, giving it time to settle and catch the beginnings of the narrative proper. Religious oaths and asseverations might be injected to fill out the line and provide a facile rhyme: in the short space (902 lines) of *Gamelyn*, for example, the author swears (in the rhyming position) four times 'by seynt Rycher' and 'by Cristes ore', twice 'by seynt Martyn' and 'by seynte Charite' and once 'by seint Iohan'; at the beginning of a line, he swears twice 'By seint Iame' and once 'by seint Iame in Gales'. 'Cristes curs' is freely and frequently offered at varying positions in the line. The *canterini* swear less frequently, although asseverations such as 'se Iddio mi vaglia' are common.[56] Like much else in these popular traditions, piety tends to fantastic extremes: religious oaths in *Athelston* are over-abundant and over-emphatic; a pious exchange between Febus and his companion is unnecessarily prolix; the pious devotion described by a Sienese abbess is heroically (and comically) exaggerated.[57]

Attempting to win some credibility and respectability for their fragile narratives, *canterini* and romancers customarily supplement their religious appeals with appeals to other external authorities. In both traditions, references to some written source supposedly underlying the narrative are most frequent, although writers pass easily from written to verbal authority, and may even mix the two:

. . . as þe story telles me,   (19)
In book iwreten we fynde-   (21)
    . . . as men me told: (68)
In romaunce as we rede.   (385, 569, 623, 779)

(*Athelston*)

(per quel che 'l libro qui chiaro mi mostra),   (112)
(according to what the book clearly shows me here),
per quel che da ciascun per vero i' sento);   (132)
according to what I hear from everyone to be the truth);
        . . . come dice il libro el vero,   (199)
    . . . as the book truly says,
        . . . secondo la storia,   (322)
        . . . according to the story,
per quel ch' i' sent'e nel libro m'informo.   (472)
according to what I hear and to what I find in the book.

(*Gibello*)[58]

It need hardly be said that no source text systematically underlies such references. Such phrases, besides suggesting some authoritative basis for the work, are chiefly of use in affording a convenient rhyme. In the tail-rhyme romances, which demand four 'b' rhymes per stanza, they occur most frequently in the tail. In *Bel Gherardino*, the first three examples ('come legger soglio'; 'ciò dicon le carte'; 'se 'l cantar non erra')[59] provide three different vowels for rhyming; in *Febus* V, 48,1, the habitual form 'se il dir non erra'[60]

80

contracts and changes to 'se io non erro' for similar purposes. Some forms refer to no authority beyond that of the author himself:

> As y ȝou tel in mi talking . . .
>
> (*Amis & Amiloun*, 484)[61]

> Io truovo d'una donna da Milano . . .
>
> (*Madonna Lionessa*, 1)[62]
>
> I tell of a lady from Milan . . .

Some short phrases of this type ('wythoute fable', 'a lo ver dir') are possessed of little authority. They are rather to be classed with the innumerable tags which simply keep popular verse in motion: 'with muche honour', 'a grande onore'; 'ful of miȝt', 'di possanza oltra missura'; 'bryȝt of ble', 'con chiara fronte'; 'wiþ gamen & play', 'con canti e festa'.[63] Some tags, such as 'armes two' or 'orecchio aperto',[64] do little but clumsily advance dramatic action; some, such as the English staple 'for the nones', do even less. But most tags in these traditions have, at least, a suggestive quality which helps—in a fragmentary but accumulative way—to create the illusion of an idyllic courtly world, in which we may discover a 'riche douke', a 'rico letto' or 'a bed of prys'.[65] In such a world, a hero would be 'queynte of gynne' ('cortese e saputo'), 'feire and gent' ('valloroso e isnello') and 'proude in pride' ('di coraggio fino').[66]

Given their imaginative potency, such descriptive elements might deserve a better name than 'tags': but they hardly deserve to be respected as genuine narrative formulae, which 'can exist as a sort of stylised verbal equivalence, where a certain set of phrases, rigorously formalised in content, are the recognised stimulus, through their traditional associations, for a certain poetic response, a form of descriptive shorthand'.[67] Clearly, the same phrase might be considered as a tag in one poem and as a formula in another: definition depends upon the inner consistency and overall quality of the work in which it features. Few *canterini* or romancers can elevate tags into formulae: yet, in one descriptive area, they can at least raise them in the right direction:

> In þe world was non here pere-
> Also whyt so lylye-flour,
> Red as rose off here colour,
> As bryȝt as blosme on brere.   (*Athelston*, 69–72)

> '. . . e donali el tuo amore,
> perch'è più bella che rosa di spina
> o giglio o viola o altro nuovo fiore!'   (*Febus*, III, 12,4–6)

> '. . . and give your love to her,
> for she is more fair than a rose on the briar
> or lily or violet or any other new flower!'

Such highly affective language, arousing sensations of physical beauty (especially feminine beauty), is one of the most characteristic and captivating features of these popular compositions. Simple, colourful natural images accumulate: Tristano's horse is 'più chiar che giglio' (14,6); Tristano and Astor are 'cavalier fioriti' (36,6—and 'arditi', 36,4); Isotta is a 'rosa di spina' (62,6) and an 'alta stella chiarita' (80,2).[68] Early on in the *cantare* of *Fiorio e Biancifiore*, Topazia—'quella rosa fresca e tenerella' (2,6)—gives birth

> . . . in una rica camera
> di magio ch'è la rosa in su la spina.   (12,3–4)

> . . . in a rich room
> in May when the rose is on the briar.

Her daughter, Biancifiore, resembles a 'fresco giglio' (14,4); she is '"asai piú chiara che non è la stella"' (68,4), a 'chiarita stella' (70,5) and a 'rosa precïosa imbalconata' (74,6). Fiorio becomes enamoured of her: his father attempts to distract him by finding two girls, 'piú belle che pesco fiorito' (57,2), who are willing to expose their charms.[69] Fiorio is unmoved. Thinking Biancifiore to be dead,

> . . . sì diceva: 'Amorosa dongella,
> cuor del mio corpo, chi mi t'ha furato?
> Se tu se' morta, rosa colorita,
> per te morò e paserò d'esta vita.'   (80,5–8)

> . . . thus he spoke: 'Lovely little lady,
> heart of my body, who has stolen you from me?
> If you are dead, coloured rose,
> I will die for you and pass from this life.'

His father promises him

> '. . . una saracina
> che più è bella che rosa di spina.'   (81,7–8)

> '. . . a Saracen girl
> who is more fair than a rose on the briar.'

But Fiorio demands his '"rosa precïosa imbalconata"' (85,8): finally he finds this '"rosa imbalconata"' (122,5),

> e Biancifior, co' lo giglio frongiuto,
> in una ciambra andaro a solazare:
> alora si congiunse 'l fino amore
> tra Fiorio e la dongella Biancifiore.   (123,5–8)

> and Biancifior, with her leafy lily,
> went off to have fun in a bedroom:
> and thus was conjoined the fin'amors
> between Fiorio and the little lady Biancifiore.

Sir Launfal is summoned by his mistress:

> For hete her cloþes down sche dede
> Almest to her gerdylstede:

Þan lay sche vncouert.
Sche was as whyt as lylye yn May,
Or snow þat sneweþ yn wynterys day-
He seygh neuer non so pert.
Þe rede rose, whan sche ys newe,
Aȝens her rode nes nauȝt of hewe,
J dar well say, yn sert.
Her here schon as gold wyre;
May noman rede here atyre,
Ne nauȝt well þenke yn hert.   (289–300)

Launfal kisses 'þat swete flour' (309) and their love is soon consummated:

For play lytyll þey sclepte þat nyȝt . . .   (349)

Such affective epithets are more abundant in the tail-rhyme romances than in the romances in four-stress couplet: this phenomenon has led Derek Pearsall to propose that the formal division 'corresponds to a more fundamental division between "epic romance" and "lyric romance", the former more prosaic, realistic, historical and martial, the latter more emotive, more concerned with love, faith, constancy and the marvellous'.[70] In form and content, the *cantari* resemble the tail-rhyme romances more closely than they do any other English verse: they would not be inappropriately described as stanzaic 'lyric romances'. But, paradoxically, neither the *cantari* nor the tail-rhyme romances develop passages of sustained lyricism with much facility or finesse: they achieve their lyric effect by continually adorning the narrative with isolated phrases, not by halting the action for lengthy lyric reflections. Attempts to develop passages of pure lyricism are generally of poor quality and of brief duration. When Tristano leaves, Isotta can summon just one word to express her grief[71]: '"Tapina!"' In the stanza following, the *canterino* attempts to develop Tristano's feelings on being fatally wounded: as usual, the hero is capable of reporting the facts, but not of reflecting upon them:

Po' che e' fu al castello arrivato,
puosesi in letto e cominciò a gridare:
'Oh me dolente lasso isventurato!
or sono io morto e non posso altro fare:
ché lo re Marco m'ha sì inaverato
ch'altri che Iddio non mi può aiutare',
Dinasso e Sagramor, pien di dolore,
sempre piagnendo cogl'occhi e col core.
(*Ultime imprese e morte di Tristano*, 67,1–8)

When he had arrived at the castle,
he got into bed and started to shout:
'Alas, sad, desolate, unfortunate me!
now I'm dead and can do no more:
for King Mark has so poisoned me
that nobody but God can help me',
Dynas and Sagremor, full of woe,
continually crying with their eyes and heart.

83

The Egerton *Floris and Blauncheflur* makes a brave attempt to articulate the hero's feelings concerning the death of his beloved:

> 'Blauncheflour!' he seide, 'Blauncheflour!'
> So swete a þing was neuer in boure.
> Of Blauncheflour is þat y meene,
> For she was come of good kyn.   (271–4)

After this incantatory repetition of the beloved's name (a device common to both traditions), the romancer ventures to attempt an apostrophe to death: typically, this soon ends as a report on the narrative action:

> 'After deeþ clepe no more y nylle,
> But slee myself now y wille.'   (287–8)

This urge to advance the action, to keep the story-line moving, is a constant feature of these popular narratives. It is appropriate that *Athelston* should open with a meeting of 'foure messangeres' on a highway: much of this poem, and of many others, is taken up with rapid journeying from place to place.[72] A Roman knight's prayer for divine assistance is answered with breathtaking speed.[73]

For authors of the *poesia d'arte*, it was important to select a story that would allow them to display their powers of *amplificatio* and *abbreviatio* to the best advantage. But the story-line itself was not of paramount importance: the rhetorical manuals devote very little space to *inventio*.[74] For popular poets and performers, however, the story was of overwhelming importance: it chiefly determined whether or not they could continue to hold their audience's attention. Consequently, all else in the *cantari* and romances subserves the need to keep the story moving. Sophisticated rhetorical figures are rare, excepting occasional brevity-formulae and (more frequently) inexpressibility topoi.[75] Dialogue is generally a crisp and rapid exchange of information. Moral reflection is confined to commonplaces and proverbial lore; moral judgements are unproblematically absolute, polarising good and evil: no attempt is made to appreciate the viewpoint of 'pagan dogs'.[76] Rhymes are simple and opportunistic;[77] syntax is unadventurous, with little subordination.

The *canterini*, we have noted, were not disposed to halt the progress of their narratives for lyric interludes: rather, they favoured a continuous narrative development, with lyric embellishment *en passant* in affective epithets, tags and phrases. *Ottava rima* excellently accommodates this complex, simultaneous need for continuous narrative development and incidental lyric accompaniment. Its success reflects the fact that this narrative form and its associated techniques were developed out of a literary situation in which the available literary modes were prevalently lyric.[78] The very name *cantare* suggests musical associations; the earliest surviving reference to the tradition (made by the jurist Odofredo, who died in 1265) complains of men who 'causa mercedis habendae', 'cantant de domino Rolando et Oliverio'.[79] This happy combination of musicality and narrative impulse also characterises the tail-rhyme romances. The tail-rhyme stanza is thought to be derived, through Anglo-Norman, from ecclesiastical sequences and responses; its most ancient forerunner in the tradition of 'lyric romance' is the *cantabile* short couplet of

King Horn. *Horn*, which dates from around 1240, has been hailed as 'the first narrative outgrowth from song or lay'.[80]

The structure of both the *cantare* and tail-rhyme stanza is quadripartite: the *ottava* rhymes hendecasyllabic lines abababcc; the tail-rhyme is typically ^{4}aab^{3}ccb^{3}ddb^{3}eeb^3. The Italian stanza, with its uniform line-length, moves the narrative forward evenly, the final couplet steadying the momentum of the alternating a and b rhymes; enjambements between stanzas are rare. But the *canterini* employed a number of devices to quicken or retard the pace of their narrative. The splendidly flexible conjunction 'onde', for example, offered a variety of options: employed at the beginning of a line, it neatly extends the span of a period and offers a stress on the first or second syllable, depending on whether or not its final vowel is elided.[81] Present participial constructions also opened up a generous variety of options in rhythm and syntax; they frequently helped keep the action moving at a lively pace:

> gridando a voce: 'L'orso mi conquide . . .'
> > (*Bel Gherardino* I, 15,3)
> crying at the top of his voice: 'The bear is beating me . . .'
>
> venne curando tutte sue ferute . . .
> > (*Brito di Bretagna*, 166)
> he moved along taking care of all his wounds . . .

Employment of the present participle allowed for postponement of the main clause:

> Leggendo un giorno del tempo passato
> un libro che mi par degli altri il fiore,
> trovai . . .   (*Brito*, 9–11)
>
> Reading one day about times past
> in a book that seems to me to be the flower of all others
> I came across . . .

But such adventurousness in syntax is uncommon, and can end in obscurity, awkwardness and repetition:

> Divisa el conto ch'essendo scoperto
> che i Norgalès era el sire di podesta,
> essendo el re di Norbelanda certo,
> bandì subitamente una sua festa
> a una dea, ch'era nel diserto
> fra tre montagne, in una gran foresta;
> così bandita quella festa bella,
> al buon Febus ‹n'› andò la novella.
>
> Avendo la novella, in sé consiglia:
> 'A questa festa . . .'   (*Febus-el-Forte* IV, 6,1–7,2)
>
> The story relates that it being discovered
> that the Norgales were superior in strength,
> the King of Norbelanda, being sure of this,

immediately announced a feast he was holding
for a goddess, which was in the desert
between three mountains, in a great forest;
this fine feast being announced in this way,
news of it came to the good Febus.

Having the news, he says to himself:
'To this feast . . .'

The tail-rhyme stanza has innate rhythmic variety, alternating movement and repose: narrative development is concentrated in the couplet, leaving extra-narrative (or lyric) elaboration for the tail. The increasing predominance of this stanza in the course of the fourteenth century suggests that most practitioners were happy with its basic capabilities. But the most competent tail-rhyme romancers were willing to stretch these capabilities and vary their options within the four-part structure: in *Athelston* and *Amis and Amiloun*, for example, tail lines are occasionally required to carry full syntactic and semantic weight in extending the duration of a period.[82]

Stylistic and syntactic features of the *cantare* and tail-rhyme romances suggest that these poems were shaped by the needs of a popular audience: but the stanzaic and metrical form also expresses the popular spirit and its cheerful compromise with more elevated poetic forms. Carducci perceptively suggests that Boccaccio sensed ('sentí') that

. . . for the long poem of the rising artisan and bourgeois generations a metre was needed that would be less solemn and perhaps less sad than that of Dante, less uniform than that of the French feudal epics; a metre in which the imagination of the poet-artificer (who was no longer singing nor contemplating but was telling stories) might become more elastic ('molleggiasse').[83]

The evolution of the tail-rhyme stanza reflects a similar desire to escape from the restrictive uniformity of the French-derived four-stress couplet while retaining its expository clarity: the developed stanza attempts to combine 'the clear articulaton of the four-stress couplet with the musical and poetic quality of the native-based three-stress line'.[84]

The spirit of compromise inherent in these stanzaic forms is clearly discernible in their contents: the *canterini* and tail-rhyme romancers are cultural mediators,[85] who render the manners and adventures of the aristocratic world available for popular consumption. They cater to a class of social aspirants, of petty bourgeois anxious to associate themselves with higher things, and, in serving such a class, they participate in a similar cultural phenomenon: the absorption of French literature into the national (or regional)[86] vernacular. The overwhelming majority of poems in both traditions depend upon translations from the French.[87] The Auchinleck Manuscript, 'now unanimously assigned to the period 1330–40',[88] has been hailed as 'the fountain-head'[89] of the tail-rhyme tradition: all six of its tail-rhyme romances have French sources. The oldest surviving *cantare* manuscript, copied in or shortly after 1343, presents a version of the distinguished French romance that inspired Boccaccio's *Filocolo: Floire et Blancheflor*.[90] The *cantare* and tail-rhyme traditions entered their most vigorous phase of development at the same historical moment: when Chaucer left for Florence in 1372, they were both in full spate.

Simultaneously, in Italy and England, great waves of translation from the French, providing popular poets with their raw materials, were encouraged and sustained by the sharp appetite of a bourgeoisie 'that appreciated the necessity, and the pleasure, of reading'.[91] As we may infer from the opening chapter of the *Filocolo*, such translations inevitably debased and obscured the subtleties of their French (and Latin) originals.[92] Often, they dismembered them: a tale extracted from Andreas Capellanus provides material for the whole of Pucci's *Brito di Brettagna*, and for an episode of Chestre's *Sir Launfal*;[93] a choice part of the Tristan legend becomes the *Ultime imprese e morte di Tristano*.[94] Tristan, or Sir Tristrem, or Tristano, becomes a household name, an object for commonplace comparison:

> Poi Enghiramo d'alto ardire s'acende;
> con la sua spada el cavalier sovrano
> scudi rompea, elmi parte e fende,
> e' suoi compagni ognun parea un Tristano . . .
>
> (Febus, III, 60,1–4)

> Then Enghiramo got fired up with lofty ardour;
> with his sword the sovereign knight
> smashed shields, slashed and cut helmets in two,
> and every one of his companions seemed to be a Tristan . . .

The surviving English Charlemagne romances are of little distinction; their Italian counterparts are no better, similarly preoccupied with bloody and interminable sequences of battles and with occasional heavy-handed moralising.[95] Such lugubriousness seems essentially foreign to the spirit of the tail-rhyme romancers and *canterini*; the *lais* of Marie de France are far more congenial. *Lanval* inspires fine flights of fancy with a fairy-mistress in *Sir Launfal*, *Liombruno* and *Bel Gherardino*; *Le Fresne* makes possible the innocent and marvellous worlds of *Lai le Freine* and *Gibello*; fond echoes of *Guigemar* are heard in numerous places. The work of Marie de France facilitates escape into a realm of magic and fantasy, far removed from mundane misery and toil; and it was, above all, just such an escape that these popular authors were looking for. The hero of *Liombruno*, in his magic boots, flies faster than the wind and, invisible under his magic cloak, plays a delightful teasing game in bed with his mistress; in *Athelston*, the Countess enters her trial by fire,

> Þat brennyd boþe fayr and lyȝt.
> Sche wente fro þe lengþe into þe þrydde;
> Stylle sche stood þe fyr amydde,
> And callyd it merye and bryȝt. (632–5)

In such poems, the distant world of aristocratic manners inspires the most colourful imaginative indulgence:

A gerfawcon sche bar on her hond;
A softe pas her palfray fond,
   Þat men her schuld beholde;
Þoruȝ Karlyon rood þat lady;
Twey whyte grehoundys ronne hyr by—
   Har colers were of golde . . .

Alora el re più chiaro che 'l cristallo
andolli drieto con una gran fiocca
di donne e di baroni senza dimoro,
con molte some d'ariento e d'oro,

   con brachi e veltri, sparvieri e falconi,
e con girfalchi ognun più verace,
con pallafreni a destro e gran ronzoni . . .[96]

Then the king more clear than crystal,
went after him with a great crowd
of ladies and of barons without delay,
with great piles of silver and of gold,

   with pointers and greyhounds, sparrowhawks and falcons,
and with gyrfalcons, each truer than the next,
with handsome palfreys and great stallions . . .

Such works occasionally boast a passing acquaintance with courtly manners and courtly language[97]: but for the most part, they rely upon an accumulation of suggestive adjectives, such as 'curteis', 'hende', 'fre' and 'goode'; 'savio', 'nobile', 'pro'' and 'cortese'. Such terms are employed with great frequency and with little precision: *cortesia* might be discovered in a hero, or in his horse; a horse might be as 'noble' as his rider.[98] Courtesy is often simply associated with spending large amounts of money:

   Þo seyde Kyng Artour, þat was hende,
   'Launfal, yf þou wylt fro me wende,
      Tak wyth þe greet spendyng!'

   Oltra misura fu tanto cortese,
   che poco tempo la poté durare . . .[99]

   He was so courteous beyond measure
   that it could not last for long . . .

Most works in these traditions are so far from the spirit of their French originals that comparisons seem pointless: they should simply be enjoyed for their own colourful, colloquial (and occasionally farcical) qualities. Messer Tristan hangs his shield on a pine and rests beneath it; Messer Astor comes along and tosses the shield into a fountain, exclaiming

   'Tu non vale una paglia,
   e teco giostra non voglio oggimai!'   (*Tristano* 17,5–6)

'You're not worth a straw,
and I don't want to joust with you any more!'

The petulant, childish exchange which follows owes little to 'le grand chant cortois'. But, occasionally, we do discover a popular writer who dares to engage more closely with his French original: the author of *La Donna del Vergiù* (a work known to Boccaccio) promises us

> . . . una storia novella
> per dare essemplo a chi intende d'amare . . . (3–4)[100]

> . . . a brand-new story
> to give an example to he who would love . . .

The story in question is that of *La Chastelaine de Vergi*, and her 'highly secret . . . love' (29); the *canterino*, given his limited (if typical) literary abilities, is doomed from the start. The French author observes the inner life of his characters with great acuity; the Italian seems palpably embarrassed by his poem's lack of narrative action.[101] The French Duchess, her advances rebuffed by the knight, nurses and broods over her injury before speaking to her husband; the Italian Duchess petitions the Duke the moment he returns from hunting. The French author can splice a literary reminiscence and a verse from a 'chançon' into his narrative with considerable finesse:

> Si est en tel point autressi
> com li chastelains de Couci,
> qui au cuer n'avoit s'amor non,
> dist en un vers d'une chançon:
> PAR DIEU, AMORS, FORT M'EST A CONSIRRER . . . (291–5)[102]

> He was in the same situation
> as the Chatelain of Couci,
> who, having nothing in his heart but his love,
> said in a verse of one of his songs:
> BY GOD, LOVE, IT PAINS ME TO RECALL . . .

The *canterino*, bereft of such abilities, nevertheless strives for them in attempting to force a dramatic climax:

> Quivi chi v'era grande strida mise
> vedendo morti amendue costoro,
> salvo che la duchessa che sen rise.
> El duca sì mugghiava com'un toro
> e raccontava sì come s'uccise
> Piramo e Tisbe alla fonte del moro;
> e dicen tutti: 'Per simile crimine
> morì Francesca con Pagol da Rimine.' (505–12)

> Then whoever was there let out a great shout
> seeing both of them to be dead,

except for the duchess, who laughed about it.
The duke was bellowing like a bull
and was telling the story of the death
of Pyramus and Thisbe at the source of the mulberry-tree;
and everyone said: 'For similar crime
Francesca died with Paul from Rimini.'

This ghastly, over-populated stanza—presenting the painful spectacle of an author stranded way beyond the limits of his competence—reminds us of the gulf that separates the *canterini* from the poets of thirteenth-century France. Some *cantari* exhibit greater literary capabilities: *Febus* VI, 16, for example, contains a respectable catalogue of men ruined in love, featuring Hercules, Hector of Troy, Sampson, Achilles, and Duke Mansidori. But it is, essentially, the sombre, tragic character of *La Chastelaine de Vergi* that defeats the *canterino*, plus the necessity of engaging with courtly ritual that he does not really comprehend. It is never clear, for example, why (apart from reasons of pure expedience) love should be secret: such restraint seems foreign to the *cantare* spirit. Brito di Brettagna feels the need to keep his love secret but succeeds for less than a stanza (17–24). Bel Gherardino, propositioned by a Queen, answers with the resolution characteristic of Marie de France's Lanval:[103]

> 'Io v'addomando e cheggio perdonanza,
> ch'i' non farei tal fallo al signor mio.'   (II, 22,1–2)

> 'I carve and beg you for your pardon,
> but I would not commit such a fault against my lord.'

But, by the end of the next stanza, he has already made love to the Queen. *Canterini* had neither the education nor the temperament to be faithful to the French courtly spirit.

As Englishmen from diverse backgrounds were attracted by the possibilities of the metrical romance, so Italian authors exploited the *cantare*. Certain members of the *famiglia* of St Catherine of Siena made the *cantare* a most effective vehicle for apostolic action;[104] such efforts are paralleled (if not equalled) in England by pious works such as *Titus and Vespasian*. Some works display a keen political sense: *Athelston* and the *Cantare della guerra degli otto santi*[105] exhibit a similar distaste for tyranny in observing power-struggles between religious and secular authorities. A number of authors are erudite: some romances, most notably *King Alisaunder*, 'smell strongly of the lamp';[106] version A of the *Cantare di Pirramo e di Tisbe*, amplifying *Metamorphoses* IV, 55–166, opens with a highly complex period which extends over two stanzas and expires with a reminiscence of *Purgatorio* XXVII, 39.[107]

Boccaccio was the first major author to involve himself with the *cantare*. It has even been suggested that Boccaccio might have originated the tradition,[108] although this is most unlikely. Boccaccio was the first to surround the *cantare* format with serious literary pretensions: the *Filostrato* prefaces its *ottave* with a prose 'Proemio' and concludes them with a lengthy *congedo*. The poem is divided into nine 'Parts' ('Parti') and adorned with authorial rubrics: every effort is made to strengthen the impression that the author is not merely telling a story, but is creating an opus. Through such efforts, Boccaccio did much to establish the *cantare* as a literary form.[109] Consequently, he was closely associated with the *cantare* throughout (and long after) the fourteenth century.[110] Most copies of the *Ninfale fiesolano*, Boccaccio's final and most distinguished essay in the *cantare* form, are found in manuscripts containing *cantari* or other popular pieces.[111] The *Filostrato*, composed in a Florentine merchant colony, was doubtless first admired and voiced abroad by intelligent artisans.[112]

In his prose 'Proemio', Boccaccio informs us that his aim in the *Filostrato* is 'cantando narrare li miei martiri' (26). This fine hendecasyllabic phrase—with its characteristic collocation of present participle and infinitive—suggests some conscious appreciation of the *ottava*'s double capabilities: his work is to be at once narrative and lyrical.

The narrative development of the *Filostrato* is, like that of most *cantari*, admirably brisk and straightforward. The work is not cluttered or burdened with extraneous erudite matter. References to sources are vague and fleeting, in the familiar *cantare* (and romance) fashion, often serving to provide a convenient rhyme: 'se 'l ver dice la storia' (I, 46,6); 's'el non erra/la storia' (I, 16,5–6); 'se non erra/la storia' (III, 90,5–6). The *Filostrato*'s actual sources, we have noted, are not readily identifiable. It was a common *canterino* practice to isolate and elaborate the most promising or eventful portions of a romance text, thereby creating a new, autonomous work[113]: the *Filostrato* appears to be the fruit of an analogous process. Trojan tales were popular among the *canterini*; Benoît's *Roman de Troie* provided the subject matter for at least one of them.[114]

Although he brushes with Vergil, Ovid and Andreas Capellanus, Boccaccio makes little use of Latin authors in the *Filostrato*. He makes greater use of Dante, slotting memorable phrases from the *Commedia* into his narrative with a breathtaking disregard for the context in which he found them.[115] Like the *canterini*, he admires and draws upon the *Commedia* without being visibly affected by its doctrine and science. In later works, his presentation of Fortune owes much to Dante[116]: in the *Filostrato* it remains primitive, even when he is imitating a Dantean passage:

> 'Pandaro,' disse Troiol 'qual fortuna
> t'ha qui guidato a vedermi languire?' (II, 2,1–2)[117]
>
> 'Pandaro,' said Troiolo, 'what fortune
> has guided you here to see me languishing?'

Although Boccaccio was later to become a great champion and expositor of Dante, the *Filostrato*'s enthusiastic and unreflective exploitation of the *Commedia* shows little more sophistication than does *Febus-el-Forte*.[118] Boccaccio's poem often speaks with popular inflections, as in this compressed account of Troiolo's languor:

> E non passava sera né mattina
> che con sospiri costui non chiamasse:
> 'O luce bella, o stella mattutina.'

91

Poi come s'ella presente ascoltasse,
mille fiate e più rosa di spina
chiamandola . . .   (V, 44,1–6)

And not an evening or a morning passed
without him calling out, with sighs:
'O fair light, o morning star.'
Then, as if she were present and listening,
calling her a thousand times and more
rose on the briar . . .

In employing the affective adjective 'tapino' (and its diminutives) to generate a convenient rhyme, Boccaccio inevitably sounds a popular register: he
rhymes 'valorosa e bella' with 'sua vita tapinella' (V, 43,2&6), 'Amico fino'
with 'tapino' (II, 16,3&5) and 'buone e belle' with 'scritte tapinelle' (II,
109,4&6). He shows an extreme fondness for other affective adjectives such as
'dolce', which he sometimes employs twice in a single stanza: 'dolce mio
signore', 'tuo dolce aspetto' (IV, 158,3&6); 'dolci baci', 'dolce ragionare' (VII,
71,1&3); 'o dolce bene', 'o dolce anima mia' (V, 24,4&6). He follows the
canterini in employing affective epithets for the evocation of female beauty:
Criseyde surpasses other women 'quanto la rosa la viola/di biltà vince' (I,
19,3–4); she has 'occhi lucenti e l'angelico viso' (I, 28,8); blushing, 'risembra-
va mattutina rosa' (II, 38,3); she seems 'in vista perla orientale' (II, 108,6).
Like the *canterini*, Boccaccio conjures up a picture of the courtly life chiefly by
accumulating such adjectives and epithets and by penning a series of lightning
sketches:

Troiolo canta e fa mirabil festa,
armeggia e dona e spende lietamente,
e spesso si rinnuova e cangia vesta,
ogni ora amando più ferventemente . . .   (II, 84,1–4)

Troiolo sings and is marvellously festive,
jousts and gives presents and cheerfully spends money,
and often gets new clothes and changes costume,
every hour loving more fervently . . .

Troiolo in guisa d'una cortesia,
con più compagni montò a cavallo
con un falcone in pugno . . .   (V, 10,1–3)

Troiolo, to act out a courtesy,
mounted his horse with many companions
with a falcon on his fist . . .

In poco d'or la sua camera piena
di donne fu e di suoni e di canti;
dall'una parte gli era Polissena
ch'un'angiola pareva ne' sembianti . . .   (VII, 84,1–4)[119]

In no time at all his room was full
of women and of music and of songs;
to one side of him was Polissena
who seemed like an angel in her looks . . .

Boccaccio, like the *canterini*, is fascinated by the outer trappings of the courtly world; and, like them, he shows a somewhat limited understanding of its inner life. For Criseida, *onestà* is a matter of personal policy and convenience:

> 'a me onesta si convien di stare.'   (II, 51,5)

> 'it suits me to stay honest.'

The fact that Criseida is 'onesta' is seen as an obstacle to the fulfilment of Troiolo's aspirations: in Chaucer, the fact that Criseyde is 'vertuous' is seen as a sign of hope.[120] For Boccaccio, *cortesia* is an elaborate game in which a man must remain 'segreto' in order to avoid public scandal;[121] the *Filostrato*'s understanding of the necessity of secrecy is little more sophisticated than that of *La Donna del Vergiù*. In *Troilus and Criseyde*, as in *La Chastelaine de Vergi*, the implications of secrecy are profound.[122]

The propensity of the *canterini* for staginess and exaggeration also affects Boccaccio: in *Filostrato* II, 7, Troiolo tells us that he has been driven to the brink of suicide a thousand times; in VII, 33 (a vulgar and inept stanza) he attempts to stab himself. In the couplet of IV, 60 (an unlikely place to begin) Troiolo embarks on a dreary apostrophe to death, punctuating it five times with the exclamation 'deh' (IV, 60,7–62,8). When language fails him, Boccaccio turns to the standard, tag-like forms of the abbreviated inexpressibility topos as readily as any *canterino*.[123] Boccaccio's description of Troiolo's final battles suggests a series of noisy, isolated brawls which—as in the *Cantare di Troia*—are summarily and unceremoniously concluded:

> . . . e dopo lungo stallo
> avendone già morti più di mille
> miseramente un dì l'uccise Achille.   (VIII, 27,6–8)

> . . . and after much delay,
> having already killed off more than a thousand,
> one day Achilles wretchedly killed him.

The preceding discussion of the *Filostrato*'s affiliations with works of popular provenance has been restricted, for the most part, to units of stylistic and narrative structure that are relatively small: from single tags and phrases to couplets and single stanzas. Larger units, such as those identified by Susan Wittig, need not be excluded from discussion: indeed, they often prove illuminating when applied to the *Filostrato-Troilus* relationship. Consider, for example, the most complex motifemic pattern discussed by Wittig in her analysis of the Middle English romances: in this motifeme, 'the lover first confesses his or her love to the helper (*confession*), who then offers to assist in some way (*promise*) and makes a plan to gain the loved one's goodwill or affection (*plan*)'.[124] Wittig then proceeds to demonstrate how this pattern is elaborated, through its constituent allomotifs, in eight Middle English romances. Chaucer's familiarity with such romances can only have deepened his appreciation of the subtle development of this motifeme in the early part of the *Filostrato*. The largest structural units identified by Wittig are the two major linking patterns separation-restoration and love-marriage.[125] These patterns, acted out in text after text, help constitute the 'horizon of the expectable'[126] for the reader of Middle English romances. Again, it was precisely as such a reader that Chaucer would have been most forcibly struck by the *Filostrato*'s originality, its breaking of the familiar horizon: for in Boccaccio's text we discover separation *without* restoration; and love *without* marriage. Perhaps it was through this double defeating of conventional romance expectations (enacted within a romance format) that the *Filostrato* first commanded Chaucer's attention.

Such large-scale analytic categories may, then, teach us something about Chaucer's general appreciation of Boccaccio's text. But the particulars of Chaucer's assessment of the specific stylistic register and social provenance of the *Filostrato* emerge only through more localised analyses of smaller narrative components. Much of the comparative analysis that now follows, then, continues our earlier engagement with smaller units of narrative and stylistic structure.

It is at once apparent that it was the *Filostrato*'s simple virtues that were most to Chaucer's liking. Boccaccio does occasionally attempt to embellish his narrative with sophisticated rhetorical figures and with ingenious verbal configurations.[127] He sometimes smoothes the flow of his verse by alliterating and makes considerable use of anaphora. *Troilus and Criseyde* is not one of Chaucer's most stylistically elaborate works[128]: Chaucer had no truck with Boccaccio's most ostentatious verbal effects (which he may well have ascribed to artistic immaturity). Fortunately, however, the Italian poem unravels its story-line straightforwardly enough, for the most part; and its author speaks with becoming candour even when considering complex possibilities[129]:

> E qual si fosse non è assai certo:
> o che Criseida non se n'accorgesse
> per l'operar di lui ch'era coverto,
> o che di ciò conoscer s'infignesse;
> ma questo n'è assai chiaro ed aperto,
> che niente pareva le calesse
> di Troiolo e dell'amor che le portava,
> ma come non amata dura stava.   (I, 48)

> And seyde he hadde a fevere and ferde amys.
> But how it was, certeyn, kan I nat seye,
> If that his lady understood nat this,
> Or feynede hire she nyste, oon of the tweye;
> But wel I rede that, by no manere weye,
> Ne semed it as that she of hym roughte,
> Or of his peyne, or whatsoevere he thoughte.   (I, 491–7)

The argument of Boccaccio's stanza divides neatly into two parts; its contents are formally announced by the first and fifth lines: first reporting what is not known about Criseida's feelings for Troiolo, it then tells us what is known. Chaucer compresses, abbreviates and amends Boccaccio's argument, but upholds its formally articulated bipartite structure. Chaucer's opening line is taken up in completing an idea developed in his previous stanza; compression is further necessitated by Chaucer's employment of rhyme royal, which contains one line fewer than the *ottava*. Having allowed himself six lines in which to translate the Italian stanza, Chaucer elects to drop Boccaccio's third line and to compress the sense of Boccaccio's couplet into a single line. Although Boccaccio's first and fifth lines do not contribute to the development of the narrative action, Chaucer decides against cutting either of them. He reduces Boccaccio's fifth line to a half-line format familiar from the English romances and fills up the rest of this line with a simple, intensifying phrase which yields his third 'b' rhyme. Neither this phrase nor the phrase 'oon of the tweye' with which it rhymes advances the narrative action. But Chaucer, like Boccaccio, recognises the useful function played by such phrases in ballasting the narrative and in regulating its rate of development.

One significant shift between these stanzas remains to be noted: whereas Boccaccio chronicles events by employing impersonal, third-person constructions, Chaucer speaks in his own person, drawing attention to his authorial role. Such a shift is typical:

> E spesse volte insieme s'avvisaro
> con rimproveri cattivi e villani . . . (VIII, 26,1–2)

> And ofte tyme, I fynde that they mette
> With blody strokes and with wordes grete . . . (V, 1758–9)

The phrase 'I fynde' has counterparts in both the *cantari* and the English romances. In his next five stanzas Chaucer departs from the Italian in order to discuss the scope and limitations of his authorial activity with his audience. On rejoining the Italian work he again injects a personal note into Boccaccio's flat chronicling of events:

> L'ira di Troiolo in tempi diversi
> a' Greci nocque molto sanza fallo . . . (VIII, 27,1–2)

> The wrath, as I bigan yow for to seye,
> Of Troilus the Grekis boughten deere. (V, 1800–1)

By cutting the phrase 'in tempi diversi' and the tag 'sanza fallo', and by opening a parenthetic space between 'ira' and 'di', Chaucer wins room for the insertion of a casual aside: that is, he employs thoughtful and painstaking art to create an impression of casualness and ease; such an impression is furthered later in the Book by the rhyming tag 'as I kan heere' (V, 1804). Although Boccaccio makes fewer personal incursions into the narrative,[130] he too cultivates a comfortable narrative manner by employing a battery of convenient tags and phrases. Some of his parenthetic asides seem strikingly 'Chaucerian' in form and mood:

> . . . sì come suole
> spesso avvenire a chi sanza difetto
> riguarda in fra le cose c'ha per mano . . . (VIII, 5,5–7)

> . . . as it is wont
> often to happen to he who, without erring,
> looks into matters that he has in hand . . .

Chaucer passes over this generalised appeal to experience, but seizes on Boccaccio's next usage of the *topos* to fashion a fine epigrammatic couplet (VIII, 7,2–4; V, 1637–8). Three stanzas earlier, he had followed yet another employment of the *topos*, this time suggesting a detached attitude towards the behaviour of lovers:

> come suole esser degli amanti usanza . . .   (VIII, 2,4)

> And as thise loveres don . . .   (V, 1572)

It is perhaps surprising to hear Boccaccio sounding and inspiring such a typically 'Chaucerian' note.[131] But in 'Parte' II, he offers a more elaborate employment of the *topos* which, in uniting author and auditors, again seems strongly reminiscent of the 'Chaucerian' manner:

> Ma come noi, per continua usanza,
> per più legne veggiam foco maggiore,
> così avvien, crescendo la speranza,
> assai sovente ancor cresce l'amore;
> e quinci Troiol con maggior possanza
> che l'usato sentì nel preso cuore
> l'alto disio spronarlo, onde i sospiri
> tornar più fier che prima e li martiri.   (II, 85)

Chaucer apparently makes no use of this stanza or the stanzas which surround it: in II, 977–9, he adopts an idea from II, 81,2–4, but then appears to ignore the Italian text until II, 981 brushes with II, 89,1. Further on in Book II, however, we find:

> But as we may alday oureselven see,
> Thorugh more wode or col, the more fir,
> Right so encrees of hope, of what it be,
> Therwith ful ofte encresseth ek desir;
> Or as an ook comth of a litel spir,
> So thorugh this lettre, which that she hym sente,
> Encressen gan desir, of which he brente.

> Wherfore I seye alwey, that day and nyght
> This Troilus gan to desiren moore
> Thanne he did erst, thorugh hope . . .   (II, 1331–40)

The first four lines of Chaucer's first stanza intelligently imitate the phrasing and structure of II, 85,1–4; his fifth offers a parallel exemplum; the couplet connects all this with the immediate facts of the narrative action. The second stanza sees Chaucer returning emphatically ('Wherfore I seye alwey') to the task of storytelling. It also sees him realigning his narrative with his source text: having employed phrases from II, 129–30 in the stanza ending at II, 1330, he links up with II, 131 in II, 1338–44, the second stanza quoted above:

> Crescea di giorno in giorno più l'ardore
> e come che speranza l'aiutasse . . .   (II, 131,1–2)

It was, apparently, this notion of hope kindling ardour which reminded Chaucer of the *topos* of II, 85. Such appeals to experience are commonplace in medieval literature: but Boccaccio's employment of the *topos*, uniting the experience of author and auditors, clearly had a particular attractiveness for the English poet. In all their writings, Chaucer and Boccaccio seem especially concerned to excite pity and compassion from their readers, and to unite author, readers and protagonists in a common bond of sympathy: such an aim is explicitly stated at the opening of the *Troilus* (22–51) and in the opening periods of both the *Fiammetta* and *Decameron*.

The *Filostrato*, then, resembles the *cantare* in its robust and energetic development of the story-line, and in its employment of stock tags and epithets to regulate and ease this development: but on speculating on the possibilities of psychological motivation (as in I, 48, quoted above) and in demanding an active and compassionate response from its readers, the *Filostrato* sets itself apart from this popular tradition. As we have seen, the *canterini* concern themselves with the fantastic, the stupefying and the marvellous, a world of gilded externals: they rarely trouble to turn their attention inwards to consider psychological motivations, or seek to involve their auditors with such complexities. The 'inner awareness' characteristic of twelfth-century French romance[132] remains quite foreign to these fourteenth-century *canterini*. Boccaccio, however, offers frequent glimpses of this inner world; and in the *Filostrato*'s opening period he suggests how he acquired such sensitivity and such powers of analysis:

> Molte fiate già, nobilissima donna, avvenne che io, il quale quasi dalla mia puerizia infino a questo tempo ne' servigi d'Amore sono stato, ritrovandomi nella sua corte intra i gentili uomini e le vaghe donne dimoranti in quella parimente con meco, udii muovere e disputare questa quistione, cioè . . . (*Proemio* 1)

> On many occasions, most beautiful lady, it has happened that I, who have been enrolled in the services of Love from my boyhood down to the present moment, finding myself in his court among noble men and beautiful women dwelling therein as my peers, heard this question mooted and disputed, namely . . .

Having made this claim for his education in the court of Love (which need not be identified with the court of King Robert or with any other historical court)[133], Boccaccio proceeds to tell of a *demande d'amour* and of the dialectical process it generates (2–5). The judgement yielded by this process is disproved by bitter experience, 'amara esperienza' (6–22); the *Filostrato* is composed as an attempt to escape from such bitterness and to atone for the unfortunate error (23–37). As a work which traces its origins back to the positing of a question in a court of Love, the *Filostrato* would have appeared particularly attractive to Chaucer, who was obviously well acquainted with such courts and such questions.[134] Such origins promise something more than a straightforward account of an amorous conquest: the reader anticipates some intelligent analysis of love's inner growth. The more mature *Filocolo*, issuing from the activity of a *brigata*, is better able to fulfil this dual promise of action and reflection than is the *Filostrato*: but the earlier work still manages some exploration of the inner life of its protagonists. This is often achieved by relocating the public dialectics of the court of Love within the private space of a single, individual mind. Chaucer was evidently impressed by the *Filostrato*'s employment of internal debate:

> Amore il facea pronto ad ogni cosa
> doversi opporre, ma d'altra parte era
> ragion che 'l contrastava . . . (IV, 16,1–3)

> Love hym made al prest to don hire byde,
> And rather dyen than she sholde go;
> But resoun seyde hym, on that other syde . . . (IV, 162–4)

Later on in Book IV, Troilus is again divided within himself by contrary forces, this time desire and reason; Boccaccio again supplies the cue for internal debate:

> 'per ch'a prender partito non s'attenta
> il cor, che d'una parte questo brama,
> e d'altra teme di non dispiacere . . .' (IV, 68,5–7)

> 'Thus am I with desir and reson twight:
> Desir for to destourben hire me redeth,
> And reson nyl nat, so myn herte dredeth.' (IV, 572–4)

Chaucer here follows Boccaccio's choice of debate structure but exploits it independently, finding the Italian phrasing and prosody deficient; such is also the case in Book II, as Chaucer tells us what Criseyde 'gan in her herte argue' (694). Whereas the arguments of Chaucer's heroine are guided by aristocratic values, and are couched in aristocratic language, the reasoning of her Italian counterpart—parts of which were to enjoy 'una vasta fortuna popolaresca'[135] —bustles with worldly energy:

> 'In every thyng, I woot, there lith mesure.' (II, 715)

> 'Chi mi vorrà se io c'invecchio mai?
> Certo nessuno . . .' (II, 71,1–2)

> 'Who will ever want me if I grow old?
> Nobody, of course . . .'

Throughout the heroine's lengthy self-interrogation, the Italian and English texts run parallel, brushing together only in isolated phrases such as '"in vita quieta"', '"wel at ese"' (II, 69,3; II, 750). But the passages terminate at similar points of impasse, with Criseyde 'biasimando e lodando' ('cursing and commending') and Criseyde 'Now hoot, now cold . . . bitwixen tweye' (78,7; 811). Although Chaucer was unimpressed by the quality of Boccaccio's language here, he evidently admired his sense of structure. Boccaccio again supplies the cue for internal debate; he also highlights the precise moment at which the protagonist's mind moves from one side of the debate to the other:

E stando alquanto, poi si rivolgea
nell'altra parte: 'Misera,' dicendo
'che vuoi tu far? Non sai tu . . .' (II, 75,1-3)

And pausing awhile, she then turned
to the other side of the case, saying: 'Wretch,
what are you up to? Don't you know . . .'

But right as when the sonne shyneth brighte
In March, that chaungeth ofte tyme his face,
And that a cloude is put with wynd to flighte,
Which oversprat the sonne as for a space,
A cloudy thought gan thorugh hire soule pace,
That overspradde hire brighte thoughtes alle,
So that for feere almost she gan to falle.

That thought was this: 'Allas! syn I am free . . .'
(II, 764-71)

The sustained magnificence and audacity of Chaucer's imagery owes
something to Boethius and nothing to Boccaccio[136]: but the *Filostrato*'s
brief, mechanical transfer between arguments certainly seems to have alerted
Chaucer to the possibilities of poetic elaboration. Another of the Italian
poem's internal debates occasions one of Chaucer's most poignant stanzas:

Pandaro con dolor tutto ascoltava,
e ver sentendol, non sapea che dirsi,
e d'una parte a star quivi il tirava
dell'amico l'amor, d'altra a partirsi
vergogna spesse volte lo 'nvitava
pel fallo di Criseida, e spedirsi
qual far dovesse seco non sapea,
e l'uno e l'altro forte gli dolea.   (VIII, 22)

This Pandarus, that al thise thynges herde,
And wiste wel he seyde a soth of this,
He nought a word ayeyn to hym answerde;
For sory of his frendes sorwe he is,
And shamed for his nece hath don amys,
And stant, astoncd of thise causes tweye,
As stille as ston; a word ne kowde he seye. (V, 1723-9)

The poems' most dynamic figure stands immobile between contrary impulses and, more painfully, is reduced to silence; Chaucer emphasises this last
fact by saving the force of 'non sapea che dirsi' for the very end of his stanza.
Pandarus' astonishment and immobility here compares with the state of the
Chaucerian dreamer before the double gate of the *Parliament of Fowls* (141–
54). Internal debate was evidently a powerful and fundamental psychological
structure for Chaucer. The only Petrarchan sonnet he elected to translate
stages an internal debate; and Chaucer took pains, in composing his first
Canticus Troili, to preserve and accentuate its debate structure.[137] In II,

1373–6, Pandarus imagines a debate between Kynde and Daunger taking place within the mind of Troilus. As we shall see, Chaucer employs allegorical personifications (most of them drawn from *Le Roman de la Rose*) when he finds his Italian source deficient in psychological analysis: but he clearly found Boccaccio's fondness for internal debate both congenial and opportune.

The *Filostrato* further qualified itself as a suitable source for Chaucer by the fertility and dense abundance of its ideas: every stanza offers two, three, four or more motifs for elaboration. Here, for example, Boccaccio develops three distinct ideas:

> Era contento Troiolo, ed in canti
> menava la sua vita e 'n allegrezza;
> l'alte bellezze ed i vaghi sembianti
> di qualunque altra donna nulla prezza,
> fuor che la sua Criseida, e tutti quanti
> gli altri uomin vivere in trista gramezza,
> a respetto di sé, seco credeva,
> tanto il suo ben gli aggradava e piaceva. (III, 72)

The ideas developed in this stanza might be summarised as follows: Troiolo was content, and led his life in singing and joyfulness; he paid no attention to female beauty, excepting that of Criseida; compared with his life, which so delighted him, he believed the life of other men to be miserable. Chaucer was so impressed by these ideas that he allocated a stanza to each of them (III, 1716–36). Boccaccio's first idea, developed over two lines, is diligently rendered by two lines of English. Chaucer improves upon Boccaccio's bald opening phrase 'Era contento' by employing the courtly, French-derived phrase 'In suffisaunce': but he upholds Boccaccio's choice of the verb *menare* ('to lede') and imitates 'in canti' with 'in singynges', a phrase found nowhere else in his writings. He then expands Boccaccio's account of Troiolo's joyful life by drawing upon *Filostrato* II, 84,1–3 (quoted above, p. 92):

> In suffisaunce, in blisse, and in singynges,
> This Troilus gan al his lif to lede.
> He spendeth, jousteth, maketh festeynges;
> He yeveth frely ofte, and chaungeth wede . . .
>   (III, 1716–9)

The last three lines of this stanza and the first three of the next add two characteristic Chaucerian emphases: Troilus' love makes him highly companionable (1720–2) and famous (1723–5). Chaucer then proceeds to develop Boccaccio's third idea:

> And, as in love, he was in swich gladnesse,
> That in his herte he demed, as I gesse,
> That ther nys lovere in this world at ese
> So wel as he; and thus gan love hym plese. (III, 1726–9)

Chaucer's third stanza offers an exquisite poetic realisation of Boccaccio's second idea:

The goodlihede or beaute which that kynde
In any other lady hadde yset
Kan nought the montance of a knotte unbynde,
Aboute his herte, of al Criseydes net.   (III, 1730–3)

Boccaccio's third line proposes a somewhat vague and hazy ideal of feminine beauty which restricts itself to externals: Chaucer, with the phrase 'goodlihede or beaute', characteristically concerns himself with both moral and aesthetic qualities.[138] For the remainder of his stanza, Chaucer takes no pains to introduce fresh ideas: he is content simply to elaborate the strain of imagery set in motion by his first four lines. In this and in dozens of other amplifications, Chaucer shows great respect for Boccaccio's text, and particularly for his powers of invention: indeed, it often appears that Chaucer wished to do the *Filostrato* justice by giving its ideas room to breathe. Sometimes, however, he found Boccaccio's powers of narrative compression most congenial:

> Ed el similemente ebbe in pensiero
> ancor più volte di volervi andare,
> di pellegrino in abito leggero,
> ma sì non si sapeva contraffare
> che gli paresse assai coprire il vero,
> né scusa degna sapeva trovare
> da dir, se fosse stato conosciuto
> in abito cotanto disparuto.   (VIII, 4)

> And ofte tyme he was in purpos grete
> Hymselven lik a pilgrym to desgise,
> To seen hire; but he may nat contrefete
> To ben unknowen of folk that weren wise,
> Ne fynde excuse aright that may suffise,
> If he among the Grekis knowen were;
> For which he wep ful ofte and many a tere.   (V, 1576–82)

Dropping 'similemente', Chaucer compresses Boccaccio's first two lines into one: 'ebbe in pensiero' is neatly rendered as 'he was in purpos grete', and 'ancor più volte' simply translated as 'ofte tyme'; the force of 'di volervi andare' is sharpened by 'To seen hire', and saved for the beginning of the third line. For the rest of the stanza, Chaucer keeps pace with Boccaccio's ideas: the phrasing of 'he may nat contrefete' is indebted to 'non si sapeva contraffare'; the phrase which follows gives concrete expression to the anxiety vaguely alluded to in Boccaccio's fifth line. The polysyllables of Boccaccio's final line are impressively sonorous but add little to the narrative: Chaucer rejects them, sealing his stanza with impressive and independent finality; his monosyllables stand like a bulwark against the feverish thinking which has gone before.

But although Chaucer benefited from the dense abundance of Boccaccio's ideas, he sometimes found their proliferation too riotous. The opening line of his next stanza aligns his text with *Filostrato* VIII, 3:

> Ei le mandò più lettere, scrivendo . . .   (VIII, 3,1)

> To hire he wroot yet ofte tyme al newe . . .   (V, 1583)

Boccaccio's stanza is again full of ideas: but Chaucer makes no use of them. The idea that Troiolo reproves Criseida—albeit 'cortesemente'—for not returning to Troy is out of keeping with Chaucer's conception both of his hero and of *curteisie*; Troilus beseeches Criseyde to return and 'holde hire trouthe' (VIII, 3,5–6; V, 1585–6).[139] Boccaccio's couplet introduces a more outrageous idea: Troiolo

> mandovvi Pandar, qualora tra essi
> o triegue o patti alcun furon promessi.   (VIII, 3,7–8)

> sent Pandaro to her, whenever there was promise
> of truce or agreement between the warring factions.

The idea that Pandaro, at this stage of the narrative, is still able to shuttle between the lovers has mind-boggling implications which Boccaccio does not trouble to explore. The reader is simply puzzled here by Boccaccio's excessive ingenuity in the same way that Erich Auerbach is puzzled by a gratuitous detail in the story of Frate Alberto.[140] As an energetic inventor of narrative detail, Boccaccio occasionally overreaches himself.

The fact that Chaucer mines almost every idea from *Filostrato* VIII, 4 and yet takes virtually nothing from the preceding stanza suggests that he was a critically discriminating reader of the Italian text. This impression is strengthened if we consider another stanza that Chaucer initially imitates, but then drops:

> Pandaro disioso di servire
> il giovinetto, il quale e' molto amava,
> lasciato lui dove gli piacque gire,
> sen gì ver dove Criseida stava;
> la qual, veggendo lui a sé venire,
> levata in piè, di lungi il salutava,
> e Pandar lei, cui per la man pigliata
> in una loggia seco l'ha menata.   (II, 34)

> This Pandarus, tho desirous to serve
> His fulle frend, than seyde in this manere . . .   (I, 1058–9)

Chaucer's 'desirous to serve' exactly translates 'disioso di servire', and the phrase 'His fulle frend' splendidly captures and compresses the sense of Boccaccio's second line, avoiding the gratuitous personal pronoun. An excessive use of personal pronouns (a characteristic feature of the *Filostrato*) and clumsy subordinate clauses make this one of Boccaccio's less distinguished *ottave*. In the space of this ill-managed, congested stanza, Pandaro moves from Troiolo's bedside to Criseida's loggia: the action advances with the rough haste typical of a *cantare* narrative. Such haste seemed inappropriate to Chaucer, who disengages with the Italian text at this point: Pandarus leaves Troilus in a thoughtful mood, and does not approach Criseyde's palace immediately,

> For everi wight that hath an hous to founde
> Ne renneth naught the werk for to bygynne
> With rakel hond, but he wol bide a stounde,

And sende his hertes line out fro withinne
Aldirfirst his purpos for to wynne.
Al this Pandare in his herte thoughte,
And caste his werk ful wisely or he wroughte.   (I, 1065–71)

Pandarus' wise forethought here contrasts with Pandaro's rash haste: over a dozen stanzas are to pass before he visits Criseyde. And, of course, Pandarus' attitude parallels that of Chaucer: as the character pauses thoughtfully before advancing his management of the love affair, so the author thinks 'ful wisely' before proceeding with his story. The responses of Chaucer and Pandarus are intimately associated. Pandarus, like Chaucer, is an unsuccessful lover who serves younger aspirants; like Chaucer, he is a littérateur. Pandarus manipulates events from within the narrative as Chaucer manipulates them from without: he is Chaucer's surrogate within the story of *Troilus and Criseyde*. It is hardly surprising, then, that Chaucer's commentary on Pandarus' diligent forethought should herald some thoughtful consideration of his own aims and intentions: this comes just four stanzas later, at the beginning of Book II, and begins with an address to the audience reminiscent of Dante's commencement of the *Purgatorio*. In this address (II, 1–49), Chaucer seeks to acquaint and involve the reader with problems facing his imaginative and artistic enterprise. Such a strategem is, of course, a vital aspect of the *Commedia*. On reaching the Sphere of the Sun, Dante makes similar demands on the reader in presenting 'that material for which I am made a scribe';[141] and, just three cantos later, we hear a plea for intellectual caution and forethought that is strikingly similar to the Chaucerian stanza quoted above:

> 'E questo ti sia sempre piombo a' piedi,
> per farti mover lento com' uom lasso
> e al sì e al no che tu non vedi:
>   ché quelli è tra li stolti bene a basso,
> che sanza distinzione afferma e nega
> ne l'un così come ne l'altro passo;
>   perch' elli 'ncontra che più volte piega
> l'oppinïon corrente in falsa parte,
> e poi l'affetto l'intelletto lega.'   (Par XIII, 112–20)

> 'And let this be always like lead to your feet,
> to make you move slowly like a weary man
> towards a yes or a no that you cannot quite see:
>   for he is truly the lowest among fools
> who affirms and denies without making distinctions
> within the one case and within the other;
>   for it often happens that a quick opinion
> inclines in the wrong direction, and after that
> the intellect is tied down by self-conceit.'

These words, spoken by St Thomas Aquinas, form part of a lengthy and complex theological discourse. They have clear artistic implications: the poet should weigh his motivations and designs most scrupulously before picking up his pen and committing his thoughts to writing.[142] Similar implications might be drawn from Chaucer's stanza which, in fact, closely imitates a passage from Geoffrey of Vinsauf's *Poetria Nova*.[143] If we consider this passage and the lines immediately following it, these artistic implications become graphically obvious:

> Si quis habet fundare domum, non currit ad actum
> Impetuosa manus: intrinseca linea cordis
> Praemetitur opus, seriemque sub ordine certo
> Interior praescribit homo, totamque figurat
> Ante manus cordis quam corporis; et status ejus
> Est prius archetypus quam sensilis. Ipsa poesis
> Spectet in hoc speculo quae lex sit danda poetis.
> Non manus ad calamum praeceps, non lingua sit ardens
> Ad verbum: neutram manibus committe regendam
> Fortunae; sed mens discreta praeambula facti,
> Ut melius fortunet opus, suspendat earum
> Officium, tractetque diu de themate secum.   (43–54)

> If a man has to lay a house's foundations, his
> impetuous hand does not rush to the task: the measuring line
> of his mind first plans out the work, and the inner man
> prescribes the work's stages in a certain order; and the hand of the mind,
> not the bodily hand, forms all in advance, so its mode of being
> is mental before it is actual. Let poetry itself
> see in this mirror what law should be given to poets.
> Let the hand not be hasty in grasping the pen, nor the tongue
> be impatient to speak; let neither be ruled by the hands
> of Fortune. But let the discrete mind, going before the act
> for the work's better fortune, suspend the operation
> of hand and tongue, and ponder at length on the theme.

It is quite clear that Chaucer pondered for years on the theme and design of the *Troilus* before setting his hand to the task of composing; the *Filostrato*, by contrast, is a youthful piece written in haste. Chaucer's obeisance to the *Poetria Nova* at this point (where Boccaccio is obviously acting with 'Impetuosa manus') functions as a private critique of the *Filostrato* and as something of a personal manifesto. Chaucer, like Dante, accepts that an artistic design should be intelligently premeditated; like Dante, he makes such meditation part of his poetry; like Dante, he shares the fruits of his thinking with his readers. And, like Dante, Chaucer shows the highest respect for *ars poetriae*, the art of poetry, the subject of Geoffrey of Vinsauf's treatise: Boccaccio's *Filostrato* (in its headlong pursuit of ideas across prosodic boundaries) does not. Paradoxically, it is in turning away from Boccaccian romance towards Dante and the rhetoricians that Chaucer comes most to resemble those romance authors of twelfth-century France, for whom 'the poem was now to be regarded as a deliberately and artfully composed work of the mind'.[144]

In the light of his own artistic experience and development, Chaucer would have recognised the *Filostrato* as a work which is securely founded upon a tradition of popular narrative. Many aspects of this tradition have counterparts in the tradition of popular romance (particularly tail-rhyme romance) that made such a fundamental contribution to Chaucer's narrative style. Each of these traditions energetically strives to adapt prestigious French precedents to the tastes of a workaday world. The basic strengths of the *Filostrato* are those of an efficient popular narrative: but it is penned by an author who claims some familiarity with aristocratic courts of Love (and with their dialectical procedures) and who proves capable of endowing his protagonists with an inner life. The poem exhibits considerable admiration for Dante, some acquaintance with common classical texts and a glorious profusion of inventive ideas which elaborate a Trojan theme in a highly original manner. Situated between *poesia popolare* and *poesia d'arte*, it draws inspiration from both traditions. Chaucer perceived that the *Filostrato* would suit him admirably as a source, if not as a poetic exemplar.

CHAPTER 6

The Making of Troilus and Criseyde

Having formed some general estimate of Chaucer's attitude towards the *Filostrato*, we may now concentrate upon the detailed business of his *makinge*. Chaucer's general restructuring and amplification of the *Filostrato* need not detain us here: this subject has been considered by a succession of scholars, and their findings have been intelligently summarised and improved upon by Robert Payne.[1] We will seek, rather, to observe the fine details of Chaucer's reactions to the language, syntax and prosody of the Italian poem. Few critics would doubt the value of such close comparative analysis, although some might question the feasibility of applying it to the works of medieval authors.[2] The vagaries of manuscript transmission certainly impede the process of detailed verbal comparison: for we cannot definitively establish what Boccaccio wrote (no autograph *Filostrato* having yet come to light), what Chaucer read, or even what Chaucer himself composed. Such uncertainties do not threaten the general conclusions reached in our last chapter: but the limitations that they impose here must be acknowledged at the outset. It would be foolhardy to hang a thesis upon a single, isolated correspondence of phrasing or syntax. For this reason we will accumulate large numbers of correspondences, juxtaposing—for the most part—complete stanzas of the two poems. The editions of Branca and of Robinson are employed throughout.[3]

   Despite such limitations, the enterprise of this chapter is, I believe, essential if our understanding of Chaucer's engagement with Italian writings is to make further progress: for nobody, to my knowledge, has ventured to estimate just how good Chaucer's grasp of Italian was.[4] We might surmise that Chaucer, as a career diplomat and civil servant, would necessarily have been an accomplished linguist,[5] although doubts have been raised[6] concerning his abilities as a Latinist. Comparative studies of the *Filostrato* and the *Troilus* might have yielded some estimate of Chaucer's abilities as Italianist: but such work has been impeded by R. A. Pratt's article of 1956.[7] Pratt proposes that Chaucer, in composing *Troilus and Criseyde*, availed himself of a French prose translation by a certain (presumably fourteenth-century) Beauvau d'Anjou. (The fact that Chaucer might have employed a French intermediary in working with the *Filostrato* does not, of course, prove that his knowledge of Italian was defective.[8]) But Carla Bozzolo has more recently argued a most convincing case for attributing the *Roman de Troilus* to Louis de Beauvau, an attribution previously advanced by Hauvette, Chiurlo and Marletta. Bozzolo assigns the *Roman* to the period 1442–58.[9] Barry Windeatt, on investigating Pratt's arguments, finds that 'the evidence for any use of Beauvau by Chaucer remains insubstantial in quantity and quality'.[10]

Comparative study of the *Filostrato* and *Troilus and Criseyde* suggests that Chaucer's understanding and appreciation of Boccaccio's language was extraordinarily acute. Many of the passages examined in the previous chapter support this proposition; subsequent investigation will, I hope, further establish that Chaucer—unlike many of his modern critics—was a serious student of the Italian language, not just a cheerful dilettante.[11] It appears that Chaucer, in reading the *Filostrato*, was concerned not simply to catch the drift of a given stanza, but to analyse and worm his way into the language from which the stanza is fashioned. Before transforming the *Filostrato*, Chaucer understood what the *Filostrato* meant.[12]

Robert Payne does not consider the *Filostrato*'s contribution to the style of the *Troilus*; he implies that Chaucer put the Italian work back on the shelf once he had extracted a 'rough structure' from it. Payne speaks of Chaucer 'tossing aside all but 2750 lines of the *Filostrato*'s 5704, compressing those into 2580, and then adding some 5660 more lines, either of his own or (more often) borrowed from Boccaccio or someone else.[13] Such statistics, coupled with the suggestion that Chaucer casually discarded over half of the *Filostrato* before beginning serious elaboration of the *Troilus*, are misleading. I shall argue that the *Filostrato* never left Chaucer's desk, or his imagination, until the English poem was complete; its contribution to the *Troilus* is much more substantial than has hitherto been recognised.

In this chapter we will examine how Chaucer utilises the phrasing and syntax of the *Filostrato* and how he employs the narrative pattern of the Italian poem to orientate the progress of his own narrative. Consideration of the techniques which Chaucer employs in amplifying stanzas from the *Filostrato* affords further opportunities to discover what Chaucer found congenial in his source. Similarly, consideration of what Chaucer chose to abbreviate or reject highlights aspects of the *Filostrato* that the English poet found inappropriate. Boccaccio's attitude towards versification (particularly the extraordinary counterpointing of syntax against metre which generates or is generated by the distinctive prose-like movement of his verse) caused Chaucer considerable misgivings: we shall see that at certain moments the English poet turns instinctively to the *Rose*, to its French derivatives and to the *Commedia* for some stable models of prosody (and for a more assured control of courtly vocabulary). Finally, having compared the *Filostrato* and the *Troilus* with a typical tail-rhyme romance, we will assess the relationship of *Troilus and Criseyde* to the traditions of illustrious and popular literature that have been outlined in these six chapters.

Chaucer's understanding of and engagement with the *Filostrato* manifests itself in a variety of ways: three of his adaptations on a single theme—wisdom—offer an initial indication of the intelligent flexibility of his response.

In I, 9,2, Boccaccio refers to Calcàs as an 'antiveduto saggio'; in I, 79,

Chaucer refers to Calkas as a 'forknowynge wise'. Chaucer understands that Boccaccio intends 'saggio' as a noun rather than as an adjective; he translates it by employing the substantive 'wise'. Chaucer further appreciates how Boccaccio has created a compound adjective in combining the participle 'veduto' with the prefix 'anti'; he similarly combines prefix and participle in 'forknowynge', a participial adjective which is apparently new both to Chaucer's writings and to the English language.[14]

Later on in Book I, Troilus (like Troiolo) imagines how he will be derided for falling in love:

> 'Che si dirà di te intra gli amanti
> se questo tuo amor fia mai saputo?
> di te si gabberebbon tutti quanti,
> di te direbbono: "ecco il provveduto . . ."'   (I, 51,1–4)

> 'What wol now every lovere seyn of the,
> If this be wist? but evere in thin absence
> Laughen in scorn, and seyn, "Loo, ther goth he
> That is the man of so gret sapience . . ."'   (I, 512–5)

Chaucer follows the first line of the Italian quite closely, although he personalises and individualises ('every lovere seyn') Boccaccio's impersonal construction. In the preceding stanza, Chaucer had employed the verb *japen* to translate Boccaccio's 'gabbare' (I, 508; I, 50,4); here he varies his translation by rendering 'si gabberebbon' as 'Laughen in scorn'. Chaucer neatly concentrates the full sense of Boccaccio's second line into four monosyllables; he thereby wins space for an expansion of the phrase 'ecco il provveduto'. Although the term 'provveduto' is employed substantively, it is constructed in the same way as 'antiveduto', combining a prefix with a past participle. In translating it, Chaucer might have employed his recent coinage 'for-knowynge', or have coined something similar: yet he chose not to do so; perhaps he wished to avoid any association (even for ironic effect) of Troilus and Calkas. His expansion, which sounds no internal echoes, renders Boccaccio's phrase most diligently: 'Loo, ther goth he' gives dramatic colour to 'ecco', and the whole of the following line is taken up with his interpretation of 'il provveduto'.

In Book II, the English hero follows his Italian counterpart in resolving to write to his beloved:

> 'Allora' disse Troiol: 'Fatto sia
> il piacer tuo; io vado e scriveraggio,
> ed Amor priego, per sua cortesia,
> lo scrivere e la lettera e 'l viaggio
> fruttevol faccia.' E di quindi s'invia
> alla camera sua, e come saggio
> alla sua donna carissima scrisse
> una lettera presto, e così disse: (II, 95)

> Quod Troilus, 'Depardieux, ich assente!
> Sith that the list, I wil arise and write;
> And blisful God prey ich with good entente,

108

The viage, and the lettre I shal endite,
So spede it; and thow, Minerva, the white,
Yif thow me wit my lettre to devyse.'
And sette hym down, and wrot right in this wyse.

(II, 1058–64)

Chaucer follows Boccaccio's structuring of the stanza quite closely here:
Troilus, like Troolo, graciously accepts the advice that he has been offered,
resolves to go and write a letter, prays for success and then prepares himself to
write. By compressing the rather diffuse narrative action of Boccaccio's final
three-and-a-half lines into just one line, Chaucer is able to extend Troilus'
speech and to squeeze in a fresh detail. At first glance, this detail—a rapid
invocation to Minerva which comes almost as an afterthought—owes nothing
to Boccaccio: Chaucer often inserts passing references to classical figures into
Boccaccio's narrative framework. But here, Chaucer's mini-invocation may
well have been inspired by a phrase in the *Filostrato*. Boccaccio's hero, we are
informed, writes wisely, 'come saggio'; Chaucer's hero prays to the goddess of
wisdom for '"wit my lettre to devyse"'.

Chaucer's most striking departure from the Italian in this stanza comes with
his substitution of 'God' for 'Amor'. This change sharply juxtaposes Christian
and pagan terms of reference as God and a Roman goddess are appealed to
within the space of a single stanza. Such juxtapositions are not uncommon in
the *Troilus*: but it is difficult to explain why Chaucer was moved to make this
particular substitution. It may be that his mind was deflected into the Christian
sphere by Boccaccio's gracious phrase 'Fatto sia/il piacer tuo', which recalls
'fiat voluntas tua' from the *paternoster*; this may also account for Troilus
exclaiming '"Depardieux"' ('"by God"'), an interjection which occurs nowhere else in the poem. All this must remain speculation. We can, however, be
more confident in assuming that Chaucer's 'viage' translates Boccaccio's
'viaggio'; 'viage' is therefore likely to mean 'journey' (that of the letter to
Criseyde), rather than 'enterprise' (as *A Chaucer Glossary* suggests).[15]

These three examples of Chaucer's writing on the theme of wisdom all testify
to his fine understanding of phrases from the Italian text, although they reflect
this understanding in differing ways. The first example sees Chaucer evolving a
concise but complex phrase which matches an Italian original; the second sees
him electing to expand a similar Italian phrase; the third sees a simple Italian
phrase triggering Chaucer's independent powers of invention. Parallels analogous to our third example afford the most generous scope for critical ingenuity:
but more precise verbal parallels provide more reliable evidence of Chaucer's
comprehension of the Italian text. And, in fact, simple parallels of phrasing, at
first glance unremarkable, often conceal much ingenuity on Chaucer's part:

'. . . i' 'l taccio per lo meglio . . .'

'. . . I hide it for the beste.' (II, 3,8; I, 581)

This comes close to being an exact translation: but we should note Chaucer's
rendering of 'taccio' as 'hide'. English has no verb corresponding to the Italian
tacere (or to the Latin *tacere*, the French *taire* or the German *schweigen*); 'taccio'
must be translated by a phrase such as 'I keep silent'. By employing the verb

hyden, Chaucer is able to keep the shape of Boccaccio's clause and to round off his stanza with a simple, emphatic phrase.

The first three stanzas of *Filostrato* VII occasion comparably simple yet highly intelligent translations from Chaucer:

> Troiol, sì com'egli è di sopra detto,
> passava tempo . . .   (VII, 1,1–2)

> This Troilus, as I byfore have told,
> Thus driveth forth . . .(V, 1100–1)

Boccaccio's opening line, with its dense subordinate clause, is imbalanced: its syllables divide 2 + 9. Chaucer restores proportion to the line by dividing it 4 + 6. He adopts the narrative formula of Boccaccio's subordinate clause: but, characteristically, he both simplifies and personalises it. He goes on to convert Boccaccio's colourless phrase 'passava tempo' ('he passed the time') into a phrase whose formulaic associations invite us to view the *aventure* of Troilus in a more detached manner.[16] Chaucer's usage of narrative formulae here raises the curtain on a fresh episode in his story; it also sees him linking up with Boccaccio's stanzas after having worked independently for over one hundred lines.[17]

In reading Boccaccio's next stanza, Chaucer came across the past participle 'beffati'; this he translates by employing the past participle 'byjaped'. Here, as often, it is necessary to consider these phrases in context to appreciate fully the neatness and economy of Chaucer's translation:

> E così stetter mezzo dì passato,
> beffati spesso dalla lor credenza,
> sì come poi mostrava esperienza.   (VII, 2,6–8)

> And thus byjaped stonden for to stare
> Aboute naught this Troilus and Pandare.   (V, 1119–20)

Chaucer often takes pains to conclude a stanza with a weighty, well-defined couplet. Here he cuts the prediction of future action in Boccaccio's final line, and wins further definition for his couplet by switching, momentarily, to the present tense. 'And thus byjaped' neatly fuses 'E così' from the sixth line of Boccaccio's stanza with 'beffati' from the seventh.

The next stanza of the *Troilus* furnishes two further examples of Chaucerian economy: each of its monosyllabic asseverations ('for aught I woot', 'so trowe I') provides an adequate translation of an Italian phrase and saves Chaucer three syllables:

> Troiolo disse: 'Anzi mangiare omai,
> per quel ch'io possa creder, non verrebbe:
> elle penrà a disbrigarsi assai
> dal vecchio padre più che non vorrebbe,
> per mio avviso; tu che ne dirai?
> Io pur mi credo che ella sarebbe
> venuta se venire ella dovesse,
> e s'a mangiar con lui non si ristesse.'   (VII, 3)

> To Pandarus this Troilus tho seyde,
> 'For aught I woot, byfor noon, sikirly,
> Into this town ne comth nat here Criseyde.
> She hath ynough to doone, hardyly,
> To wynnen from hire fader, so trowe I.
> Hire olde fader wol yet make hire dyne
> Er that she go; God yeve hys herte pyne!'   (V, 1121–7)

Boccaccio's third and fourth lines are not easy to translate: 'disbrigarsi' ('to disentangle oneself') and *penare* ('to experience difficulty') are not common verbs, and the positions of 'assai' and 'non vorrebbe' in the line—dictated by exigences of rhyme—are potentially confusing.[18] But Chaucer evidently understood the meaning of these lines; he adapts them most skilfully in V, 1124–5.

Chaucer's couplet arouses complex sensations in the reader. Troilus paints a vivid picture of a pathetic '"olde fader"' who is determined to dine with his daughter: yet, the reader appreciates, the true pathos here lies in Troilus' energetic self-deception. Boccaccio provides suggestions for all this, but in dividing them between his first and last lines he dissipates much of their pathetic potential. By rendering 'anzi mangiare' as 'byfor noon', Chaucer saves Boccaccio's suggestions for his couplet; and once again, Chaucer's couplet is splendidly concentrated and well-defined.

Chaucer's translation of *Filostrato* VII, 29 provides a further impressive example of his resolution to build climactically towards a memorable couplet. Here, as often, the autonomy of Boccaccio's couplet is much eroded by enjambement and elision:

> 'Oh me, Criseida, qual sottile ingegno,
> qual piacer nuovo, qual vaga bellezza,
> qual cruccio verso me, qual giusto sdegno,
> qual fallo mio o qual fiera stranezza,
> l'animo tuo altiero ad altro segno
> han potuto recare? Oh me, fermezza
> a me promessa, oh me, fede e leanza,
> chi v'ha gittate dalla mia amanza?'   (VII, 29)

> 'O, my Criseyde, allas! what subtilte,
> What newe lust, what beaute, what science,
> What wratthe of juste cause have ye to me?
> What gilt of me, what fel experience,
> Hath fro me raft, allas! thyn advertence?
> O trust, O feyth, O depe aseuraunce,
> Who hath me reft Criseyde, al my plesaunce?'   (V, 1254–60)

Chaucer's translations of Boccaccio's terms here are so intelligent and precise that they might almost have served as a glossary for a fourteenth-century English reader of the *Filostrato*. Chaucer translates 'sottile ingegno' by forming a noun from the adjective 'sottile' which corresponds to the sense of the substantive 'ingegno': *subtilte* invariably has associations with mental ingenuity in Chaucer. 'Newe lust' crisply translates 'piacer nuovo'; 'beaute' translates 'bellezza'. Chaucer drops 'vaga' (one of Boccaccio's favourite adjectives)[19] to introduce 'science' (one of Chaucer's favourite nouns)[20] and to create a three-fold pattern of appeal which matches and balances that of the stanza's penultimate line. Chaucer flattens the two-fold appeal of Boccaccio's third line into a single question, but his phrase 'wratthe of juste cause' splendidly combines the senses of 'cruccio' and 'giusto sdegno'. 'Gilt of me' neatly renders 'fallo mio'; 'fel experience' intelligently interprets 'fiera stranezza', its choice of adjective being particularly apt.[21] Up to this point— the end of the fourth line—Chaucer has kept pace with Boccaccio's stanza. Boccaccio's object, verb and complement have not yet been reached; if Chaucer is to secure the relative autonomy of his couplet, he will need to compress these into his next line. Chaucer achieves such compression with great assurance: his choice of 'raft' as verb and 'advertence' as object is quite inspired.

Of the three qualities which feature in Chaucer's penultimate line, 'feyth' directly translates 'fede' while 'trust' and 'depe aseuraunce' correspond more loosely to 'fermezza/a me promessa' and 'leanza'. The couplet, once again, brings a subtle shift of emphasis from Chaucer. Whereas Troiolo continues his appeal to Criseida, Troilus' appeal drifts away from any fixed point of address. Troilus, momentarily, speaks into a void. This subtle shift is beautifully accompanied by a modulation between the first four syllables of the fifth line and the first four of the seventh; the verb *reven* is employed again to fine effect.

I would like to draw attention to one last detail of this particular Chaucerian translation: whereas Troiolo opens his apostrophe with ' "Oh me, Criseida" ', Troilus begins ' "O my Criseyde" '. The change is slight. It may be that Chaucer's text had 'mia' for 'me', or that Chaucer misunderstood: but it seems highly likely that Chaucer would have recognised 'Oh me' (and its variant forms)[22] as an exclamation approximating to the English 'allas'; and, in fact, we find that two of Boccaccio's usages of the exclamation in this stanza bring forth an 'allas!' from Chaucer. I think it probable that Chaucer consciously decided to insert the possessive adjective 'my' into V, 1254; if we juxtapose the opening of his previous stanza with its Italian counterpart,[23] we may deduce what provoked him to do this:

> 'La tua Criseida, oh me, m'ha ingannato,
> di cui io più che d'altra mi fidava,
> ella ha altrui il suo amor donato . . .'   (VII, 26,1–3)

> 'My lady bryght, Criseyde, hath me bytrayed,
> In whom I trusted most of any wight.
> She elliswere hath now here herte apayed.'   (V, 1247–9)

This juxtaposition elicits a most striking contrast: whereas Troiolo disassociates himself from Criseida in speaking (to Pandaro) of ' "la tua Criseida" ' (' "your Criseida" '), Troilus speaks of ' "my lady bryght" '. With such a change, Chaucer repudiates Troiolo's repudiation of his beloved. Chaucer's wish to emphasise the continuing selfless devotion of Troilus to Criseyde also accounts, I would suggest, for the reappearance of the possessive adjective in V, 1254. It accounts for the suppression of the self-referential quality of

Troiolo's '"fermezza/a me promessa"' (VII, 29,6–7). It may also account for the translation of 'altrui' (VII, 26,3, 'another person') as if it were 'altrove' ('elsewhere') in V, 1249. The thought that Criseyde may have bestowed her love 'elliswhere' is painful but comfortingly vague; it shields Troilus from the more painful admission that Criseyde has taken another man.

Chaucer's adaptation of *Filostrato* IV, 80 follows Boccaccio's initial appeal to experience and adheres to the general development of Boccaccio's argument: but only one Chaucerian phrase represents a studied imitation of the Italian. This phrase, however, is splendidly effective: Chaucer sets it like a jewel at the centre of his stanza:

> Ma come noi veggiamo ch'egli avviene,
> che l'una donna l'altra a visitare
> ne' casi nuovi va se le vuol bene,
> così sen venner molte a dimorare
> con Criseida il giorno, tutte piene
> di pietosa allegrezza, ed a contare
> le cominciaron per ordine il fatto,
> com'ella era renduta, e con che patto.   (IV, 80)

> But as men seen in towne, and al aboute,
> That wommen usen frendes to visite,
> So to Criseyde of wommen com a route,
> For pitous joie, and wenden hire delite;
> And with hire tales, deere ynough a myte,
> Thise wommen, which that in the cite dwelle,
> They sette hem down, and seyde as I shall telle.   (IV, 680–6)

Boccaccio's oxymoron 'pietosa allegrezza' finely captures the conflicting feelings of the women who visit Criseida: although they pity her for having to leave Troy, they are stimulated by their own company and excited by their role as social commentators. Chaucer shows his admiration for Boccaccio's phrasing in speaking of the 'pitous joie' of the Trojan women.

The register and flavour of Chaucer's phrasing often reveals a subtle understanding of the Italian text even when it does not represent a *verbum pro verbo* translation:

> Saziar non si poteva il giovinetto
> di ragionar con Pandaro . . .   (III, 63,1–2)

> This is o word for al; this Troilus
> Was nevere ful to speke of this matere . . .   (III, 1660–1)

A Chaucer Glossary glosses the phrase 'ful to speke' as 'sated with talking', recording it as an instance (apparently unique in this sense) of Chaucer's usage of the adjective *ful*. Chaucer was evidently influenced here by Boccaccio's association of *saziare* (a verb usually associated with eating) and *ragionare*.

The primary meaning of the Italian noun *pensiero* is 'thought; idea'[24]: but *il pensiero* is usually—especially in poetic contexts—an unhappy process. Chaucer understood the sad overtones of Troiolo's 'pensiero'[25]:

Aveagli già amore il sonno tolto,
e minuito il cibo, ed il pensiero
multiplicato sì che già nel volto
ne dava pallidezza segno vero . . .   (I, 47,1–4)

And fro this forth tho refte hym love his slep,
And made his mete his foo, and ek his sorwe
Gan multiplie, that, whoso tok kep,
It shewed in his hewe both eve and morwe.   (I, 484–7)

Boccaccio's first three lines are patterned and structured by a sequence of
three past participles. This sequence is generated by the auxiliary verb which
features in the stanza's opening phrase ('Aveagli') and is subsequently understood by ellipsis. Chaucer adopts Boccaccio's three-fold patterning, but avoids
verbal auxiliaries and employs three independent verbs: *reven*; *maken*; *ginnen*.
Despite this change, Chaucer's lines still owe much to the Italian: 'love'
('amore') remains the subject of his main clause; a similar clausal subordinator
('that'; 'sì che') introduces the dependent clause at a similar point in the stanza.
English monosyllables prove, once again, most economical: for example,
although Chaucer requires six words to translate the awkward phrase 'minuito
il cibo', his paraphrase costs only six syllables. It is interesting to note that
Chaucer again elects to fill the space that such economy wins him not with extra
narrative detail but with phrases which enhance the illusion of an easy-going
narrative style: 'and fro this forth'; 'whoso tok kep'; 'both eve and morwe'.

The presence of certain phrasings in *Troilus and Criseyde* may best be
accounted for—and their meaning more securely established—by referring to
the *Filostrato*. The scientific and dialectical connotations of the term 'discese'
employed in *Filostrato* VI, 12,5 are preserved by the English 'descendeth' (V,
859)[26]; the noun phrase 'un accusarla' in IV, 69,3 inspires 'hire accusement'
(IV, 556), a phrase containing a substantive which occurs nowhere else in
Chaucer's writings. The usage of the verb *convenirsi* in a rhyming position at II,
111,1 probably accounts for the impressive presence (unique in the *Troilus*) of
the adjective 'covenable' in II, 1137; the adjective 'molesta' in IV, 102,6
certainly inspired what is the only verifiable Chaucerian usage of the verb
'moleste' (IV, 880).[27] The phrase 'con cambiata/faccia'—which troubles the
modern translator—[28] is straightforwardly rendered by Chaucer as 'with a
chaunged face' (IV, 68). The highly unusual[29] participial adjective 'malvissuto' (IV, 38,1) inspires the coinage 'myslyved' (IV, 330). In III, 349, Chaucer's
remarkable consideration of sighs ('sikes') as 'richesse' borrows from
Boccaccio's 'sospir . . . a gran divizia' (III, 11,5). This last Chaucerian
adaptation forms part of a close and sustained engagement with an Italian
stanza:

Chi poria dire intera la letizia
che l'anima di Troiolo sentiva,
udendo Pandar? Ché la sua tristizia,
com' più parlava, più scemando giva.
Li sospir, ch'egli aveva a gran divizia,
gli dieder luogo e la pena cattiva
si dipartì, e 'l viso lagrimoso,
bene sperando, divenne gioioso.   (III, 11)

Who myghte tellen half the joie or feste
Which that the soule of Troilus tho felte,
Heryng th'effect of Pandarus byheste?
His olde wo, that made his herte swelte,
Gan tho for joie wasten and tomelte,
And al the richesse of his sikes sore
At ones fledde; he felte of hem namore. (III, 344–50)

Here, as often, Chaucer begins by imitating Boccaccio quite closely; he then proceeds to elaborate his stanza more independently, although details from the Italian text figure in this elaboration. To appreciate just how closely Chaucer adheres to the letter and spirit of the Italian stanza, we may compare his handiwork with that of a modern translator:

Who could describe all the joy that Troiolo felt in his heart as he listened to Pandaro? For the more he heard, the further his grief diminished. He gained respite from the sighs that had overwhelmed him, his desperate suffering was allayed, and his sad looks were cheered by hopes of happiness.[30]

Clearly, if Chaucer had worked from a prose text similar to that of Havely, his verse would have differed markedly from the stanza he derives from the *Filostrato*.

The modern translator makes 'Troiolo' the subject of a first subordinate clause; he translates 'anima' ('soul') as 'heart' and tucks this away in a locative phrase; he transforms the present participial phrase 'udendo Pandar' into a temporal clause featuring a perfect verb. Chaucer correctly translates 'anima' as 'soule' and follows Boccaccio in making 'the soule of Troilus' ('l'anima di Troiol') the subject of his subordinate clause. Correctly translating 'udendo' as 'heryng', he upholds Boccaccio's usage of the present participle.

Havely catches the sense of Boccaccio's next sentence: but whereas Boccaccio has 'com' più parlava' (with Pandaro actively talking), Havely has 'the more he heard' (with Troiolo actively listening). This change of verb is dictated (I presume) by the desire to concentrate upon Troiolo; similar reasoning accounts for a change at the beginning of the next sentence, where 'He' (Troiolo) supplants 'Li sospir' as initial subject. Such changes combine to draw us away from the Italian stanza, for Boccaccio concentrates not upon the hero but upon the hero's parts and attributes: his soul; his sadness; his sighs; his wretched pain.[31] Chaucer follows Boccaccio's choice of emphasis; as 'Troiolo' is nowhere the subject of a sentence in the Italian stanza, so 'Troilus' ('he') does not figure as subject in the English until the intensification of the final half-line.

Modern translations of the *Filostrato* (bound by the constraints of modern syntax and vocabulary) inevitably obscure many of Chaucer's diligent imitations of Boccaccio's phrasing and syntax. For example, the present participial constructions which are one of the *Filostrato*'s most distinctive attributes exert an important, if limited, influence on the syntax, style and prosody of the *Troilus*:

Immaginando affanno né sospiro
poter per cotal donna esser perduto . . . (I, 35, 1–2)

He imagined that neither trouble nor suffering for such a lady's sake
could be wasted . . .   (p. 28)

> Imaginynge that travaille nor grame
> Ne myghte for so goodly oon be lorn . . .   (I, 372–73)[32]

Present participles in English and Italian perpetually tempt poets with the
offer of an easy rhyme: Chaucer yields to this temptation much less often than
Boccaccio, but occasionally (as here) he follows the Italian initiative:

> Così adunque andandosi gabbando
> or d'uno or d'altro Troiolo, e sovente
> or questa donna or quella rimirando . . .   (I, 26,1–3)

> Withinne the temple he wente hym forth pleyinge,
> This Troilus, of every wight aboute,
> On this lady, and now on that, lokynge . . .   (I, 267–9)

Boccaccio's opening line juxtaposes two present participles: although
Chaucer converts the first of these into a simple past tense, he nevertheless
captures the reflexive quality of Boccaccio's 'andandosi gabbando'.

In III, 1534–40 Chaucer follows Boccaccio in introducing his stanza with a
past participle ('Tornato'; 'Retorned') and his couplet with a present participle
('pensando'; 'Thynkyng'). Chaucer's fine stanza owes as much to Boccaccio's
syntactic framework as it does to his phrasing[33]:

> Tornato Troiol nel real palagio,
> tacitamente se n'entrò nel letto
> per dormir s'el potesse alquanto ad agio,
> ma non gli poté sonno entrar nel petto,
> sì gli facean nuovi pensier disagio,
> rammemorando il lasciato diletto,
> pensando seco quanto più valea
> Criseida, che el non si credea.   (III, 53)

> Retorned to his real paleys soone,
> He softe into his bed gan for to slynke,
> To slepe longe, as he was wont to doone.
> But al for nought; he may wel ligge and wynke,
> But slep ne may ther in his herte synke,
> Thynkyng how she, for whom desir hym brende,
> A thousand fold was worth more than he wende.
>   (III, 1534–40)

Chaucer's stanza is expertly organised into three parts. The first follows the
Italian quite closely. In the second, anaphora augments the effect of rhyme in
forming a tightly concentrated centre to the stanza from which the couplet may
flow. And although the second half of the sixth line carries the sense of
Boccaccio's sixth line, the couplet flows most beautifully; the potential of
Boccaccio's final cramped and hurried half-line is fully realised.

Of course, Chaucer often chose to go against the patterns of Boccaccio's syntax. In his next stanza, for example, Chaucer eschews Boccaccio's usage of the present participle; in the stanza after this he introduces a present participle where Boccaccio employs the present tense:

> El giva ciascuno atto rivolgendo
> nel suo pensiero e 'l savio ragionare . . .   (III, 54,1–2)
>
> And in his thought gan up and down to wynde
> Hire wordes alle, and every countenaunce . . .   (III, 1541–2)
>
> grazie infinite ne rende ad Amore . . .   (III, 55,4)
>
> Thonkynge Love he so wel hire bisette . . .   (III, 1552)

Chaucer's first translation here draws upon an earlier triumph in rendering awkward phrasing:

> seco nel cor ciascuna paroletta
> rivolvendo di Pandaro . . .   (II, 68,3–4)
>
> And every word gan up and down to wynde
> That he had seyd . . .   (II, 601–2)

Here we may consider how Chaucer imitates Boccaccio (upholding his choice of present participle) in concluding one stanza and in beginning the next:

> pensando che amore a molti aperto,
> noia acquistava e non gioia per merto.
>
> Ed oltre a questo, assai più altre cose . . .   (I, 36,7–37,1)

> . . .—for he thought that a love that was made known to many people would reap sorrow rather than joy as its reward.

> And he also thought of trying a great many other ways . . .   (p. 28)

> Remembryng hym that love to wide yblowe
> Yelt bittre fruyt, though swete seed be sowe.
>
> And over al this, yet muchel more he thoughte . . .   (I, 384–6)

It is difficult to decide whether or not the two couplets here should be underlined. Chaucer's fine metaphoric language greatly improves upon the plainness of Boccaccio's *sententia*: yet the Italian text provides Chaucer not only with a *sententia* for elaboration,[34] but also with a present participle by which such elaboration may be tethered grammatically to the main body of the stanza. The modern translation again conceals the correspondence of present participles. It also obscures the similarity between the opening phrases of the next stanza by translating 'oltre' as if it were 'anche'. This is especially unfortunate as Chaucer's translation of 'Ed oltre a' is, like that of 'rivolvendo' in II, 601, re-employed at a later point in the narrative:

> 'Ed oltre a ciò, questa città si vede
> piena di belle donne e graziose . . .' (IV, 48,1–2)

'And moreover this city appears to be full of lovely and graceful women
. . .' (p. 62)

> 'And over al this, as thow wel woost thiselve,
> This town is ful of ladys al aboute . . .' (IV, 400–1)

Turning to another episode from the *Troilus*, we find that Chaucer in fact
settled on a satisfactory translation of the prepositional phrase 'oltre a' at an
early point in his narrative. These lines furnish us with a further fascinating
example of Chaucer's adaptation of a Boccaccian present participle:

> Piacendo questa sotto il nero manto
> oltre ad ogni altra a Troiol . . . (I, 30,1–2)

Since this lady in the black cloak pleased Troiolo above all others
. . . (p. 27)

> She, this in blak, likynge to Troilus
> Over alle thing . . . (I, 309–10)

Boccaccio's use of participles, then, excites a variety of responses from
Chaucer; it seems evident that Chaucer considered each usage with the same
discriminating respect that he shows for all aspects of Boccaccio's syntax.
Chaucer's close analysis of the Italian text is again evident in his imitation of
phrases from I, 30,1–2. Here he adopts the constituent parts of Boccaccio's
lines but reorders them; elsewhere he sometimes follows Boccaccio's ordering
remarkably closely:

> Nell'opere opportune alla lor guerra
> egli era sempre nell'armi il primiero . . . (III, 90,1–2)

He was always the foremost in furthering the campaign on their side
with feats of arms. (p. 56)

> In alle nedes, for the townes werre,
> He was, and ay, the first in armes dyght . . . (III, 1772–3)

Robinson's punctuation suggests that Chaucer's lines may be divided into
five constituent parts: we find that the order of these parts corresponds exactly
to that of the equivalent phrases in the Italian. However, when Boccaccio's
phrasing and syntax prove intractable Chaucer shows himself quite willing to
depart from them:

> Di Pandar crebbe allora la pietate
> ed il disio di ciò voler sapere.
> Ond'el seguì: 'Se la nostra amistate . . .' (II, 4,1–3)

With that Pandaro's pity increased at that—as did his desire to find out
the truth—and so he replied: 'If our friendship . . .' (p. 31)

This Pandare, that neigh malt for wo and routhe,
Ful ofte seyde, 'Allas! what may this be?
Now frend,' quod he, 'if evere love or trouthe . . .'   (I, 582–4)

Chaucer here avoids getting into the kind of tangle that the modern translator finds himself in by recasting Boccaccio's syntax and by entering into direct speech a line earlier than the Italian: what Boccaccio reports of Pandaro, Pandarus expresses for himself. Such ingenuity from Chaucer is not uncommon: he often improves upon his source simply by converting reported action into speech,[35] or vice versa:

'Così piangendo, in amorosa erranza
dimoro, lasso, e non so che mi fare . . .'   (IV, 70,1–2)

Thus wepyng that he koude nevere cesse,
He seyde, 'Allas! how shal I, wrecche, fare?'   (IV, 575–6)

The stanzas immediately preceding these lines are given over to the speeches of Troiolo and Troilus. Chaucer follows the pattern of Boccaccio's 'Così piangendo' in IV, 575 but ducks momentarily out of direct speech: he probably wished to avoid the somewhat maudlin spectacle of a hero reporting upon his own 'wepyng'.

Chaucer's understanding of the Italian text manifests itself in adaptations of difficult or idiomatic passages. Chaucer finds a delightfully appropriate English equivalent for Pandaro's *sotto voce* comment in VII, 10,7–8 (V, 1174–6) and evidently understands Boccaccio's usage of the idiom *avere gola a* in IV, 32,5 (IV, 285).[36] Here he clearly understands the grammatical function of the term 'tanto':

'Oh,' disse Pandar 'com'hai tu potuto
tenermi tanto tal foco nascoso?'   (II, 9,1–2)

'Oh—' said Pandaro, 'how could you have kept so ardent a passion as this concealed from me?'   (p. 31)

'How hastow thus unkyndely and longe
Hid this fro me, thow fol?' quod Pandarus.   (I, 617–8)

Havely apparently takes 'tanto' to be an adjective premodifying the noun 'foco' (which he translates as 'passion'). Chaucer sees 'tanto' as an adverbial phrase (in which 'per' and 'tempo' are understood by ellipsis). Maintaining the ellipsis, Chaucer translates 'tanto' with the adverb 'longe'. Chaucer's reading of the line is the correct one: 'tal' is the adjective which premodifies 'foco', not 'tanto'.

Another correct interpretation of the term 'tanto' figures in Chaucer's adaptation of the dense and difficult couplet which concludes Troiolo's apostrophe to Death ('Morte'):

'tu n'uccidi ben tanti oltre al volere,
che ben puoi fare a me questo piacere.'   (IV, 62,7–8)

> 'Syn that thou sleest so fele in sondry wyse
> Ayens hire wil, unpreyed, day and nyght,
> Do me at my requeste this servise:' (IV, 512–4)

Boccaccio's apostrophe expires in a rush of words: Chaucer, we have noted, generally favours a more measured, recapitulative couplet; here he transfers Troiolo's petition to the head of his stanza and dilutes its breathless compactness. At other times, however, he is pleased to imitate the dense quality of Boccaccio's phrasing:

> . . . sì com'egli avviene
> che colui ch'ama mal volentier crede
> cosa ch'accresca amando le sue pene . . . (VIII, 7,2–4)

> . . . for it is usual for a lover to be reluctant to believe anything that will add to his sufferings in love. (p. 98)

> For with ful yvel wille list hym to leve,
> That loveth wel, in swich cas, though hym greve.
>
> (V, 1637–8)

Boccaccio introduces his sententious appeal to experience with the familiar formula 'sì com'egli avviene'. In the *Troilus*, such weighty utterances are most often housed in the couplet; Chaucer—doubtless alerted by Boccaccio's introductory formula—transfers Boccaccio's *sententia* from the main body of the stanza to its appropriate place. In a footnote, Havely argues against the interpretation of earlier translators,[37] who

> . . . assume that *mal* modifies *ama*, and translate: 'he who loveth ill, willingly believeth . . .' But *male* is well attested in the sense of 'not' or 'hardly' (GDLI, *male* [advb.], 15). Cp., for example, Inf. XVIII, 52. (p. 204)

I feel sure that Havely is right here: but for confirmation we may turn to the *Troilus*. Chaucer translates the phrase 'colui ch'ama' as 'hym . . . / That loveth' and 'mal volentier crede' as 'with ful yvel wille list . . . to leve'. Chaucer evidently takes 'mal' in the sense that Havely suggests to be appropriate; and yet his paraphrase still manages to incorporate the literal flavour of 'mal' that the earlier translators include and Havely obscures. Here, as often, modern translators of the *Filostrato* would be well advised to look to Chaucer for guidance.

I hope that the foregoing analyses have helped substantiate my claim that Chaucer understood Boccaccio's language extraordinarily well. The *Filostrato* may initially have commended itself to the English poet through the strength and originality of its plot: but its syntax and phrasing also came to exert a considerable influence on the elaboration of the *Troilus*.

In chapter III, we considered the way in which Chaucer in the *Troilus* develops the fiction of following Lollius, an ancient author whose role corresponds to that of Ilario in the *Filocolo*. At the surface of his fictional world, Chaucer purports to be translating from ancient Latin: but beneath its surface we discover him energetically practising translation from modern Italian. Posture and practice seemingly constitute distinct aspects of Chaucer's creative enterprise; the gap between them is never apparently bridged. But here, at least, we can consider these aspects in the closest juxtaposition:

> 'se Calcàs per ambage e per errori
> qui non ci mena . . .' (VI, 17,3–4)

> 'And but if Calkas lede us with ambages,
> That is to seyn, with double wordes slye,
> Swiche as men clepen a word with two visages . . .'
>
> (V, 897–9)

Considering *Troilus* I, 1065–71 (above, pp. 102–4), we observed Chaucer reacting to his Italian source by invoking the guidance of a Latin rhetorician, Geoffrey of Vinsauf; here, on discovering an impressive Latinate noun in the Italian ('ambage'), he poses as one who glosses a Latin term, employing a suggestive formula ('that is to seyn')—familiar from *Boece*—to enhance the effect. Neither of these reactions to the *Filostrato* halts or detracts from the development of the narrative action. The earlier example can be taken simply as a passing reflection on Pandarus' thoughtful plotting of Troilus' love suit. The later example, which glosses a difficult or unfamiliar word, acquires dramatic appropriateness in being spoken by Diomede, a man who characteristically shows himself sensitive to the fact that Criseyde, in passing over to the Greeks, is embracing an unfamiliar culture.

As we have seen, Chaucer introduces many new words to English in translating from Boccaccio's Italian: but, typically, he draws attention to his translation practice only in appropriating a word of high Latin pedigree. There seems little doubt that he *did* recognise 'ambages' as a noun of Latin origin; he may have recalled it from Vergil's *Aeneid*:

> Talibus ex adyto dictis Cumaea Sibylla
> horrendas canit ambages antroque remugit,
> obscuris vera involvens . . . (VI, 98–100)

> With such words the Cumaean Sibyl sings from her shrine
> her fearsome enigmas and echoes booming out from the cavern,
> enfolding the truth with darkness . . .

Here 'ambages' fall from the mouth of the Cumaean Sibyl: discovered in such a context, the term offers impressive suggestive potential to a poem that seriously concerns itself with the problem of truth and true speaking in a pagan world. The *Troilus* is one such poem; the *Commedia*[38] is another:

> Né per ambage, in che la gente folle
> già s'inviscava pria che fosse anciso
> l'Agnel di Dio che le peccata tolle,
>   ma per chiare parole e con preciso
> latin rispuose quello amor paterno . . . (Par XVII, 31–35)

Not in enigmas, in which the foolish people
were once entangled before the slaying
of the Lamb of God who takes away sins,
but in plain language and in precise
terms that paternal love replied . . .

A similarly sharp distinction between the languages of pagan fiction and of Christian truthfulness is drawn by Chaucer in concluding both the *Troilus* and *The Canterbury Tales*.

Boccaccio's employment of the term 'ambage' may, then, have sent Chaucer to Dante and from Dante to Vergil; it may have sent him to a text (perhaps glossed) of the *Aeneid*; it may have sent him to a French translation of a Latin text.[39] Whatever the case, or combination of cases, the range of possibilities opened up by Boccaccio's 'ambage' stands as fitting testimony to the rich potential of his text as a Chaucerian source.

In 1355, Pierre Bersuire employed 'ambages' as a French noun in translating Livy from Latin into French.[40] In composing the *Troilus*, Chaucer is similarly concerned to expand his native lexicon, and thereby to increase the creative potential of the English language: he too attempts to introduce 'ambages' to his vernacular. The considerable contribution made by Boccaccio's vocabulary and phrasing to this process of lexical expansion is nowhere acknowledged by Chaucer. And on the only occasion that Chaucer draws attention to his introduction of a new word to the English language in *Troilus and Criseyde* he disguises his indebtedness to the Italian by affecting the pose of a glossator of Latin. The fact that 'ambages' took root in French and fell upon stony ground in English might be seen as offering Boccaccio some measure of historical revenge and of poetic justice.[41]

Chaucer's fundamental indebtedness to the *Filostrato*'s narrative framework is readily apparent from a brief examination of the table of parallels provided by F. N. Robinson.[42] Many divergences in sensibility and attitude (much discussed by English critics) set the English poet apart from Boccaccio: but for all that, Chaucer continues to employ stanzas from the *Filostrato* until his *Troilus* is virtually complete; Book V reveals parallels with the Italian work as impressive and sustained as any in Book I.[43] The *Troilus* does not 'grow away from' its Italian source. The pattern of the *Filostrato*'s 'tale' (I, 263) is firmly imprinted on Chaucer's mind. When he excurses from his source, this pattern is not forgotten; he can generally be observed to be moving away *from* or back *towards* Boccaccio's poem. The *Filostrato* orientates the progress of *Troilus and Criseyde* from start to finish.

Chaucer's first sustained digression from his source comes with the insertion of seven stanzas (I, 218–66) between imitations of *Filostrato* I, 25 and I, 26. But in fact, the English poet begins to move away from Boccaccio's text even in translating the opening line of I, 25:

O ciechità delle mondane menti. . . .

O blynde world, O blynde entencioun!   (I, 211)

The term *entencioun* occurs far more frequently in *Boece* than anywhere else

122

in Chaucer's writings: its presence here lends philosophical precision to Boccaccio's somewhat vague exclamation at worldly blindness and adumbrates the discussion of natural law which follows. This discussion is first conducted in a comic vein with the example of 'proude Bayard' (I, 218), but is then more seriously applied to the case of Troilus. For four stanzas Chaucer develops a didactic, authorish posture in preaching to his audience of lovers on the 'ensample' (I, 232) of Troilus. Two important (and closely associated) strains of imagery are delicately introduced during this excursus: that of Fortune's wheel (I, 215–16) and that of the navigational imagery which describes how Troilus' heart is steered (I, 228).[44] Having moved a considerable distance from his source text, Chaucer spends an entire stanza in realigning himself with it. The distinction that he draws here between 'my tale' and 'other thing collateral' is most instructive:

> But for to tellen forth in special
> As of this kynges sone of which I tolde,
> And leten other thing collateral,
> Of hym thenke I my tale forth to holde,
> Bothe of his joie and of his cares colde;
> And al his werk, as touching this matere,
> For I it gan, I wol therto refere.   (I, 260–6)

From this it seems that Chaucer appraised the *Filostrato* much as we have suggested: as a source providing an excellent story-line ('tale') which may be embellished, expanded and supplemented from time to time with incidental authorial commentary ('other thing collateral').[45] It is a notable feature of the *Troilus* that Chaucer most often speaks and poses as an *auctour* when working away from his Italian source. Poised to embark on his lengthiest and most ambitious departure from the *Filostrato* (III, 442–1309, the very heart of the *Troilus*), Chaucer seems almost overwhelmed with authorial self-consciousness: he confesses his own uncertainties (III, 442–8), nervously discusses his own strategy of writing (III, 491–504) and makes several references to 'myn' (imaginary Latin) 'auctour' (III, 502–3, 575–8).

Having worked away from the *Filostrato* for well over one hundred stanzas, Chaucer rejoins it with remarkable ease:

> Lungo sarebbe a raccontar la festa,
> ed impossible a dire il diletto . . .   (III, 31,1–2)

> Of hire delit, or joies oon the leeste,
> Were impossible to my wit to seye . . .   (III, 1310–11)

He then proceeds to employ (to a greater or lesser extent) every one of Boccaccio's next thirty-four stanzas (III, 32–65; III, 1310–1680). It seems that even in setting out for uncharted territory in III, 442 Chaucer definitely envisaged rejoining the *Filostrato*. Chaucer often terminates a sustained bout of independent elaboration by hooking up most emphatically with his source text as if to orientate himself and draw breath:

> 'Ben puoi dunque veder ch'Amor t'ha posto
> in loco degno della tua virtute;

sta' dunque fermo nell'alto proposto
e bene spera della tua salute,
la quale io credo che seguirà tosto
se tu col pianto tuo non la rifiute.
Tu sei di lei ed ella di te degno,
ed io ci adoprerò tutto 'l mio 'ngegno'.   (II, 24)

'And sith that God of Love hath the bistowed
In place digne unto thi worthinesse,
Stond faste, for to good port hastow rowed;
And of thiself, for any hevynesse,
Hope alwey wel; for, but if drerinesse
Or over-haste oure bothe labour shende,
I hope of this to maken a good ende.'   (I, 967–73)

Having worked independently for eleven stanzas (I, 890–966), Chaucer
re-establishes contact with his Italian source here most decisively;[46] and yet,
remarkably, no flaw appears in the seamless garment of Pandarus' discourse.
The craft which Chaucer employs in rejoining the *Filostrato* is sometimes
exquisitely subtle: earlier in Book I, in the space of a single line, he realigns
himself with Boccaccio's narrative while yet sounding a final echo of the wheel
of Fortune imagery that has been developed over his last three stanzas
(I, 834–54):

'. . . orsù, lascia 'l tapino
pianto che fai . . .'   (II, 16,5–6)

'Lat be thy wo and tornyng to the grounde . . .'   (I, 856)

Between terminating one 'Parte' of his *Filostrato* and beginning another,
Boccaccio habitually outlines and introduces the next phase of his narrative in a
lengthy rubric. Chaucer, we have noted, builds such authorial reflections into
the fabric of his poem. On four occasions,[47] Chaucer ignores Boccaccio's
structural divisions and continues his narrative without a break. These
continuations are finely crafted: for example, having imitated the final stanza of
the *Filostrato*'s fifth 'Parte', Chaucer proceeds directly to an imitation of the
first stanza of *Filostrato* VI. Once again, Chaucer wins fresh impetus and
dramatic force for his narrative by transferring and recasting Boccaccio's
reported action into direct speech:

Dall'altra parte in sul lito del mare,
con poche donne, tra le genti armate,
stava Criseida, ed in lagrime amare
da lei eran le notti consumate . . .   (VI, 1,1–4)

Upon that other syde ek was Criseyde,
With wommen fewe, among the Grekis stronge;
For which ful ofte a day 'Allas!' she seyde,
'That I was born! Wel may myn herte longe . . .'

(V, 687–90)

The ghostly presence of the *Filostrato* may sometimes be discerned beneath
Chaucer's narrative surface even when the English poet appears to have put the
Italian text to one side. In beginning Book II, Chaucer develops his narrative
independently for almost three hundred lines. Halfway through this independent development, however, we find:

> Quivi con risa e con dolci parole,
> con lieti motti e con ragionamenti
> parentevoli assai, sì come suole
> farsi talvolta tra congiunte genti . . .   (II, 35,1–4)

> So after this, with many wordes glade,
> And frendly tales, and with merie chiere,
> Of this and that they pleide, and gonnen wade
> In many an unkouth glad and dep matere,
> As frendes doon whan thei ben mette yfere . . .
>
> (II, 148–52)

I think it likely that Chaucer consciously referred to the *Filostrato* at this
point: for he is influenced here not by the cadences of Boccaccio's language,
but simply by the details of his narrative. Chaucer's imagination rarely seems
to have been swayed simply by the rhythms of Boccaccio's verse.[48] (The
cadences of the *Commedia*, however, exerted a continuous influence on the
young Boccaccio: his opening line here is obviously (if not consciously)
modelled on *Inferno* XVIII, 91).

In the midst of Chaucer's lengthiest independent elaboration we encounter
a most unexpected (and hitherto unnoticed) borrowing from Boccaccio's
text:

> ora i polsi fregando ed or la faccia
> bagnandogli sovente, come accorte
> persone, s'ingegnavan rivocare,
> ma poco ancor valeva l'adoprare.   (IV, 19,5–8)

> 'Now speke to me, for it am I, Criseyde!'
> But al for nought; yit myght he nought abreyde.

> Therwith his pous and paumes of his hondes
> They gan to frote, and wete his temples tweyne . . .
>
> (III, 1112–5)

Here it seems most likely that Chaucer deliberately resorted to his Italian
source text in order to appropriate a number of narrative details. The passage
he imitates forms part of the *Filostrato*'s fourth 'Parte': Troiolo, having heard
the Trojan parliament pronounce that Criseida should be handed over to the
Greeks, faints, wounded with 'alto duol' (IV, 18,8); Priamo, Ettore and his
brothers attempt to revive him. Chaucer evidently found such high public
melodrama—worthy of a popular romance—inappropriate: but he judged
such a collapse fitting when transferred to the private drama played out at the
centre of his poem. Clearly, then, Chaucer had read ahead in the *Filostrato* very
carefully before embarking on his greatest independent excursus.

Having considered the ways in which Chaucer introduces and concludes extensive digressions from his source, I would like, briefly, to draw attention to a technique that he characteristically employs in more restricted amplifications of Boccaccio's text. This technique is quite simple: Chaucer sometimes expands an *ottava* by dividing it into two parts and devoting a stanza to each part. I have been able to identify twenty-nine examples of this technique.[49] Their distribution is interesting: eight of them occur in the first three Books of the *Troilus*, and the other twenty-one in the last two. This suggests that Chaucer may have evolved the technique in the actual process of composing his poem.[50] The distribution of examples in *Troilus* IV and V usefully draws attention to the parts and qualities of the *Filostrato* that Chaucer found admirable and amenable: for it seems reasonable to assume that Chaucer would only have expanded his source in this way when he was happy with its potentialities. Two examples from the middle of Book IV—where such expansions are densely distributed—bear this out:

> Né potea ritenere alcun sospiro,
> e tal fiata alcuna lagrimetta
> cadendo, dava segno del martiro
> nel qual l'anima sua era costretta;   (IV, 84,1–4)

> For which no lenger myghte she restreyne
> Hir teeris, so they gonnen up to welle,
> That yaven signes of the bittre peyne
> In which hir spirit was, and moste dwelle;
> Remembryng hir, fro heven into which helle
> She fallen was, syn she forgoth the syghte
> Of Troilus, and sorwfully she sighte.   (IV, 708–14)

> ma quelle stolte che le facean giro,
> credevan per pietà la giovinetta
> far ciò, ch'avesse d'abbandonar esse,
> le quali esser solean sue compagnesse.   (IV, 84,5–8)

> And thilke fooles sittynge hire aboute
> Wenden that she wepte and siked sore
> Bycause that she sholde out of that route
> Departe, and nevere pleye with hem more.
> And they that hadde yknowen hire of yore
> Seigh hire so wepe, and thoughte it kyndenesse,
> And ech of hem wepte eke for hire destresse.   (IV, 715–21)

In the space of a stanza, Boccaccio moves from considering the outward manifestations of Criseida's grief to reporting the way in which these signs are interpreted by the circle of women that surrounds her. Chaucer, respecting the balanced structure of this *ottava*, allots a stanza to each of its two equal parts. He imitates Boccaccio's first four lines of external description very closely and then, typically, moves inwards to consider Criseyde's secret thoughts. Although the last three lines of Chaucer's stanza depart from the *Filostrato*, their syntax and prosody exhibit powerfully Boccaccian characteristics: a present participle introduces the dependent clause; enjambements and mid-line pauses unsettle the equilibrium of the lines. For once, the firm articulation of the Chaucerian couplet is eroded; Chaucer successfully conveys the inner agitation of his heroine.

In his next stanza (IV, 722–8), Chaucer simply expands Boccaccio's succinct portrayal of Criseida's female companions (IV, 85). Boccaccio rarely succeeds in evoking pathos through lyricism: but here—and elsewhere[51]—he creates a most poignant effect by dramatic means in surrounding private grief with a social circle. Chaucer much admired this section of the *Filostrato*: he closely imitates all eight of the *ottave* following the rubric at IV, 78 and devotes two stanzas to IV, 79 (IV, 666–79) as well as to IV, 84. He ends by adopting Boccaccio's assessment of the effect that the words of these foolish women have on the heroine:

> . . . né erano altro che grattarla
> nelle calcagne, ove il capo prudea . . . (IV, 85,5–6)

> But swich an ese therwith they hire wroughte,
> Right as a man is esed for to feele,
> For ache of hed, to clawen hym on his heele! (IV, 726–8)

Chaucer's refined (or mock-refined) rendering of Boccaccio's epigrammatic colloquialism testifies further to his exceptional abilities as an Italianist. Boccaccio's lines here are redolent of the *cantare* manner[52]; in fact the whole of this colourful, rapidly-narrated episode owes much to the *cantare*. The *ottava* at IV, 81 employs the quadripartite structure typical of the *cantare* stanza in reporting the various reactions of the Trojan women to Criseida's imminent departure. Chaucer found this congenial: the first six lines of his equivalent stanza (IV, 687–93) adhere closely to the structure and content of Boccaccio's *ottava*. A four-part *ottava* facilitates the task of a translator or adaptor by offering its ideas in simple two-line units.[53] In his final expansion of an *ottava* into two stanzas (V, 1744–57), Chaucer adopts three ideas from a quadripartite Boccaccian stanza (VIII, 25,1–4,7–8) and casts one aside (VIII, 25,5–6). The brusque and summary manner in which Boccaccio orders events in VIII, 25 proves congenial to Chaucer because, at this late stage of the narrative, he is earnestly attempting to detach himself and his emotions from the story of Troilus. Earlier on, however, Chaucer characteristically endeavours to smooth away the rough edges of Boccaccio's narrative manner and to slow its somewhat hectic rate of development:

> Chi potrebbe giammai narrare appieno
> ciò che Criseida nel pianto dicea?
> Certo non io, ch'al fatto il dir vien meno,
> tant'era la sua noia cruda e rea. (IV, 95,1–4)

> How myghte it evere yred ben or ysonge,
> The pleynte that she made in hire destresse?
> I not; but, as for me, my litel tonge,
> If I discryven wolde hire hevynesse,
> It sholde make hire sorwe seme lesse
> That that it was, and childisshly deface
> Hire heigh compleynte, and therefore ich it pace.
>
> (IV, 799–805)

Ma mentre tai lamenti si facieno,
Pandaro venne, a cui non si tenea
uscio giammai, e 'n camera sen gio
là dov'ella faceva il pianto rio.   (IV, 95,5–8)

Pandare, which that sent from Troilus
Was to Criseyde—as ye han herd devyse
That for the beste it was acorded thus,
And he ful glad to doon hym that servyse—
Unto Criseyde, in a ful secree wise,
Ther as she lay in torment and in rage,
Com hire to telle al hoolly his message . . .   (IV, 806–12)

Although he asks 'how' rather than 'who' ('chi'), Chaucer adopts
Boccaccio's employment of an inexpressibility topos couched in terms of an
answered question. In extending this topos over an entire stanza, Chaucer
personalises its reflective quality. Once again, such reflections may be read as a
private commentary on his source: for Boccaccio *does* attempt to render the
heroine's 'pleynte', albeit not in full ('appieno', IV, 95,1). In the two stanzas
preceding IV, 95, Boccaccio's heroine berates her absent father and bewails her
own state. Chaucer makes no use of these verses, which are certainly cliché-
ridden and woodenly melodramatic: little better, in fact, than the 'compleynt'
of Dido in *The House of Fame*,[54] a passage which the mature Chaucer could
hardly have recalled without some embarrassment:

'Oimè lassa, trista e dolorosa,
ch'a me convien portar la penitenza
del tuo peccato! Cotanto noiosa
vita non meritai per mia fallanza.
O verità del ciel, luce pietosa . . .'   (IV, 94,1–5)

'Woe is me, abandoned, sad and grieving,
for it falls to me to do penance
for your sin! Such a vexatious
life I did not deserve through fault of my own.
O heavenly truth, piteous light . . .

'Allas!' quod she, 'my swete herte,
Have pitee on my sorwes smerte,
And slee me not! goo nought awey!
O woful Dido, wel-awey!'   (HF 315–8)

The sudden arrival of Pandaro in the second half of *Filostrato* IV, 95
certainly makes Boccaccio's usage of the inexpressibility topos seem somewhat
perfunctory: Boccaccio again seems to be writing 'with rakel hond'.[55] By
reflecting on the way in which a 'litel tonge' may 'childisshly deface' a 'heigh
compleynte', Chaucer fills out his first stanza and postpones the arrival of
Pandarus until his second. In this second stanza, Chaucer states his subject
immediately ('Pandare') but does not reach his main verb ('Com') until the
beginning of the final line. He is content to devote most of the intervening
space to a résumé of past events; this is introduced by a phrase ('as ye han herd')
which confirms his intimacy with his auditors.

Chaucer sometimes exploits the space created by the expansion of a single *ottava* into two stanzas by introducing classical material: in I, 704–7 he introduces proverbial lore, (possibly derived from Ovid or Seneca) and in III, 374–5 a reference to Achilles; in IV, 299–301 he refers to Oedipus ('Edippe') and in V, 599–602 to Juno's hatred of the Thebans. But as a rule, Chaucer seems content simply to expand his text along the lines mapped out by the *Filostrato*: again, it is as if he wishes to do justice to Boccaccio's fecund (sometimes riotous) powers of invention.

Chaucer demonstrates as much skill in abbreviating his source as he does in amplifying it. In Book V, for example, we see him reducing a sequence of eight *ottave* from *Filostrato* VII (18–25) to five stanzas of rhyme royal (1212–46). Here, as often, it is instructive to consider what Chaucer cuts from his source. In VII, 21, for example, Priamo (in a tone of voice which recalls the affective, *cantare*-like simplicity of the *Ninfale fiesolano*)[56] entreats his son Troiolo to disclose the cause of his misery: '"Dilmi, figliuolo . . ."' (VII, 21,7). Such pathos does not suit Chaucer here: he deprives Priam of direct speech and fuses VII, 21 with VII, 22. Similarly, many of Criseida's final words to Troiolo in *Filostrato* IV are found unfitting for the *Troilus*. Much is cut and much compressed: for example, the first three *ottave* of Criseida's expatiation on the 'evil things' ('cose ree', IV, 147,6) that may follow as consequences of Troiolo's flight from Troy (IV, 147–9) are packed into a single English stanza (IV, 1555–61); and in the stanza following, Criseida's frothy circumlocutions are supplanted by a crisp, argumentative style that reminds us that Criseyde is the niece of Pandarus:

> 'As alday happeth after anger game . . .'
> . . . .
> 'For hastif man ne wanteth nevere care.'   (IV, 1563,1568)

Three stanzas later, Criseida's long-winded (pseudo-courtly) style again contrasts with Criseyde's incisiveness:

> 'Ed oltre a questo vo' che tu riguardi
> a ciò che quasi d'ogni cosa avviene:'   (IV, 152,1–2)

> 'And in addition to this I wish you to take notice
> of that which holds in almost every case:'

> 'And forthi sle with resoun al this hete!'   (IV, 1583)

Criseyde supports her case in this stanza with three pithy proverbs, whereas Criseida begins a rambling, two-stanza embroidery of a theme ('familiarity breeds contempt') derived from Andreas Capellanus.[57] Seven stanzas later, Criseida launches another polite appeal (adapted from Dante's appeal to Vergil in *Inferno* XXVI, 66); Chaucer again naturalises the artificial, pseudo-courtly quality of Boccaccio's language:

> 'Ond'io ti priego, se 'l mio priego vale . . .'   (IV, 160,1)

> 'Therefore I pray you, if my prayer be of value . . .'

> 'Forthi with al myn herte I yow biseke . . .'   (IV, 1632)

Chaucer seeks out and fuses the essential content of *Filostrato* IV, 160–1, in simple, unaffected language (IV, 1632–8). We may observe, here, the technique of amplification discussed above employed in reverse: Chaucer derives a single stanza from two *ottave*. Incidences of this pattern of abbreviation are not, however, numerous enough to warrant much discussion; it seems more germane to conclude this brief section by re-emphasising the notable contribution made by English monosyllables to the cause of economy in translation:

E fatto questo, con animo forte
la propria spada del fodero trasse,
tutto disposto di prender la morte,
acciocché il suo spirto seguitasse
quel della donna con sì trista sorte,
e nell'inferno con lei abitasse,
poi che aspra fortuna e duro amore
di questa vita lui cacciava fore. (IV, 120)

And after this, with sterne and cruel herte,
His swerd anon out of his shethe he twighte,
Hymself to slen, how sore that hym smerte,
So that his soule hire soule folwen myghte
Ther as the doom of Mynos wolde it dighte;
Syn Love and cruel Fortune it ne wolde,
That in this world he lenger lyven sholde. (IV, 1184–90)

Chaucer's seven-line stanza contains nine words more than Boccaccio's *ottava*. Chaucer's economical employment of monosyllables is augmented by skilful powers of compression. The essence of Boccaccio's third line is captured in just three words ('Hymself to slen'). Boccaccio's next two lines are rendered in one: Chaucer transforms the phrase 'quel della donna' into 'hire soule' and inserts this into the middle of his fourth line; he cuts 'con sì trista sorte', a weak phrase which serves to supply Boccaccio's third 'a' rhyme. Chaucer now has three lines in which to translate the last three lines of the *ottava*; he elects, characteristically, to classicise Boccaccio's infernal vision by introducing the ancient (and Dantean) figure of Minos.

In incorporating ideas from *Filostrato* III, 78 into his *prohemium* to Book III, Chaucer packs more words into his seven lines than Boccaccio can fit into eight. Skilfully compressing each of Boccaccio's first three ideas, Chaucer gains the effect of *anaphora* on 'Ye'. Having disposed of Boccaccio's first five-and-a-half lines in just over three lines, Chaucer is able to rearrange and develop the ideas introduced by the Boccaccian relative adverb 'onde' in a more leisurely fashion:

Tu 'n unità le case e le cittadi,
li regni e le province e 'l mondo tutto

tien', bella dea; tu dell'amistadi
se' cagion certa e del lor caro frutto;
tu sola le nascose qualitadi
delle cose conosci, onde il costrutto
vi metti tal, che fai maravigliare
chi tua potenza non sa ragguardare.   (III, 78)

Ye holden regne and hous in unitee;
Ye sothfast cause of frendshipe ben also;
Ye knowe al thilke covered qualitee
Of thynges, which that folk on wondren so,
Whan they kan nought construe how it may jo
She loveth hym, or whi he loveth here,
As whi this fissh, and naught that, comth to were.

(III, 29–35)

This juxtaposition reminds us that whereas the mature Chaucer is a skilled and experienced versifier, the youthful Boccaccio has yet to discover his métier as a prose writer. As we have noted, Boccaccio's respect for the restraints of poetic form is somewhat limited: his first main verb here arrives with a sudden thump ('tien''), and his positioning of 'onde' is particularly awkward. It is ironic that *Troilus and Criseyde* has so often been discussed as if it were a novel (and especially ironic that Meech should have contributed to such discussion)[58]: for much of Chaucer's translating of the *Filostrato* is analogous to a movement from prose to verse.[59]

The language of the *Filostrato* repeatedly endeavours to break loose from the conventional constraints of verse and to develop a prose-like impetus. For example, although the first two lines of IV, 13 are end-stopped, the rest of this stanza develops its argument with scant reference to line-endings, an argument which is extended (as in III, 78) with an awkwardly-positioned 'onde'. And although the first two lines of VII, 6 are end-stopped, the rest of this stanza (which features a sequence of four mid-line copulative 'e's) is governed by a prose-like logic. Having pursued his argument across a line-ending, Boccaccio often elects to catch his breath by coming to a dead halt in the first half of the subsequent line: to this end he favours terms with a heavily-stressed final syllable such as 'incominciò'.[60] He is fond of separating the subject of a lengthy sentence from the main verb and of filling the intervening space with subordinate clauses introduced (most typically) by relative pronouns such as 'il quale'[61]; in IV, 112 he rounds off an extraordinary prose-like stanza by rhyming 'i quali' with 'vostri mali'. Chaucer exhibits great skill in containing the flow of Boccaccio's ideas within tighter (or more conventional) constraints of versification. Some *ottave*, however, lie beyond his powers of redemption:

Pandaro, presa la lettera pia,
n'andò verso Criseida, la quale
come 'l vide venir, la compagnia
con la quale era lasciata, cotale
gli si fé 'ncontro parte della via,
qual pare in vista perla orientale,
temendo e disiando; e' salutarsi
du lunge assai, poi per le man pigliarsi.   (II, 108)

> Pandaro, having taken the pious letter,
> went off towards Criseida, who
> on seeing him coming, having left
> the company with which she was, she
> went along part of the way to meet him,
> who seems like an oriental pearl to look at,
> fearing and desiring; and greeting one another
> from afar, they then took one another by the hands.

This clumsy and confusing stanza, with its glut of personal and relative pronouns, is not much improved by the *cantare*-style simile in its sixth line which, in rhyming 'orientale' with 'la quale' and 'cotale', provides Boccaccio's third 'b' rhyme. Such *ottave* are not a rarity in the *Filostrato*: Boccaccio seems particularly prone to drop into a prose-like rhythm when shifting his protagonists from place to place or when chronicling a quick succession of events. Chaucer reacts to such stanzas in varying ways. He aligns himself with the first line of *Filostrato* II, 108 in II, 1093 but goes on to elaborate and enliven his stanza quite independently. He passes over four prosaic, business-like stanzas in which final arrangements are made for Troiolo's nocturnal encounter with Criseida (III, 21–24), but keeps determinedly abreast of four stanzas in which Troiolo's fears about Criseida's disloyalty are confirmed (VIII, 8–11; V, 1646–73). In adapting (rewriting and versifying) certain prose-like Boccaccian *ottave* Chaucer takes great pains:

> E questo detto, il suo Pandaro prese
> per mano, e 'l viso alquanto si dipinse
> con falso riso, e del palagio scese,
> a varie cagion con gli altri finse
> ch'eran con lui, per nasconder l'offese
> ch'el sentiva d'amor; ma poi ch'attinse
> con gli occhi di Criseida la magione
> chiusa, sentì novella turbagione.   (V, 51)

> And having said this, his Pandaro he took
> by the hand, and his face he somewhat painted
> with a false smile, and left the palace,
> and trumped up various excuses with the others
> who were with him, to hide the suffering
> that he was feeling from love; but when he reached
> with his eyes of Criseida the mansion
> closed, he felt new perturbation.

> And therwithal, his meyne for to blende,
> A cause he fond in towne for to go,
> And to Criseydes hous they gonnen wende.
> But Lord! this sely Troilus was wo!
> Hym thoughte his sorwful herte braste a-two.
> For, whan he saugh hire dores spered alle,
> Wel neigh for sorwe adoun he gan to falle.   (V, 526–32)

This *ottava* is drawn from one of the areas of the *Filostrato* that Chaucer most admired, or made most use of; even though no exact verbal correspondences arise when it is juxtaposed with the Chaucerian stanza quoted above, there is no doubting the appropriateness of this juxtaposition. In his first five-and-a-half lines, Boccaccio packs a prodigious quantity of information into a string of short clauses which show scant respect for line-endings; he then introduces a longer clause with a tortuous and confusing word order before squeezing in one last short clause. The word which bears most weight in this *ottava* is the 'ma' which introduces a turn in the argument analogous to that in a well-made sonnet. A more disciplined poet would not, perhaps, have left such a vital conjunction stranded in mid-line. Chaucer, in seeking to improve on Boccaccio's stanza, might have elected to make his turn in the couplet.[62] But, with a characteristically explosive authorial ejaculation, he turns earlier rather than later; this allows him to surround the crucial information in his penultimate line with two lines of emotional intensification. The whole of Chaucer's stanza, constructed line-by-line, exhibits great poetic balance and control; his first three lines offer a splendid and economical digest of the information piled up in the first five-and-a-half lines of Boccaccio's *ottava*.

Chaucer makes intelligent use of many *ottave* whose prose-like qualities inhibit extensive literal imitation. He sometimes selects a single motif from an Italian stanza as a starting point for his own poetic elaboration. In IV, 115 Boccaccio devotes an entire stanza to describing the sighs, cries and tears of his lovers; he tells us in his final line that these tears 'amare fossero oltre lor natura'. Chaucer tells of tears that 'bittre weren, out of teris kynde' (IV, 1136) before going on to develop an exquisite comparison with the tears of Myrrha ('Mirra'). In similar fashion, he passes over most of the apostrophic melodrama of *Filostrato* IV, 62 before lighting on an idea couched in its couplet and making this the starting point for his own more balanced and thoughtful poetic development (IV, 512–8).

Chaucer persistently endeavours to divert the prose-like current of Boccaccio's language into more conventional poetic channels. He frequently substitutes proper nouns for personal pronouns and curtails the processions of relative pronouns which stretch out Boccaccio's sentences. So in beginning his Book III *prohemium*, Chaucer follows Boccaccio (III, 74) in enjambing between his first two lines (and in entering into a first subordinate clause) but then terminates his sentence at the end of his second line. Boccaccio, typically, extends his period with a 'dal quale' in the second half of his second line. This necessitates further enjambement; continuing his period right through the *ottava*, he reaches his main verb in his final line.

The prose-like rhythms which permeate Boccaccio's *ottave* vitiate attempted adaptations of epic similes from Dante and Vergil: Boccaccio proves unable to hold the balance between two halves of a comparison. In *Inferno* XII, 22–25 Dante (likening the movement of the Minotaur to that of a wounded bull) creates a delicate equilibrium by balancing 'Qual è' at the beginning of one tercet with 'vid' io' at the beginning of another. Chaucer, following Boccaccio's appropriation of the Dantean passage (IV, 27), matches 'Right as' with 'Right so' (IV, 239–42); in the *Troilus*, as in the *Commedia*, two lines separate these clinching phrases. In the *Filostrato*, however, the whole structure of the simile seems close to collapse. Boccaccio begins by adapting the Vergilian formula 'non aliter' ('Né altrimenti') and reaches the second half of his comparison in his fifth line: but his second 'clinching phrase' is surrounded by so much enjambement that it offers little resistance to the momentum of a prose period in full spate. Nine stanzas before this, (IV, 18) Boccaccio's attempt to adapt a simile from *Aeneid* IX, 435–7 ends in similar disarray. On this occasion he balances 'Qual' against 'tale' in his fourth line: but he leaves this 'tale' stranded in mid-line and, incredibly, fails to end-stop a single line of his *ottava* until his final line where, once again, he finds his main verb. Chaucer passes over this *ottava*: but he upholds Boccaccio's choice of rhetorical form (epic simile) and theme (natural decay) in turning to a Dantean simile which features bare autumnal branches (*Inferno* III, 112–17; IV, 225–31). Chaucer again respects Dante's construction of the simile by balancing phrases at the beginning of his first and fourth lines ('Come', 'And as'; 'similemente', 'Lith Troilus'). Chaucer enhances the balance and stability of his stanza by alliterating and by repeating 'biraft'; the second appearance of this participial adjective yields an internal rhyme with 'ilaft'. Chaucer charges his stanza with a metamorphic suggestiveness in describing the way in which Troilus is bound 'in the blake bark of care' (IV, 229). In his final line, however, he takes the trouble of anchoring such poetic virtuosity to the immediate facts of his narrative. Directed by Boccaccio to Dante, Chaucer builds upon Dante's example to achieve one of the most accomplished stanzas of the *Troilus*:

> And as in wynter leves ben biraft,
> Ech after other, til the tree be bare,
> So that ther nys but bark and braunche ilaft,
> Lith Troilus, byraft of ech welfare,
> Ibounden in the blake bark of care,
> Disposed wood out of his wit to breyde,
> So sore hym sat the chaungynge of Criseyde.   (IV, 225–31)

In discussing the verse of Machaut and Chaucer, James Wimsatt observes that 'in court poetry the forces of disorder and dissolution could be kept under control within the tight constraints of form and convention'.[63] The *Troilus* takes shape within such constraints: the *Filostrato*, however, sees a simultaneous slackening of the outer constraints of prosody and of the inner constraints of courtesy:

> 'Io credo certo ch'ogni donna in voglia
> vive amorosa, e null'altro l'affrena
> che tema di vergogna; e s'a tal doglia
> onestamente medicina piena
> si può donar, folle è chi non la spoglia . . .'   (II, 27,1–5)

> 'I believe for certain that every woman in desire
> lives amorously, and nothing else reins her back
> but fear of scandal; and if to such pain
> a full dose of medicine might honestly
> be applied, she who does not strip off such pain is crazy . . .'

Pandaro's argument here, developed without regard for line-endings, debases (drags down from a higher to a lower social level) the language of *amour cortois*. Such debasement is a characteristic feature of a work in which the term 'cortese' itself is (as in the *cantare* tradition) pressed into service as a decorative epithet affording a convenient rhyme. Troiolo awaits Criseida:

> 'La donna cortese
> tosto verrà, ed io sarò giocondo . . .'   (III, 25,6–7)

> 'The courteous lady
> will soon be here, and I'll be cheerful . . .'

Boccaccio employs terms such as 'valore' and 'valorosa' with great frequency and little precision. At their most intimate moment, his lovers experience 'l'ultimo valore' of love, whereas Troilus and Criseyde 'Felten in love the grete worthynesse' (III, 32,8; III, 1316). Pandaro urges that no woman is '"più valorosa"' than Criseida; it inevitably follows (through exigences of rhyme) that none is '"più graziosa"': Pandarus maintains that no woman is '"more bountevous/Of hire estat"' nor '"more gracious/For to do wel"' (II, 22,1,3; I, 883–4,885–6). The *Filostrato*'s imperfect control of courtly terminology complements its imperfect versification: both imperfections attest to a lack of *mesure*, the vital quality which governs the social and poetic procedures of the *Troilus*:

> So whan it liked hire to go to reste,
> And voided weren thei that voiden oughte,
> She seyde . . .   (II, 911–13)

Chaucer's measured, unhurried lines here create (particularly through the delicate balance of 'voided weren' against 'voiden oughte') a sense of a world in which social proprieties are scrupulously (but unostentatiously) observed. This sense is strengthened just five stanzas later when Troilus, under the pressure of intense emotion, restrains himself from questioning Pandarus until such proprieties have been observed and secrecy is ensured:

> With al the haste goodly that they myghte,
> They spedde hem fro the soper unto bedde;
> And every wight out at the dore hym dyghte,
> And where hym liste upon his wey him spedde.
> But Troilus . . .   (II, 946–50)

Once again, Chaucer's evocation of a social order in which such domestic procedures are quietly observed is complemented by the unhurried development of his end-stopped lines: Boccaccio's enjambements belong to a different world. Pandaro, in lecturing Troiolo, explicitly insists on the importance of secrecy: news of Criseida's sexual compliance must not find its way '"into the vulgar mouth"' ('"alla bocca del vulgo"', II, 25,5). But such solicitude simply forms part of a practical strategy of seduction: the young Boccaccio's insensitivity to the spiritual dimension of secrecy compares with that of the *canterino* who struggled with *La Chastelaine de Vergi*.

At critical moments in the development of their courtship, Troiolo and Criseida are each persuaded by the brute force of Pandaro's crude arguments.[64] At comparable moments, Chaucer turns instinctively away from

135

Boccaccio towards the French poets he had admired and imitated since his youth. In Book I, for example, Pandarus concludes a vigorous assault against Troilus' wanhope by appropriating arguments from the *Roman de la Rose* (20859–63; I, 810–12) and from Machaut's *Remede de Fortune* (1636–48; I, 813–19). Such arguments prove effective:

> Of that word took hede Troilus . . .   (I, 820)

In II, 820–931 Criseyde is similarly moved by the persuasive force of Antigone's song: the arguments and the lyricism which make her better disposed towards love are developed from a set of Machaut lyrics which 'includes two lays, two balades, and a virelai'.[65] Later in Book II Chaucer puts his schooling in the figurative language of the *Rose* to good use in revealing the inner workings of his heroine's psyche where Boccaccio confines himself to the description of externals:

> Poi si [Pandaro] partì, ed ella dall'un canto
> della camera sua, ove più rada
> usanza di venire ad ogni altro era,
> a scriver giù si pose in tal manera: (II, 120,5–8)

> Then he left, and she in a corner
> of her room, to which most infrequently
> was there occasion for anyone else to come,
> set herself down to write in such a way:

> And into a closet, for t'avise hire bettre,
> She wente allone, and gan hire herte unfettre
> Out of desdaynes prison but a lite,
> And sette hire down, and gan a lettre write . . .   (II, 1215–8)

Four stanzas later Pandarus employs the language of the *Rose* in referring to Criseyde's desire to maintain ' "the forme of daunger" ' (II, 1243); a little later he imagines a debate between Kynde and Daunger staged within Criseyde's mind (II, 1373–6); and finally, as Troilus and Criseyde consummate their love, Chaucer himself steps in to ward off 'thow foule daunger' and 'thow feere' (III, 1321). The 'daungerous' behaviour of Criseyde is largely modelled on that of Machaut's ladies, as are her subtle powers of argument, her rhetorical skill and her penchant for proffering momentous oaths of loyalty. Troilus' agonised inner conflicts recall those of certain Machaut heroes, as does his abiding concern to discover 'trouthe' in his lady.[66]

Machaut and the poets of the *Rose* also provide Chaucer with models of versification and with a fund of poetic motifs for the incidental embellishment of his work.[67] Their influence in the *Troilus* makes itself felt even when Chaucer appears to be following Boccaccio. In V, 218–45, for example, Troilus' complaint borrows material from Boccaccio (V, 20–21, 24–25) but develops it in a restrained and formal manner that is reminiscent of the French poets. Boccaccio's popular epithets are rejected ('misero dolente', 'cuor del corpo mio', 'lasso più ch'altro', 'o dolce bene', 'o caro mio diporto', 'o bella donna', 'o dolce anima mia') or refined beyond recognition: 'dolce anima bella' becomes 'my righte lode-sterre' (V, 25,1; V, 232). Boccaccio's brightest ideas are developed within tighter bounds of versification:

> '. . . ora abbracciando
> vado il piumaccio . . .' (V, 20,5–6)

> 'And graspe aboute I may, but in this place,
> Save a pilowe, I fynde naught t'enbrace.' (V, 223–4)

Anguished, semi-rhetorical questions appear in every Chaucerian stanza and anaphora is employed to fine effect. Chaucer end-stops every line until the middle of his final stanza, where his sudden departure from the norm (V, 242–5) proves brilliantly effective: the balance and restraint of Troilus' complaint is broken by one final anguished outburst.

In previous chapters we have considered ways in which the *Roman de la Rose* precedes the *Commedia* as an extended vernacular narrative. In passing from the poets of the *Rose* and their continuators, Chaucer's personal poetic evolution traces, in a sense, this historical movement. James Wimsatt rightly insists[68] that Chaucer did not abandon the French love poets on discovering the Italians; I would reinforce his point by proposing that Chaucer's apprenticeship among French texts actually primed him, in many ways, for his encounter with the *Commedia*. We discover, in examining the *Troilus*, that Chaucer often turns from Boccaccio towards Dante and the French poets for similar reasons: for a more sophisticated, first-hand understanding of *curteisie* and for standards of versification which might attest to such understanding.

In adapting the *Rose*, the poet of *Il Fiore* (perhaps Dante himself) launched a forthright attack against 'i borghesi' (CXVIII, 5&10), the mercantile and entrepreneurial class that had encroached upon traditional aristocratic domains, forcing the nobility into debt and reducing them to the level of basket-makers (CXVIII, 8). La Vechia voices the essential wisdom of this world in which everything is for sale: she instructs Bellacoglienza in the art of feminine 'mercatantia' (CLVII, 8) until her disciple is fit and willing to 'far mercato' (CXCIV, 5). La Vechia, like the merchants of medieval Italy, makes much use of courtly language: the term 'cortese' is frequently on her lips, and concepts such as 'franchezza' are subtly redefined.[69] The *Filostrato*, composed within a Florentine merchant colony, undoubtedly perpetuates this popular debasement of aristocratic language. Its appropriation of Dantean phrasings contributes to this process. The unreflective enthusiasm for the *Commedia* evident in the *Filostrato* (and in numerous *cantari* and other popular pieces) would not, one feels, have amused the great poet. It certainly would not have amused Petrarch, who (in writing to Boccaccio in 1359) lamented the fact that Dante's verse was 'acclaimed and declaimed . . . by "ignorant oafs in taverns and market places"'.[70] *Troilus and Criseyde*, however, attests to a mature, deeply-meditated feeling for the *Commedia* (and for the art of poetry) which even Dante (if not Petrarch) might have admired. Certain Dantean scenes cast long and subtle shadows over the *Troilus*: Chaucer (as an author of romances) was undoubtedly alive to the moral issues raised by a reading of *Inferno* V; and his reading of the first nine tercets of *Inferno* XXX certainly alerted him to ways in which the disaster of Thebes foreshadows that of Troy.[71]

The sophisticated ways in which Chaucer adverts to the *Commedia* in fashioning his *Troilus* contrast markedly with the cheerful robustness of Boccaccio's usage of Dante. The Dantean tercet which Chaucer so carefully incorporates into his final stanza (*Paradiso* XIV, 28–30) is squeezed by Boccaccio into a single line and allowed no especial prominence (II, 41,4). Chaucer does, however, occasionally follow Boccaccio's initiative in mining the *Commedia* for more routine poetic requirements: in III, 1688–94, for example, he draws upon two inexpressibility topoi from different areas of the *Paradiso* (XIX, 7–9; XXIV, 25–27). The *Filostrato*'s forthright adaptation of Dantean effects was, I believe, of especial interest to Chaucer in demonstrating how a tale of secular love might be embellished and ennobled without losing its fundamental romance character. For the narrator of *Troilus and Criseyde* often speaks with two distinct voices:

> Now lat us stynte of Troilus a stounde . . .
> . . . .
> And thus he dryeth forth his aventure.   (I, 1086,1092)

> Owt of thise blake wawes for to saylle,
> O wynd, o wynd, the weder gynneth clere;
> For in this see the boot hath swych travaylle,
> Of my connyng, that unneth I it steere.   (II, 1–4)[72]

Here Chaucer ends the first Book of his *Troilus* as a romancer[73] and begins the second as a follower of Dante. Such shifts in authorial identity are a characteristic feature of Chaucer's poem. In the stanzas following the *prohemium* to Book III, for example, Chaucer works hard to recover his posture as an unpretentious romancer. (In *Anelida and Arcite* he was, apparently, unable to effect such a recovery after Anelida's lengthy *compleynt*). He enlivens the ending of his first narrative stanza with an authorial exclamation; five stanzas later he slackens the pace of his narration by rhyming his couplet with two romance tags:

> God leve hym werken as he kan devyse!   (III, 56)

> His resons, as I may my rymes holde,
> I wol yow telle, as techen bokes olde.   (III, 90–91)

In III, 106 Troilus addresses Criseyde as '"wommanliche wif"', a phrase which he employs again in III, 1296. Criseyde reminds us that she is a romance heroine by warning Troilus that although he is a '"kynges sone"' he will enjoy no more '"sovereignete"' over her in love than she deems appropriate (III, 169–72). Six stanzas later Chaucer closes one narrative episode and opens another by employing one of his favourite forms of tag phrase[74] and by shifting his scenery with the ostentation typical of a romancer:

> . . . it joie was to here.

> Now lat hire wende unto hire owen place,
> And torne we to Troilus ayein . . .   (III, 217–9)

The form of this tag phrase may be compared with a line from *Amis and Amiloun*; the same tail-rhyme romance provides a parallel to the deliberate change of scene engineered by Chaucer in III, 218 (and in II, 687–9, III, 1583–6, and V, 195–6) and combines this with an authorial interjection reminiscent of III, 56:

> Þat semly was on to se.   (534)

> Lete we sir Amiloun stille be
> Wiþ his wiif in his cuntre—
> God leue hem wele to fare—
> & of sir Amis telle we . . .   (337–40)

Derek Pearsall has suggested that *Amis and Amiloun* 'has some claim to be regarded as the typically best English romance'.[75] *Amis*, the *Troilus* and the *Filostrato* have much in common which sets them apart from the *Commedia*. Their authors cultivate an easy-going narrative manner: they employ recapitulatory formulae, repeat phrases or entire lines and predict the future outcome of present actions.[76] The rhymes of the *Commedia* strive for perpetual, ingenious variety: these authors ease their task of rhyming by introducing numerous references to sources, religious oaths, stock phrases and standard epithets. Chaucer takes full advantage of the fact that his heroine's name rhymes with *seyde*.[77] He employs variations of the romancer's simile 'stille as any ston' on five occasions in the *Troilus* and rhymes on *ston* six times.[78] He rhymes on *two* on over twenty occasions; these include the romance tags 'eyen two' (III, 1352, IV, 750) and 'armes two' (IV, 911). Chaucer turns to Petrarch for his first *Canticus Troili*: but in the latter part of his poem Troilus' song is often that of Amis[79]:

> His song was, 'Waileway!'   (984)

> For which his song ful ofte is 'weylaway!'   (IV, 1166)

The author of *Amis*, like Chaucer and Boccaccio, makes effective use of internal debate[80]; and he too chooses to accentuate the isolated misery of his heroine by surrounding her with cheerful female companions[81]:

> Vp hir ros þat swete wiʒt,
> In-to þe gardine sche went ful riʒt
> Wiþ maidens hende & fre.
> þe somers day was fair & briʒt,
> þe sonne him schon þurch lem of liʒt,
> þat semly was on to se.
> Sche herd þe foules gret & smale,
> þe swete note of þe niʒtingale
> Ful mirily sing on tre;
> Ac hir hert was so hard ibrouʒt,
> On loue-longing was al hir þouʒt,
> No miʒt hir gamen no gle.   (529–40)

In such a stanza we may discern a 'hierarchy of semantic features'[82]: some elements are more essential to the development of the story than others. These less essential elements (often located in the shorter lines) make the art of poetic composition less exacting; they also allow the audience momentary relaxations of concentration. Chaucer and Boccaccio seem similarly determined to cultivate an easy-going narrative manner which will not over-tax their auditors. This presents a radical contrast to the demands exacted from the solitary reader who struggles to follow Dante through his great poem. There are no inessential phrases, no momentary resting-places, in the *Commedia*; the faint-hearted reader is actively encouraged to abandon his attempt to read the poem.[83]

Chaucer's choice of the *Filostrato* as the source of his great *tragedye* is unlikely to have been a happy historical accident. Chaucer's knowledge of Italian was, we have noted, extraordinarily good: he knew just what he was choosing (and, presumably, paying for) in adopting Boccaccio's poem. The author of the *Filostrato*, Chaucer would have realised, shares his reverence for Dante: but he also shares his fondness for a tradition of stanzaic narrative which draws much of its peculiar vigour from popular, oral-derived origins. Chaucer's discriminating adherence to the style and conventions of the English romances was, it would seem, a matter of deliberate choice.[84] In the final Book of the *Troilus* Chaucer leans especially heavily upon the conventions of romance: it is as if he wishes to push his protagonists (brought to imaginative life by his artistry) back into the world of artifice.[85] To this end he elects to follow Boccaccio's summary, *cantare*-like account[86] of Troiolo's death, emitting a cry ('weilawey') and a pious exclamation ('save only Goddes wille!') that are quite typical of an English romancer:

> . . . e dopo lungo stallo,
> avendone già morti più di mille,
> miseramente un dì l'uccise Achille.   (VIII, 27,6–8)

> But weilawey, save only Goddes wille!
> Despitously hym slough the fierse Achille.   (V, 1805–6)

This couplet provides one ending to the story of Troilus; the remaining nine stanzas provide another which bears witness to Chaucer's highest artistic pretensions.[87] The very last of these stanzas sees Chaucer turning to Dante: it is the *Commedia*, Chaucer suggests, that stands before him as his pattern of versification, of style and of Christian propriety:

> Quell' uno e due e tre che sempre vive
> e regna sempre in tre e 'n due e 'n uno,
> non circunscritto, e tutto circunscrive . . .
>
>   (Par XIV, 28–30)

> Thow oon, and two, and thre, eterne on lyve,
> That regnest ay in thre, and two, and oon,
> Uncircumscript, and al maist circumscrive,
> Us from visible and invisible foon
> Defende, and to thy mercy, everichon,
> So make us, Jesus, for thi mercy digne,
> For love of mayde and moder thyn benigne.
>   Amen.

CHAPTER 7

Chaucer and Boccaccio among
Illustrious and Popular Traditions

As an author of romances and as a disciple of Dante, Chaucer was admirably served by Boccaccio's *Teseida*. Chaucer scholars have subjected the *Teseida* to much close scrutiny in recent years.[1] Little can be added to their findings here, although I would suggest that their accounts of the *Teseida* (often overshadowed by their accounts of the exceedingly sombre *Knight's Tale*) have often made Boccaccio's poem seem more sombre than it really is. Here, having briefly considered the *Teseida*'s literary affiliations, we will limit ourselves to noting how Boccaccio's poem meets Chaucer's requirements in works as diverse as *The Knight's Tale* and *The Parliament of Fowls*. Discussion of the *Parliament* brings us full circle, back to the *Amorosa Visione* and to Boccaccio's early Florentine period. And further exploration of this period leads to a final assessment of Chaucer and Boccaccio as poets working within a European complex of illustrious and popular traditions.

Although the *Teseida* strives to turn itself into an instant vernacular classic by surrounding its verses with erudite commentary, its fundamental affiliations are with the *cantare*. This fact was obvious to the compiler of the *Cantare dei Cantari*, a sequence of fifty-nine *ottave* which set out the supposed repertoire of a gifted *canterino*: the twelve Books of the *Teseida* are numbered among *cantari* dedicated to Theban subjects.[2] It has been argued that the *Teseida* owes more to the *cantare* than does the *Filostrato*[3]; it certainly contains an abundance of the *cantare*-like traits observable in the earlier narrative.[4] Chaucer doubtless perceived that the momentum generated by the *Teseida*'s narrative is, essentially, the rude vigour of a popular romance. In spite of its epic pretensions, the *Teseida* fails to achieve the gravity of movement that characterises *The Knight's Tale*: its protagonists, like *cantare* characters, rush hurriedly from place to place as if transported by magic carpet. In the opening Book—which Chaucer cuts almost entirely[5]—the warfare waged between Teseo's men and the Amazon women has farcical qualities reminiscent of many *cantare* (and popular English romance) passages: Teseo mocks the '"cowardly and pathetic exertions"' ('"vile e tristo adoperare"') of his '"sad little soldiers"' ('"cavalier

141

dolenti"') as they are haplessly deluged in pitch, oil and soap.[6] Ipolita, the Amazon commander, seems to be a close relative of the *cantare* warrior Madonna Lionessa. In gazing upon Ipolita, Teseo remembers his rape of Elena: he recalls a past conquest even in conceiving of a future one (I, 130), a phenomenon which must have struck Chaucer as a gross lapse of decorum. Such lapses are ruthlessly weeded out by the English poet, who supplants Boccaccio's casual and complacent *cortesia* with his own more urgent and profoundly-meditated *curteisie*. When Teseo first comes across the young knights locked in combat, he is an admiring spectator (V, 82): Theseus furiously intervenes, incensed that these knights should fight like wild animals,

> 'Withouten juge or oother officere,
> As it were in a lystes roially.' (I, 1712–3)

Following Arcite's funeral, Teseo attempts to console his subjects with lengthy philosophical reflections (XII, 6–19). This attempt, mercilessly derided by Branca,[7] prompts Chaucer to turn to Boethius.[8] The somewhat flat-footed logic which opens Teseo's speech is transferred to Egeus:

> 'Così come alcun che mai non visse
> non morì mai, così si pò vedere
> ch'alcun non visse mai che non morisse;
> e noi che ora viviam, quando piacere
> sarà di quel che 'l mondo circunscrisse,
> perciò morremo: adunque sostenere
> il piacer dell'iddii lieti dobbiamo,
> poi ch'ad esso resister non possiamo.' (XII, 6)

> 'Right as ther dyed nevere man,' quod he,
> 'That he ne lyvede in erthe in some degree,
> Right so ther lyvede never man,' he seyde,
> 'In al this world, that som tyme he ne deyde.
> This world nys but a thurghfare ful of wo,
> And we been pilgrymes, passynge to and fro.
> Deeth is an ende of every worldly soore.' (I, 2843–9)

Here, as often, Boccaccio's language flows freely and easily, colloquial in style and (despite the seriousness of the theme) almost cheerful in tone. Here, as often, the development of a prose-like momentum erodes prosodic constraints: the autonomy of the couplet is once again sacrificed; the initial logical sequence is cramped and enjambed into three lines. In adopting this sequence Chaucer resorts to the 'Right as . . . Right so' construction which he employs to order an epic simile in the *Troilus*.[9] Every thought in the seven-line speech of Egeus is developed and ordered within the line unit. Such ordering highlights the inexorable movement of the couplets; and the reflections added by Chaucer in the last three lines augment the sense of gloomy inevitability which hangs over the entire *Tale*. Such an atmosphere is worlds (perhaps genres) apart from that which prevails in the *Teseida*: Boccaccio's poem has the sunny disposition characteristic of the best (and most typical) *cantari*. The delightful battle of wits waged between Ipolita and Teseo in the opening Book is close in spirit to certain Canterbury narratives, but not to *The Knight's Tale*; its imaginative territory borders on that of the Merchant, the Franklin and the Wife of Bath.

Chaucer evidently admired the straightforward narrative qualities of the *Teseida*; but he also appreciated passages in which Boccaccio presses his claim to be considered as an illustrious poet extending the enterprise of Dante and the *auctores*.[10] It appears that, from the first, the *Teseida* served Chaucer as an artist's pattern-book, a repository of poetic and iconographic motifs which may embellish and lend distinction to a 'tale'.[11] The invocation to Venus and the Muses at the beginning of the second Book of *The House of Fame* apparently borrows inspiration from the *Teseida*'s opening *ottave*; and these same *ottave* are more diligently imitated at the beginning of *Anelida and Arcite*[12]: the example of the *Teseida* was evidently instrumental in convincing Chaucer of the need to abandon octosyllabic couplets. Stanzas from the *Teseida* made a notable contribution to the most distinguished of Chaucerian dream poems, *The Parliament of Fowls*. By the time he came to compose the *Parliament*, Chaucer had little to learn from Boccaccio's versification: and yet he chose to devote almost one hundred lines (which, as J. A. W. Bennett observes,[13] amounts to almost a sixth of his narrative) to stanzas derived from the *Teseida*'s seventh Book. This represents the lengthiest bout of sustained imitation in Chaucerian dream poetry, excepting, of course, *The Romaunt of the Rose*.

Chaucer obviously appreciated the intelligent manner in which iconographic details from the *Rose* and the *Commedia* are absorbed into the *Teseida*'s description of the temple of Venus and its environs. A similar imaginative terrain is explored in greater detail in the Boccaccian dream vision composed just a few years later, the *Amorosa Visione*. Bennett analyses the *Teseida* stanzas in considerable detail but has little to say about 'the park of pleasure described in Boccaccio's *Amorosa Visione*' because 'that carried a quite unambiguous welcome over its portal'.[14] The inscription to which Bennett refers (III, 16–21) is certainly welcoming: but so is the description above the ' "narrow gateway" ' (' "piccola porta" ') that stands next to it (II, 64–69). Before crossing the threshold that leads to the garden, the Italian dreamer (like his counterpart in the *Parliament*) is pulled by conflicting impulses.[15] And he subsequently discovers that even within the garden, ambiguities abound. This *locus amoenus*[16] is irrigated by a fountain that directs streams of water in three different directions (XXXVIII, 19–XXXIX, 69). The first stream, issuing from the head of a lion (signifying nobility) flows towards the east, the direction traditionally taken by every genuine prayer and godward aspiration; this represents ' "amore onesto" ', ' "honest love" '.[17] The second, representing ' "amore per diletto" ' (' "love for pleasure" '), issues from the head of a bull (signifying sensual impetuosity) and flows towards the south, the traditional seat of fiery passions. The third, representing ' "amore per utilità" ' (' "love for gain" '), flows from the head of a wolf (signifying covetousness) and meanders towards the cold north.

But the dreamer is oblivious to such subtle demarcations on first entering the garden; his delighted reaction is as spontaneous and subjective as that of his English counterpart:

Ahi quanto egli era bello il luogo ov'io
era venuto, e quanto era contento
dentro da me l'ardente mio disio!   (XXXVIII (A), 19–21)

Ah, how beautiful it was, the place that I
had come to, and how happy it was
within me, my ardent desire!

But, Lord, so was I glad and wel begoon!
For overal where that I myne eyen caste
Were treës clad with leves that ay shal laste,
Ech in his kynde, of colour fresh and green . . .   (171–4)

The explosive release of tension in these lines marks the escape of each dreamer from oppressive *sentence* into joyful *solas*: Chaucer has been burdened by the daunting extra-terrestrial teaching of African, and Boccaccio by the monotonous accumulation of disastrous case histories pointed out by his female guide in the fifth and final *triumph*, that of Fortune. Chaucer now abandons himself to describing the delights of the garden, a place where 'swetnesse everemore inow is' (185): a place of perfect climate (204–5) and everlasting daylight (209–10) in which a man might enjoy eternal youth and good health (207) in perpetual spring (173). Such a place corresponds to the portion of the Italian garden watered by the first and most noble stream:

Herba non v'ha, né frutti che smarriti
teman dell'autunno, ma tuttora
con frutti e frondi be' verdi e fioriti
    ivi dimoran, né mai si scolora
prato, ma bel di variati fiori
la state e 'l verno sempre vi dimora.   (XXXIX (A), 37–42)

There was no grass nor fruits there which feared
to perish in autumn, but continually
with fruits and leaves, beautifully green and flowering
    they dwelt there, nor did the meadow ever become
discoloured, but beautiful with diverse flowers
flourished perpetually through summer and winter.

Teseida VII contains no such picture of eternal spring; its garden of Venus corresponds to that watered by the *Visione*'s second stream. This area is just as beautiful ('similmente è bello') as the first, but is subject to the laws of temporal change:

Ogni pratel di quel lito è contento
di mutar condizione a tempo e loco,
secondo c'ha 'l vigore acceso e spento.
    Rallegrasi ogni animale e gioco
vi fa, secondo che amor lo strigne
sotto la forza sua o molto o poco.

(XXXIX (A), 52–57)

Every little meadow by that stream is content
to change condition with time and place,
depending whether fertility is there active or exhausted.
    Every animal gladdens itself and makes
sport there, in such measure as love compels it
in accordance with its power, great or small.

Here each and every creature is touched by and responds to the power of love appropriate to its particular capacities. Such a place, inhabited by 'every cheerful bird' ('ogni gaio uccello', 48), corresponds to the domain of Chaucer's Nature. The English birds are similarly joyful in their subjection to natural laws: their assembly concludes with a song to Nature which celebrates summer's annual triumph over the darkness and inhospitability of winter (680–92).

Not a single tree or green or living plant is discovered in the third portion of the Italian garden, which is a sad and dessicated plain ('secca la pianura trista'). Although bleached white, part of it is tinged by a dark colour ('color perso') from the disgusting stream (XXXIX, 61–69). A similarly baleful landscape is evoked by the black letters above the *Parliament*'s double gateway. These speak of a place where

> '. . . nevere tre shal fruyt ne leves bere.
> This strem yow ledeth to the sorweful were
> There as the fish in prysoun is al drye . . .'   (137–9)

The stream advertised here has much in common with that which flows from the jaws of Boccaccio's wolf-head. It is not, of course, quite the same: a dry and barren atmosphere similar to that evoked by these black letters is breathed by the English dreamer within the temple of Venus. But there are impressive parallels in the various ways in which the English and Italian poets explore the single subject of love in these dream poems. Boccaccio sees three different garden landscapes watered by a single fountain; Chaucer passes through three domains, presided over by African, Venus and Nature.[18] Each poet skilfully exploits the poetic license afforded by a dream-vision framework; and each deliberately relinquishes such license once the spell of the vision is broken. The end of each vision is marked by a transition from the preterite to a present tense which pictures the author preparing himself for future labours.[19] Boccaccio follows the teaching of his virtuous guide, observing keenly in the hope of writing again (L, 49–51); Chaucer returns to his books, hoping

> . . . to rede so som day
> That I shal mete som thyng for to fare
> The bet, and thus to rede I nyl nat spare.   (697–9)

Perhaps the range of Chaucer's industrious reading extended to the *Amorosa Visione*. His second dream poem certainly has much in common with the cantos dedicated to the *triumphs*; and the imaginative terrain explored in the *Parliament* compares with that set out in the later part of the Italian vision. John Norton-Smith is obviously aware of such correspondences in suggesting that Boccaccio's poem influences 'the structural *idée*' of the *Parliament*, and that 'the pattern of the *Visione* explains the close thematic connection between the *Parliament* and the *House of Fame*'.[20]

But comparison of the *Amorosa Visione* and *The Parliament of Fowls* yields contrasts as well as congruences. In his *Parliament*, Chaucer has obviously learned from earlier struggles and embarrassments. His poem features catalogues of heroes and heroines, birds and trees, but never becomes cluttered with detail. It draws upon a remarkable range of illustrious sources, but successfully absorbs them into a coherent unity. It features a verse form which demands disciplined ingenuity, but is not gratuitously elaborate. In short, the poem employs great craft in creating a thoroughly convincing impression of naturalness and ease. The *Visione*, we have noted, sags and buckles under the strain of ambitions which outrun Boccaccio's poetic competence.

Similar ambitions are somewhat more successfully realised in the *Comedia delle ninfe fiorentine*, a *prosimetrum* composed shortly before the *Visione* in the period 1341–2.[21] Alternating passages of prose and *terza rima*, it tells how a young rustic, Ameto, becomes enamoured of a noblewoman, Lia. Under the influence of this love, Ameto is educated within a circle of seven women (representing the seven cardinal virtues) and—like the narrator of the *Caccia* before him—is transformed from 'beast' to 'man'[22]; he ends by singing in honour of the Trinity. Like the *Visione*, the *Comedia delle ninfe* inherits the pedagogical strain of the *Tesoretto*: but it also begins to develop a greater freedom and clarity of narrative style which anticipates that of the *Ninfale fiesolano*. This delightful work is the only Boccaccian poem which can sustain comparison with the artful naturalness of Chaucer's *Parliament*. Composed just a few years before the *Decameron* began to take shape,[23] the *Ninfale* represents a watershed in Boccaccio's cultural evolution. It is his last full-length vernacular poem.

The *Ninfale fiesolano* tells how a simple pagan rustic, Africo, becomes enamoured of Mensola, a young nymph dedicated to Diana. Unlike his fortunate predecessor Ameto, Africo has no virtuous story-tellers to enlighten him; he seeks to consummate his love in a manner that can only provoke outrage among the pagan gods. His parents, blameless countryfolk, become frightened and confused by his infatuation. The inadequacy of their responses to Africo's love-sickness arouses much pathos: Africo's mother first hears his lover's cry of '"Omè, omè"' whilst standing in a little garden ('orticello') by her wooden house (132); she can only think to prepare him a bath, a 'bagnuolo' for her 'figliuolo' (151). The poem's accretion of domestic and familial detail (and of affective diminutives) excites *pietà* from its readers in much the same way that Chaucer's adaptation of the Dantean Ugolino episode moves our *pitee*.[24]

Although the *Ninfale* is set in pagan times it contains very little classical matter; the only required reading for the poem is Ovid's *Metamorphoses*. And the influence of Ovid is discernible not so much in isolated textual borrowings as in the poem's total effect: the metamorphoses which conclude the *Ninfale* come as authentic realisations of the poem's inner logic, not as incidental ornaments to the narrative. The poem's later verses seem especially close in spirit to certain Chaucerian scenes, particularly those depicting the ineluctable tragedy of a hapless heroine. On learning of her pregnancy from the ancient nymph Sinedecchia, Mensola—like many of Chaucer's good women—responds eloquently through bodily gesture[25]:

Niente a questo Mensola risponde,
ma, per vergogna, in grembo il capo pose
a Sinedecchia, e 'l bel viso nasconde . . .   (387,1–3)

Nothing to this does Mensola say in response,
But, for shame, her head she lay down in the lap
of Sinedecchia, and hides her fair face . . .

Mensola's transgression will inevitably excite the wrath of the goddess
Diana; her last days are full of pathos. Her son Pruneo is born; she makes him a
little dress ('gonnella', 404,6) and they are playing happily together by the
river-bank when the deity arrives. Diana, speaking in 'chiaro latino' (409,5),
exposes the guilt of Mensola, who attempts to flee but is transformed into
water. The goddess follows a logic that is impeccable but inhuman. The name
of Mensola is assumed by the river that absorbs the young woman. The
metamorphosis becomes a sad symbol of mankind's inability to cope with the
greater powers that shape and determine our existence. Chaucer's mature art
contains many such symbols; his *Troilus* presents 'a world controlled by forces
that have human faces, but not human hearts'.[26]

The *Ninfale fiesolano* represents Boccaccio's third and final essay in *cantare*
form (and, in retrospect, his farewell to vernacular poetry in general). The
poem succeeds so convincingly because Boccaccio allows the popular form to
realise its innate potential, unencumbered by extraneous erudite matter. The
narrator speaks with the ingenuous straightforwardness of a *canterino* ('vi vo
contar . . .', 9,5) and employs the full range of narrative techniques associated
with the *cantare*.[27] Appeals to written authority ('come molti libri fan chiarez-
za', 458,4) supplement appeals to the narrator's own experience ('sì com'io
sento', 449,6) and recapitulative formulae (311,7–8). Affective epithets (such
as the ever-popular 'cuor del corpo mio')[28] and floral formulae (such as 'fresco
giglio', 74,6, 'fresca rosa aulente', 255,5 and 'rosa novella', 296,1) contribute to
Boccaccio's delightful evocation of an idyllic pagan world. But although such a
world is primarily a realm of pleasant fantasy, it does not exclude mundane
human realities: Boccaccio's poem is energised by a sharpness of psychological
insight that is foreign to its native popular tradition. In this it resembles
Chaucer's *Franklin's Tale*, which makes comparable use of popular romance
conventions, yet maintains a similarly sharp sense of human frailty. Each poem
evokes a world which is at once fantastic yet familiar, pagan yet contemporary.

Antonio Pucci, Florentine town-crier and author of *Brito di Brettagna* and
Madonna Lionessa, was moved to address an admiring sonnet to Boccaccio in
which he speaks 'as a son to a father'.[29] Pucci (who was born *circa* 1310 and died
at Florence in 1388)[30] was, in fact, several years older than Boccaccio; his form
of address deferentially observes the distance between a lesser and a greater
poet. But it is interesting to note that this semi-educated *canterino* should think
it appropriate to address Boccaccio at all: he evidently felt that he and
Boccaccio had something in common. Like Boccaccio, he compiled a
Zibaldone[31]; and he too attracted some attention as a literary man:

'Deh fammi una canzon, fammi un sonetto'
mi dice alcun ch'ha la memoria scema,
e parli pur che, datomi la tema,
i' ne debba cavare un gran diletto.[32]

'Go on, do me a canzone, do me a sonnet'
some half-brained someone says to me,
and it seems to him that, once I'm given the theme,
I should dig one out to provide great pleasure.

There is no evidence that Boccaccio ever acknowledged Pucci's sonnet. In later years (as he increasingly subjected himself to Petrarch's influence and to Petrarch's disdain for popular verse), Boccaccio came to hold himself aloof from the *cantare*. In his *Corbaccio* (which dates from around 1365) Boccaccio satirises an amorous widow's fondness for *cantare* stories (which include the *Cantare di Fiorio e Biancifiore*, one of the sources of his own *Filocolo*).[33] But it is unlikely that such disparaging references managed to erode the association of Boccaccio with the *cantare* that persisted in the popular mind.[34] The association was doubtless still strong when Chaucer first visited Florence.

Chaucer certainly does not encourage us to associate him with the English romances. Derek Pearsall suggests that 'the only debt . . . which Chaucer can be proved to owe to earlier English poetry is one which he thought worth paying in withering scorn'[35]; he goes on to depict Chaucer turning to French and Italian texts. But one of the lessons that Chaucer learned on turning to Boccaccio was, in fact, how a writer might present himself as an illustrious poet whilst utilising a popular native tradition of stanzaic narrative. The piece of 'withering scorn' that Pearsall alludes to is, of course, *The Tale of Sir Thopas*. In accentuating the characteristic traits of the tail-rhyme tradition Chaucer creates a narrative that has much in common with the *cantare*. This Italian tradition gave rise to the two Boccaccian poems which, in turn, made possible the greatest of Chaucerian romances: *The Knight's Tale* and the *Troilus*. The suggestion that Chaucer, in parodying the Middle English rhyming romances, is 'biting the hand that fed him'[36] remains illuminating when Chaucer's domestic circumstances are viewed within their appropriate European context.

Pearsall's characterisation of *Sir Thopas* as 'withering scorn' seems to mistake the enterprise (and certainly the tone) of Chaucer's tail-rhyme romance: for it is possible to poke fun at a literary trait (or set of traits) without renouncing the right to use it. Elsewhere in *The Canterbury Tales*, for example, we discover Chaucer drawing upon a favourite romancer's (and *canterino*'s) strategy. This has been wittily identified by Wittig as 'the *meanwhile-back-at-the-ranch* motifeme'[37]:

> Now lat us turne agayn to Januarie,
> That in the gardyn with his faire May
> Syngeth ful murier than the papejay . . .
>
> (CT IV, 2320–2)

Proserpyne and Pluto have just concluded a most violent altercation; Damyan is poised to do business in the pear tree; and yet Chaucer's Merchant finds time to shift his scene with studied (almost elegant) deliberateness. Such a shift undoubtedly gains in comic effect by echoing similarly deliberate transitions at similarly awkward moments in numerous popular compositions. But Chaucer was quite willing to employ the same device to serious effect elsewhere, most notably in his *Troilus*.[38] And Boccaccio's *Ninfale fiesolano* contains a generous number of comparable transitions.[39]

The true intentions of European medieval poets–writing at Florence or Naples, Avignon or London—are extraordinarily difficult to define: a gulf of uncertain dimensions divides what they purport to be doing from what they actually do. The right hand of the illustrious poet knows not what the left hand is leafing through. But it is attractive to think that in the *Ninfale fiesolano* and *Sir Thopas* Boccaccio and Chaucer (who were both anxious to be publicly associated with the illustrious poets) are privately acknowledging their indebtedness to more humble traditions of vernacular verse. It is clear that much of their characteristic narrative vitality is tapped from such popular roots. C. S. Lewis has observed that 'as a form, the Italian epic illustrates the conversion . . . of a popular *genre* to literary respectability'.[40] By 'Italian epic', Lewis means that tradition of extended narrative in *ottava rima* formed by Pulci, Boiardo, Ariosto and Tasso.[41] Lewis does not seem to realise that this tradition originates with Boccaccio's *Teseida*; for it was Boccaccio who first set in motion the 'conversion' process that Lewis himself describes so well:

> When the 'literary' poets arrive they take up the extravagances of popular romance with a smile—a smile half of amusement and half of affection —like men returning to something that had charmed their childhood. They too will write of giants and 'orcs', of fairies and flying horses, of Saracens foaming at the mouth. They will do it with an occasional gravity, referring us to Turpin whenever the adventures are most preposterous, and it will be great fun. But they find that their pleasure is not only the pleasure of mockery. Even while you laugh at it, the old incantation works. Willy-nilly the fairies allure, the monsters alarm, the labyrinthine adventures draw you on.[42]

The Tale of Sir Thopas dramatises a similarly amused and affectionate return to poetic childhood. It encourages us to measure the prodigious development experienced by English poetry in the course of Chaucer's lifetime. But it also reminds us that this humble species of narrative 'represents the vigorous wild stock upon which were grafted Chaucer's other more literary and sophisticated styles'.[43] One of these styles, that which predominates in *The Knight's Tale*, sees Chaucer (like Tasso two centuries later) exploring the more sombre possibilities of this 'Italian epic' tradition. But we more often discover Chaucer employing less sombre (but no less sophisticated) styles to explore those adventurous and fantastic themes (with their attendant 'fairies and flying horses') that are more typical of this *ottava rima* tradition; more typical of Boccaccio's early writings; and more typical, too, of English romance. For Chaucer is not, on the whole, a sombre poet; nor is he, compared with Dante and Petrarch, a markedly serious or single-minded one. The *Commedia* and the *Canzoniere*, deliberately restricted in stylistic range and generic variety, are consciously difficult and exclusive. *The Canterbury Tales*, by contrast, is endlessly accommodating. It seems only appropriate to close this account of Chaucer's Italian adventures with the English voice that he chose for himself as a Canterbury pilgrim. In Harry Bailey's opinion, '"this may wel be rym dogerel"' (VII, 925); but in the pilgrim Chaucer's opinion, '"it is the beste rym I kan"' (VII, 928). Perhaps Chaucer is, after all, open to the suggestion that 'the beste rym he koude', for all its lofty, illustrious and European pretensions, still bears a family resemblance to those popular English 'romances of prys':

> Now holde youre mouth, *par charitee*,
> Bothe knyght and lady free,
>   And herkneth to my spelle;
> Of bataille and of chivalry,
> And of ladyes love-drury
>   Anon I wol yow telle.
>
> Men speken of romances of prys,
> Of Horn child and of Ypotys,
>   Of Beves and sir Gy,
> Of sir Lybeux and Pleyndamour,—
> But sir Thopas, he bereth the flour
>   Of roial chivalry!   (VII, 891–902)

Conclusion

When visiting Florence in the spring of 1373, Chaucer may have heard Boccaccio referred to as the distinguished elder statesman of Tuscan culture who was to deliver a series of lectures on Dante's *Commedia* at the church of Santo Stefano di Badia. He may have associated Boccaccio with the performances of *cantari* which took place regularly at the Piazza San Martino.[1] He may have associated him with both church and piazza and have formed a mental image of Boccaccio as a writer who gains inspiration from (and lends inspiration to) both illustrious and popular traditions of vernacular narrative. But even if Chaucer had never heard Boccaccio mentioned by name—which seems most unlikely—he was nevertheless capable of forming a comparable mental image simply through his reading of Boccaccio's works: for comparative study of the *Troilus* and the *Filostrato* suggests that Chaucer was a diligent and discerning Italianist. His own willingness to draw inspiration from a generous range of literary forms and styles qualified him to recognise a similar willingness in the Italian poet. The remarkable variety of influences operative in Boccaccio's early writings (which proved so congenial to Chaucer) reflects the extraordinary circumstances of Boccaccio's upbringing and literary formation at Angevin Naples.

Chaucer's verse and Boccaccio's early writings hold the ancient Latin poets in the highest regard. Both poets are fascinated by the relationship of their Christian epoch to the world of pagan antiquity; and both are evidently convinced that their relationship to the *auctores* lends definition to their own enterprise as vernacular authors. Each writer is similarly conscious of the power and prestige of the French vernacular, for each grew to maturity in an environment in which French culture was deeply and firmly rooted. Each poet derives much material from French romances, and each is familiar with the frameworks and narrative procedures of French dream poetry and the *dits amoreux*. The *Roman de la Rose* was of fundamental importance to both writers. Boccaccio's *Amorosa Visione*—which prepared the way for the Petrarchan *Trionfi*—extends the enterprise of transitional works, such as Brunetto Latini's *Tesoretto*, which had prepared the way for the *Commedia* by adapting the lessons of the *Rose* to Italian conditions. Five generations of

Italian poets participate in this Italianising of the *Rose*: Brunetto; Durante; Dante; Boccaccio; Petrarch. Chaucer's Englishing of the *Rose* begins with diligent, close translation and becomes ever more subtle as his poetic career progresses. The sheer, concentrated brilliance of Chaucer's single-handed achievement in fashioning a *vulgaris illustris* from the scant resources of a retarded native vernacular has no parallel in the history of European poetry.

For both Chaucer and Boccaccio, the *Commedia* stands as the supreme model of what a vernacular poet might achieve. Boccaccio was, from the first, a tireless champion of Dante's reputation, and he made extensive use of the *Commedia*'s verse form. Chaucer was more wary of bringing the form and content of the *Commedia* within the bounds of his own *makinge*: but he outshines Boccaccio in furthering the aesthetic and poetic principles of the *Commedia*. Chaucer is the more convincing continuator of Dante's great example of vernacular eloquence.

Chaucer was evidently alert to Boccaccio's imperfect comprehension of aristocratic values and vocabulary. Although he shared Boccaccio's mercantile origins (and later worked in close collaboration with Italian merchants), Chaucer was distanced from such origins by his education in an aristocratic household. Boccaccio remained an outsider to the courtly world; his poetic evocations of *cortesia* actually furthered the debasement of courtly language that Petrarch found cause to complain of whilst lamenting the popular reception of Dante's *Commedia*. Perhaps this was why Chaucer was anxious to publicise his admiration for Petrarch and Dante whilst passing over Boccaccio in silence. It is quite evident that Chaucer, in completing his *Troilus*, is willing to countenance association with the greatest of poetic masters, ancient and modern. Had he acknowledged Boccaccio by name, this might have prompted comparisons that he was willing to avoid. And when, unsolicited, we make such comparisons, we discover that the literary strategy pursued throughout Boccaccio's early writings is essentially similar to that developed throughout Chaucer's career: the marriage of popular and illustrious traditions. It is, after all, this fruitful union which makes possible the variegated and densely-peopled worlds of the *Decameron* and *The Canterbury Tales*.

Bibliography

With the exception of a few essential works of reference, the bibliography is restricted to works cited or alluded to in the text. The bibliography is organised under the following headings, which refer to the language of the primary material under consideration:

A   English
B   French (with Anglo-Norman and Provençal)
C   Italian (with Neapolitan)
D   Latin
E   European and General

Each heading is sub-divided as follows:

(i) Primary sources
(ii) Secondary sources

For a detailed guide to writings on and by Boccaccio, see Enzo Esposito, *Boccacciana. Bibliografia delle edizioni e degli scritti critici (1939–1974)* (Ravenna, 1976). See also Enrico Giaccherini, 'Chaucer and the Italian Trecento: a Bibliography', in Boitani, *Italian Trecento*, pp. 297–304.

A(i) English

Andrew, Malcolm and Ronald Waldron, eds, *The Poems of the Pearl Manuscript*, York Medieval Texts, second series (London, 1978)
Bliss, A. J., ed., *Sir Launfal* (London, 1960)
———, ed., *Sir Orfeo*, second edition (Oxford, 1966)
Brewer, D. S., ed., *The Parlement of Foulys* (London, 1960)
———, ed., Geoffrey Chaucer, *The Works 1532. With supplementary material from the Editions of 1542, 1561, 1598 and 1602*, Scolar Press Facsimile (Menston, 1969)
Brook, G. L., ed., *The Harley Lyrics*, fourth edition (Manchester, 1968)

Bryan, W. F. and G. Dempster, *Sources and Analogues of Chaucer's Canterbury Tales* (Chicago, 1941)

Caxton, W., ed., *The book of fame made by G. Chaucer* (Westminster, London, 1486?)

Crow, M. M. and C. C. Olson, eds, *Chaucer Life-Records* (Oxford, 1966)

Cunningham, see Pearsall

De Vries, F. C., ed., *Floris and Blauncheflur* (Groningen, 1966)

Dempster, see Bryan

DiMarco, V. and L. Perelman, eds, *The Middle English Letter of Alexander to Aristotle, Costerus*, NS, 13 (Amsterdam, 1978)

Fellows, Jennifer L., 'Sir Beves of Hampton: Study and Edition', unpublished Ph.D. dissertation, Cambridge University, 5 vols (1980)

Fox, Denton, ed., *The Poems of Robert Henryson* (Oxford, 1981)

French, W. H. and C. B. Hale, eds, *Middle English Metrical Romances* (New York, 1930)

Gibbs, A. C., ed., *Middle English Romances*, York Medieval Texts (London, 1966)

Hale, see French

Hall, Joseph, ed., *King Horn* (Oxford, 1901)

Hausknecht, Emil, ed., *Floris and Blauncheflur* (Berlin, 1885)

Kölbing, E., ed., *The Romance of Sir Beues of Hamtoun*, EETS, ES, 46, 48, 65 (1885–94)

Leach, MacEdward, ed., *Amis and Amiloun*, EETS, OS, 203 (1937)

McNeill, G. P., ed., *Sir Tristrem*, Scottish Text Society (1886)

O'Sullivan, M. I., ed., *Firumbras and Otuel and Roland*, EETS, OS, 198 (1935)

Olson, see Crow

Pearsall, Derek and I. C. Cunningham, eds, *The Auchinleck Manuscript, National Library of Scotland Advocates' MS 19.2.1*, a facsimile (London, 1977)

Pearsall, Derek, ed., *Piers Plowman by William Langland. An edition of the C-text* (London, 1978)

Perelman, see DiMarco

Robinson, F. N., ed., *The Works of Geoffrey Chaucer*, second edition (OUP, London, 1966)

Root, R. K., ed., *The Book of Troilus and Criseyde* (Princeton, 1926)

Sands, D. B., ed., *Middle English Verse Romances* (New York, 1966)

Schmidt, A. V. C. and Nicholas Jacobs, eds, *Medieval English Romances, Two Parts* (London, 1980)

Skeat, W. W., ed., *The Tale of Gamelyn* (Oxford, 1893)

———, ed., *The Complete Works of Geoffrey Chaucer*, 7 vols (Oxford, 1894–7)

Sutherland, R., *'The Romaunt of the Rose' and 'Le Roman de la Rose'. A Parallel-Text Edition* (Oxford, 1967)

Trounce, A. McI., ed., *Athelston*, EETS, OS, 224 (1951)

Waldron, see Andrew

Wattie, Margaret, ed., *The Middle English Lai le Freine*, Smith College Studies in Modern Languages, 10, number 4 (Northampton, Mass., 1929)

Windeatt, B. A., ed., Geoffrey Chaucer, *Troilus and Criseyde. A New Edition of 'The Book of Troilus'* (London & NY, 1984)

Zupita, J., ed., *Guy of Warwick*, EETS, ES, 42, 49, 59 (1883, 1887, 1891)

Barney, Stephen A., ed., *Chaucer's 'Troilus'. Essays in Criticism* (London, 1980)

Baugh, A. C., ed., *A Literary History of England* (New York, 1948)

———, 'The Middle English Romances: Some Questions of Creation, Presentation and Preservation', *Speculum*, 42 (1967), 1–31

Bennett, J. A. W., *The Parlement of Foules. An Interpretation* (Oxford, 1957)

———, *Chaucer's 'Book of Fame'. An Exposition of the 'House of Fame'* (Oxford, 1968)

———, 'Little Gidding. A Poem of Pentecost', *Ampleforth Journal*, 79 (1974), Part I, 60–73

———, 'Chaucer, Dante and Boccaccio', *Accademia Nazionale dei Lincei*, Quaderno 234 (Rome, 1977)

———, see also Heyworth

Benson, David C., *The History of Troy in Middle English Literature* (Woodbridge, Suffolk, 1980)

Benson, Larry D., 'The Literary Character of Anglo-Saxon Poetry', PMLA, 81 (1966), 334–41

Benson, Robert G., *Medieval Body Language: A Study of the Use of Gesture in Chaucer's Poetry*, Anglistica, 21 (Copenhagen, 1980)

Billings, Anna Hunt, *A Guide to the Middle English Romances* (New York, 1901; reprinted NY, 1967)

Bloomfield, Morton W., 'Distance and Predestination in *Troilus and Criseyde*', PMLA, 72 (1957), 14–26

Boitani, Piero, *Chaucer and Boccaccio*, Medium Aevum Monographs, NS, VIII (Oxford, 1977)

———, *English Medieval Narrative in the Thirteenth and Fourteenth Centuries*, translated by J. K. Hall (Cambridge, 1982)

———, ed., *Chaucer and the Italian Trecento* (Cambridge, 1983)

———, 'Style, Iconography and Narrative: the Lesson of the *Teseida*', in Boitani, *Trecento*, 185–199

Brewer, D. S., ed., *Chaucer and Chaucerians* (London, 1966)

———, 'The relationship of Chaucer to the English and European traditions', in Brewer, *Chaucer and Chaucerians*, 1–38

———, *Towards a Chaucerian Poetic*, Sir Israel Gollancz Memorial Lecture, British Academy, 1974 (London, 1974)

———, ed., *Writers and their Background: Geoffrey Chaucer* (London, 1974)

———, *Chaucer and his world* (London, 1978)

———, ed., *Chaucer: The Critical Heritage*, 2 vols (London, 1978)

Brink, Bernhard ten, *Geschichte der Englischen Litteratur*, 2 vols (Berlin, 1877; Strasbourg, 1893)

Brunner, Karl, 'Chaucer's *House of Fame*', *Rivista di letterature moderne*, NS, I (1950–1), 344–50

Burnley, J. D., *Chaucer's Language and the Philosophers' Tradition* (Cambridge, 1979)

Burrow, John, *Ricardian Poetry* (London, 1971)

———, *Medieval Writers and Their Work. Middle English Literature and its Background 1100–1500* (Oxford, 1982)

———, 'Introduction' to Scattergood and Sherborne, *English Court Culture*, ix

Child, C. G., 'Chaucer's *House of Fame* and Boccaccio's *Amoroso Visione*', MLN, 10 (1895), 190–92

Childs, Wendy, 'Anglo-Italian Contacts in the Fourteenth Century', in Boitani, *Trecento*, 65–87

Clanchy, M. T., *From Memory to Written Record. England 1066–1307* (London, 1979)

Clemen, Wolfgang, *Chaucer's Early Poetry*, translated by C. A. M. Sym (London, 1963)

Clogan, P. M., 'Chaucer and the *Thebaid* Scholia', SP, 61 (1964), 599–615

Clough, Cecil H., 'Introduction: Culture and Society', in *Profession, Vocation and Culture in Later Medieval England. Essays dedicated to the Memory of A. R. Myers* (Liverpool, 1982), 1–2

Coleman, Janet, *Piers Plowman and the 'Moderni'* (Rome, 1981)

———, 'English Culture in the Fourteenth Century', in Boitani, *Trecento*, 32–63

Cummings, Hubertis M., *The Indebtedness of Chaucer's Works to the Italian Works of Boccaccio (A Review and Summary)* (Cincinnati, 1916; reprinted NY, 1965)

Davis, Norman et al., eds, *A Chaucer Glossary* (Oxford, 1979)

Du Boulay, F. R. H., 'The Historical Chaucer', in Brewer, *Writers*, 33–57

Fansler, D. J., *Chaucer and the Roman de la Rose* (New York, 1914)

Ford, Boris, ed., *The New Pelican Guide to English Literature*, 10 vols (Harmondsworth, 1982–4). Vol I, Part One, *Medieval Literature: Chaucer and the Alliterative Tradition*

Fowler, Alastair, *Triumphal Forms. Structural patterns in Elizabethan poetry* (Cambridge, 1970)

Gist, M. A., *Love and War in the Middle English Romances* (Philadelphia and London, 1947)

Glasscoe, Marion, ed., *The Medieval Mystical Tradition in England. Dartington 1984* (Cambridge, 1984)

Green, R. F., 'The *Familia Regis* and the *Familia Cupidinis*', in Scattergood and Sherborne, *English Court Culture*, 87–108

Hammond, E. P., *Chaucer: A Bibliographical Manual* (New York, 1908)

Harbert, Bruce, 'Chaucer and the Latin Classics', in Brewer, *Writers and their Background*, 137–53

Hartung, A. E., see Severs

Havely, N. R., *Chaucer's Boccaccio* (Cambridge, 1980)

Heyworth, P. L., ed., *Medieval Studies for J. A. W. Bennett* (Oxford, 1981)

Hoffman, Richard L., *Ovid and the Canterbury Tales* (OUP, London, 1966)

Howard, Donald R., *The Idea of the Canterbury Tales* (Berkeley, 1976)

———, *Writers and Pilgrims. Medieval Pilgrimage Narratives and Their Posterity* (Berkeley, 1980)

Hulbert, J. R., *Chaucer's Official Life*. The University of Chicago, A Dissertation (Wisconsin, 1912)

James, M. R., Medieval Manuscripts. Part III of Biblioteca Pepysiana, *A Descriptive Catalogue of the Library of Samuel Pepys*, 4 parts (London, 1914–22)

Jordan, Robert, 'Chaucerian Romance?', in Haidu, *Approaches*, 223–34

Kane, George, *Middle English Literature* (London, 1951)

Kean, P. M., *Chaucer and the Making of English Poetry*, 2 vols (London, 1972)

Kennedy, A. G., see Tatlock

Koeppel, E., 'Chauceriana', *Anglia*, 14 (1891–2), 227–67

Koonce, B. G., *Chaucer and the Tradition of Fame* (Princeton, 1966)

Kurath, Hans et al., eds, *Middle English Dictionary*, A–O, incomplete (Michigan and OUP, London, 1954)

Larner, John, 'Chaucer's Italy', in Boitani, *Trecento*, 7–32

Lewis, C. S., 'What Chaucer Really Did to *Il Filostrato*', *Essays and Studies by Members of the English Association*, 17 (1932), 56–75

———, *The Allegory of Love* (Oxford, 1936)

———, *The Discarded Image* (Cambridge, 1964)

Loomis, L. H., 'Chaucer and the Breton Lays of the Auchinleck MS', SP, 38 (1941), 14–33

———, 'The Auchinleck Manuscript and a Possible London Bookshop of 1330–1340', PMLA, 57 (1942), 595–627

Lowes, J. L., '*The Franklin's Tale*, the *Teseide*, and the *Filocolo*', MP, 15 (1917–8), 689–728

Mann, Jill, *Chaucer and Medieval Estates Satire. The Literature of Social Classes and the 'General Prologue' to the 'Canterbury Tales'* (Cambridge, 1973)

———, 'Chaucerian Themes and Style in the *Franklin's Tale*', in Ford, *Chaucer and the Alliterative Tradition*, 133–53

Martin, Judith E., 'Studies in Some Early Middle English Romances', unpublished Ph.D. dissertation, Cambridge University (1968)

Mathew, Gervase, *The Court of Richard II* (London, 1968)

McCall, John P., '*Troilus and Criseyde*', in CCS (see Rowland), 446–463

McGrady, Donald, 'Chaucer and the *Decameron* Reconsidered', CR, 12 (1977–8), 1–26

Meech, S. B., 'Chaucer and an Italian Translation of the *Heroides*', PMLA, 45 (1930), 110–28

———, *Design in Chaucer's 'Troilus'* (Syracuse UP, 1959; reprinted NY, 1969)

Mehl, Dieter, *The Middle English Romances of the Thirteenth and Fourteenth Centuries* (London, 1968)

Minnis, A. J., *Chaucer and Pagan Antiquity* (Cambridge, 1982)

Murray, James A. H. et al, eds, *The Oxford English Dictionary* (Oxford, 1933)

Muscatine, Charles, *Chaucer and the French Tradition* (Berkeley, 1957)

———, *Poetry and Crisis in the Age of Chaucer* (Notre Dame, 1972)

Norton-Smith, John, *Geoffrey Chaucer* (London, 1974)

———, 'Chaucer's *Anelida and Arcite*', in Heyworth, *Studies for J. A. W. Bennett*, 81–99

Orme, Nicholas, 'The Education of the Courtier', in Scattergood and Sherborne, *English Court Culture*, 63–85

Owings, M. A., *The Arts in the Middle English Romances* (New York, 1952)

Owst, G. W., *Literature and Pulpit in Medieval England* (Cambridge, 1933)

Palmer, John N., 'The Historical Context of the *Book of Duchess*': a Revision', CR, 8 (1973–4), 253–61

Payne, Robert O., *The Key of Remembrance: A Study of Chaucer's Poetics* (New Haven, 1963)

———, 'Chaucer and the Art of Rhetoric', in CCS, 42–64

Pearsall, Derek, 'The Development of Middle English Romance', *Medieval Studies*, 27 (1965), 91–116

———, *Old English and Middle English Poetry* (London, 1977)

—, 'The Troilus Frontispiece and Chaucer's Audience', *The Yearbook of English Studies*, 7 (1977), 68–74

Pratt, R. A., 'Chaucer and *Le Roman de Troyle et de Criseida*', SP, 53 (1956), 509–39

Rajna, Pio, 'Le origini della novella narrata dal "Frankeleyn" nei *Canterbury Tales* del Chaucer', *Romania*, 32 (1903), 204–67

Ramsey, Lee C., *Chivalric Romances. Popular Literature in Medieval England* (Bloomington, 1983)

Robbins, R. H., ed., *Chaucer at Albany* (New York, 1975)

—, 'Geoffroi Chaucier, Poète Français, Father of English Poetry', CR, 13 (1978–9), 93–115

Robinson, Ian, *Chaucer and the English Tradition* (Cambridge, 1972)

Rowland, Beryl, ed., *Companion to Chaucer Studies*, revised edition (New York and Oxford, 1979)

Ruggiers, Paul G., 'The Italian Influence on Chaucer', in CCS, 160–84

Salter, Elizabeth, 'Chaucer and Internationalism', *Studies in the Age of Chaucer*, 2 (1980), 71–79

—, *Fourteenth-Century English Poetry. Contexts and Readings* (Oxford, 1983)

Scattergood, V. J. and J. W. Sherborne, eds, *English Court Culture in the Later Middle Ages* (London, 1983)

Scattergood, V. J., 'Literary Culture at the Court of Richard II', in Scattergood and Sherborne, 29–43

Schlauch, Margaret, 'Chaucer's Prose Rhythms', PMLA, 65 (1950), 568–89

—, 'The Art of Chaucer's Prose', in Brewer, *Chaucer and Chaucerians*, 140–63

Schoeck, Richard J. and Jerome Taylor, eds, *Chaucer Criticism*, 2 vols (Notre Dame and London, 1961)

Severs, J. Burke, ed. vols 1–2, and Albert E. Hartung, ed. vols 3–6, *A Manual of Writings in Middle English*, incomplete (Hamden, Connecticut, 1967–)

Shannon, E. F., 'Chaucer and Lucan's *Pharsalia*', MP, 16 (1918–19), 609–14

—, *Chaucer and the Roman Poets* (Cambridge, Mass., 1929)

Sherborne, J. W., see Scattergood

—, 'Aspects of English Court Culture in the Later Fourteenth Century', in Scattergood and Sherborne, 1–27

Shook, Laurence, K., '*The House of Fame*', in CCS, 414–27

Smalley, Beryl, *English Friars and Antiquity in the Early Fourteenth Century* (Oxford, 1960)

Spearing, A. C., *Criticism and Medieval Poetry*, second edition (London, 1972)

—, *Medieval Dream-Poetry* (Cambridge, 1976)

Strohm, Paul, 'Chaucer's Audience', *Literature and History*, 5 (1977), 26–41

Sypherd, W. O., *Studies in Chaucer's Hous of Fame* (London, 1907)

Takada, Yasunari, 'On the Consummation of Troilus' Love: Chaucer's *Troilus and Criseyde*, III. 1247–60', *Studies in Language and Culture*, 8 (1982), 103–129

Tatlock, J. S. P. and A. G. Kennedy, *A Concordance to the Complete Works of Geoffrey Chaucer and to the Romaunt of the Rose* (Washington, 1927)

Thrupp, Sylvia, L., *The Merchant Class of Medieval London (1300–1500)* (Chicago, 1948)

Trounce, A. McI., 'The English Tail-rhyme Romances', *Medium Aevum*, 1 (1932), 87–108, 168–82, 2 (1933), 34–57, 189–98, 3 (1934), 30–50

Wallace, David J., 'Chaucer and the Poets of the Pieno Trecento', *Comparison*, 13 (1982), 98–119

——, 'Chaucer and Boccaccio's Early Writings', in Boitani, *Trecento*, 141–62

——, 'Some Amendments to the Apparatus of Robinson's *Works of Chaucer*', *Notes and Queries*, NS, 30 (1983), p. 202

——, 'Mystics and Followers in Siena and East Anglia: A study in Taxonomy, Class and Cultural Mediation', in Glasscoe, *Mystical Tradition*, 169–191

Wells, J. E., *A Manual of the Writings in Middle English* (New Haven, 1916)

Wetherbee, Winthrop, 'The Descent from Bliss: *Troilus* III. 1310–1582', in Barney, *Chaucer's 'Troilus'*, 297–317

Wheeler, Bonnie, 'Dante, Chaucer and the Ending of *Troilus and Criseyde*', *Philological Quarterly*, 61 (1982), 105–123

Wilkins, Nigel, 'Music and Poetry at Court: England and France in the Late Middle Ages', in Scattergood and Sherborne, 183–204

Wimsatt, James I., *Chaucer and the French Love Poets. The Literary Background of the Book of the Duchess* (Chapel Hill, 1968)

——, 'Machaut's *Lay de Confort* and Chaucer's *Book of the Duchess*', in Robbins, *Chaucer at Albany*, 11–26

——, 'Guillaume de Machaut and Chaucer's *Troilus and Criseyde*', *Medium Aevum*, 45 (1976), 277–93

——, *Chaucer and the Poems of 'Ch'* (Cambridge, 1982)

Windeatt, Barry A., 'The "Paynted Process": Italian to English in Chaucer's *Troilus*', *English Miscellany*, 26–27 (1977–8), 79–103

——, '"Love that Oughte Ben Secree" in Chaucer's *Troilus*', CR, 14 (1979–80), 116–31

——, *Chaucer's Dream Poetry: Sources and Analogues* (Cambridge, 1982)

——, 'Chaucer and the *Filostrato*', in Boitani, *Trecento*, 163–83

Wise, B. A., *The Influence of Statius Upon Chaucer* (Baltimore, 1911; reprinted NY, 1967)

Wittig, Susan, *Stylistic and narrative structures in the Middle English Romances* (Austin and London, 1978)

Zacher, Christian K., *Curiosity and Pilgrimage. The Literature of Discovery in Fourteenth-Century England* (Baltimore, 1976)

B(i)   French (with Anglo-Norman and Provençal)

Baird, J. L. and J. R. Kane, *La Querelle de la Rose: Letters and Documents* (Chapel Hill, 1978)

Conlon, D. J., ed., *Le Rommant de 'Guy de Warwik' et de 'Herolt d'Ardenne'* (Chapel Hill, 1971)

Ewert, Alfred, ed., *Gui de Warewic. Roman du XIIIe siècle*, 2 vols (Paris, 1932)

——, ed., Marie de France, *Lais* (Oxford, 1944)

Gschwind, Ulrich, ed., *Le Roman de Flamenca*, 2 Parts, Romanica Helvetica, 86A, 86B (Berne, 1976)

Hoepffner, Ernst, ed., *Les Oeuvres de Guillaume de Machaut*, 3 vols (Paris, 1908–21)

Kane, J. R., see Baird

Krüger, Felicitas, ed., *Li romanz de Floire et Blancheflor*, Romanische Studien, 45 (Berlin, 1938)

Lecoy, Félix, ed., *Le Roman de la Rose*, 3 vols (Paris, 1975–9)

du Méril, M. Edéléstand, ed., *Floire et Blanceflor* (Paris, 1856)

Oulmont, Charles, *Les Débats du Clerc et du Chevalier dans la littérature poétique du Moyen-Age* (Paris, 1911)

Pelan, M. M., ed., *Floire et Blancheflor*, revised edition (Paris, 1956)

——, ed., *Floire et Blancheflor. Seconde Version* (Paris, 1975)

Scheler, Auguste, ed., *Oeuvres de Froissart: Poésies*, 3 vols (Brussels, 1870–72)

Stürzinger, J. J., ed., Guillaume de Deguileville, *Le pèlerinage de vie humaine* (London, 1893)

Sutherland, see A(i), Sutherland

Wahle, Hermann, ed., *Die Pharsale des Nicholas von Verona* (Marburg, 1888)

Whitehead, F., ed., *La Chastelaine de Vergi*, second edition (Manchester, 1951)

B(ii)   French (with Anglo-Norman and Provençal)

Badel, Pierre-Yves, *Le Roman de la Rose au XIVe siècle. Étude de la réception de l'oeuvre* (Geneva, 1980)

Bozzolo, Carla, *Manuscrits des traductions françaises d'oeuvres de Boccace. XVe siècle* (Padua, 1973)

Dahlberg, Charles, tr., *The Romance of the Rose* (Princeton, 1971)

Duggan, Joseph, *The Song of Roland: Formulaic Style and Poetic Craft* (Berkeley, 1973)

Fleming, John V., 'The Moral Reputation of the *Roman de la Rose* before 1400', *Romance Philology*, 18 (1964–5), 430–35

——, *The 'Roman de la Rose'. A Study in Allegory and Iconography* (Princeton, 1969)

Guilbert, L. et al., eds, *Grand Larousse de la langue française*, 7 vols (Paris, 1971–8)

Hanning, Robert W., *The Individual in Twelfth-Century Romance* (New Haven and London, 1977)

Kelly, Douglas, 'The Source and Meaning of *Conjointure* in Chrétien's *Erec* 14', *Viator*, 1 (1970), pp. 179–200

Luria, Maxwell, *A Reader's Guide to the 'Roman de la Rose'* (Hamden, Connecticut, 1982)

Muscatine, Charles, 'The Emergence of Psychological Allegory in Old French Romance', PMLA, 68, 1160–82

Reinhold, Joachim, *Floire et Blancheflor. Étude de littérature comparée* (Paris, 1906)

Vinaver, Eugène, *The Rise of Romance* (Oxford, 1971)

West, G. D., *An Index of Proper Names in French Arthurian Prose Romances* (Toronto, 1978)

Wimsatt, James I., see A(ii), Wimsatt
Zumthor, Paul, *Essai de poétique médiévale* (Paris, 1972)

C(i)   *Italian (with Neapolitan)*

Altamura, Antonio, 'Un'ignota redazione del cantare di Florio e Bianco-
fiore—Contributo alla storia del *Filocolo*', *Biblion*, I (1946–7), 92–133
Balduino, Armando, ed., *Cantari del Trecento* (Milan, 1970)
———, ed., see Branca, *Opere di GB*, Vol. III
Barbi, M. et al, eds, *Le opere di Dante. Testo critico della Società Dantesca
Italiana*, second edition (Florence, 1960)
———, see Busnelli
Battaglia, Salvatore, ed., Andrea Capellano, *Trattato d'Amore. Testo latino del
sec. XII con due traduzioni toscane inedite del sec. XIV* (Rome, 1947)
Bensa, Enrico, *Francesco di Marco da Prato. Notizie e documenti sulla mercatura
italiana del secolo XIV* (Milan, 1928)
Biagi, Ovido, *Zibaldone Boccaccesco Laurenziano*, see D(i), Biagi
Bigi, Emilio, ed., commentary by G. Ponte, *Opere di Francesco Petrarca*,
second edition (Milan, 1964)
Branca, Vittore, ed., *Amorosa Visione* (Florence, 1944)
Branca, Vittore, ed., *Tutte le opere di Giovanni Boccaccio*, 12 vols, incomplete
(Milan, 1964–), 6 vols to date:
Vol. I   V. Branca, *Profilo biografico*
          V. Branca, ed., *Caccia di Diana*
          A. E. Quaglio, ed., *Filocolo*
Vol. II   V. Branca, ed., *Filostrato*
          A. Limentani, ed., *Teseida delle nozze d'Emilia*
          A. E. Quaglio, ed., *Comedia delle ninfe fiorentine*
Vol. III V. Branca, ed., *Amorosa Visione*
          A. Balduino, ed., *Ninfale fiesolano*
          P. G. Ricci, ed., *Trattatello in laude di Dante*
Vol. IV   V. Branca, ed., *Decameron*
Vol. VI   G. Padoan, ed., *Esposizioni sopra la Comedìa di Dante*
Vol. X   V. Zaccaria, ed., *De mulieribus claris*
Bruscoli, N., ed., Giovanni Boccaccio, *L'Ameto. Lettere. Il Corbaccio*, Sd'I,
182 (Bari, 1940)
Busnelli, G. and G. Vandelli, eds, Dante Alighieri, *Il Convivio*, second edition
with an appendix by A. E. Quaglio (Florence, 1964)
Castets, Ferdinand, ed., *Il Fiore. Poëme italien du XIIIe siècle, en CCXXXII
sonnets imité du Roman de la Rose par Durante* (Paris, 1881)
Chiappelli, L., 'Una lettera mercantile del 1330 e la crisi del commercio
italiano nella prima metà del Trecento', ASI, 82 (1924), 229–56
Claricio, Girolamo, ed., *Amorosa Visione di Messer Giov. Bocc.* (Milan, 1521)
Clogan, Paul M., 'Two Verse Commentaries on the Ending of Boccaccio's
Filostrato', M&H, NS, 7, 147–52
Contini, Gianfranco, ed., *Poeti del Duecento*, 2 vols (Milan–Naples, 1960)
Corti, Gino, 'Consigli sulla mercatura di un anonimo trecentista', ASI, 110
(1952), 114–9

Crescini, V., ed., *Il Cantare di Fiorio e Biancifiore*, 2 vols (Bologna, 1889–1899)

De Robertis, Domenico, 'Cantari antichi', *Studi di filologia italiana*, 28 (1970), 67–175

Del Lungo, I., *Dino Compagni e la sua cronica*, 3 vols (Florence, 1879–87)

Di Benedetto, L., ed., *Poemetti allegorico-didattici del secolo XIII*, Sd'I, 184 (Bari, 1941)

Favati, Guido, ed., *Il Novellino* (Genoa, 1970)

Federzoni, L., ed., see C(ii), Carducci

de' Ferrari, Gabriel Giolito, ed., *Amorosa Visione di M. Gio. Bocc.* (Venice, 1549)

Limentani, Alberto, *Dal Roman de Palamedés ai Cantari di Febus-el-Forte* (Bologna, 1962)

———, ed., see Branca, *Opere di GB*, Vol. II

Marti, M., ed., *Poeti del Dolce stil nuovo* (Florence, 1969)

———, ed., see Segre

McKenzie, K., ed., Antonio Pucci, *Le noie*, Elliott Monographs, 26 (Princeton and Paris, 1931)

Neri, F., et al., eds, Francesco Petrarca, *Rime · Trionfi e Poesie Latine* (Milan–Naples, 1951)

Padoan, G., ed., see Branca, *Opere di GB*, Vol. VI

Pellegrini, C., ed., Benedetto Alberti, *Della Famiglia* (Florence, 1946)

Petrocchi, Giorgio, ed., Dante Alighieri, *La Commedia secondo l'antica vulgata*, 4 vols (Milan, 1966–7)

Quaglio, A. E., ed., see Branca, *Opere di GB*, Vols I, II

———, see Busnelli

Rajna, Pio, 'Il Cantare dei Cantari e il Serventese del Maestro di tutti l'Arti', *Zeitschrift für Romanische Philologie*, 2 (1878), 220–54, 419–37

Ricci, P. G., ed., Giovanni Boccaccio, *Opere in versi. Corbaccio. Trattatello in Laude di Dante. Prose Latine. Epistole* (Milan–Naples, 1965)

———, ed., see Branca, *Opere di GB*, Vol. III

Salinari, Carlo and Natalino Sapegno, eds, *Elegia di madonna Fiammetta* (Turin, 1976)

Sapegno, Natalino, ed., *Poeti minori del Trecento* (Milan–Naples, 1952)

———, ed., *Rimatori del tardo Trecento* (Rome, 1967)

———, ed., see Salinari

Schiaffini, A., ed., Paolo da Certaldo, *Libro di buoni costumi* (Florence, 1945)

Segre, Cesare, ed., *Volgarizzamenti del Due e Trecento* (Turin, 1953)

—— and Mario Marti, eds, *La Prosa del Duecento* (Milan–Naples, 1959)

Simonelli, Maria, ed., Dante Alighieri, *Il Convivio* (Bologna, 1966)

Sinclair, John D., tr., *The Divine Comedy of Dante Alighieri*, 3 vols (OUP, London, 1971)

Vandelli, G., ed., see Busnelli

Varanini, G., ed., *Cantari religiosi senesi del Trecento*, Sd'I, 230 (Bari, 1965)

C(ii)   *Italian (with Neapolitan)*

Alessio, G, see Battisti

Altamura, Antonio, *La letteratura dell'età angioina* (Naples, 1952)

————, see C(i), Altamura

Balduino, Armando, 'Tradizione canterina e tonalità popolareggianti nel *Ninfale fiesolano*', SsB, 2 (1964), 25–80

Ballerini, Carlo, ed., *Atti del convegno di Nimega sul Boccaccio (28–29–30 Ottobre 1975)* (Bologna, 1976)

Barbina, Alfredo, ed., *Concordanze del 'Decameron'*, 2 vols (Florence, 1969)

Battaglia, Salvatore, *Grande Dizionario della Lingua Italiana*, A-MED (9 vols), incomplete (Turin, 1961–)

Battisti, C. and G. Alessio, eds, *Dizionario Etimologico Italiano*, 5 vols (Florence, 1950–7)

Bec, Christian, *Les marchands écrivains. Affaires et humanisme à Florence 1375–1434* (Paris, 1967)

Benedetto, L. F., *Il 'Roman de la Rose' e la letteratura italiana*, Beihefte zur Zeitschrift für Romanische Philologie, 21 (Halle, 1910)

Thomas G. Bergin, *Boccaccio* (New York, 1981)

————, see Wilkins

Billanovich, G., 'Dalla *Commedia* e dall'*Amorosa Visione* ai *Trionfi*', GSLI, 123 (1946), 1–52

————, *Petrarca letterato. I. Lo Scrittoio del Petrarca* (Rome, 1947)

————, 'Tra Dante e Petrarca', IMU, 8 (1965), 1–44

Bosco, Umberto, ed., *Enciclopedia Dantesca*, 6 vols (Rome, 1970–8)

Branca, D., *I romanzi italiani di Tristano e la Tavola Ritonda* (Florence, 1968)

Branca, Vittore, *Il cantare trecentesco e il Boccaccio del Filostrato e del Teseida* (Florence, 1936)

————, 'Per la genesi dei *Trionfi*', *Rinascita*, 4 (1941), 681–708

————, 'L'*Amorosa Visione* (tradizione, significati, fortuna)', ASNSP, second series, 11 (1942), 20–47

————, 'Nostalgie tardogotiche e gusto del fiabesco nella tradizione narrativa dei cantari', in Pighi, *Studi in onore di Flora*, 88–108

————, *Giovanni Boccaccio. Profilo biografico*, see Branca, *Opere di GB*, Vol. I

————, *Boccaccio medievale*, third edition (Florence, 1970)

————, 'Giovanni Boccaccio, rinnovatore dei generi letterari', in Ballerini, *Convegno di Nimega*, 13–35

Brand, C. P., *Ludovico Ariosto. A preface to the 'Orlando Furioso'* (Edinburgh, 1974)

Carducci, Giosue, 'Ai parentali di Giovanni Boccacci', *Edizione nazionale delle opere di Giosue Carducci*, directed by L. Federzoni, 30 vols (Bologna, 1945–62), XI, 311–334

Casella, M. T., 'Nuovi argomenti per l'attribuzione del volgarizzamento di Valerio Massimo al Boccaccio', SsB, 10 (1977–8), 109–21

Ceva, Bianca, *Brunetto Latini. L'Uomo e l'Opera* (Milan–Naples, 1965)

Contini, Gianfranco, 'Un nodo della cultura medievale: la serie *Roman de la Rose—Fiore—Divina Commedia*', LI, 25 (1973), 162–189

Contini, Gianfranco, 'Fiore, Il', ED, II, 895–901

Croce, Benedetto, *Poesia popolare e poesia d'arte* (Bari, 1933)

Davidsohn, R., *Forschungen zur älteren Geschichte von Florenz*, 4 vols (Berlin, 1896–1908)

Debenedetti, S., 'Troilo cantore', GSLI, 66 (1915), 414–25

De Robertis, Domenico, 'Per la storia del testo della canzone "La dolce vista e 'l bel guardo soave"', *Studi di filologia italiana*, 10 (1952), 5–24

————, 'Problemi di metodo nell'edizione dei cantari', in *Studi e problemi di critica testuale. Convegno di Studi di Filologia italiana nel Centenario della Commissione per i Testi di Lingua (7–9 aprile 1960)* (Bologna, 1961), 119–38

Di Benedetto, F., see E(i), Di Benedetto, 'Considerazioni sullo Zibaldone Laurenziano'

Di Stefano, G., 'Dionigi da Borgo San Sepolcro, amico del Petrarca e maestro del Boccaccio', *Atti dell'Accademia delle Scienze di Torino. II. Classe di scienze morali, storiche e filologiche*, 96 (1961–2), 272–314

Dionisotti, C., 'Appunti su antichi testi', IMU, 7 (1964), 99–131

Folena, G., ed., see Parodi

Foster, Kenelm, *The Two Dantes and Other Studies* (London, 1977)

————, *Petrarch. Poet and Humanist* (Edinburgh, 1984)

Franceschetti, Antonio, 'Rassegna di studi sui cantari', LI, 25 (1973), 556–74

Ghisalberti, A. M., ed., *Dizionario biografico degli italiani*, AARON-COLLEGNO (22 vols), incomplete (Rome, 1960–)

Gozzi, Maria, 'Ricerche storiche intorno a Binduccio dello Scelto', SsB, 3 (1965), 25–39

————, 'Sulle fonti del *Filostrato*. Le narrazioni di argomento troiano', SsB, 5 (1968), 123–209

Griffin, N. E. and A. B. Myrick, tr., *The Filostrato of Giovanni Boccaccio: A Translation with Parallel Text* (London, 1929; reprinted NY, 1967)

Hollander, Robert, *Boccaccio's Two Venuses* (New York, 1977)

Hyde, J. K., *Society and Politics in Medieval Italy. The Evolution of the Civil Life, 1000–1350* (London, 1973)

Kirkham, Victoria, 'Reckoning with Boccaccio's "Questioni d'amore"', MLN, 89 (1974), 47–59

Kirkpatrick, Robin, *Dante's Paradiso and the Limitations of Modern Criticism* (Cambridge, 1978)

Léonard, E. G., *Boccace et Naples* (Paris, 1944)

————, *Les Angevins de Naples* (Paris, 1954)

Lovera, Luciano, ed., *Concordanza della Commedia di Dante Alighieri*, 3 vols (Turin, 1975)

Malagoli, Luigi, 'Timbro della prosa e motivi dell'arte del Boccaccio nel *Filocolo*', *Studi mediolatini e volgari*, 6–7 (1959), 97–111

Marletta, F., 'Di alcuni rapporti del *Filostrato* del Boccaccio con la poesia popolare', in *Miscellanea a Carlo Pascal* (Catania, 1913), 201–19

Mazzoni, Francesco, 'Latini, Brunetto', ED, III, 579–88

Melli, E., 'Riecheggiamenti danteschi in un cantare toscano del secolo XIV', *Filologia romanza*, 5 (1958), 82–87

Monteverdi, Angelo, 'Un libro d'Ovidio e un passo del *Filocolo*', in Hatcher and Selig, *Studia in honorem Spitzer* (see E(ii), Selig), 335–340

Muscetta, Carlo, *Giovanni Boccaccio* (Bari, 1972)

Myrick, see Griffin

Padoan, Giorgio, 'Mondo aristocratico e mondo comunale nell'ideologia e nell'arte di Giovanni Boccaccio', SsB, 2 (1964), 81–216

————, 'Petrarca, Boccaccio e la scoperta delle Canarie', IMU, 7 (1964), 263–77

————, 'Teseo "figura redemptoris" e il cristianesimo di Stazio', in G. Padoan, *Il pio Enea, l'empio Ulisse* (Ravenna, 1977), 125–150

————, 'Boccaccio, Giovanni', ED, I, 645–50

Parodi, E. G., *Lingua e letteratura. Studi di Teoria linguistica e di Storia dell'italiano antico*, edited by G. Folena, 2 vols (Venice, 1957)

————, 'La cultura e lo stile del Boccaccio' (1913), in Parodi, *Lingua e letteratura*, 470–79

————, 'Osservazioni sul *cursus* nelle opere latine e volgari del Boccaccio' (1913), in Parodi, *Lingua e letteratura*, 480–92

Petronio, Giuseppe, ed., *Dizionario enciclopedico della letteratura italiana*, 6 vols (Bari, 1966–70)

Pighi, G. B. et al., eds, *Studi di varia umanità in onore di Francesco Flora* (Milan, 1963)

Previté-Orton, C. W., 'Italy, 1250–1290', in Bury, *Medieval History* (see E(ii), Bury), VI, 166–204

Quaglio, A. E., 'Valerio Massimo e il *Filocolo* di Giovanni Boccaccio', CNeo, 20 (1960), 45–77

————, 'Tra fonti e testo del *Filocolo*', GSLI, 139 (1962), 321–369, 513–540

————, 'Boccaccio e Lucano: una concordanza e una fonte dal *Filocolo* all'*Amorosa Visione*', CNeo, 23 (1963), 153–71

Ramat, Rafaello, 'Boccaccio 1340–1344', *Belfagor*, 19 (1964), 17–30, 154–74

Reynolds, Barbara, ed., *The Cambridge Italian Dictionary*, 2 vols (Cambridge, 1962, 1981)

Ricci, P. G., 'Notizie e documenti per la biografia del Boccaccio. 4. L'incontro napoletano con Cino da Pistoia', SsB, 5 (1968), 1–18

Richards, Earl Jeffrey, *Dante and the 'Roman de la Rose'. An Investigation into the Vernacular Narrative Context of the 'Commedia'* (Tübingen, 1981)

Roncaglia, Aurelio, 'Per la storia dell'ottava rima', CNeo, 25 (1965), 5–14

Ryan, Christopher, John, 'The Theme of Free Will in Dante's Minor Works, with Particular Reference to Aspects of the Cultural Background' (unpublished Ph.D. dissertation, Cambridge University, 1978)

Ryder, Alan, *The Kingdom of Naples Under Alfonso the Magnanimous* (Oxford, 1976)

Sabatini, Francesco, *Napoli angioina: cultura e società* (Naples, 1975)

Sapegno, Natalino, *Storia letteraria del Trecento* (Milan–Naples, 1963)

————, *Pagine di storia letteraria*, second edition, (Palermo, 1966)

————, 'Antonio Pucci', in Sapegno, *Pagine*, 133–181

————, *Il Trecento*, third edition (Milan, 1973)

Sapori, A., *Studi di storia economica medievale*, second edition (Florence, 1947)

Silber, Gordon R., 'Alleged Imitations of Petrarch in the *Filostrato*', MP, 37 (1939–40), 113–24

Vallone, A., 'Lectura Dantis', ED, III, 606–9

Vanossi, Luigi, 'Detto d'Amore', ED, II, 393–5

Velli, Giuseppe, 'Cultura e *Imitatio* nel primo Boccaccio', ASNSP, series II, 37 (1968), 65–93

Weise, Georg, *L'Italia e il mondo gotico* (Florence, 1956)

Weiss, Roberto, *The Renaissance Discovery of Classical Antiquity* (Oxford, 1969)

Wilkins, E. H., *A History of Italian Literature* (London, 1954); revised by T. G. Bergin (Cambridge, Mass., 1974)

————, 'Boccaccio's first octave', *Italica*, 33 (1956), 19

D(i)   Latin

Battaglia, Salvatore, ed., see C(i), Battaglia (for Andreas Capellanus, *De Amore*)

Biagi, Ovido, *Lo Zibaldone Boccaccesco Mediceo Laurenziano Plut. XXIX–8*, a facsimile (Florence, 1915)

Bigi, Emilio, ed., *Opere di Petrarca*, see C(i), Bigi

Camera, M., ed., *Annali delle Due Sicilie*, 2 vols (Naples, 1841–60)

Di Benedetto, F., 'Considerazioni sullo Zibaldone Laurenziano del Boccaccio e restauro testuale della prima redazione del *Faunus*', IMU, 14 (1971), 91–129

Gallo, Ernest, *The 'Poetria Nova' and its Sources in Early Rhetorical Doctrine* (The Hague–Paris, 1971)

Marigo, A., ed. and tr., Dante Alighieri, *De Vulgari Eloquentia*, third edition, updated by P. G. Ricci (Florence, 1957)

Martellotti, G. et al., eds, Francesco Petrarca, *Prose* (Milan–Naples, 1955)

Massèra, A. F., ed., Giovanni Boccaccio, *Opere Latine Minori*, Sd'I, 111 (Bari, 1928)

Neri, F., ed., Petrarca, *Rime . . . Poesie Latine*, see C(i), Neri

Ricci, see Marigo

Ricci, P. G., ed., Boccaccio, *Opere in versi . . . Prose Latine. Epistole*, see C(i), Ricci

Romano, V., ed., Giovanni Boccaccio, *Genealogia deorum gentilium*, 2 vols, Sd'I, 200–1 (Bari, 1951)

Rossi, V., ed., Francesco Petrarca, *Le Familiari*, 4 vols (Florence, 1933–42)

Zaccaria, V., ed., see C(i), Branca, *Opere di GB*, Vol. X

D(ii)   Latin

Glare, P. G. W., ed., *Oxford Latin Dictionary* (Oxford, 1982)

Osgood, Charles G., tr., *Boccaccio on Poetry* (Princeton, 1930)

E(ii)   European and General

Auerbach, Erich, *Literary Language and Its Public in Late Latin Antiquity and in the Middle Ages*, translated by Ralph Manheim (London, 1965)

Auerbach, Erich, *Mimesis. The Representation of Reality in Western Literature*, translated by Willard R. Trask (Princeton, 1968)

Bloomfield, Morton, W., 'The Problem of the Hero in the Later Medieval Period', in Burns and Reagan, *Concepts*, 27–48

Burns, N. T. and C. J. Reagan, *Concepts of the Hero in the Middle Ages and Renaissance* (London, 1976)

Bury, J. B., ed., *The Cambridge Medieval History*, 8 vols (Cambridge, 1911–36)

Culler, Jonathan, *Structuralist Poetics* (London, 1975)

Curtius, E. R., *European Literature and the Latin Middle Ages*, translated by Willard R. Trask (London, 1953)

Daiches, David and Anthony Thorlby, eds, *The Mediaeval World* (London, 1973)

Ebel, Uda, 'Die literarischen Formen der Jenseits- und Endzeitsvisionen', in Frappier, *Grundriss, VI: La Littérature Didactique, Allégorique et Satirique*, 2 vols, I, 181–215

Foley, John Miles, ed., *Oral Traditional Literature. A Festschrift for Albert Bates Lord* (Columbus, Ohio, 1981)

Ford, Boris, *New Pelican Guide* (see A(ii)), *1. Medieval Literature. Part Two: The European Inheritance*

Frappier, Jean et al, *Grundriss der Romanischen Literaturen des Mittelalters*, incomplete (Heidelberg, 1968–)

Goldin, Frederick, *The Mirror of Narcissus in the Courtly Love Lyric* (New York, 1967)

Gordon, R. K., *The Story of Troilus as told by Benoît de Sainte-Maure, Giovanni Boccaccio (translated into English prose), Geoffrey Chaucer and Robert Henryson* (London, 1934)

Haidu, Peter, ed., *Approaches to Medieval Romance*, Yale French Studies, 51 (1974)

Hatcher, A. G. and K. L. Selig, eds, *Studia philologica et litteraria in honorem L. Spitzer* (Bern, 1958)

Hausknecht, Emil, 'Die verbreitung der sage von Flore und Blancheflor ausserhalb Englands', in Hausknecht, *Floris and Blauncheflur* (see A(i), Hausknecht), 1–88

Jauss, Hans Robert, 'Die Minneallegorie als esoterische Form einer neuen ars amandi', in Frappier, *Grundriss*, VI, I, 224–44

——, *Toward an Aesthetic of Reception*, translated by Timothy Bahti (Minneapolis, 1982)

Kelly, Douglas, 'Matière and *genera dicendi* in Medieval Romance', in Haidu, *Approaches*, 147–59

Lopez, R. S. and I. W. Raymond, *Medieval Trade in the Mediterranean World* (London, 1955)

Murphy, James J., *Rhetoric in the Middle Ages. A History of Rhetorical Theory from Saint Augustine to the Renaissance* (Berkeley, Los Angeles and London, 1974)

Ong, Walter J., *Orality and Literacy. The Technologizing of the Word* (London and NY, 1982)

Raymond, I. W., see Lopez

Reagan, C. J., see Burns

Scaglione, Aldo, 'Boccaccio, Chaucer and the Mercantile Ethic', in Daiches and Thorlby, *Mediaeval World*, 579–600

Selig, K. L., ed., see Hatcher

Spitzer, Leo, 'Note on the Poetic and Empirical "I" in Medieval Authors', *Traditio*, 4 (1946), 414–422

Thorlby, Anthony, see Daiches

Young, Karl, *The Origin and Development of the Story of Troilus and Criseyde* (Chaucer Society, 1908; reprinted NY, 1968)

Notes

Introduction pp. 1–2

1 For Chaucer's use of the *Teseida* (which is discussed briefly in chapter 7 below) see Piero Boitani, *Chaucer and Boccaccio*, Medium Aevum Monographs, NS, VIII (Oxford, 1977).

2 *The Origin and Development of the Story of Troilus and Criseyde* (Chaucer Society, 1908; reprinted New York, 1968), p. 181.

3 *The Indebtedness of Chaucer's Works to the Italian Works of Boccaccio (A Review and Summary)* (Cincinnati, 1916; reprinted NY, 1965), Preface and p. 198.

4 Meech tells us that his work received encouragement in its early stages from 'Professor Karl Young, who made me a Chaucerian': see *Design in Chaucer's 'Troilus'* (Syracuse UP, 1959; reprinted NY, 1969), p. ix.

5 The essay first appeared in *Essays and Studies by Members of the English Association*, 17 (1932), pp. 56–75; I quote from this source. The essay is reprinted in *Chaucer: The Critical Heritage*, edited by Derek Brewer, 2 vols (London, 1978), II, 468–85; *Chaucer's 'Troilus'. Essays in Criticism*, edited by Stephen A. Barney (London, 1980), pp. 37–54. It appears in abridged form in *Chaucer Criticism*, edited by Richard J. Schoeck and Jerome Taylor, 2 vols (Notre Dame & London, 1961), II, 16–33.

6 Lewis, p. 56.

7 See Lewis, pp. 59, 61, 62, 66.

8 *Design*, pp. vii–viii. There is no evidence for the historical existence of the 'Maria d'Aquino' that Meech supposes Boccaccio to have courted: see Vittore Branca, *Giovanni Boccaccio. Profilo biografico* in *Tutte le opere di Giovanni Boccaccio*, edited by V. Branca, 12 vols, incomplete (Milan, 1964–), I, pp. 27–28.

9 Elizabeth Salter, 'Chaucer and Internationalism', *Studies in the Age of Chaucer*, 2 (1980), 71–79 (p. 71).

10 Vittore Branca, *Boccaccio medievale* (Florence, 1956[1], 1964[2], 1970[3]). I employ the third edition, in which Branca admits that his choice of title was 'scopertamente polemico' (p. X).

Chapter 1: Accommodating Dante pp. 5–22

1 For details of Chaucer's 1373 visit to Genoa and Florence, see *Chaucer Life-Records*, edited by M. M. Crow and C. C. Olson (Oxford, 1966), pp. 32–40; D. S. Brewer, *Chaucer and his world* (London, 1978), pp. 119–31.

2 See Branca, *Profilo*, pp. 82–3.

168

3 See the edition by P. G. Ricci in Branca, *Opere di GB*, Volume III; and see Branca, *Profilo*, p. 108.

4 See *Esposizioni sopra la Comedìa di Dante*, edited by G. Padoan in Branca, *Opere di GB*, Volume VI. See also G. Padoan, 'Boccaccio, Giovanni', in *Enciclopedia Dantesca*, edited by Umberto Bosco, 6 vols (Rome, 1970–8), I, 645–50; A. Vallone, 'Lectura Dantis', ED III, 606–9.

5 See Padoan, ED I, 648. Boccaccio was appointed on 25 August (Padoan, *Esposizioni*, p. XV).

6 See 'Franco Sacchetti' in *Rimatori del tardo Trecento*, edited by Natalino Sapegno (Rome, 1967), pp. 3–83; for the *canzone* lamenting Boccaccio ('Or è mancata ogni poesia') see pp. 61–6.

7 All these datings are approximate: see Branca, *Opere di GB*, II, 3–5; I, 47; II, 231.

8 For the date of the *Visione*, see Branca, *Opere di GB*, III, 3–6. For the political and social conditions surrounding its composition, see Branca, *Profilo*, pp. 53–66; Rafaello Ramat, 'Boccaccio 1340–1344', *Belfagor* 19 (1964), pp. 17–30, 154–74.

9 My translation of Branca, *Opere di GB*, III, 3.

10 Ramat sees the *Visione* as 'l'opera più grossamente macchinosa e poeticamente povera' of Boccaccio (*1340–1344*, p. 154); Branca refers to 'questo mediocrissimo poemetto' (*Opere di GB*, III, 20) and Carlo Muscetta, *Giovanni Boccaccio* (Bari, 1972) is similarly uncomplimentary (pp. 110–14). Gabriel Giolito de' Ferrari, the third six-teenth-century publisher of the B text (Venice, 1549), offers an intriguing account of the poem's defects in his preface ('Ai Lettori'). He proposes that Boccaccio 'nel verso fu meno che mediocre', but believes the work to be worthy of notice because it is 'molto dotta, piacevole, e piena di bellissime moralità, e in ultimo di questo eccellente Autore . . .'.

11 E. H. Wilkins believed AV to be only half-complete: see *A History of Italian Literature* (London, 1954), p. 105; Wilkins, *History*, revised by T. G. Bergin (Cambridge Mass., 1974), p. 105. This, however, seems most unlikely. For a consider-ation of HF as a poem of crisis, see Charles Muscatine, *Poetry and Crisis in the Age of Chaucer* (Notre Dame & London, 1972), pp. 108–132.

12 See E. Koeppel, 'Chauceriana', *Anglia*, 14 (1891–2), 227–67 (pp. 234–8); C. G. Child, 'Chaucer's *House of Fame* and Boccaccio's *Amorosa Visione*', *Modern Language Notes*, 10 (1895), pp. 190–92; Cummings, *Indebtedness*, pp. 13–32; J. L. Lowes, 'The Franklin's Tale, the Teseide, and the Filocolo', *Modern Philology*, 15 (1917–18), pp. 689–728.

The case for the influence of AV on HF was advanced by Koeppel and Child and dismissed by Cummings. Lowes exposed some of the glaring deficiencies of Cummings' methods: but Cummings work (the only book on Boccaccio listed or referred to in the second edition of F. N. Robinson's *The Works of Geoffrey Chaucer*) has enjoyed a long and misleading influence. Cummings' synopsis of the *Visione* (pp. 14–16) is so distorted and inaccurate that his claim that 'in this summary of the A.V. one finds no marked similarities to any of Chaucer's narratives' (p. 16) can hardly be denied.

13 The poem survives in two versions, referred to by V. Branca as 'A' and 'B' in his editions which appear in *Opere di GB*, Volume III. Version A survives in 8 MSS; the earliest B text is that printed by Girolamo Claricio in 1521. Branca's claim that the B text represents Boccaccio's own revisions seems to be generally accepted: see *Opere di GB*, III, 19, 541–9. Branca concedes, however, that there are clear signs that Claricio tinkered with Boccaccio's text (p. 546).

14 See D. S. Brewer, 'The relationship of Chaucer to the English and European traditions', in *Chaucer and Chaucerians*, edited by D. S. Brewer (London, 1966), pp. 1–38; John Burrow, *Ricardian Poetry* (London, 1971), pp. 12–23, 35–46; P. M. Kean, *Chaucer and the Making of English Poetry*, Volume I, *Love Vision and Debate* (London, 1972), pp. 1–23. I find myself in broad agreement with the findings of these scholars. For the view that Chaucer's poetic language is minimally indebted to that of his English

predecessors, see Derek Pearsall, *Old English and Middle English Poetry* (London, 1977), pp. 199–200.

15 See Robinson, *Works*, p. 782. The text of *Havelock* follows that in Part One of *Medieval English Romances*, edited by A. V. C. Schmidt and Nicholas Jacobs, Two Parts (London, 1980).

16 The text of *Sir Orfeo* follows that in Schmidt and Jacobs, Part One, which is based on the Auchinleck MS (MS Advocates' 19.2.1 in the National Library of Scotland). See also *Sir Orfeo*, edited by A. J. Bliss, second edition (Oxford, 1966), which provides excellent editions of all three extant versions of the poem.

17 Chaucer's mastery of syntax does, from the first, set him apart from the English romancers: see Pearsall, *OE & ME Poetry*, p. 200. The same holds true for Boccaccio and the *canterini*: see below, p. 85.

18 For parallels between SO and Chaucer's MerchT, FranklT, WBT, see L. H. Loomis, 'Chaucer and the Breton Lays of the Auchinleck MS', *Studies in Philology*, 38 (1941), 14–33 (pp. 24–29); Bliss, *Sir Orfeo*, pp. xlviii–ix. The series of sudden and gruesome deaths depicted within the temple of Mars in KnT I (A) 1995–2026 may well draw inspiration from SO 387–402.

19 In explaining *voussoir* ('vousour', SO 363) Schmidt and Jacobs remark that this is 'a surprisingly technical term for an unlearned poet' (I, 202–3).

20 Karl Brunner, 'Chaucer's *House of Fame*', *Rivista di letteratura moderne*, NS, 1 (1950–1), 344–50 goes as far as declaring Chaucer's edifice to be 'ganz und gar eine gotische Kirche des 14. Jahrhunderts' (p. 346).

21 Kean, *Making*, I, 111.

22 Chaucer adverts to his translation of the *Rose* in LGW F 327–31, G 253–57. See Ronald Sutherland, *'The Romaunt of the Rose' and 'Le Roman de la Rose'. A Parallel-Text Edition* (Oxford, 1967).

Sutherland concludes his 'Introduction' by affirming that there is 'no reason to doubt that Fragment A of the *Romaunt*, save for a few revisions, is Chaucer's genuine work' (p. xxxiv).

23 For this dating, see John N. Palmer, 'The Historical Context of the *Book of the Duchess*: a Revision', *The Chaucer Review*, 8 (1973–4), pp. 253–61.

24 For an excellent account of this tradition, see James Wimsatt, *Chaucer and the French Love Poets. The Literary Background of the Book of the Duchess* (Chapel Hill, 1968).

25 In Machaut's *Dit de la Fonteinne amoreuse*, written in 1360, the poet-narrator overhears a young lord (his patron) deliver a fifty-stanza complaint; having written it down, he later presents the lord with his own poem, thereby meeting his demand for a suitable complaint. See Wimsatt, *Love Poets*, pp. 112–17; Wimsatt, 'Machaut's *Lay de Confort* and Chaucer's *Book of the Duchess*' in *Chaucer at Albany*, edited by R. H. Robbins (New York, 1975), 11–26 (pp. 14–15). Wimsatt argues that Chaucer's BD played an active part in extending the tradition of the *dits amoreux* by influencing Froissart's *Dit dou bleu Chevalier* (*Love Poets*, pp. 129–33).

26 See Salter, *Internationalism*, pp. 75–76.

27 R. H. Robbins, 'Geoffroi Chaucier, Poète Français, Father of English Poetry', CR, 13 (1978–9), pp. 93–115.

28 *The Allegory of Love* (Oxford, 1936), p. 164. Lewis examines BD 985–93. See also Brewer, *English and European traditions*, pp. 2–8.

29 *Studies in Chaucer's House of Fame* (London, 1907), p. 13.

30 See, for example, pp. 44–72. Sypherd's work is 'still indispensable' (Laurence K. Shook, 'The House of Fame' in *Companion to Chaucer Studies*, edited by Beryl Rowland (NY and Oxford, 1979), 414–27 (p. 414)).

31 Charles Muscatine, *Chaucer and the French Tradition* (Berkeley and London, 1957), p. 7.

32 *Chaucer and the Roman de la Rose* (New York, 1914), p. 73.

33 Wolfgang Clemen, *Chaucer's Early Poetry*, translated by C. A. M. Sym (London,

1963), p. 67. See also J. A. W. Bennett, *Chaucer's 'Book of Fame'* (Oxford, 1968): Bennett begins his first chapter by tracing parallels between BD and HF. His book provides the most exhaustive exposition of the classical traditions behind HF.

34 All quotations follow Dante Alighieri, *La Commedia secondo l'antica vulgata*, edited by Giorgio Petrocchi, 4 vols (Milan, 1966–7).

35 For a refinement of this bald synopsis, see *De Vulgari Eloquentia*, edited and translated by A. Marigo, third edition updated by P. G. Ricci (Florence, 1957), pp. CXX–CXXI.

36 Bernhard ten Brink saw HF as a deliberate attempt 'eine Art Gegenstück zu Dantes gewaltiger Dichtung zu liefern': see *Geschichte der Englischen Litteratur*, 2 vols (Berlin, 1877; Strasbourg, 1893), II, 106–111 (p. 111). See also B. G. Koonce, *Chaucer and the Tradition of Fame* (Princeton, 1966).

37 See Erich Auerbach, *Literary Language and Its Public in Late Latin Antiquity and in the Middle Ages*, translated by Ralph Manheim (London, 1965), pp. 317–20.

38 Inf XV, 85 (' "come l'uom s'etterna" '). For the text of the *Tesoretto*, see *Poeti del Duecento*, edited by Gianfranco Contini, 2 vols (Milan–Naples, 1960), II, 175–277. For a succinct account of Brunetto's writings and their significance, see Francesco Mazzoni, 'Brunetto Latini', ED III, 579–88.

39 See L. F. Benedetto, *Il 'Roman de la Rose' e la letteratura italiana* (Halle, 1910), pp. 89–100, 163; Bianca Ceva, *Brunetto Latini. L'Uomo e l'Opera* (Milan–Naples, 1965), p. 92; *Dizionario enciclopedico della letteratura italiana*, edited by Guiseppe Petronio, 6 vols (Bari, 1966–70); ED III, 580; Uda Ebel, 'Die literarischen Formen der Jenseits- und Endzeitvisionen', in *Grundriss der Romanischen Literaturen des Mittelalters*, edited by Jean Frappier et al., *VI: La Littérature Didactique, Allégorique et Satirique*, 2 vols (Heidelberg, 1968–70), I, 181–215 (pp. 213–14).

40 See 411–26; 909–14; 1113–24; 2900–2. It is possible that Brunetto originally intended to write a *prosimetrum* in the style of Boethius, Bernardus Silvestris and Alanus de Insulis: see Contini, II, 215.

41 Both works date from the period 1260–6; they show similarities in points of detail and in general organisation. Brunetto refers readers to his 'gran Tesoro' in *Tesoretto* 1350–6. In Inf XV, 119–20 Brunetto commends ' "il mio Tesoro" ' to Dante.

42 See Ceva, pp. 92–3; Contini, II, 183; H. R. Jauss, 'Die Minneallegorie als esoterische Form einer neuen *ars amandi*', *Grundriss*, VI, I, 224–44 (pp. 241–3).

43 See 1453–86, where Larghezza warns against spending money in brothels, in taverns and on capons, partridge and fish; and see the worldly advice offered by Cortesia (esp. 1747–56).

44 The major segment of the poem ends with this Retraction; the part which follows, referred to as *La Penetenza*, seems somewhat autonomous: see Contini, II, 259.

45 The 'fino amico caro' referred to may be Rustico di Filippo, dedicatee of Brunetto's metrical letter *Il Favolello*.

46 See *Le Roman de la Rose*, edited by F. Lecoy, 3 vols (Paris, 1975–9), 1606–12; Rom, Fragment A, 1605–12; LGW F 315–18, G 241–4. On *curiositas*, see Christian K. Zacher, *Curiosity and Pilgrimage* (Baltimore, 1976), pp. 18–41.

47 See Robert O. Payne, *The Key of Remembrance: A Study of Chaucer's Poetics* (New Haven, 1963); Payne, 'Chaucer and the Art of Rhetoric' in CCS, pp. 42–64. Brunetto's *Rettorica* (which dates from the period of his French exile) is a translation of and commentary on the first seventeen chapters of Cicero's *De Inventione*.

48 See Benedetto, pp. 89–100 and passim; and see above, pp. 53–7.

49 For the influence of the *Tesoretto* on these two poems, see Mazzoni, ED III, 585; the *Detto* is seen as 'autenticamente "brunettiano" '. Both poems have been attributed to Dante; each survives in a unique version which was copied by the same hand: see Luigi Vanossi, '*Detto d'Amore*', ED II, 393–5; DELI II, 288; G. Contini, '*Fiore, Il*', ED II, 895–901. Both poems are contained in *Poemetti allegorico-didattici del secolo XIII*,

edited by L. Di Benedetto, Scrittori d'Italia 184 (Bari, 1941). Quotations from *Il Fiore*, however, follow the edition of Ferdinand Castets (Paris, 1881).

50 See DELI III, 283–4.

51 Branca notes numerous echoes in his earlier edition of the poem (Florence, 1944), pp. 387–496.

52 See G. Billanovich, 'Dalla *Commedia* e dall'*Amorosa Visione* ai *Trionfi*', *Giornale storico della letteratura italiana*, 123 (1946), pp. 1–52.

53 Quoted in V. Branca, 'Per la genesi dei *Trionfi*', *Rinascita*, 4 (1941), 681–708 (p. 686).

54 Adapted from Branca's replication of Claricio's title-page in *Opere di GB*, III, 541–2.

55 See Billanovich, *Ai Trionfi*, p. 29.

56 See Wimsatt, *Love Poets*, pp. 49–69 (esp. 53–57).

57 Wimsatt notes (p. 125) that the majority of *dits* do not have a dream frame comparable to that of RR; neither does the *Tesoretto*, *Detto d'Amore*, *Il Fiore* or *L'Intelligenza*. For Machaut, see *Les Oeuvres de Guillaume de Machaut*, edited by Ernst Hoepffner, 3 vols (Paris, 1908–21); for Froissart, see *Oeuvres de Froissart: Poésies*, edited by Auguste Scheler, 3 vols (Brussels, 1870–2).

58 Wimsatt, p. 111. The allegorical identity of Boccaccio's female guide remains uncertain, although it has been much disputed: Crescini sees her as 'Fortezza', Branca as 'Virtù' and Muscetta as 'Venere celeste': see Muscetta, p. 111.

59 Compare, for example, the following lengthy discourses by the female guides on Fortune; both are punctuated by brief comments from the unhappy auditor: AV (A) XXXI, 65–XXXVI, 66; RF 2403–3076.

60 See Wimsatt, *Love Poets*, p. 120.

61 See *Olympia* in Giovanni Boccaccio, *Opere in versi. Corbaccio. Trattatello in Laude di Dante. Prose Latine. Epistole*, edited by P. G. Ricci (Milan–Naples, 1965), pp. 672–91 (lines 1–7). The *Buccolicum carmen* was completed by 1369: see Branca, *Profilo*, pp. 182–3.

62 See Sypherd, pp. 128–32; and see V. Branca, 'L'*Amorosa Visione* (tradizione, significati, fortuna)', *Annali della R. Scuola normale superiore di Pisa*, second series, 11 (1942), 20–47 (pp. 46–47).

63 Branca, *Opere di GB*, III, 12 (my translation).

64 See (A&B): XXXVI, 31–3; XLIX, 73–88; and see Branca, *L'AV (tradizione)*, p. 30.

65 XI (A), 19 ('morning star'); XXVII (A), 28 ('into his control'). For Boccaccio's use of such *cantare* phrases and epithets, see above, pp. 90–97. It is interesting to note that both these phrases were later revised: the popular adjective 'mattutina' is replaced by the solemnly classical 'micante' (XI (B), 19) and 'in sua balia' becomes 'in le sue mani' (XXVIII (B), 28).

66 See Branca's discussion of Boccaccio's usage of the adjective 'gentile' (*Opere di GB*, III, 558).

67 See above, p. 75.

68 DVE II, vi, 7 ('whom loving solicitude invites me ("nos") to visit').

69 In a letter dated 28 August 1341, Boccaccio laments the death of Dionigi di Borgo San Sepolcro, the man who did most to kindle his early interest in classical learning. For the text of this *epistola* (which survives only in an Italian translation) see Ricci, *Opere in versi*, pp. 1074–7; for its (disputed) date, see Branca, *Profilo*, p. 53. For Dionigi, see above, pp. 25–6.

70 These glosses were probably not completed until Boccaccio had returned to Florence: see Branca, *Profilo*, p. 47.

71 See Inf II, 7–9; Purg I, 7–12, XXIX, 37–42.

72 See Fs I, 1–5; Tes III, 1–2; AV II (A&B), 1–18.

73 This process is readily discernible in HF even without the aid of the rubrics ('Proem'; 'The Invocation', etc.) with which modern editors draw it to our attention:

see *The Complete Works of Geoffrey Chaucer*, edited by Walter W. Skeat, 7 vols (Oxford, 1894–7), III; Robinson, *Works*. Skeat and Robinson fail to inform us that there is no MS or early textual authority for their rubrics.

74 Boccaccio associates himself with Orfeo in the neo-Dantean invocation which opens the *Visione*'s second canto (A&B, II, 8).

In the Middle Ages (building upon the precedent of Ovid, Met X, 78–85), Orpheus' artful manipulation of nature was associated with pederasty, the perversion of nature. Writers who abused their natural talents could come under similar suspicions: see, for example, RR 19599–656.

75 See (A&B) XXVIII, 67–69; HF 321–2, 334–5, 340. Such parallels between lovers are examined by Child, pp. 190–92.

76 See (A&B) XXV, 61–69; HF 388–396. These reports derive (ultimately) from the direct speech of *Heroides* II. In AV (B) 'Fillis' becomes 'Fillida'.

77 Given the immense popularity of the *Heroides* it is probable that both writers made use of derivative and intermediary texts: see Robinson, notes to 388ff, 391, 392, 405–26 (p. 781). S. B. Meech presents a remarkably persuasive case for Chaucer's acquaintance with Filippo Ceffi's *Heroides* translation: see 'Chaucer and an Italian Translation of the *Heroides*', PMLA, 45 (1930), pp. 110–28.

78 A and B texts differ here in points of detail. My summary follows the A text. Many of the correspondences which appear between AV and HF are due, of course, to their usage of common sources.

79 See III, 1–IV, 3. This rebellion is staged in front of a double gate comparable to that in PF 123–54.

80 The relevant passages are set out and considered by Koeppel (pp. 235–8) and Sypherd (pp. 109–113).

81 For Statius' supposed Toulosan citizenship, see Branca, *Opere di GB*, III, 590; and see Purg XXI, 89.

82 Robinson erroneously notes that AV 'has no parallel list' (note to 1460, p. 786).

83 Note to 1547, p. 786.

84 The autonomy is but momentary, as Boccaccio's guide explains:

'Ver è ch'alcun più ch'altro valoroso
meritò fama, ma se 'l mondo dura
è perirà il suo nome glorioso.' (XXX (A), 22–24)

Time sweeps away Fame: here we see the sequence of the Petrarchan *Trionfi* in miniature.

85 Derek Brewer, *Towards a Chaucerian Poetic*, Sir Israel Gollancz Memorial Lecture, British Academy 1974 (London, 1974), p. 8.

86 For the view that the *Anelida* ends complete, see J. Norton Smith, 'Chaucer's *Anelida and Arcite*', in *Medieval Studies for J. A. W. Bennett*, edited by P. L. Heyworth (Oxford, 1981), pp. 81–99.

87 All but two of the stanzas in Anelida's *compleynt* consist of nine lines. Stanza 75 of the *Intelligenza* is quoted above, p. 12: this may have furnished Chaucer with a name for his heroine. Stanzas 15–58 of this poem describe the gems in the lady's crown: these include 'berillo' (25, 1–9; see HF, 1184).

Chapter 2: Cultural Formations   pp. 23–37

1 For the view that Boccaccio is unrivalled as a literary innovator, see Vittore Branca, 'Giovanni Boccaccio, rinnovatore dei generi letterari', in *Atti del convegno di Nimega sul Boccaccio (28–29–30 Ottobre 1975)*, edited by Carlo Ballerini (Bologna, 1976), pp. 13–35.

2 The scholarly reconstruction of Boccaccio's Naples has made steady progress over the last hundred years and has recently received fresh impetus through two important works: Francesco Sabatini, *Napoli angioina: cultura e società* (Naples, 1975); N. R.

Havely, *Chaucer's Boccaccio* (Cambridge, 1980), pp. 1–12. Havely's succinct and suggestive essay does not take Sabatini's monumental study into account.

3 See the edition of the *Caccia* by Branca in Branca, *Opere di GB*, Volume I.

4 See Branca, *Profilo*, pp. 15, 50–53; E. G. Léonard, *Boccace et Naples* (Paris, 1944), p. 19.

5 See E. G. Léonard, *Les Angevins de Naples* (Paris, 1954), p. 476; Alan Ryder, *The Kingdom of Naples Under Alfonso the Magnanimous* (Oxford, 1976), pp. 16–17.

6 Much precious material from the Neapolitan State Archives was destroyed by German soldiers in 1943 as a reprisal measure: but many of Robert's legislative and judicial acts are recorded in *Annali delle Due Sicilie*, edited by M. Camera, 2 vols (Naples, 1841–60), vol. II.

An assassination attempt took place on 17 April 1330 as the royal family was seated at table. (This event may have lent a certain topical piquancy to the poisoned peacock episode in Fc II, 32–40). Barbaric punishments were meted out to the son, servant and daughters of the assailant: see *Annali*, II, 362–3.

7 See *Comedia delle ninfe fiorentine*, edited by A. E. Quaglio in Branca, *Opere di GB*, Vol. II, XXXV–XXXVIII; *Elegia di madonna Fiammetta*, edited by C. Salinari & N. Sapegno (Turin, 1976), II, p. 36.

8 CN XXXVIII, 109 ('la mobile pompa dei grandi'); *Elegia*, II, p. 36 ('lieta, pacifica, abbondevole, magnifica, e sotto ad un solo re').

9 'Mondo aristocratico e mondo comunale nell'ideologia e nell'arte di Giovanni Boccaccio', *Studi sul Boccaccio*, 2 (1964), pp. 81–216.

10 See Padoan, pp. 114, 88–90.

11 See Branca, *Profilo*, pp. 101–4, 129–33, 168–73.

12 For the Italian text, see Ricci, *Opere in versi*, 1150–93 (pp. 1158–60). Only the concluding sentences of the Latin original survive: see Ricci, p. 1193.

13 For Boccaccino's career at Naples, see Branca, *Profilo*, pp. 13–16; R. Davidsohn, *Forschungen zur älteren Geschichte von Florenz*, 4 vols (Berlin, 1896–1908), III, 181 (register 907), 182 (911), 184 (922, 926, 927), 187 (942). In a document dated 4 February 1329 King Robert refers to 'Buccacius de Certaldo de societate Bardorum de Florencia, consiliarius, cambellanus, mercator, familiaris et fidelis noster' (*Forschungen* III, 187 (942)).

14 See Branca, *Profilo*, pp. 17–19, 30.

15 See Antonio Altamura, *La letteratura dell'età angioina* (Naples, 1952), pp. 12–16; Beryl Smalley, *English Friars and Antiquity in the Early Fourteenth Century* (Oxford, 1960), p. 274; Havely, pp. 3–5.

16 Robert's attempts to etymologise Greek names prove inaccurate (and occasionally comical), recalling the efforts of the young Boccaccio: see Altamura, pp. 11–12.

17 See Sabatini, pp. 28, 71–75, 226 (note 44), 243–6.

18 See Branca, *Profilo*, p. 34; Sabatini, p. 76; Havely, p. 4.

19 See Sabatini, p. 77.

20 See Altamura, pp. 85–86; Sabatini, pp. 77–78.

21 See the edition of V. Romano, 2 vols, Sd'I 200–1 (Bari, 1951); and see Charles G. Osgood, *Boccaccio on Poetry* (Princeton, 1930), a translation (with useful notes) of the Preface and Books XIV–XV of the *Genealogia*.

22 Smalley, *Friars*, p. 290.

23 See Branca, *Profilo*, p. 34.

24 See Sabatini, pp. 78–9; G. Di Stefano, 'Dionigi da Borgo San Sepolcro, amico del Petrarca e maestro del Boccaccio', *Atti dell'Accademia delle Scienze di Torino. II. Classe di scienze morali, storiche e filologiche*, 96 (1961–2), 272–314 (pp. 289–303). It is possible that Boccaccio embarked upon a translation of V. Maximus whilst at Naples: see Sabatini, pp. 106, 258 (note 216); M. T. Casella, 'Nuovi argomenti per l'attribuzione del volgarizzamento di Valerio Massimo al Boccaccio', SsB, 10 (1977–8), pp. 109–21.

25 See G. Billanovich, *Petrarca letterato. I. Lo Scrittoio del Petrarca* (Rome, 1947), pp. 62–66; Roberto Weiss, *The Renaissance Discovery of Classical Antiquity* (Oxford,

1969), p. 43. For the *Familiares*, see Francesco Petrarca, *Le Familiari*, edited by V. Rossi, 4 vols (Florence, 1933–42).

26 See *Opere di Francesco Petrarca*, edited by Emilio Bigi, commentary by G. Ponte, second edition (Milan, 1964), pp. 406–13.

27 See *Lo Zibaldone Boccaccesco Mediceo Laurenziano Plut. XXIX–8*, a facsimile prefaced by Ovido Biagi (Florence, 1915); F. Di Benedetto, 'Considerazioni sullo Zibaldone Laurenziano del Boccaccio e restauro testuale della prima redazione del *Faunus*', *Italia medioevale e umanistica*, 14 (1971), pp. 91–129.

28 Such is the dating given in Giovanni Boccaccio, *Opere Latine Minori*, edited by A. F. Massèra, Sd'I 111 (Bari, 1928), pp. 109–24.

29 Some folios in this MS have been transposed: see Di Benedetto, p. 97.

30 See Di Benedetto, p. 98. Biagi's facsimile begins with fol. 45v: for this extraordinary page, see Di Benedetto, p. 104, note 3. For the *Epistola* and its influence, see *The Middle English Letter of Alexander to Aristotle*, edited by V. DiMarco & L. Perelman, *Costerus*, NS, 13 (Amsterdam, 1978), pp. 16–29.

31 See Di Benedetto, pp. 97–102.

32 Di Benedetto, p. 99.

33 See G. Billanovich, 'Tra Dante e Petrarca', IMU, 8 (1965), 1–44 (p. 43).

34 For the date of the *Zibaldone Magliabechiano*, see G. Padoan, 'Petrarca, Boccaccio e la scoperta delle Canarie', IMU, 7 (1964), 263–77 (pp. 276–7).

35 See Branca, *Profilo*, pp. 48–49; Sabatini, pp. 79–80. Petrarch was examined at Naples and crowned at Rome. Robert did not accompany him to Rome; Boccaccio was almost certainly not present at either ceremony.

36 See Francesco Petrarca, *Prose*, edited by G. Martellotti et al (Milan–Naples, 1955), pp. 276–83 (an extract from *Rerum memorandarum libri*, I, 37); Havely, pp. 3, 191 (note 39); and see Par VIII, 76–84, 145–8.

37 See *Familiares* V, 6, quoted by Branca, *Profilo*, p. 21, note 1. Robert 'equitavit ad justras' on six occasions in the first five months of 1337. A colourful and informed account of a Neapolitan joust appears in *Elegia* V, pp. 86–88. For the *Trionfi*, see Francesco Petrarca, *Rime Trionfi e Poesie Latine*, edited by F. Neri et al. (Milan–Naples, 1951).

38 See *Triumphus Cupidinis* III, 79–81. Smalley observes that 'Petrarch despised both Charlemagne and chivalry as un-Roman' (*Friars*, p. 292).

39 See Benedetto, *Rose*, pp. 164–8.

40 See the allegorical personifications in *Triumphus Pudicitie*, 76–90, especially 'Bella Accoglienza' (85) and 'Timor d'infamia' (87); and see above, p. 13.

41 See Smalley, *Friars*, p. 291.

42 Sabatini, p. 34.

43 See Sabatini, pp. 34–37; Aurelio Roncaglia, 'Per la storia dell'ottava rima', *Cultura Neolatina*, 25 (1965), 5–14 (pp. 10–11); RR 6601–6734, 18697–9.

44 All details concerning the work of these translators follow Sabatini, pp. 38–39, 232.

45 See Branca, *Boccaccio medievale*, pp. 301–7.

46 See Léonard, *Angevins de Naples*, pp. 246–7.

47 See tables I–X following p. 517 in Léonard, *Angevins de Naples*.

48 For notable examples, see Sabatini, pp. 39–40; Smalley, p. 92.

49 See Havely, p. 7, and above, p. 34.

50 See Roncaglia, *Ottava rima*, pp. 5–14.

51 See James I. Wimsatt, *Chaucer and the Poems of 'Ch'* (Cambridge, 1982).

52 See E. H. Wilkins, 'Boccaccio's first octave', *Italica*, 33 (1956), p. 19; Roncaglia, pp. 5–11.

53 See Branca, *Opere di GB*, III, 629–30.

54 See the editions of P. G. Ricci in Branca, *Opere di GB*, Vol. III: I, 123; II & III, 76. *Redazione* I dates from some time after June 1351, II from around 1360 and III from before 1372: see Branca, *Profilo*, p. 108, note 1.

55 See Branca, *Profilo*, pp. 23, 26–27.

56 Léonard, *Boccace et Naples*, p. 51.

57 See A. R. Myers, 'The Wealth of Richard Lyons', in *Essays in Medieval History presented to Bertie Wilkinson*, edited by T. H. Sandquist & M. R. Powicke (Toronto, 1969), pp. 301–329.

58 See Altamura, *Età angioina*, pp. 92–93; Léonard, *Boccace et Naples*, p. 117.

59 Boccaccio reports this (with a mixture of anger and derision) in his letter to Nelli: see Ricci, *Opere in versi*, pp. 1186–7.

60 See Léonard, *Boccace et Naples*, p. 113.

61 See Léonard, pp. 14–18; Branca, *Profilo*, p. 24. For Acciaiuoli's will, see Léonard, pp. 21–22.

62 See the edition of Guido Favati (Genoa, 1970). The work dates from between 1281–1300 (see Favati, pp. 59–60).

63 In 1308 a group of Genoans expressed their loyalty to a new *società* by meeting in church to swear on the Bible; the meeting was attended by two poultry dealers. See R. S. Lopez & I. W. Raymond, *Medieval Trade in the Mediterranean World* (London, 1955), pp. 191–2.

64 'Fiori di parlare, di belle cortesie e di belli risposi e di belle valentie, di belli donari e di belli amori.'

65 See Branca, *Boccaccio medievale*, pp. 3–10.

66 Gino Corti, 'Consigli sulla mercatura di un anonimo trecentista', *Archivio storico italiano*, 110 (1952), 114–19 (p. 119):

E vuolsi saper tenere i' libro e lle scritture, e scrivere e rispondere alle lettere: la quale non è pichola nè pocho bella praticha, e ispeziale quella del sapere dettare. Però che de' grandi amici abbiamo è lla linghua, quando l'uomo la sa bene usare; e chosì per lo contradio, quando l'uomo nolla sa usare.

See also Paolo da Certaldo, *Libro di buoni costumi*, edited by A. Schiaffini (Florence, 1945); Benedetto Alberti, *Della Famiglia*, edited by C. Pellegrini (Florence, 1946), esp. pp. 321–2.

67 Branca, *Profilo*, p. 19.

68 See Enrico Bensa, *Francesco di Marco da Prato. Notizie e documenti sulla mercatura italiana del secolo XIV* (Milan, 1928), p. 291 and passim.

69 See L. Chiappelli, 'Una lettera mercantile del 1330, e la crisi del commercio italiano nella prima metà del Trecento', ASI, 82 (1924), 229–56 (lines 141–8, 167–73); Corti, *Consigli*, p. 119.

70 Corti, p. 119:

Ella t'i(n)segnia che ttu no' debi intendere niuna scrittura per lo testo, ma per la intenzione. E no' dire: La tale altorità o 'l tale amaestramento dicie chosì; ma di' in te medesimo che fu così la 'ntenzione di costui, quando egli iscrisse questo.

71 See C. Battisti & G. Alessio, *Dizionario Etimologico Italiano*, 5 vols (Florence, 1950–7), II, 1034; S. Battaglia, *Grande Dizionario della Lingua Italiana*, 9 vols, incomplete (Turin, 1961–), III, 383–7 (esp. 385, 20). The etymology of the OF (& ME) *compaignie* is, of course, similar.

72 Bensa, p. 292 (an extract from a contract dated 25 Oct. 1367); Fc IV, 50, 7–8.

73 See A. Sapori, *Studi di storia economica medievale*, second edition (Florence, 1947), pp. 640–42; I. Del Lungo, *Dino Compagni e la sua cronica*, 3 vols (Florence, 1879–87), I, 366–7; J. K. Hyde, *Society and Politics in Medieval Italy. The Evolution of the Civil Life, 1000–1350* (London, 1973), pp. 176–7.

74 Text from Sapori, p. 642 (lines 12–13).

75 See Sabatini, p. 94; DELI I, 238. Boccaccio is thought to have met Graziolo: see Branca, *Profilo*, pp. 34–35.

76 See DVE II, ii, 9; *Rime* (ed. Neri), LXX, XCII, CCLXXXVII.

77 See P. G. Ricci, 'Notizie e documenti per la biografia del Boccaccio. 4. L'incontro napoletano con Cino da Pistoia', SsB, 5 (1968), 1–18 (pp. 6–7).

78 See D. De Robertis, 'Per la storia del testo dalla canzone "La dolce vista e 'l bel

guardo soave"', *Studi di filologia italiana*, 10 (1952), 5–24 (pp. 7–9). Boccaccio draws upon this canzone in Fs V, 62–5, *ottave* which constitute the earliest record of Cino's poem.

79 See N. Sapegno, *Il Trecento*, third edition (Milan, 1973), pp. 44–48. References to Cino's verse follow M. Marti, *Poeti del Dolce stil nuovo* (Florence, 1969).

80 See Sabatini, p. 57.

81 See Ricci, *Notizie*, pp. 3–5; Branca, *Profilo*, pp. 30–32.

82 CLXV, 20–21: 'without a language/in which subtle distinctions may be made'.

83 See Sabatini, p. 94. Dante's work was attacked on theological and political grounds at Florence in the 1330s: see Padoan, *Boccaccio*, ED I, 649; Vernani, DELI V, 430.

84 See Sabatini, p. 98.

85 Camera, *Annali*, II, 413 (dated 22 June 1335): 'cantando et cantari faciendo matinatas, et fidem conjugalem sollicitabat'.

86 *Annali*, II, 411–12 (dated 15 Jan 1335).

87 See Chapter V below.

88 See Sabatini, pp. 119–24; Altamura, pp. 57–66.

89 See 'Epistola napoletana' in Giovanni Boccaccio, *L'Ameto. Lettere. Il Corbaccio*, edited by N. Bruscoli, Sd'I 182 (Bari, 1940), pp. 157–8.

90 'abbate Ia. Boccaccio . . . e nin juorno ni notte perzí fa schitto ca scribere.'

91 For dating and commentary, see Sabatini, pp. 106–110.

92 See *Caccia*, ed. Branca, in *Opere di GB*, I, pp. 6–7.

93 See *Vita nuova*, edited by M. Barbi in *Le opere di Dante. Testo critico della Società Dantesca Italiana*, second edition by M. Barbi et al (Florence, 1960), XLII; CD I, 53–55, XVIII, 49–51.

94 See CD XVII, 29, VN XXIII, 60; CD XVII, 43–58, Purg XXVIII, esp. 35, 40–41, 64–66.

95 See Purg XXVIII, 7–36.

96 See BD 30–61, 354–8; HF 614–28.

97 Both poems date from the 1330s. The *Chasse*, like the *Caccia*, features a number of huntresses (with their dogs) who represent local noblewomen: see Wimsatt, *Love Poets*, pp. 39–44; and for further French parallels, see Branca, *Opere di GB*, I, 6–7.

98 The unhappy heroine of Boccaccio's *Elegia di madonna Fiammetta* keeps to her room to shut society out: but society goes on the offensive, invading her chamber with musical instruments to woo her back to itself (VI, p. 104). Fiammetta's most desperate attempt to end her asocial existence is frustrated by a cry that brings a whole society to her: servants, husband, sisters, relatives and friends come running to her room (VI, p. 129).

99 See IV, 4; for the Barrili, see *Opere di GB*, I, 681–2 and Havely, p. 4.

100 See XVII, 46; and see chapter V below. Boccaccio employs a *cantare*-like formula in getting the narrative action of CD under way (I, 16).

101 See, for example, XI, 24–30.

102 See *Convivio* I, ii, 3 in the edition of Maria Simonelli (Bologna, 1966): 'Non si concede per li rettorici alcuno di se medesimo sanza necessaria cagione parlare . . .'.

103 See *The Court of Richard II* (London, 1968), pp. 1–6.

104 See, for example, V. J. Scattergood, 'Literary Culture at the Court of Richard II', in *English Court Culture in the Later Middle Ages*, edited by V. J. Scattergood & J. W. Sherborne (London, 1983), 29–43 (p. 30).

105 'The Troilus Frontispiece and Chaucer's Audience', *The Yearbook of English Studies*, 7 (1977), 68–74 (p. 73). See also Paul Strohm, 'Chaucer's Audience', *Literature and History*, 5 (1977), 26–41 (pp. 30–34).

106 Walter Map, *De Nugis Curialium*, translated by Tupper & Ogle, quoted by J. A. Burrow. 'Introduction' to Scattergood & Sherborne, p. ix.

107 See T&C I, 171; LGW F Prologue, 496–7.

108 See J. W. Sherborne, 'Aspects of English Court Culture in the Later Fourteenth

Century', in Scattergood & Sherborne, 1–27 (p. 23); Janet Coleman, 'English Culture in the Fourteenth Century', in Boitani, *Trecento*, 32–63 (pp. 59–60).

109 See Scattergood, pp. 38–40. For a more detailed account of Chaucer's associates in the royal household, see James Root Hulbert, *Chaucer's Official Life*, The University of Chicago, A Dissertation (Wisconsin, 1912).

110 See Coleman, pp. 46–55.

111 Nigel Wilkins, 'Music and Poetry at Court: England and France in the Late Middle Ages', in Scattergood & Sherborne, 183–204 (p. 183).

112 See Wilkins, pp. 183–4.

113 See Wimsatt, *The Poems of 'Ch'*, pp. 51–60, 66–8.

114 F. R. H. Du Boulay, 'The Historical Chaucer', in Brewer, *Writers*, 33–57 (p. 39); for the suggested revision, see Pearsall, *Frontispiece*, p. 73 and note 4.

115 See John Larner, 'Chaucer's Italy', in Boitani, *Trecento*, 7–32 (p. 18).

116 See Scattergood, pp. 34–6.

117 *Familiares* XXI, 15 (a letter addressed to Boccaccio), lines 175–9.

118 See Crow & Olson, pp. 9–11.

119 Sylvia L. Thrupp, *The Merchant Class of Medieval London (1300–1500)* (Chicago, 1948), p. 210.

120 Aldo Scaglione sees Chaucer and Boccaccio as 'two of the most delightfully "bourgeois" souls ever to leave records in literature'. See 'Boccaccio, Chaucer and the Mercantile Ethic', in *The Mediaeval World*, edited by David Daiches & Anthony Thorlby (London, 1973), 579–600 (p. 582).

121 *Mercantile Ethic*, p. 582.

122 Nicholas Orme, 'The Education of the Courtier', in Scattergood & Sherborne, 63–85 (p. 82).

123 See Crow & Olson, pp. 13–18.

124 See Cecil H. Clough, 'Introduction: Culture and Society', in *Profession, Vocation and Culture in Later Medieval England. Essays dedicated to the Memory of A. R. Myers* (Liverpool, 1982), pp. 1–2; Thrupp, chapter VI, pp. 234–87, 'Trade and Gentility'.

125 *Historical Chaucer*, p. 37.

126 Wendy Childs, 'Anglo-Italian Contacts in the Fourteenth Century', in Boitani, *Trecento*, 65–87 (p. 68)

127 See Childs, p. 68.

128 For Bromyard, see G. R. Owst, *Literature and Pulpit in Medieval England* (Cambridge, 1933), pp. 352–3. See also Thrupp, pp. xv-xvii; Larner, p. 10. For a detailed account of the literary activity of Florentine merchants in the later fourteenth century, see Christian Bec, *Les marchands écrivains. Affaires et humanisme à Florence 1375–1434* (Paris, 1967).

Chapter 3: Organising an Opus pp. 39–60

1 For a more detailed account of the *Filocolo*'s intricate plot (and its numerous sub-plots), see Thomas G. Bergin, *Boccaccio* (New York, 1981), pp. 74–84.

2 See *Filocolo*, edited by A. E. Quaglio, in Branca, *Tutte le Opere di GB*, Vol. I. For a good analysis of the *Filocolo*'s language, see Luigi Malagoli, 'Timbro della prosa e motivi dell'arte del Boccaccio nel *Filoclolo*', *Studi mediolatini e volgari*, 6–7 (1959), pp. 97–111. E. G. Parodi asserts that the style of the *Filocolo* is, 'in fin de' conti', comparable to that of the *Decameron*, and that this style exerts a powerful hold over Italian prose 'fino quasi al Manzoni': see 'La cultura e lo stile del Boccaccio' (1913), in Parodi, *Lingua e letteratura. Studi di Teoria linguistica e di Storia dell'italiano antico*, edited by G. Folena, 2 vols (Venice, 1957), 470–79, (pp. 475–6). In a later essay (collected in the same volume) Parodi suggests that this style owes much to the *cursus*: see 'Osservazioni sul *cursus* nelle opere latine e volgari del Boccaccio' (1913), 480–492 (p. 488). For the *Filocolo*, the *Decameron* and the *cursus*, see Branca,

Boccaccio medievale, pp. 45–85. For the influence of the *cursus* on Chaucer's prose, see Margaret Schlauch, 'Chaucer's Prose Rhythms', PMLA, 65 (1950), pp. 568–589; Schlauch, 'The art of Chaucer's prose', in Brewer, *Chaucer and Chaucerians*, 140–163 (pp. 156–162).

3 See Young, *Development*, pp. 139–181; Lowes, *Franklin's Tale*, pp. 705–28; W. F. Bryan and G. Dempster, *Sources and Analogues of Chaucer's Canterbury Tales* (Chicago, 1941), p. 377. Young, speaking of the *Filocolo*, refers to 'the dull and pedantic prose of the Italian romance' (p. 180); Lowes asserts that the '*Teseide* is a work of art; the *Filocolo* falls short of that enviable distinction' (p. 706).

4 See *Floire et Blancheflor*, revised edition by M. M. Pelan (Paris, 1956), pp. XII–XIII. Pelan fixes a date for her MS of version I between 1155–73; this places it 'parmi les premiers romans'.

5 See *Le Roman de Flamenca*, edited by Ulrich Gschwind, 2 Parts, Romanica Helvetica 86A, 86B (Berne, 1976), I, lines 4475–96; Joachim Reinhold, *Floire et Blancheflor. Étude de littérature comparée* (Paris, 1906), pp. 9–11; Pelan (I), pp. XXII–XXIII; *Intelligenza* 75 (quoted above, pp. 12–13).

6 The distinguishing adjectives 'aristocratique' and 'populaire' were first applied to the two versions by M. Edélestand du Méril in introducing his editions entitled *Floire et Blancheflor* (Paris, 1856), pp. xix–xxii. Reinhold doubted their appropriateness (p. 82) and Felicitas Krüger rejected them, maintaining that both versions were intended 'für höfischritterliche Kreise': see *Li romanz de Floire et Blancheflor*, ed. Krüger, Romanische Studien 45 (Berlin, 1938), p. VII. The new epithets were introduced by Pelan (I, p. XIII) and welcomed by F. C. De Vries in his edition of the ME *Floris and Blauncheflur* (Groningen, 1966), p. 54, note 62. A. C. Gibbs, in prefacing extracts from the ME version in *Middle English Romances*, York Medieval Texts (London, 1966) returns to the original distinction by employing the terms 'aristocratic' and 'popular' (p. 76).

For information on MSS see the editions above and that of M. M. Pelan, *Floire et Blancheflor. Seconde Version* (Paris, 1975). All references to the romances are to the editions of Pelan (versions I and II).

7 See 'Die verbreitung der sage von Flore und Blancheflor ausserhalb Englands' in *Floris and Blauncheflur*, edited by Emil Hausknecht (Berlin, 1885), pp. 1–88; and see De Vries, pp. 54–55.

8 Reinhold, p. 31 ('drily summarised').

9 See *Cantari del Trecento*, edited by Armando Balduino (Milan, 1970), pp. 34–36, 259–60.

10 Many conclusions reached by nineteenth-century investigators are untenable because the editions from which they worked (those of du Méril) do not record all MS variants; the best edition of the OF version I is said to contain 'serious defects': see De Vries, pp. 6, 56.

Quaglio, in his excellent edition of Fc, says virtually nothing about Boccaccio's possible acquaintance with either of the French versions. Tasso maintained that the *cantare* version represented a verse imitation of Fc made for public recitation: see Hausknecht, p. 27. A similar suggestion is made by Angelo Monteverdi, 'Un libro d'Ovidio e un passo del *Filocolo*', in *Studia philologica et litteraria in honorem L. Spitzer*, edited by A. G. Hatcher and K. L. Selig (Bern, 1958), pp. 335–340. This suggestion is rejected by Quaglio and Balduino; see Balduino, *Cantari*, pp. 34,259. In fact Ludovico Dolce (1508–66) did attempt to make a version of Fc in *ottave*, with disastrous results: see Hausknecht, pp. 34–5; DELI, II, 313.

11 See above, p. 27.

12 Such a positive historical connection between the prefatory chapter and the main story of the *Filocolo* would supplement the obvious thematic symmetry already existing between them: the battle of the righteous Charles against the enemy of the Church, Manfred, obviously mirrors that between the Christian pilgrims and the pagan King Felice. In fact, this equation between Manfred and the Saracens realised by Boccaccio's

adoption of the *Floire et Blancheflor* story was anticipated by Jean de Meun, who maintained that the Swabian and his followers '". . . firent pis que Sarradin/de conmencier bataille amere/contre Sainte Iglise . . ."' (6726–8).

13 As a consequence of this treaty, signed in 1269, Charles Martel (grandson of Charles d'Anjou and Robert's elder brother) succeeded to the title of King of Hungary: see C. W. Previté-Orton, 'Italy, 1250–1290' in *The Cambridge Medieval History*, planned by J. B. Bury, 8 vols (Cambridge, 1911–36), VI, 166–204 (p. 191). Dante had immense admiration for Charles Martel: in Par VIII, 37–148 Charles quotes the opening line of a Dantean *canzone* and proceeds to survey the geography and history of the Angevin empire.

14 I, 1, 26: '"un picciolo libretto volgarmente parlando"'.

15 See *Il Cantare di Fiorio e Biancifiore*, edited by V. Crescini, 2 vols (Bologna, 1889–1899), I, 48–56; Balduino, pp. 19, 35. The MS in question is Biblioteca Nazionale Centrale, Florence, Cod. Magliabechiano VIII 1416; I quote from Balduino's edition of this MS. Antonio Altamura has argued for the existence of a fourteenth-century Neapolitan tradition of this *cantare*, but his case (based upon an edition printed at Naples in 1481) is not convincing: see 'Un'ignota redazione del cantare di Florio e Biancofiore—Contributo alla storia del *Filocolo*', *Biblion*, 1 (1946 –7), pp. 92–133.

16 See Quaglio, *Opere di GB*, I, 739–40 (note 8).

17 Pelan I, XIII ('in a perverted form').

18 Pelan (II, pp. 25–26) finds just 23 brief resemblances; see also Reinhold, pp. 81–118.

19 See Reinhold, pp. 112–15, 118.

20 See Pelan I, XVI–XX; Krüger, pp. xxii–xxiii.

21 I, 121. The pagan king is at Naples when he hears news of the defeat of the Christian pilgrims; no MS variants are recorded for this line.

22 2 MSS have 'deux cents' and one has 'sept': but 'plus de sept anz' may be a 'formule pour situer le roman dans le passé' (Pelan I, p. 140).

23 See Pelan I, p. 139. Pelan's puzzlement leads her to speculate that the opening of version I might have been added by a later copyist: but there is no MS evidence to support this.

24 See *Guy of Warwick*, edited by J. Zupita, EETS, ES, 42, 49, 59 (London, 1883, 1887, 1891).

25 See below, p. 190. Chaucer mentions 'sir Gy' in *Sir Thopas*, VII, 899.

26 See Smalley, passim and pp. 155–6 (for Holcot compared with Boccaccio) and pp. 161–3 (for Holcot's extravagant moralising of medieval history).

27 For example: the speech of 'Juno' (the Church) to 'colui che per lei tenea il santo uficio' (the Pope) in I, 1,4–9 is indebted to that of Juno to Eolus in *Aeneid* I, 65–75; the flood with which Jove punishes the sins of Lycaon in V, 8, 1 merges *Genesis* 7, 17–24 with Met I, 163–312.

28 A. E. Quaglio, 'Tra fonti e testo del *Filocolo*', GSLI, 139 (1962), 321–369, 513–540 ('picked up by ear from a distance', p. 327). Quaglio gives a useful summary of Boccaccio's attitudes towards each of the five writers in Fc V, 97, 4–6.

29 In the *Filocolo* Boccaccio evidently regards Lucan as a poet; he later regards him as a metrical historian: see *Esposizioni*, Canto IV (I), 130 (p. 203).

30 See A. E. Quaglio, 'Boccaccio e Lucano: una concordanza e una fonte dal *Filocolo* all'*Amorosa Visione*', CNeo, 23 (1963), pp. 153–171; Giuseppe Velli, 'Cultura e *Imitatio* nel primo Boccaccio', ASNSP, series II, 37 (1968), pp. 65–93.

31 See Fc I, 29, 10 (and note 10, p. 744); Fc I, 30, 16 (and note 14, p. 745). For an account of Boccaccio's employment of Statius in the *Teseida*, see Boitani, *Chaucer and Boccaccio*, pp. 9–13, 32–34.

32 See V, 97, 7–8; and see II, 17, 14, where Biancifiore expresses her desperate willingness to be converted into a book so that Florio might read her.

33 In V, 37, 1 Florio forgives Fileno, 'giurando per se medesimo che di perfetto

amore l'amerà per inanzi, e le preterite cose sì come fanciullesche metterà in oblio . . .': compare I *Corinthians* 13, 4–11.

34 For example, the very first tale of the *Decameron* (recounting the death of Ser Cepparello) employs the adjective 'santo' 21 times, often to great ironic effect. See *Decameron*, edited by V. Branca in Branca, *Opere di GB*, Vol. IV.

35 'Sulmona, riposta patria del nobilissimo poeta Ovidio'. Sulmona is described as being 'secluded' because it is surrounded by the mountains of the Abruzzi region.

36 Florio adopts the alias of 'Filocolo' in III, 75, 4; I refer to the *Filocolo*'s hero as 'Florio' throughout to avoid confusion.

37 The *Filocolo* draws upon the full range of Ovid's writings: see Quaglio, *Tra fonti*, pp. 337–38. The series of laments which punctuate the narrative following the separation of the lovers in Book II are (inevitably) heavily indebted to the *Heroides*: see, for example, II, 17, 4–18 (and notes, pp. 764–7).

38 For a fine account of Dante's simultaneous attachment to Christianity and paganism, see Kenelm Foster, *The Two Dantes and Other Studies* (London, 1977), pp. 156–253.

39 See Chapter IV below.

40 An abundance of verbal echoes testifies that the *Vita nuova* figured prominently in Boccaccio's mind as he wrote the *Filocolo*: the 'story' of love, separation and reconciliation that the *Vita nuova* and the *Commedia* combine to tell closely parallels that of Boccaccio's romance.

41 See Fc III, 33, 1–14, IV, 1, 1–5 and compare Inf XX, 52–99, Purg V, 67–129, Par XI, 43–72.

42 The phrase (employed in discussing the *Commedia*) is that of Morton W. Bloomfield, 'The Problem of the Hero in the Later Medieval Period', in *Concepts of the Hero in the Middle Ages and Renaissance*, edited by N. T. Burns and C. J. Reagan (London, 1976), 27–48 (p. 36).

43 See esp. II, 44–46. Ascalion is appointed to teach Florio (and Biancifiore) in I, 45, 4.

44 See Fc III, 67, 12; Inf XXVI, 119–20.

45 Boccaccio's most impressive adherence to a classical text in the *Filocolo* is, perhaps, his imitation of Lucan. This predates the French verse *Pharsale* composed by the Italian Nicholas of Verona in 1343: see *Die Pharsale des Nicholas von Verona*, edited by Hermann Wahle (Marburg, 1888), p. VI and lines 1930–37.

In imitating Lucan, Boccaccio sometimes exhibits 'una aderanza rispettosa alla lettera del verso che rammenta la tecnica dei traduttori medievali' (Quaglio, *Lucano*, p. 160). But at other moments, Boccaccio's concentration upon one area of a classical text is interrupted by the memory of another and the two are fused in a colourful *contaminatio* (see Velli, pp. 91–93). Like Chaucer, Boccaccio was not averse to taking short cuts to classical learning; both poets make good use of Valerius Maximus' anecdotal and encyclopaedic *Facta et dicta memorabilia*: see A. E. Quaglio, 'Valerio Massimo e il *Filocolo* di Giovanni Boccaccio', CNeo, 20 (1960), pp. 45–77; S&A, pp. 642–44, 662–63. And both poets are happy to employ an Italian translation of a classical text: see Quaglio, *Valerio Massimo*, pp. 46–77; Meech, *Italian Translation* (see above, p. 173, note 77).

46 See '*Troilus and Criseyde*' in CCS, pp. 446–463.

47 McCall, p. 449.

48 McCall, p. 449.

49 McCall, p. 449. The article quoted is Morton W. Bloomfield, 'Distance and Predestination in *Troilus and Criseyde*', PMLA, 72 (1957), pp. 14–26.

50 See II, 18, 31, 49; V, 1037, 1051, 1088, 1094, 1651, 1653.

51 See V, 97, 10 (quoted above, p. 45) and (for the conversion) V, 52, 4–71, 17.

52 For the importance of the fiction of a Latin source for medieval vernacular writers, see Leo Spitzer, 'Note on the Poetic and the Empirical "I" in Medieval Authors', *Traditio*, 4 (1946), 414–422 (p. 415 & note 3).

53 See above p. 84.

54 Payne, *Key*, p. 89.

55 Claudian is also featured in HF (as a poet associated with Hell): see HF 1507–12.

56 See E. F. Shannon, 'Chaucer and Lucan's Pharsalia', MP, 16 (1918–19), pp. 609–14; B. A. Wise, *The Influence of Statius upon Chaucer* (Baltimore, 1911; reprinted New York, 1967); P. M. Clogan, 'Chaucer and the *Thebaid* Scholia', SP, 61 (1964), pp. 599–615. Clogan speaks of Chaucer's 'perpetual admiration' for Statius (p. 615).

57 See above, p. 10.

58 E. F. Shannon, *Chaucer and the Roman Poets* (Cambridge, Mass., 1929), p. 375.

59 Richard L. Hoffman, *Ovid and the Canterbury Tales* (OUP, London, 1966), p. 207.

60 Foundations for such an exercise have been laid by E. P. Hammond, *Chaucer: A Bibliographical Manual* (New York, 1908), pp. 84–105.

61 DVE II, vi, 7. In this chapter of *De Vulgari* Dante cites one of his own compositions as eleventh and last in a series of 'illustres cantiones' drawn from various romance vernaculars. He asserts that these *canzoni* exemplify the highest standards of construction ('supremam . . . contructionem'); he adds that it might have proved useful to consider the 'regulatos . . . poetas, Virgilium videlicet, Ovidium Metamorfoseos, Statium atque Lucanum. . . '.
The studied casualness with which Dante turns to ancient Latin authors as alternatives for imitation attests to his extraordinary confidence in the capabilities of the vernacular.

62 The pattern of Boccaccio's choice (four *auctores* and two vernacular poets) conforms to that of Jean de Meun; Chaucer's conforms to Dante's. Chaucer and Boccaccio include the four poets cited in DVE II, vi, 7; Statius is absent from *Inferno* IV because he is reserved for a greater role later in the *Commedia*.

63 Such modesty is not a feature of the equivalent passages in the *Rose* and *Commedia*. Both these earlier passages are prophetic: Jean locates his own writing in the future; Dante takes his place among the great *auctores* before the *Commedia* has got fully under way.

64 For helpful observations of continuities between the *Rose* and *Commedia*, see Benedetto, *Rose*, pp. 1–164; G. Contini, 'Un nodo della cultura medievale: la serie *Roman de la Rose—Fiore—Divina Commedia*', *Lettere Italiane*, 25 (1973), pp. 162–189; Earl Jeffrey Richards, *Dante and the 'Roman de la Rose'. An Investigation into the Vernacular Narrative Context of the 'Commedia'* (Tübingen, 1981).

65 I follow the transcription adopted by John V. Fleming, *The 'Roman de la Rose'. A Study in Allegory and Iconography* (Princeton, 1969), p. 18. Premierfait's translations of Boccaccio's *De Casibus Virorum Illustrium* date from 1400 and 1409, and his *Decameron* translation dates from 1411–14; Fleming describes him as 'the leading "Romance philologist" of his day'. For a more sceptical view of the value of Premierfait's comparison of the *Commedia* and the *Rose*, see Pierre-Yves Badel, *Le Roman de la Rose au XIVe siècle. Étude de la réception de l'oeuvre* (Geneva, 1980), pp. 488–9.

66 In a letter to Pierre Col dated 2 October 1402, Christine argues enthusiastically for the superiority of the *Commedia* over the *Rose*: 'But if you wish to hear paradise and hell described more subtly and, theologically, portrayed more advantageously, poetically, and efficaciously, read the book of Dante, or have it explained to you, because it is written splendidly in the Florentine language' (translated by Maxwell Luria in Luria, *A Reader's Guide to the 'Roman de la Rose'* (Hamden, Connecticut, 1982), p. 201). See also J. L. Baird and J. R. Kane, *La Querelle de la Rose: Letters and Documents* (Chapel Hill, 1978); Badel, pp. 431–482.

67 See Fleming, p. 19. Laurent directs us to the Book of the *Aeneid* which recounts Aeneas' descent to the underworld. It is worth noting that Vergil's hero, before seeking the depths of Hell, seeks the heights where Apollo sits enthroned: 'at pius Aeneas arces, quibus altus Apollo/praesidet . . ./. . . petit' (VI, 9–11). Dante begins his *Commedia*

with an upward ascent (Inf I, 13–30) but is forced to descend to the infernal underworld before ascending to the celestial vision. The 'ordre' of *Aeneid* VI was certainly imprinted on Dante's mind as he began his *Commedia*: in Inf II, 32 the protagonist cries '"Io non Enëa . . . sono"'.

68 See John V. Fleming, 'The Moral Reputation of the *Roman de la Rose* before 1400', *Romance Philology*, 18 (1964–5), pp. 430–35.

69 See lines 9–14 in the edition of J. J. Stürzinger (London, 1893).

70 *Cleanness* 1057 in *The Poems of the Pearl Manuscript*, edited by Malcolm Andrew and Ronald Waldron, York Medieval Texts, second series (London, 1978). The speech referred to is RR 7689–7764.

71 CT X, 1083–4.

72 V, 11: '"ched i' son tu' deo"'. For a brief but illuminating discussion of moral and ethical issues in the *Fiore*, see Christopher J. Ryan, 'The Theme of Free Will in Dante's Minor Works, with Particular Reference to Aspects of the Cultural Background' (unpublished dissertation, Cambridge University, 1978), pp. 284–296.

73 For the notion of a 'poetic I' in medieval authors, see Spitzer, *Poetic and Empirical* '*I*'.

74 For a convenient summary of past analyses, see Richards, pp. 32–41.

75 See Richards, pp. 106–8 and *passim*.

76 See Contini, *Nodo*; Contini, '*Il Fiore*', ED II, 895–901; Mazzoni, *Latini*.

77 The Italian feminisation of the French Bel Acueil helps move the *Fiore* away from pure allegory towards conventional (romance) narrative. None of Guillaume's continuators matches or approaches his exquisite control of allegory. For a fine account of Guillaume's art, see Charles Muscatine, 'The Emergence of Psychological Allegory in Old French Romance', PMLA, 68 (1953), pp. 1160–82.

78 Ryan, p. 284.

79 The following description of the 'story' of the *Rose* could be applied to the *Commedia*: 'ha inizio il racconto, che in sintesi è la storia di un lungo viaggio per la conquista della Rosa; viaggio pieno di imprevisti, con l'intervento di numerosi personaggi che contrastano o favoriscono quella conquista' (DELI, IV, 584). For a deliberate comparison of the two stories, see Castets, p. XVII.

80 Par XXIV, 2 ('benedetto Agnello'). References to shepherds, sheep, lambs and pasture abound in the *Paradiso*.

81 The definition of tragedy formulated in Chaucer's Boethius translation envisages a period of prosperity preceding a miserable decline. A hero must rise before he can fall; comedy precedes tragedy:
'(Glose. Tragedye is to seyn a dite of a prosperite for a tyme, that endeth in wrecchidnesse.)' (*Boece* II, Prosa 2, 70–72).

82 For the mixture of estates in CT, see Jill Mann, *Chaucer and Medieval Estates Satire* (Cambridge, 1973). In the *Filocolo*'s first *brigata* we have a number of nuns, a king's daughter and a student of canon law (as Boccaccio identifies himself in I, 1, 30), with 'alcuno compagno' (I, 1, 23).

83 This image of the nut and nutshell was a commonplace of medieval commentators: see Giorgio Padoan, 'Teseo "figura redemptoris" e il cristianesimo di Stazio' in *Il pio Enea, l'empio Ulisse* (Ravenna, 1977), 125–150 (pp. 134–5). And see *The Prologue to The Fables* in *The Poems of Robert Henryson*, edited by Denton Fox (Oxford, 1981), p. 3, lines 15–21; CT VII, 3443.

84 Quoted by Richards, p. 53. For Boncompagno and his influence see James J. Murphy, *Rhetoric in the Middle Ages. A History of Rhetorical Theory from Saint Augustine to the Renaissance* (Berkeley, Los Angeles & London, 1974), pp. 244–268; *Dizionario biografico degli italiani*, edited by A. M. Ghisalberti, 22 vols, incomplete (Rome, 1960–), XI, 720–25.

85 See Richards, pp. 18–20. Guido delle Colonne's *Historia destructionis Troiae* was more widely respected as a historical document than the French verse romance from

which it was translated, Benoît de Sainte Maure's *Roman de Troie*. Guido's *Historia* is in Latin prose.

86 Boccaccio's pursuit of his lady is figured as a hunt in which the lady is a ' "fagiana" ' (hen pheasant). The phrase ' "le imprese cose" ' probably refers to the mercantile career mapped out for Boccaccio by his father.

87 *Opere di GB*, II, 925, note 102: 'il valore della poesia amorosa, la potenza delle rime d'amore'.

88 *La prosa del Duecento*, edited by Cesare Segre and Mario Marti (Milan–Naples, 1959), p. 134, paragraph 4: 'e rettorica quella scienza per la quale noi sapemo ornatamente dire e dettare'. See also E. R. Curtius, *European Literature and the Latin Middle Ages*, translated by W. R. Trask (London, 1953), p. 71.

89 See *Tesoretto* 1610–12.

90 See Inf II, 67–69; Inf XVIII, 91–93.

91 See CT V, 716–727. Schlauch notes that the Retraction reveals 'almost no concern for *cursus*' and suggests that it 'may be designated as *stylus humilis*' (*Prose Rhythms*, p. 584).

92 The verses of Boethius' Lady Philosophy sugar the pill of her prose teachings: see *Boece* I, pr. 5, 68–78; I, pr. 6, 91–102. Brunetto is dissatisfied with rhyme, as 'le parole rimate/ascondon la sentenza/e mutan la 'ntendenza . . .' (*Tesoretto* 416–18; and see above, p. 10 and note 40). The Latin root of 'prose' is 'prorsus' or 'prosus', 'following a straight line, not oblique': see the *Oxford Latin Dictionary*, edited by P. G. W. Glare (Oxford, 1982), pp. 1498–9.

93 On the relationship of the metaphorical to the 'historical' and the 'real' in CT, see Donald R. Howard, *The Idea of the Canterbury Tales* (Berkeley, 1976); Howard, *Writers and Pilgrims. Medieval Pilgrimage Narratives and Their Posterity* (Berkeley, 1980), pp. 77–103.

Chapter 4: Pagans at the Threshold of Enlightenment   pp. 61–72

1 See Kenelm Foster, *Petrarch. Poet and Humanist* (Edinburgh, 1984), pp. 52–3.

2 See *Rime*, ed. Neri, III, CCCLXVI, 13; and see Foster, *Petrarch*, pp. 43–7.

3 See *Piers Plowman by William Langland. An edition of the C-text*, by Derek Pearsall (London, 1978), XII, 73–87; XIV, 131–217; XX, 403–71.

4 *Chaucer and Pagan Antiquity* (Cambridge, 1982).

5 See Auchinleck MS, ed. Zupita, stanzas 23–24 (p. 400). Despite such differing intentions, the *Filocolo* and *Sir Guy* make comparable use of stock romance incidents and episodes. For example, the English romance features a chess game played at Alexandria between Fabour, son of a Saracen king, and Sadok, son of a sultan (Auchinleck MS, stanzas 56–57); the *Filocolo* features a chess game played at Alexandria between Florio, son of a Saracen king, and Sadoc, keeper of a sultan's tower (IV, 96). For equivalent scenes (in verse and prose respectively) see *Gui de Warewic. Roman du XIIIᵉ siècle*, edited by Alfred Ewert, 2 vols (Paris, 1932), 7973–92; *Le Rommant de 'Guy de Warwik' et de 'Herolt d'Ardenne'*, edited by D. J. Conlon (Chapel Hill, 1971), 152, 44–57. Boccaccio (like Chaucer) may well have heard of Sir Guy: the Anglo-Norman romance spawned imitations right across Europe (see Ewert, pp. VIII–IX; Conlon, pp. 14–15).

6 See Young, pp. 139–81; see also Robinson, *Works of Chaucer*, p. 824, note to T&C III, 512–1190. The *Filostrato* exerts virtually no influence on T&C III, 442–1309.

7 This division of influences cannot, of course, be rigidly insisted upon: Boccaccio's reading of the *Rose* would inevitably have been coloured by his devotion to Dante; and incidents from both works would doubtless have fused in Boccaccio's mind with details drawn from a greater body of literature.

8 See Par XII, 80 ('oh madre sua veramente Giovanna'); RR 10535–644. It is interesting to note that this prediction of Boccaccio's poetic powers is immediately

followed by an exhibition of them in a scene of metamorphosis, a mode of writing highly esteemed by Dante and the poets of the *Rose*; after this scene Florio refers us back to the prophecy (IV, 5,4).

9 See: Inf XIII, 25–57; Met V, 632–38, IX, 656–665; Frederick Goldin, *The Mirror of Narcissus in the Courtly Love Lyric* (NY, 1967). Richards 'tentatively' suggests that the Dantean earthly paradise 'might reflect a careful integration of the *Rose*'s attitude towards Ovid's version of the story of Narcissus' (p. 88).

10 See IV, 1,1; IV, 5,5–6; IV, 9,1–2; and see above, p. 48 and note 43.

11 See Fc IV, 10,2–11,12; *Fiore* XXXIII–IV.

12 'Moscardo' is 'a name given loosely to the spotted flycatcher, sparrow-hawk and red-footed falcon' (*The Cambridge Italian Dictionary*, edited by Barbara Reynolds, 2 vols (Cambridge, 1962, 1981), I, 491).

13 The 'fagiana' is, we later learn, Boccaccio's beloved (V, 8,36, quoted above, p. 58). Fiammetta, elected queen of the Neapolitan *brigata*, is, we are later told, a king's daughter; her true name is Maria (IV, 16,4–5). Maria, the governor of the *Filocolo*'s first *brigata*, is Boccaccio's beloved. The pheasant is often associated with the Virgin Mary in medieval visual iconography.

It is interesting to note that the thirteenth-century debate poem *Blancheflor et Florence* features a court of birds which discusses a *demande d'amour*: see *Blancheflor et Florence* in Charles Oulmont, *Les Débats du Clerc et du Chevalier dans la littérature poétique du Moyen-Age* (Paris, 1911), 167–183 (lines 342–414). This assembly (like Boccaccio's gathering of birds) erupts into violence.

14 See *The Parlement of Foulys*, edited by D. S. Brewer (London, 1960), p. 11.

15 See Fc IV, 13,7–10, PF 491–616; Fc IV, 14,3, PF 673–692.

16 See IV, 13,7, quoted above, p. 64.

17 See IV, 12,1, quoted above, p. 63.

18 See *Opere di GB*, I, 851, note 37.

19 See Purg XXXIII, 34–78 (esp. 46, 50). In these tercets Dante is charged to record things whose significance he cannot at that moment comprehend.

20 See Purg XXIX, 55–7, where Dante looks in vain for Vergil to interpret the advancing pageant of Christian revelation: 'I turned round full of wonder/to the good Vergil, and he answered me/with an expression charged with no less amazement.'

21 IV, 16,4: ' "per cui quella piaga, che il prevaricamento della prima madre aperse, richiuse" '.

22 For a detailed account of this parliament, see Victoria Kirkham, 'Reckoning with Boccaccio's "Questioni d'amore" ', MLN, 89 (1974), pp. 47–59.

23 Foster, 'Dante and Eros' in *The Two Dantes*, 37–55 (p. 48). The opening line of Boccaccio's *ballata* recalls the opening line of the *Convivio*'s first *canzone* (a line quoted by Charles Martel in Par VIII, 37).

24 IV, 43,13: ' " 'vera reina delli regni miei' " '.

25 See *Teseida delle nozze di Emilia*, edited by A. Limentani in Branca, *Opere di GB*, vol. II, gloss to VII, 50 (pp. 462–472). Boccaccio maintains that 'Venere è doppia, perciò che l'una si può e dee intendere per ciascuno onesto e licito disiderio, sì come è disiderare d'avere moglie per avere figliuoli, e simili a questo . . . La seconda Venere è quella per la quale ogni lascivia è disiderata, e che volgarmente è chiamata dea d'amore . . .' (p. 463). See also Robert Hollander, *Boccaccio's Two Venuses* (New York, 1977), pp. 59–65.

26 This sounds like a *cantare* tag: but it maintains the association of Fiammetta and her eyes with Venus, the morning star.

27 *The Divine Comedy of Dante Alighieri*, translation and comment by John D. Sinclair, 3 vols (OUP, London, 1971), II, 415. See also *Convivio* III, xiv, 5; Dante Alighieri, *Il Convivio*, edited with commentary by G. Busnelli and G. Vandelli, introduced by M. Barbi, second edition with an appendix by A. E. Quaglio (Florence, 1964), p. 148. Dante follows Aquinas in distinguishing between *lux* (*luce*, the light at its source), *lumen* (*lume*, the luminosity of the diaphanous medium through which light

travels), *radius* (*raggio*, the direct line of light from its source to the object it strikes) and *splendor* (*splendore*, reflected light).

28 See P. Rajna, 'Le origini della novella narrata dal "Frankeleyn" nei *Canterbury Tales* del Chaucer', *Romania*, 32 (1903), pp. 204–267; Young, *Origin*, p. 181; S&A, p. 377.

29 Lowes complained that Rajna's parallels 'suffer . . . in being torn from their context' (*Franklin's Tale*, p. 720).

30 The *brigata*'s debating is intelligible to pagans because it is deliberately restricted to worldly ('"mondani"') delights and misfortunes: see IV, 56,1; and see my article 'Chaucer and the Poets of the Pieno Trecento', *Comparison*, 13 (1982), 98–119, esp. pp. 104–6.

31 See Fc IV, 31,8, CT V, 906–917, 1245–55; Fc IV, 37–8, CT V, 1306–27. It is interesting to note that Aurelius prays to Apollo in V, 1031–7 almost as if he were a garden god, '"governour/Of every plaunte, herbe, tree, and flour"'; Tarolfo is challenged to produce a garden '"d'erbe e di fiori e d'alberi e di frutti copioso"' (IV, 31,8).

32 See Fc IV, 31,5, CT V, 829–36; and see *Ars Amatoria* I, 475–6, *Ex Ponto* IV, 10,5.

33 See Fc IV, 31,23–35 (imitated from Met VII, 179–293: see Velli, pp. 91–93 and above, p. 181, note 45); CT V, 1273–1296.

34 See CT V, 865–893; T&C IV, 958–1078.

35 *The Franklin's Tale* is much closer to Fc IV, 31 than to Dec X, 5: see Lowes, *Franklin's Tale*, p. 720; S&A, p. 377. Compared with the *Filocolo* story, the *Decameron* analogue reveals a considerable shift in imaginative emphasis: its interest centres on the magnificence of a great lord, 'messere Ansaldo Gradense' (X, 5,4). Ansaldo is not an active figure: action revolves about him; the 'far fare' construction is often employed in the expedition of his affairs. Whereas the *Filocolo* suitor promises the magician half of everything he possess (IV, 31,19) and the English suitor twice as much as everything (V, 1227–31, 1571–5), Ansaldo is not threatened with personal or financial embarrass- ment. He does not trouble to confront the wife directly until all conditions have been fulfilled; and then the wife come to *his* house (X, 5,18).

The narrator of *Decameron* X, 5 declares that for him, the most impressive feature of the story is Ansaldo's 'liberalità' (X, 5,26; see also X, 5,3). In telling his brief tale he exhibits a singleness of imaginative concentration and a bare economy of style that are quite different from the language and procedure of the two analogues. Chaucer must sometimes have despaired at the rambling luxuriance of the *Filocolo*'s prose style: the prolix description of a sunrise in Fc IV, 31,10 may have provoked the satirically verbose sunset of CT V, 1016–18. But such a fulsome, digressive style was doubtless more congenial (and more useful) to Chaucer than the potted, streamlined economy of the *Decameron* tale: for example, the lecture on outer poverty and inner riches delivered in Fc IV, 31,18 is similar in letter and spirit to that delivered by Chaucer's Loathly Lady in CT III, 1177–1206.

36 See Fc IV, 74,1–20, Purg XXIX–XXXII; and see Quaglio, *Opere di GB*, I, 887–8.

37 See Purg XXVIII, 7–18, 55–56, 143; PF 201–3, 186, 173.

38 See Purg XXVII, 37–39, 94–96; XXVIII, 64–66 (for Beatrice compared to Venus), 71–75; XXIX, 4–6; XXXII, 64–66; XXXIII, 46–51, 69.

39 See Janet Coleman, *Piers Plowman and the 'Moderni'* (Rome, 1981), pp. 118–9.

40 See CT IV, 1729–35. The poet referred to is Martianus Capella, whose 5th century *De nuptiis Philologiae et Mercuri* opens with a prayer to Hymen.

41 For an illuminating account of the literary history of Hymen and his place in the *Troilus*, see Yasunari Takada, 'On the Consummation of Troilus' Love: Chaucer's *Troilus and Criseyde*, III. 1247–60', *Studies in Language and Culture*, 8 (1982), 103–129 (pp. 110–127).

42 This extraordinary statue is first described in IV, 85,8. Its features conform with

those traditionally associated with Cupid, with one remarkable exception: '"ma egli non ha gli occhi fasciati come molti il figurano, anzi gli ha quivi belli e piacevoli, e per pupilla di ciascuno è un carbuncolo, che in quella camera tenebre essere non lasciano per alcun tempo, ma luminosa e chiara come se il sole vi ferisse la tengono."'

43 Ingenious music follows each marriage: compare RR 20991–21022, Fc IV, 121,5–6. (The four musical trees in Fc IV, 121,6 are first described in IV, 85, 9). After her marriage, Biancifiore tells us of the ingenious ways in which she employed the Cupid statue as a substitute for Florio. For her, as for Pygmalion, such pathetic ingenuity serves, at least, as a palliative to torment: see RR 20854–6, 20907–81; Fc IV, 124, 1–4.

44 Genius explicitly compares the brilliance and efficacy of this three-faceted gem to the inferior qualities of the '"cristauz doubles"' situated in the well of Narcissus (20409–430). This progression within the *Rose* has a counterpart in the *Commedia* as Dante moves from gazing upon the Venus-like eyes of his beloved (Purg XXVIII, 64–66) to contemplation of the final Trinitarian vision: a comparison of RR 20495–568 and Par XXXIII, 76–145 elicits many striking parallels. A cognate movement occurs within *Filocolo* IV as we move from the scene illuminated by the Venus-like light reflected by Fiammetta's eyes (43,14) to the scene enacted within the tower.

The self-luminous carbuncle is, of course, a stock feature of European romance; it is also discussed by scholarly authors such as Marbode of Rennes and Isidore of Seville: see M. A. Owings, *The Arts in the Middle English Romances* (New York, 1952), pp. 143–4. The Sultan's pavilion in *Guy of Warwick* is surmounted by a golden, effulgent eagle and by 'a stone, that gaue grete lyght' (3642). The tower at Alexandria in *Floire et Blancheflor* (version I) is similarly surmounted by a carbuncle (which, in lighting up the surrounding terrain like a prison search-light (I, 1633–46) performs a defensive as well as a decorative function). On reading the French romance, Boccaccio was inspired to locate carbuncles *within* the tower and to charge them with iconographic suggestiveness borrowed from the *Rose*.

45 See *The Romance of the Rose*, translated by Charles Dahlberg (Princeton, 1971), p. 420.

46 See RR 20479–80, 20491–3. The olive symbolises the cross; its fruit is Christ.

47 The presence of the goddess of chastity at the wedding confirms that Florio's intentions are honest. (Troilus appeals to Diana in III, 731–2). Young (pp. 140–8) discerns the influence of the *Filocolo*'s marriage scenes in many details of the equivalent scenes in the *Troilus*, including Troilus' oaths of sincerity (III, 1142–5) and the exchange of rings (III, 1368).

48 See Purg XXVIII, 64–66, Fc II, 48,13 (and p. 789, note 13).

49 See Robinson, p. 823, note to lines 39–42. Chaucer was intimately familiar with St Bernard's prayer to the Virgin in Par XXXIII; he makes extensive use of it in the *Invocacio ad Mariam* which forms part of his *Second Nun's Prologue* (see Robinson, pp. 756–7).

50 Compare Par XXXIII, 14–16, T&C III, 1261–4.

51 For further adumbrations voiced by Troilus in Book III, see 1282, 1599–1600.

52 Alastair Fowler notes that III, 1271 is the central line of the central stanza of Chaucer's poem: see *Triumphal Forms* (Cambridge, 1970), p. 65.

53 See Minnis, pp. 10, 99–101 and (for a translation of the relevant Trevet gloss), pp. 145–6.

54 See Minnis, pp. 95–9. For a stimulating exploration of the treacherous terrain which extends between the 'heigh . . . place' at the centre of the *Troilus* (III, 1271) and the barren wastes of Book IV, see Winthrop Wetherbee, 'The Descent from Bliss: *Troilus* III. 1310–1582', in Barney, *Chaucer's 'Troilus'*, pp. 297–317.

55 See esp. V. 1828–32, 1849–53.

56 George Kane, *Middle English Literature* (London, 1951), p. 48.

57 See *The Discarded Image* (Cambridge, 1964), pp. 45–91.

58 The phrase is that of John of Wales, quoted by Minnis, p. 31.

1 Branca, *Opere di GB*, II, 846–72, notes more than one hundred parallels of phrasing and dramatic situation between the works: see esp. p. 854, note 22; 858,11; 861,65 & 77; 863,12; 867,26; 869,62.

2 R. K. Gordon, *The Story of Troilus as told by Benoît de Sainte-Maure, Giovanni Boccaccio (translated into English prose), Geoffrey Chaucer and Robert Henryson* (London, 1934), p. xiii. In 'The Fortunes of Troilus' (Appendix A to *Chaucer's Boccaccio*), N. R. Havely offers a more detailed and sophisticated account of the story of Troilus: but as his title suggests, Havely's perspective remains close to that of Gordon. It is salutary to note that the *Filostrato* may, viewed from the perspective of Italian literary history, be seen as being of marginal importance: the *Filocolo* is much more significant. (See N. Sapegno, *Storia letteraria del Trecento* (Milan–Naples, 1963), pp. 291–2.

3 Branca, *Opere di GB*, II, 7, notes that the extensive researches of Young and Pernicone have only managed to demonstrate Boccaccio's indebtedness to Benoît in little more than one hundred of his 5704 verses. Branca (pp. 5–7) notes Boccaccio's indebtedness to Guido delle Colonne's *Historia Troiana*, his probable indebtedness to Dares and Dictys and his possible use of Binduccio dello Scelto's Italian prose translation of Benoît. Quaglio observes that the 'disperato problema' of the *Filostrato*'s central source is still unresolved (*Tra Fonti*, p. 361, note 2).

4 Maria Gozzi, 'Sulle fonti del *Filostrato*. Le narrazioni di argomento troiano', SsB,5 (1968), pp. 123–209.

5 The texts compared with the *Filostrato* are as follows: Guido de Columnis, *Historia destructionis Troiae*; *Le Roman de Troie en prose*, anonymous; Benoît de Sainte-Maure, *Roman de Troie*; Binduccio dello Scelto, *Libro de la storia di Troia*; *Istorietta troiana*, anonymous; 'Romanzo barberiniano', anonymous. For full details of texts and manuscripts, see Gozzi, pp. 126–8. For a full account of Guido and his influence on English writers, see David C. Benson, *The History of Troy in Middle English Literature* (Woodbridge, Suffolk, 1980). The work of dello Scelto survives in a single manuscript, copied at Siena in 1322; it is a faithful translation of the southern version of the *Roman de Troie en prose*: see M. Gozzi, 'Ricerche storiche intorno a Binduccio dello Scelto', SsB, 3 (1965), pp. 25–39. The last two works listed above are also in prose, the first in Italian and the second in Latin.

6 Gozzi, *Fonti*, p. 126.

7 Gozzi, *Fonti*, pp. 207–9.

8 See above, p. 2.

9 See Gordon R. Silber, 'Alleged Imitations of Petrarch in the *Filostrato*', MP, 37 (1939–40), pp. 113–24.

10 F. Marletta, 'Di alcuni rapporti del *Filostrato* del Boccaccio con la poesia popolare' in *Miscellanea a Carlo Pascal* (Catania, 1913), pp. 201–19. For further discussion of the *Filostrato*'s popular fortune, see S. Debenedetti, 'Troilo cantore', GSLI, 66 (1915), pp. 414–25.

11 See above, p. 31 and note 78; and see Branca, *Opere di GB*, II, 865.

12 The phrase is translated from V. Branca, *Il cantare trecentesco e il Boccaccio del Filostrato e del Teseida* (Florence, 1936), p. 70.

13 Boccaccio makes a more impressive and sustained imitation of the *Convivio*'s expository style in two lengthy glosses to Tes VII: see *Opere di GB*, II, 453–6, 462–72. The content of this Fs passage (esp. VII, 99) is echoed in AV XXXIII (and in CT III, 1109–64).

14 Fs VIII, 29 and 30–33; T&C V, 1835–41 and 1842–8. The suspicion that Boccaccio is more interested in exploiting a literary posture in these verses than in offering moral guidance is confirmed by the rubric that precedes them; 'Parla l'autore a' giovani amadori assai brievemente, mostrando più nelle mature che nelle giovinette donne porre amore.'

15 This canzone, which appears in Florence, Biblioteca Nazionale Centrale MS II,

II, 38, was copied by one Rigo d'Allessandro Rondinelli. Paul M. Clogan, in 'Two Verse Commentaries on the Ending of Boccaccio's *Filostrato*', M&H, NS, 7, 147–52, provides a transcription (pp. 148–50).

16 See above, pp. 133–8.

17 See Branca, *Profilo*, pp. 40–41.

18 See Antonio Pucci, *Le noie*, edited by K. McKenzie (Princeton & Paris, 1931), p. xxxix. This poem is in *terza rima*.

19 See *Proprietà di Mercato Vecchio*, in *Poeti minori del Trecento*, edited by N. Sapegno (Milan–Naples, 1952), pp. 403–10. Pucci also employed *terzine* in his *Centiloquio*, a popularisation of G. Villani's *Cronica*: see DELI, IV, 467–8.

20 See N. Sapegno, 'Antonio Pucci', in *Pagine di storia letteraria*, second edition (Palermo, 1966), 133–181 (p. 149).

21 Boccaccio's utilitarian attitude towards the sonnet form in the *Teseida* may be gauged by his first introductory rubric: 'Sonetto nel quale si contiene uno argomento generale a tutto il libro.' (*Opere di GB*, II, 251). Boccaccio may have been inspired to employ such sonnets by the metrical arguments (some perhaps as old as the sixth century) which preceded each book of the *Thebaid*. The Latin argument in the T&C MSS after V, 1498 was probably derived from such sources: see Robinson, pp. 835–6. Although Chaucer could hardly have admired the poetic quality of Boccaccio's sonnets, he may well have appreciated their decorative, classicising effect.

22 The term *cantare* may be employed in three distinct ways, indicating: 1) a tradition of narrative; 2) a specific poem within that tradition; 3) a specific portion of such a poem (corresponding to a *fitt* of an English tail-rhyme romance). So within the *cantare* tradition, we discover the *cantare* of *Febus-el-Forte*, composed of six *cantari*.

23 See Branca, *Il cantare* (cited above, p. 188 note 12), pp. 54–55.

24 Branca (*Il cantare*, p. 4) explicitly accepts the distinction between popular and aristocratic poetry established by Croce's 1933 study. It is encouraging to note that twenty years earlier, Marletta had concluded his essay by arguing that '"la poesia culta e la popolare"' should not be treated as mutually exclusive entities: much passed between them. (See Marletta, *Di alcuni rapporti*, p. 219).

25 Boitani, maintaining that 'nothing more exhaustive' can be added to Branca's study, proceeds to summarise Branca's findings (*Chaucer and Boccaccio*, pp. 40–41). In fact, there has been a great flowering of *cantare* studies since Branca's work of 1936: see Antonio Franceschetti, 'Rassegna di studi sui cantari', LI, 25 (1973), pp. 556–74. Havely notes that the *cantari* and the English tail-rhyme romances share certain characteristics: see *Chaucer's Boccaccio*, p. 7.

26 Dieter Mehl, *The Middle English Romances of the Thirteenth and Fourteenth Centuries* (London, 1968), p. 28. In similar vein, Robert Jordan argues that application of the generic term 'romance' to Chaucerian narrative creates two taxonomic alternatives: 'either all of Chaucer's narratives are romances . . . or the Chaucer canon contains no such genre as romance' ('Chaucerian Romance?', in *Approaches to Medieval Romance*, edited by Peter Haidu, Yale French Studies, 51 (1974), 223–34 (p. 233)). Jordan further suggests that 'the generic boundaries formulated by modern scholarship' are of little use when applied to Chaucerian narrative structure. I would suggest, however, that the kind of structural analyses performed or made possible by Hans Robert Jauss offer considerable potential for Chaucer studies. See, for example, 'Genres and Medieval Literature', in *Toward an Aesthetic of Reception*, translated by Timothy Bahti (Minneapolis, 1982), 76–109 (pp. 83–7), where romance is generically differentiated from epic and the novella.

27 Mehl, p. 31, is referring to the three-fold division ('De France, et de Bretaigne, et de Rome . . .') proposed by Jean Bodel in his *Chanson des Saisnes*. Baugh and Sands (and others before them) accept Bodel's divisions, although they find it necessary to invent additional 'matters' for the English romance: see *A Literary History of England*, edited by A. C. Baugh (NY, 1948), pp. 174–5; D. B. Sands, *Middle English Verse*

Romances (NY, 1966), p. 2. See also Douglas Kelly, '*Matière* and *genera dicendi* in Medieval Romance', in Haidu, *Approaches*, 147–59, esp. p. 151.

28 Derek Pearsall, 'The Development of Middle English Romance', *Medieval Studies*, 27 (1965), 91–116 (p. 91).

29 For the text of this enigmatic poem, see Pio Rajna, 'Il Cantare dei Cantari e il Serventese del Maestro di tutti l'Arti', *Zeitschrift für Romanische Philologie*, 2 (1878), pp. 220–54 & 419–37; and see below, p. 141.

30 Vittore Branca observes that 'ottava e cantari sono termini . . . saldate l'una all'altra': see 'Nostalgie tardogotiche e gusto del fiabesco nella tradizione narrativa dei cantari', in *Studi di varia umanità in onore di Francesco Flora*, edited by G. B. Pighi et al. (Milan, 1963), 88–108 (p. 91).

31 See A. Balduino, 'Traduzione canterina e tonalità popolareggianti nel *Ninfale fiesolano*', SsB, 2 (1964), 25–80 (pp. 28–29). A *strambotto* is 'a folk-lyric of 8 or 6 lines' (CID, I, 787); a *rispetto* is a 'love poem in a stanza of eight or six lines (a popular art-form, esp. of the Tuscan countryside)'. (CID, I, 673).

32 Marletta, *Di alcuni rapporti*, p. 202, describes a 12 stanza *serenata* which borrows 3 stanzas from the *Filostrato*.

33 Branca, *Il cantare*, pp. ix–x. Considering the ways in which romances were presented by professional story-tellers, Baugh (like Branca) concedes that certain works were evidently too lengthy to have been intended for 'the market place or the tavern': see A. C. Baugh, 'The Middle English Romances: Some Questions of Creation, Presentation and Preservation', *Speculum*, 42 (1967), 1–31 (p. 19).

34 Pearsall, *Development*, p. 91.

35 Balduino, *Cantari*, p. 8.

36 See Domenico De Robertis, 'Problemi di metodo nell'edizione dei cantari', in *Studi e problemi di critica testuale. Convegno di Studi di Filologia italiana nel Centenario della Commissione per i Testi di Lingua (7–9 aprile 1960)*, (Bologna, 1961), pp. 119–38. Franceschetti (*Rassegna*, p. 566) and Balduino (*Cantari*, p. 24) respect the rigorous guidelines established by De Robertis, who insists that a *cantare* can only be held to be as old as the MS that contains it, even though the legend or story it narrates is almost certainly much older. De Robertis lists all *cantari* firmly dateable before 1375 (excluding those of Pucci) in 'Cantari antichi', *Studi di filologia italiana*, 28 (1970), 67–175 (pp. 67–77).

37 See Branca, *Il cantare*, p. X; Pearsall, *Development*, p. 92.

38 Pearsall, *Development*, p. 97, note 12; Jennifer L. Fellows, '*Sir Beves of Hampton*: Study and Edition', unpublished Ph.D. dissertation, Cambridge University, 5 vols (1980). *Cantare* MSS raise uncertainties comparable to those discussed by Pearsall: see Franceschetti, *Rassegna*, pp. 566–7.

39 'The scribe is no longer a copyist; he has become a poet' (Baugh, *Some Questions*, p. 29). Baugh's equation is suggestive, but not universally applicable: for example, although *Lai Le Freine* and *Roland and Vernagu* were copied into the same gathering (37) of the Auchinleck MS by the same man ('scribe 1'), they nevertheless display great differences in literary merit. It seems clear that versifier and copyist (or perhaps translator, versifier and copyist) made independent contributions to the production process of each Auchinleck romance: see *The Auchinleck Manuscript. National Library of Scotland Advocates' MS 19.2.1*, a facsimile introduced by Derek Pearsall and I. C. Cunningham (London, 1977), pp. viii–xi. And see De Robertis, *Problemi*, pp. 122–3.

40 L. H. Loomis, in 'The Auchinleck Manuscript and a Possible London Bookshop of 1330–1340', PMLA, 57 (1942), 595–627, remarks on 'the little insistence there was anywhere on the accurate copying of secular English texts' (p. 622). This state of affairs is lamented in *Chaucer's Wordes unto Adam, His Owne Scriveyn* (Robinson, *Works of Chaucer*, p. 534).

41 See Baugh, *Some Questions*, passim; Franceschetti, *Rassegna*, pp. 560–1, upholding the meticulous considerations of De Robertis, *Problemi*, pp. 129–31. These two Italian scholars define a *canterino* as, strictly speaking, a creative fabricator (or

popular poet), distinguishing his function from that of a copyist or public performer. Inevitably, critical discussions find it difficult to observe such distinctions with much consistency, and the term *canterino* is used somewhat loosely. (In many instances, of course, the *canterino* may have been his own copyist and performer). Loomis observes comparable ambiguities surrounding discussions of 'minstrels', who are sometimes spoken of as authors and sometimes as 'oral "publishers" of . . . popular poetry' (*Bookshop*, p. 595).

42 'The trouble with assumptions about oral tradition is that, in the nature of things, no other evidence is likely to be forthcoming' (Pearsall, *OE & ME Poetry*, p. 154). For differing views of this highly problematic relationship between oral and literate composition, see Larry D. Benson, 'The Literary Character of Anglo-Saxon Poetry', PMLA, 81 (1966), pp. 334–41; *Oral Traditional Literature. A Festschrift for Albert Lord Bates*, edited by John Miles Foley (Columbus, Ohio, 1981); Walter J. Ong, *Orality and Literacy. The Technologizing of the Word* (London & NY, 1982). See also M. T. Clanchy, *From Memory to Written Record. England 1066–1307* (London, 1979), pp. 211–2.

43 Baugh, *Some Questions*, p. 29, my addition in brackets. Baugh's account may be compared with that of Balduino, *Cantari*, p. 9.

44 *Floris and Blauncheflur*, ed. De Vries, lines 595–8 (pp. 92–94). Subsequent references to F&B follow De Vries' edition from MS Egerton 2862.

45 Pearsall (*Development*, p. 93) and Baugh (*Some Questions*, p. 26) isolate some interesting moments in the general process of winnowing out minstrel material from English romances. This process was by no means complete in either the romance or *cantare* tradition by the fifteenth century.

46 See Branca, *Il cantare*, pp. 54–56. For the essential functions of redundancy, see Ong, pp. 39–41; Susan Wittig, *Stylistic and narrative structures in the Middle English Romances* (Austin & London, 1978), pp. 12–16, 125–6, 181–2.

47 See John Burrow, *Medieval Writers and Their Work. Middle English Literature and its Background 1100–1500* (Oxford, 1982), p. 47. See also Ong's account of 'the tenaciousness of orality' (pp. 115–6). A little earlier, Ong gives a timely reminder that rhetoric has much in common with the oral traditions which, in modern critical discourse, are often opposed to it: 'rhetoric retained much of the old oral feeling for thought and expression as basically agonistic and formulaic' (p. 110).

48 *The Tale of Gamelyn*, edited by W. W. Skeat (Oxford, 1893). Six variations of this appeal are contained in *Gamelyn*; *canterini*, beginning new *cantari* (divisions of a longer work) similarly repeat and vary their opening formulae. Other means of dividing segments of narrative are sometimes employed: in *King Horn* and *Febus-el-Forte*, for example, fresh narrative episodes often begin after sunrise. For F-e-F, see Alberto Limentani, *Dal Roman de Palamedés ai Cantari di Febus-el-Forte* (Bologna, 1962). For KH, see *King Horn*, edited by Joseph Hall (Oxford, 1901). Hall edits all 3 MSS; I refer to his edition of Cambridge University Library MS Gg. 4.27.2.

49 The author of *Emaré* insists that minstrels should, '. . . at her bygynnyng/Speke of þat ryghtwes Kyng/That made bothe see and sonde.' See *Emaré* in *Middle English Metrical Romances*, edited by W. H. French and C. B. Hale (NY, 1930), pp. 421–55; lines quoted (16–18) are from the second stanza. Schmidt and Jacobs note that 'opening with a prayer is especially found in tail-rhyme romances' (I, 187).

50 Text from French & Hale, pp. 381–419. The content and structure of this stanza is closely paralleled by the opening of *Athelston* (edited by A. McI. Trounce, EETS, OS, 224 (1951)). The second *cantare* of *Il Bel Gherardino* (in Balduino, *Cantari*, pp. 71–99) also opens with an appeal to the Trinity.

51 This *cantare* is the work of Antonio Pucci: text from Sapegno, *Poeti minori*, pp. 869–81.

52 Many *canterini* (doubtless inspired by Dante's example) appeal for 'grazia' or 'grazia nella mente' to inspire their compositions: English romance writers appeal for 'grace' as sinners, but not for literary inspiration.

53 In Balduino, *Cantari*, pp. 147–60.

54 See above, pp. 8–10, 15–16.

55 Text from Balduino, *Cantari*, pp. 237–51.

56 See, for example, *Bel Gherardino* I, 37,8.

57 See *Athelston* 168–9, where full-blooded oaths by different speakers conclude one stanza and begin another; see F-e-F V, 32–33 and SCS 35.

58 Text from Sapegno, *Poeti minori*, pp. 914–37.

59 BG: I, 3,4; I, 12,3; I, 14,4.

60 See, for example, *Ultime imprese e morte di Tristano* (in Balduino, *Cantari*, pp. 101–27), 4,4. These two forms are included in a list of 'formule varie' in Limentani, *Febus*, p. xxxiii. In *The Romance of Sir Beues of Hamtoun*, (edited by E. Kölbing, EETS, ES, 46,48,65 (1885–94)), C. Schmirgel offers two appendices which are useful for comparative purposes: I, 'Typical Expressions' (pp. xlv–lxiv), and II, 'Repetitions Within the Poem' (pp. lxiv–lxvi).

61 Edited by MacEdward Leach, EETS, OS, 203 (1937).

62 This *cantare*, the work of Antonio Pucci, appears in Sapegno, *Poeti minori*, pp. 882–95.

63 F&B 636; SCS 25,1; A&A 2252, F-e-F I, 1,5; A&A 2447; F-e-F VI, 52,7; A&A 1888; *Spagna* 391. Extracts from *Spagna*, a poem in 40 *cantari*, are given by Sapegno, *Poeti minori*, pp. 896–913. I follow this text.

64 KH 430; SCS 31,1.

65 A&A 265; F-e-F I, 23,7; *Sir Launfal*, edited by A. J. Bliss (London, 1960), line 283.

66 SL 536 (BG II, 47,6); F&B 245 (F-e-F II, 30,1); A&A 1793 (BB 367).

67 Pearsall, *OE & ME Poetry*, p. 149. Pearsall offers a subtle and succinct discussion of the distinction between tags and formulae. For an alternative formulation of this qualitative divide, see Judith E. Martin, 'Studies in Some Early Middle English Romances', unpublished Ph.D. dissertation, Cambridge University (1968), p. 268.

68 See *Ultime imprese e morte di Tristano*.

69 See above, p. 43.

70 Pearsall, *Development*, p. 96.

71 UIMT 66,6: ' "wretch!" '.

72 In BG, I, 39 the Pope, overcome with curiosity, rides (with 'altri baroni') five miles out of Rome to see Bel Gherardino and company: 'contra a costoro andaro per vedelli' (I, 39,8). In *Sir Launfal*, King Arthur sees two knights, 'And aȝens ham he gan wende' (152). Both authors are similarly impatient in developing their narrative; it is interesting to note that they employ similar prepositions ('contra', 'aȝens') in the phrases quoted.

73 See above, p. 43.

74 Geoffrey of Vinsauf, for example, devotes just 28 of his 2121 lines to *inventio* (lines 43–70): see Ernest Gallo, *The 'Poetria Nova' and its Sources in Early Rhetorical Doctrine* (The Hague-Paris, 1971), pp. 16–17, 136–7. Payne notes that 'for Chaucer as for his thirteenth-century preceptors, the action of a narrative poem is all potential, and ultimately is only what the realization of a style can make of it' (*Key*, pp. 179–80).

75 See, for example: Gam 877; F&B 367, 825–6; BG I, 11,5–6, I, 23,3, I, 42,2, II, 46,8; Gib 418, 422.

76 KH 598 features the epithet 'heþene honde'; CFB exploits the fortunate rhyming of 'cristiani', 'pagani' and 'cani' (see above, p. 43).

77 Heroes' names are mercilessly exploited for rhyming purposes: 'Febusso' encourages employment of the tag 'senza noia o busso' (F-e-F: II, 58,6; VI, 2,5); Liombruno is rhymed with 'pruno' (L 281–5) and Roulond with 'hys bronde' (*Otuel & Roland*, 578–9: see *Firumbras and Otuel and Roland*, edited by M. I. O'Sullivan, EETS, OS, 198 (1935)).

78 See Sapegno, *Storia letteraria*, pp. 388–9.

79 See Branca, *Nostalgie*, p. 88; Franceschetti, *Rassegna*, p. 571. In discussing the

cantare, we should remember that a vital element—the musical accompaniment—has perished: see Branca, *Il cantare*, p. 3.

80 Pearsall, *Development*, p. 105. A variety of tail-rhyme stanzas are employed (to great effect) by the lyrics in MS Harley 2253, which dates from around 1314–25: see *The Harley Lyrics*, edited by G. L. Brook, fourth edition (Manchester, 1968).

81 See, for example: BG I, 44,6; UIMT 55, 8; F-e-F VI, 38,2; *Cantare di Pirramo e di Tisbe*, (Redazione A), 33,6. For this last work, see Balduino, *Cantari*, pp. 129–45. Employed as a final conjunction (with the subjunctive), *onde* means 'so that'; 'in order to'; 'so as to'. As a relative adverb, *onde* may mean: 'whence, from where, from which, with which, wherewith' (CID, I,519).

82 See, for example: A, 371, 446, 533; A&A 150, 237.

83 Giosue Carducci, 'Ai parentali di Giovanni Boccacci', *Edizione nazionale delle opere di Giosue Carducci*, directed by L. Federzoni, 30 vols (Bologna, 1945–62), XI, 311–334 (p. 322).

84 Pearsall, *Development*, p. 108. In the course of his excellent article (esp. pp. 105–112), Pearsall observes the stages of this evolutionary process.

85 See Sapegno, *Poeti minori*, p. 809; Pearsall, *Development*, pp. 91–92, *OE & ME Poetry*, p. 146. See also David Wallace, 'Mystics and Followers in Siena and East Anglia: A study in Taxonomy, Class and Cultural Mediation', in *The Medieval Mystical Tradition in England. Dartington 1984*, edited by Marion Glasscoe (Cambridge, 1984).

86 Both the *cantare* and the tail-rhyme traditions are regional in character. The *cantare* was firmly centred in Tuscany, although it later spread further afield. There are contemporary references to a Franco-Venetian *cantare* tradition, but textual evidence is lacking: see Franceschetti, *Rassegna*, pp. 572–3. A. McI. Trounce, in 'The English Tail-rhyme Romances', *Medium Aevum*, 1 (1932), pp. 87–108, 168–82, 2 (1933), 34–57, 189–98, 3 (1934), 30–50 argues that the tail-rhyme romances formed an east-midland tradition. Mehl (*The ME Romances*, p. 34) accepts this thesis; Pearsall (among others) is more wary, feeling that Trounce over-states his case, but nevertheless proposes that 'the tradition is centred in the east-midlands but shifts northwards towards the end of the century'. (*Development*, p. 109; and see Pearsall, *OE & ME Poetry*, pp. 148, 318).

87 See *A Manual of Writings in Middle English 1050–1500*, edited by J. Burke Severs (vols 1–2) and by Albert E. Hartung (vols 3–6), incomplete (Hamden, Connecticut, 1967–), vol. I, *Romances*, pp. 11–12; Baugh, *History*, p. 174; and Balduino, *Cantari*, p. 21, who notes that the *cantare* has the characteristics of 'una letteratura "riflessa"'. Pearsall (*OE & ME Poetry*, pp. 143–4) observes that 'whereas most English romances of the thirteenth century are derived directly from Anglo-Norman originals, the majority of fourteenth century romances are derived, at one or two removes, from French'. Limentani, in *Febus*, pp. V–CXXI, offers a detailed and illuminating account of the metamorphosis of the *Roman de Palamedés* into the *Cantari di Febus-el-Forte* by way of an Italian prose translation; he then presents excellent editions of the relevant texts.

88 Pearsall and Cunningham, *Auchinleck MS*, p. vii.

89 Trounce, *English Tail-rhyme*, 1 (1932), p. 94.

90 See above, pp. 42–4 and p. 180, note 15.

91 *Volgarizzamenti del Due e Trecento*, edited by C. Segre (Turin, 1953), p. 13. Segre remarks on the popularity of French romances throughout Italy in the thirteenth and fourteenth centuries. For the popularisation of French romance in England, see Lee C. Ramsey, *Chivalric Romances. Popular Literature in Medieval England* (Bloomington, 1983), esp. pp. 1–25 ('The French Book').

92 See Fc I, 1,25–26, and pp. 42–4 above.

93 See Sapegno, *Poeti minori*, p. 869; Bliss, *Sir Launfal*, pp. 24–31. Typically, Pucci's hero derives his name from a misunderstanding of the Latin 'Brito miles'; the adjective 'Brito' (Breton) is mistaken for a proper noun. Andreas' *De Amore* was popular reading in Italy: Pucci commends it in lines 9–10 of *Brito* (quoted above, p. 85).

94 See Balduino, *Cantari*, pp. 103–4. The Tristan legend was particularly popular in fourteenth-century Italy: see D. Branca, *I romanzi italiani di Tristano e la Tavola Ritonda* (Florence, 1968). Outside Malory, only one romance centred on Tristan survives in English: but *Sir Tristrem* (c.1300) is an important transitional work which heralds the way both for the developed tail-rhyme stanza and for the greater popularity of Arthurian subjects in the fourteenth century. See Baugh, *History*, pp. 189–93; Pearsall, *Development*, pp. 107–8.

95 See Baugh, *History*, pp. 185–9 and *Some Questions*, p. 20; Severs, *Romances*, pp. 80–100; Anna Hunt Billings, *A Guide to the Middle English Romances* (NY, 1901; reprinted NY, 1967), pp. 47–84; Margaret Adlum Gist, *Love and War in the Middle English Romances* (Philadelphia & London, 1947), pp. 113–90. Although the earliest reference to the *cantare* (see above, p. 84) mentions Carolingian heroes, no fourteenth-century Charlemagne *cantari* survive: *Spagna* and its partial derivative *Orlando*, thought by Sapegno to date from the later fourteenth century, are now thought to date from after 1400. See Franceschetti, *Rassegna*, pp. 558–9.

96 *Sir Launfal*, 961–6; *Febus* VI, 33,5—34,3. For further examples, see SO 281–313, CFB 25–26.

97 Gamelyn's father 'cowde of norture ynough · and mochil of game' (Gam 4); Bel Gherardino professes to know how to serve at table (BG II, 20). The circumlocutory styles of BG I, 33 and CFB 129 attempt, it seems, to imitate courtly diction.

98 See F-e-F V, 43 (and Sp. 309–24); A 338–9.

99 SL 79–81; BG I, 7,1–2. Authors in both traditions characteristically display a warm (mercenary) interest in money matters. See also AV XIV (A), 55–84 and HF 1348–9 (and above, p. 18).

100 The text follows Sapegno, *Poeti minori*, pp. 824–42. The poem's title, like that of *Brito*, represents a mistranslation: see *Poeti minori*, p. 824. Boccaccio refers to this *cantare* in Dec III, Conclusione, 8; he alludes to BG and F-e-F in *Corbaccio* (see Ricci, *Opere in Versi*, p. 528).

101 See esp. DdV 105–6, where the *canterino* seems almost to announce a fresh start to the narrative action.

102 The text follows *La Chastelaine de Vergi*, edited by F. Whitehead, second edition (Manchester, 1951).

103 See *Lanval* 269–74 in Marie de France, *Lais*, edited by A. Ewert (Oxford, 1944). A similar situation arises in *Guingamor*, a lay which Ewert (p. xvi) does not attribute to Marie.

104 See *Cantari religiosi senesi del Trecento*, edited by G. Varanini, Sd'I 230 (Bari, 1965); Wallace, *Mystics and Followers*, pp. 170–183.

105 This fascinating poem, probably composed in the spring of 1376, appears in Balduino, *Cantari*, pp. 237–51.

106 Baugh, *Some Questions*, p. 2.

107 Four *cantare* versions of this Ovidian legend have survived: 'redazione A' is the only one which can securely be regarded as a Trecento text. See Balduino, *Cantari*, pp. 131–2.

108 See C. Dionisotti, 'Appunti su antichi testi', IMU, 7 (1964), 77–131 (pp. 99–131); Roncaglia, *Ottova rima*, pp. 5–14. The arguments of these critics are most ably summarised and analysed by Balduino, *Cantari*, pp. 19–21, 257–9, and by Franceschetti, *Rassegna*, pp. 570–4.

109 Franceschetti observes that 'a questo punto delle ricerche ci sembra molto più probabile che, forma metrica a parte, sia stato il Boccaccio a nobilitare e a fissare, addottandola, quella tradizione più che a costituirla' (*Rassegna*, p. 572).

110 Branca, noting the traditional assignation of two *cantari* to Boccaccio (the *Ruffianella* and Niccolò Cicerchia's *Passione*) suggests that this indicates 'come egli fu sentito per tutto il Trecento quasi come un *canterino*'. (*Il cantare*, p. 57). See also Varanini, *Cantari religiosi senesi*, pp. 539–42; Balduino, *Cantari*, p. 163.

111 See Balduino, *Tradizione canterina*, p. 79, note 2.

112 The *Decameron's* earliest admirers were from the merchant class: see above, p. 29.

113 See above, p. 87; and see Balduino, *Cantari*, p. 104. The editor or director of the Auchinleck MS was similarly willing to dismember a continuous French source in order to generate two or three English romances: see Loomis, *Bookshop*, p. 612.

114 See Rajna, *Cantare dei Cantari*, pp. 231–45.

115 See, for example: II, 41,4–5, using Par XIV, 28–30; II, 135,8, using Purg III, 78; VI, 27,5, using Par XXV, 4.

116 See Branca, *Opere di GB*, II, 4–5.

117 These lines owe something to Inf XV, 46–47: but the image of Fortune as a guiding force compares with that of BG II, 11,8. The casual way in which the *Filostrato* employs the term 'fortuna' might be compared with PT 8–9. In imitating Fs II, 2,1–2, Chaucer renders ' "fortuna" ' as ' "cas . . . or aventure" ' (T&C I, 568).

118 See E. Melli, 'Riecheggiamenti danteschi in un cantare toscano del secolo XIV', *Filologia romanza*, 5 (1958), pp. 82–87. Limentani (*Febus*, p. XVIII) amends and extends Melli's list of Dantean echoes in *Febus*. See also Fs II, 72,6, which employs Inf II, 106 as a link in a chain of the most mundane, self-absorbed logic.

119 See also VII, 62,1–3; and see V, 40,1–5, which features a rapid journey and a ceremonious meeting of the kind noted above, p. 84 (and note 72).

120 Compare Fs II, 23,1–3, T&C I, 897–900.

121 In Fs II, 54,2, Pandaro describes Troiolo as a ' "segreto uom" '. In II, 11,1–4, Pandaro reveals that he has failed in love by breaching the rules of secrecy: Chaucer ignores this revelation.

122 See Barry Windeatt, ' "Love that Oughte Ben Secree" in Chaucer's *Troilus*', CR, 14 (1979–80), pp. 116–31.

123 See, for example, I, 49,2 ('che dir non si poria'), and IV, 95–102, which features three such examples.

124 Wittig, *Structures*, p. 70.

125 See Wittig, p. 179.

126 Jauss, *Aesthetic of Reception*, p. 79.

127 See, for example: III, 59,1–2; III, 65,1–2; IV, 65,4; VI, 19,7–8; III, 94; IV, 60; IV, 107.

128 See Payne, *Key*, p. 191.

129 To draw attention to the *Filostrato's* contribution to the language of the *Troilus*, I have underlined equivalent phrases in the Italian and English texts; ideas paraphrased or recast from the Italian are not underlined. Such a simple expedient is only intended as an approximate, initial guide to Chaucer's imitations.

130 Most of Boccaccio's authorial posturing is confined to the rubrics which punctuate his narrative at frequent intervals: in these rubrics he habitually refers to himself impersonally as 'l'autore'.

131 On Chaucer's characteristic and frequent appeals 'to *common* human experience', see Jill Mann, 'Chaucerian Themes and Style in the *Franklin's Tale*', in *The New Pelican Guide to English Literature*, edited by Boris Ford, *1. Medieval Literature. Part One: Chaucer and the Alliterative Tradition* (Harmondsworth, 1982), 133–53 (p. 137).

132 See Eugène Vinaver, *The Rise of Romance* (Oxford, 1971); Robert W. Hanning, *The Individual in Twelfth-Century Romance* (New Haven & London, 1977).

133 On reading Boccaccio's early writings we may imagine, as Richard Firth Green imagines on reading LGW, 'the presence of a tight-knit group of initiates playing with literary and social conventions at which we can now but guess' ('The *Familia Regis* and the *Familia Cupidinis*', in Scattergood & Sherborne, 87–108 (p. 106)). But, Green argues, there is no reason to ascribe the genesis of LGW to historical, formally-constituted courts of love; and there is less reason, as I have argued in chapter II, to seek such origins for CD, Fc and Fs.

134 See CT V, 1622; and see Brewer, *Parlement*, pp. 7–13.

135 Branca, *Opere di GB*, II, 851, note 34.

136 Chaucer's stanza is partly indebted to the third *metrum* of *De Consolatione Philosophiae*, where the clouds of ignorance and confusion surrounding the narrator are first pierced by sunlight. Chaucer is audacious in reversing the movement of the Latin imagery—in describing how Criseyde's 'brighte thoughtes' are clouded over with 'feere'—and in enlisting such powerful natural images to describe a change of expression on a woman's face. This imagery colours the development of subsequent stanzas: see II, 781, 806.

137 In I, 400–20, Chaucer imitates *Canzoniere* CXXXII (see Neri, *Rime*, p. 194). Petrarch finds himself 'fra sì contrari venti': Troilus is ' "possed to and fro" ', ' "bitwixen wyndes two, / That in contrarie stonden evere mo" '.

138 For a detailed account of such qualities in Chaucer, see J. D. Burnley, *Chaucer's Language and the Philosophers' Tradition* (Cambridge, 1979).

139 For Chaucer's conception of *curteisie* (and of the related term, *gentillesse*), see Burnley, pp. 151–70.

140 See *Mimesis*, translated by Willard R. Trask (Princeton, 1968), p. 208.

141 Par X, 27. In the *prohemium* to Book II, Chaucer is similarly concerned to present himself as a humble mediator of prescribed material.

142 For a more sophisticated and informed discussion of these *terzine* and their implications, see Robin Kirkpatrick, *Dante's Paradiso and the Limitations of Modern Criticism* (Cambridge, 1978), pp. 28–30 and *passim*.

143 I follow the edition of Gallo, cited above, p. 192, note 74; my translation. On Chaucer's translation, see Robinson, p. 818, note to 1065ff.

144 Jordan, *Chaucerian Romance?*, p. 225 (summarising Vinaver, *Rise of Romance*, pp. 36–7). As Jordan points out, it is this resemblance, or half resemblance, to the poets of twelfth-century France which makes Chaucer's exceptional artistic practice seem, historically speaking, decadent.

Chapter 6: The Making of Troilus and Criseyde   pp. 106–140

1 See Payne, *Key*, pp. 177–88.

2 Problems associated with the close reading of medieval texts are identified and discussed by A. C. Spearing, *Criticism and Medieval Poetry*, second edition (London, 1972), pp. 1–27.

3 For explanations of editorial practice, see Branca, *Opere di GB*, II, 839–44; Robinson, *Works of Chaucer*, pp. xl–xli, 905–6. The list of variant readings in Robinson may be supplemented by those in *The Book of Troilus and Criseyde*, edited by R. K. Root (Princeton, 1926). All textual parallels adduced by my comparisons of Fs and T&C have been checked against (and are upheld by) the new Windeatt text of the *Troilus*, always excepting obvious differences in editorial punctuation and spelling. See Geoffrey Chaucer, *Troilus and Criseyde. A New Edition of 'The Book of Troilus'*, by B. A. Windeatt (London & NY, 1984).

4 Barry Windeatt has recently provided materials which help in forming such an estimate: see 'Chaucer and the *Filostrato*', in Boitani, *Trecento*, pp. 163–183; and see his *New Edition*, pp. 3–24.

5 See Paul G. Ruggiers, 'The Italian Influence on Chaucer', in CCS, 160–84 (p. 161).

6 See Bruce Harbert, 'Chaucer and the Latin Classics', in Brewer, *Writers*, 137–153 (pp. 145–8).

7 See R. A. Pratt, 'Chaucer and *Le Roman de Troyle et de Criseida*', SP, 53 (1956), pp. 509–39. Robinson draws attention to these 'new discoveries of Professor Pratt' (p. 812).

8 It seems that T. S. Eliot was influenced by the Temple Classics translation of Inf XV in composing *Little Gidding*: see J. A. W. Bennett, '*Little Gidding*. A Poem of Pentecost', *Ampleforth Journal*, 79 (1974), Part I, 60–73 (pp. 65–66). This does not prove that Eliot's Italian was defective.

9 Carla Bozzolo, *Manuscrits des traductions françaises d'oeuvres de Boccace. XVe siècle* (Padua, 1973), pp. 29–33.

10 *New Edition*, p. 19.

11 For a vigorous example of modern dilettantism, see Ian Robinson, *Chaucer and the English Tradition* (Cambridge, 1972), pp. 248–65.

12 As we shall see, Chaucer's understanding of Boccaccio's Italian sometimes surpasses that of the *Filostrato*'s most recent (and most competent) English translator, N. R. Havely.

13 *Key*, p. 176.

14 See OED, *foreknow* (b); MED *for(e-knouen)*.

15 See *A Chaucer Glossary*, compiled by Norman Davis et al. (Oxford, 1979), *viage* (2).

16 'Thus driveth forth' echoes a phrase in V, 680 and recalls I, 1092 (see above, p. 138), a line which is repeated at V, 1540.

17 The last readily identifiable parallel in phrasing came with VI, 31, 1 and V, 989. (The phrase 'of which he was ful feyn' (V, 1013) may owe something to 'fu assai caro' (VI, 32,2); 'seco venne pensando' (VI, 33,7) may have inspired Chaucer's usage of the present participle in 'Retornyng in hire soule ay up and down' (V, 1023)). I shall argue below that when Chaucer rejoins Boccaccio's text after having elaborated his narrative independently, he often rejoins it most emphatically: here he makes continuous and extensive use of the first eleven stanzas of *Filostrato* VII.

18 We cannot, of course, straightforwardly equate our own difficulties with those of Chaucer. As Chaucer's word order was highly flexible, comparable flexibility in the *Filostrato* may not have troubled him. But the two verbs in question do seem to have been comparatively rare: *penare* does not feature in the *Commedia* (although it appears nine times in the *Decameron*); *disbrigare* appears only once in the *Commedia* (albeit in the memorable context of *Inferno* XXXIII, 116) and does not appear in the *Decameron*.

19 The adjective *vaga*, which has a broad range of application, appears forty-four times in the *Decameron*; the phrase 'vaga bellezza' appears at III, 8,25; IV, Intro 31; X, 8,78.

20 *Science* is featured forty-five times in Chaucer's writings (including nineteen usages in *Boece*). In the *Troilus* it appears only twice (I, 67; V, 1255). In speculating that 'science' may have drawn Criseyde's attention away from him, Troilus is probably thinking of the influence of Calkas, 'That in science so expert was . . .' (I, 67).

21 ME *fel* derives from OF *fel*, 'fierce, savage'; its range of meaning corresponds closely to that of the Italian *fiera*.

22 The form 'oh me' occurs once in the *Commedia* (Inf XXVIII, 123) and 'omè' five times. The form 'oimè' occurs frequently in the *Decameron*, and in the *Canzoniere* too (but not as frequently as Petrarch's imitators lead one to expect).

23 The Italian counterpart is VII, 26. Chaucer makes no use of VII, 28. In VII, 27, Troiolo interprets his own dream; Chaucer saves this stanza until V, 1513–19 and makes Cassandra the interpreter.

24 CID, I, 555.

25 Chaucer's understanding was doubtless aided by the fact that ME *thought* could have similarly distressful overtones (which modern English *thought* has lost): see OED, *thought* (5).

26 Compare the meanings of *descenden* and *discendere* given by MED (7) and by GDLI (9).

27 *Covenable* features most prominently in scientific and theological contexts (see MED, *covenable* (1–6)); all but two of the verifiably Chaucerian usages occur in prose works. The verb 'moleste' appears in Rom 5274.

28 See Fs IV, 4,5–6 and Havely, pp. 57,201.

29 'Malvissuto' does not appear in Dec; it is not listed in CID.

30 Havely, *Chaucer's Boccaccio*, p. 47. Subsequent page references to this work are given in the text in brackets.

31 See also Chaucer's translation of Fs III, 53,4 (III, 1538, quoted above, p. 116) where 'slep' ('sonno') is accorded a similarly active role.

32 For another close Chaucerian imitation of an Italian stanza beginning with a present participial phrase, see IV, 127–30 (and Fs IV, 12,1–3).

33 Compare also Fs IV, 83, T&C IV, 701–7; Fs IV, 69,1–3, T&C IV, 554–6. In translating Fs IV, 69,3 Havely (p. 64)—but not Chaucer—misses Boccaccio's sudden switch to the present tense.

34 Boccaccio's *sententia* was a popular commonplace (see Branca, *Opere di GB*,II, 849). It is featured as the thirteenth of the 'rules of love' in *De Amore* II, viii: 'Amor raro consuevit durare vulgatus'. See Andrea Capellano, *Trattato d'Amore. Testo latino del sec. XII con due traduzioni toscane inedite del sec. XIV*, edited by Salvatore Battaglia (Rome, 1947), pp. 358–9.

35 See, for example, Fs VII, 10,6–7 and T&C V, 1170.

36 'Gola' means 'throat'; 'avere gola a qualcosa' means 'to have an appetite for something, to desire something'. The expression is still current although, curiously, it is not listed in CID.

37 See N. E. Griffin & A. B. Myrick, *The Filostrato of Giovanni Boccaccio: A Translation with Parallel Text* (London, 1929; reprinted NY, 1967).

38 *Ambages* is not a rare noun in classical Latin: see Glare, *Oxford Latin Dictionary*, ambages. It occurs three times in the *Aeneid*: I, 342; VI, 29,99. Dante employs the term 'ambage' only once in the *Commedia*; there seems little doubt that, in doing so, he is thinking of *Aeneid* VI, 99.

39 For the idea that Boccaccio sometimes signposts Chaucer back to Dante, see J.A.W. Bennett, 'Chaucer, Dante and Boccaccio', in Boitani, *Trecento*, 89–113 (pp. 94–109); for an additional practical example, see above, p. 134. I can see nothing in the context of Fs VI, 17,3–4 which might have done this, excepting the word 'ambage' itself. Bersuire's Livy translation (discussed above) is the kind of French text that might possibly have served Chaucer here.

40 See L. Guilbert, et al., *Grand Larousse de la langue française*, 7 vols (Paris, 1971–8), Vol I, XCIII and *ambages*.

41 T&C V, 897 is the only incidence of *ambages* recorded by MED. OED records a number of incidences (none earlier than 1520), but notes that 'there has been a growing tendency to look upon it as merely L[atin]' (*ambage*).

42 See *Works of Chaucer*, p. 813. I have found Robinson's table to be substantially correct in its particulars; it has been of great use. Some additions and amendments are offered in my article 'Some Amendments to the Apparatus of Robinson's *Works of Chaucer*', *Notes and Queries*, NS, 30 (1983), p. 202.

43 See, for example, above pp. 110–12; and compare Fs VII, 10 & T&C V, 1170–76, Fs VIII, 14 & T&C V, 1688–94.

44 Employing such imagery, Troilus attempts (tragically) to forge a link between his love for Criseyde and the force which orders the universe: see I, 416; III, 1291; IV, 282; V, 641.

45 The ensemble of 'tale' and 'other thing collateral' bears an interesting relationship to the concept of *conjointure* established by Chrétien de Troyes in opening *Erec et Enide*. *Conjointure* (a term adapted from a well-known passage of Horace's *De Arte Poetica*) means ' "a whole made out of several parts" or simply "arrangement" '; as such, 'it is not a substitute for the *conte*, but something which a skilful poet can and must superimpose upon it' (Vinaver, *Rise of Romance*, pp. 36–7). See also Douglas Kelly, 'The Source and Meaning of *Conjointure* in Chrétien's *Erec* 14', *Viator*, 1 (1970), pp. 179–200.

46 For further notable examples of sedulous imitation following independent elaboration, compare: Fs II, 128,6–8, T&C II, 1321–3; III, 5, III, 239–45; III, 11, III, 344–50 (quoted above, p. 115); IV, 137, IV, 1422–8.

47 Compare: I, 57–II, 1 & I, 540–553; V, 71–VI, 1 & V, 680–93; VI, 34–VII, 1 & V, 1093–1106; VII, 106–VIII, 1 & V, 1555–68.

48 In VI, 533 Chaucer's 'non hardyment' owes more to the musicality of Boccaccio's verb phrase 'non ardirai' than it does to the literal sense: but such an instance is rare. The noun 'hardyment' appears nowhere else in Chaucer.

49 The twenty-nine examples that I have been able to identify are listed below. Where possible I have indicated in brackets the way in which Boccaccio's *ottava* is divided up by Chaucer. The presence of '½' simply indicates that Chaucer divides Boccaccio's ideas somewhere other than at the end of a line. In several cases (indicated with an asterisk) Chaucer reorders the sequence of Boccaccio's ideas.

Filostrato	*Troilus & Criseyde*	
I, 8	I, 64–77	
I, 28	I, 288–301	(3 + 5)
II, 13	I, 701–14	(3 + 5)
II, 33	I, 1044–57	(5 + 3)
II, 118	II, 1191–1204	(4 + 4)
III, 15	III, 372–85	(⋆)
III, 16	III, 386–99	(5 + 3)
III, 40	III, 1394–1407	(4 + 4)
III, 94	IV, 1–14	(3 + 5)
IV, 4	IV, 57–70	(4 + 4)
IV, 13	IV, 134–47	(4½ + 3½)
IV, 30	IV, 260–73	(5 + 3)
IV, 34	IV, 295–308	(3 + 5)
IV, 68	IV, 561–74	(4 + 4)
IV, 75	IV, 617–30	(4 + 4)
IV, 79	IV, 666–79	(⋆)
IV, 84	IV, 708–21	(4 + 4)
IV, 95	IV, 799–812	(4 + 4)
IV, 96	IV, 813–26	(6 + 2)
IV, 107	IV, 918–31	(6 + 2)
IV, 118	IV, 1156–69	(⋆)
IV, 131	IV, 1331–7, 1345–51	(2½ + 5½)

(between these 2 stanzas translating IV, 131, Chaucer inserts a stanza translating IV, 134)

V, 22	V, 281–94	(5½ + 2½)
V, 33	V, 386–99	(3 + 5)
V, 50	V, 512–25	(5½ + 2½)
V, 57	V, 589–602	(6 + 2)
V, 70	V, 666–79	(⋆)
VI, 15	V, 876–889	(4 + 4)
VIII, 25	V, 1744–57	(4 + 4)

50 In T&C I, 64–77 Chaucer spreads the ideas of Fs I, 8 over two stanzas rather than dividing them up and developing them separately as he does later in the *Troilus*; consequently, these two early stanzas prove somewhat repetitive.

51 See above, p. 34.

52 See Branca, *Opere di GB*, II, 860, note 59. But note also Par XVII, 129, where Cacciaguida urges Dante to write a vision that will set readers of bad conscience scratching: '"e lascia pur grattar dov'è la rogna"'.

53 See, for example, Fs IV, 40 where the *ottava*'s quadripartite structure is (as in many *cantare* stanzas) accentuated by the use of anaphora. Chaucer passed over all four ideas in this *ottava* of lyric complaint.

54 See HF 300–60 (and above, pp. 7, 16). Dido's words are identified as a 'compleynt' in HF 362.

55 T&C I, 1067: see above, pp. 102–4, where I discuss an earlier 'private commentary'.

56 See below, p. 146–7.

57 See Branca, *Opere di GB*, II, 862, note 90.

58 See *Design*, p. vi.

59 Chaucer's rendering of the *Filostrato* often brings an increase in expressive vehemence and intensity: see Barry Windeatt, 'The "Paynted Proces": Italian to English in Chaucer's *Troilus*', *English Miscellany*, 26–27 (1977–8), pp. 79–103. It is important to emphasise that Chaucer often achieves such intensification by compressing loose Italian arguments into single lines: for example, in translating Fs IV, 50 in IV, 435–41 he achieves expressive vehemence but avoids enjambement.

60 See, for example: IV, 15,3; IV, 50,2; VII, 51,7; VIII, 11,3&7.

61 See, for example: I, 40; V, 6. Chaucer sometimes separates subject from main verb to great poetic effect: see above, p. 128 and CT I, 1–12.

62 Chaucer does this elsewhere: see V, 27.

63 *Machaut's 'Lay de Confort'*, p. 18.

64 See II, 29, 1–3; II, 55,1 (and above, p. 75).

65 James Wimsatt, 'Guillaume de Machaut and Chaucer's *Troilus and Criseyde*', *Medium Aevum*, 45 (1976), 277–93 (p. 291). Wimsatt examines the song and its sources in some detail (pp. 287–91).

66 On Criseyde, see Wimsatt, *Machaut and 'Troilus'*, pp. 285–7; on Troilus, see pp. 279–82, 284–6.

67 For example: T&C IV, 519–20 adapts RR 6352–3; V, 1373–9 adapts some of the paradoxes piled up in RR 4263–4300; IV, 1–11 borrows from the account of Fortune in JRB 684–93.

68 See *Machaut and 'Troilus'*, p. 277.

69 La Vechia's advice on discerning the true purposes of a correspondent is remarkably similar in spirit to that offered by the author of a treatise for novice merchants (see above, p. 30): 'O s'alcun ti mandasse alcuno scritto,/Sì guarda ben la sua intenzione,/Ched e' non abia fintamente scritto.' (CLXXI, 9–11). For examples of 'cortese', see *Fiore* CXLII, 4; CXLIII, 13; CXLV, 1; CXLVI, 7. For 'franchezza' (and the argument that women are 'franche nate'), see CLXXXIII.

70 Foster, *Petrarch*, p. 29, translating a passage from *Familiares* XXI, 15 (cited above, p. 36).

71 For evidence of Chaucer's familiarity with these passages, see T&C III, 988–990 (Inf V, 103); III, 1625–8 & IV, 481–3 (V, 121–3); IV, 1538–40 & V, 599–602 (XXX, 1–4).

72 Compare Purg I, 1–3.

73 Peter Haidu observes that 'the basic narrative vocabulary of romance is *avanture*' ('Introduction' to Haidu, *Approaches*, 3–11 (p. 4)).

74 For similar phrases, see: T&C II, 817, III, 1228; PF 175. The phrase 'that joye it was to here' supplies a rhyme in LGW F 140 and a complete tail in *Sir Thopas* (VII, 768).

75 *Development*, p. 110.

76 Typical recapitulative phrases are: Fs III, 4,1 ('com'è detto avanti'); T&C III, 1394 ('of whom that I yow seye'); A&A 901 ('as y ʒou say'). In Fs I, 38,7 Boccaccio repeats a line (I, 26,7) 'secondo gli usi canterini' (Branca, *Opere di GB*, II, 849, note 21); in I, 31,1 he repeats a phrase from the final line of the preceding stanza, an expedient which is also 'di tradizione canterina, per aiutar la memoria di chi recitava' (Branca, *Opere di GB*, II, p. 849, note 23). T&C II, 637 closely resembles SqTl V, 558; and see above, p. 197, note 16. A&A 265–6 repeats the couplet at 229–30. For predictions of future narrative developments—which Branca (*Opere di GB*, II, 863, note 10) again denotes as characteristic 'della tecnica narrativa popolaresca e dei cantari'—see Fs V, 14,7–8 and VI, 8 (which Chaucer imitates in the stanza V, 764–770). See also T&C III, 1383–6 and A&A 1354–6 (which anticipates 2131–2).

77 On the habitual use of predicate formulae which feature *seyde* in the ME romances, see Wittig, pp. 19–20; on predicate formulae in general, see Joseph

Duggan, *The Song of Roland: Formulaic Style and Poetic Craft* (Berkeley, 1973), pp. 108–9.

78 II, 600; II, 1494; III, 699; IV, 354; V, 1729. II, 600; II, 1228; II, 1494; III, 891; IV, 354; IV, 467.

79 The term 'weylawey' is used on thirteen occasions, the first being in III, 304.

80 See A&A 637–51, 1273–84, 2281–2304 and above, pp. 98–100. In A&A 1273 the indecisive knight is (like Pandarus in V, 1729) 'stille so ston'.

81 See above, pp. 126–7. Belisaunt sends the maidens away on the arrival of Amis (565–7).

82 Jonathan Culler, *Structuralist Poetics* (London, 1975), p. 53.

83 See Par II, 1–9.

84 John Burrow observes that 'Gower stands off from the [popular English romance] traditions so generously represented in the work of Chaucer' (*Ricardian Poetry*, p. 29; my addition in brackets).

85 The set-piece descriptions of Diomede, Criseyde and Troilus in conventional romance terms in V, 799–840 inevitably distance us from these characters. This distancing effect is continued when the narrative proper resumes in V, 840: Diomede, pressing on with his seduction, is said to be 'as fressh as braunche in May' (V, 844; and see V, 847, 848 and 854).

86 Discussed and translated above, p. 93.

87 This brief account of the ending of T&C, which necessarily concentrates upon stylistic register, may be supplemented by the fine article by Bonnie Wheeler, 'Dante, Chaucer and the Ending of *Troilus and Criseyde*', *Philological Quarterly*, 61 (1982), pp. 105–123.

Chapter 7: Chaucer and Boccaccio   pp. 141–149

1 See Piero Boitani, *Chaucer and Boccaccio*; Boitani, *English Medieval Narrative in the Thirteenth and Fourteenth Centuries*, translated by J. K. Hall (Cambridge, 1982), pp. 193–202; Boitani, 'Style, Iconography and Narrative: the Lesson of the *Teseida*', in Boitani, *Trecento*, pp. 185–199; Burrow, *Medieval Writers*, pp. 57–8; Elizabeth Salter, *Fourteenth-Century English Poetry. Contexts and Readings* (Oxford, 1983), pp. 130–181.

2 See Rajna, *Cantare dei Cantari*, esp. *ottava* 26 (p. 430). Both of the surviving MSS of this poem are thought to date from the first half of the fifteenth century: see Rajna, pp. 419–25.

3 See Branca, *Cantare trecentesco*, p. 57, note 1.

4 Limentani diligently records such traits in his excellent edition of the *Teseida*.

5 For a convenient table of correspondences between KnT and Tes, see Robinson, p. 670. There is no firm evidence to suggest that Chaucer's copy of Tes contained Boccaccio's glosses. Limentani's edition of Tes is based upon the autograph MS (Biblioteca Laurenziana, Florence, Cod. Acquisti e Doni 325).

6 See Tes I, 52 and 61–65. The warfare described here has few epic qualities; it suggests, rather, the conditions prevailing in a squabble between two medieval towns, and parallels a passage in F-e-F (III, 22). Boccaccio's battle descriptions are, compared with those of Chaucer and the best English romancers, remarkably inept.

7 See *Cantare trecentesco*, pp. 69–70. Branca is also troubled by the tenor of Palemone's response: 'è il linguaggio che si userebbe in un mercato!' (p. 70).

8 See Robinson, *Works of Chaucer*, p. 682, notes to 2837, 2987 ff.

9 See above, p. 134.

10 See Tes XII, 84 and above, p. 41.

11 For an artist's pattern-book (dating from around 1400 and featuring numerous sketches of various birds) see Magdalene College, Cambridge, MS Pepys 1916; and see Bibliotheca Pepysiana, *A Descriptive Catalogue of the Library of Samuel Pepys*, 4 parts (London, 1914–22), Part III (by M. R. James), *Medieval Manuscripts*, pp. 47–51. For

the distinction that Chaucer draws between 'my tale' and 'other thing collateral' in composing the *Troilus*, see above, pp. 123, 198.

12 See Tes I, 1–3; HF 518–22; Anel 1–21.

13 See *The Parlement of Foules. An Interpretation* (Oxford, 1957), p. 82. The stanzas in question are Tes VII, 50–66, PF 183–280. For translations and discussion of the Italian stanzas, see Brewer, *Parlement*, pp. 43–45, 138–40; Havely, pp. 129–30, 208–9; B. A. Windeatt, *Chaucer's Dream Poetry: Sources and Analogues* (Cambridge, 1982), pp. xiii–xiv, 81–83.

14 *The Parlement*, p. 62.

15 See AV (A&B) III, 61–75, PF 141–54.

16 'The *locus amoenus* or "beautiful place", which became the heavenly landscape of literary visions and dreams, is basically a Mediterranean landscape, an ideal originating in Greece, Italy and Palestine' (A. C. Spearing, *Medieval Dream-Poetry* (Cambridge, 1976), p. 17). The garden of the *Visione* conforms closely to the typical *locus* that Spearing proceeds to describe; it is particularly indebted to the garden of Love presented by Andreas Capellanus in *De Amore* (see *Opere di GB*, III, 708–9).

17 The three streams in the *Visione* are symbolic representations of the three kinds of love defined by Fiammetta in the *Filocolo*'s garden parliament: see Fc IV, 44,3–7 (from which I quote in the text); *Opere di GB*, I, 872; III, 710.

18 Windeatt observes that the juxtaposition of these three domains presents 'a comprehensive range of the ways that love is to be known and expressed' (*Chaucer's Dream Poetry*, p. xiv).

19 See AV (A&B) L, 43–51; PF 693–9.

20 *Geoffrey Chaucer* (London, 1974), p. xi. We are promised a 'later treatment' of these ideas, which are set out in a brief 'Author's Note'.

21 See Quaglio in *Opere di GB*, II, 667–8.

22 See CN XLVI, 5; CD XVIII, 10–12 (and above, p. 35).

23 See *Ninfale fiesolano*, edited by Armando Balduino in *Opere di GB*, III, 275–6.

24 See Inf XXXIII, 13–75; CT VII, 2407–62.

25 See Robert G. Benson, *Medieval Body Language: A Study of the Use of Gesture in Chaucer's Poetry*, Anglistica, 21 (Copenhagen, 1980), esp. pp. 111–6.

26 Windeatt, *'Paynted Proces'*, p. 103.

27 For a full account of these techniques in NF, see Balduino, *Tradizione canterina*, pp. 30–74.

28 See NF 242,7; 286,2; and see above, pp. 82, 136.

29 See McKenzie, *Le noie*, p. XXIII: 'come a padre figlio'.

30 See Sapegno, *Poeti minori*, p. 349.

31 See Sapegno, *Pagine*, pp. 141–2.

32 For the full text of Pucci's delightful seventeen-line *sonetto*, see Sapegno, *Poeti minori*, p. 351; I quote lines 1–4. In lines 5–8 Pucci complains that the effort of poetic composition keeps him awake at night, tossing and turning in his bed 'cento e cento volte'. Chaucer might have sympathised: see BD 1–15, 221–69.

33 See Ricci, *Opere in versi*, pp. 528, 540.

34 See above, p. 91.

35 *OE & ME Poetry*, p. 199.

36 Brewer, *English and European Traditions*, p. 4.

37 *Stylistic and narrative structures*, p. 61.

38 See above, p. 138.

39 See NF 9,2–6; 30,8; 41,5–6; 116,1; 328,1–2; 372,7–8; 433,3–5.

40 *Allegory of Love*, p. 299. This conversion of the 'popular' to the 'respectable' often proves essential for the formation of new, 'official' genres to supercede those that, through continual reproduction, have lost their expressive potential: see Jauss, *Aesthetic of Reception*, p. 106.

41 For a succinct account of this tradition, see C. P. Brand, *Ludovico Ariosto. A preface to the 'Orlando Furioso'* (Edinburgh, 1974), pp. 46–56.

42 *Allegory of Love*, p. 299.
43 Burrow, *Ricardian Poetry*, p. 21 (summarising pp. 12–21).

Conclusion   p. 151

1 See Branca, *Nostalgie*, p. 91; McKenzie, *Le noie*, pp. XLVII–XLVIII.

Index

de' Ferrari, Gabriel Giolito, 169
Fiore, 12, 54–6, 62, 137, 172
Fiorio e Biancifiore, Cantare di, 40, 42–4, 78, 82, 148
Flamenca, 40
Fleming, John V., 182
Floire et Blancheflor (French romances), 40–46, 86, 187
Florence, 5, 6, 23–5, 28, 87, 147–9, 151
Floris and Blancheflour (English romance), 40, 72
Floris and Blauncheflur (Egerton MS), 78, 84
Fortune, 11–13, 20–21, 91, 104, 123, 144, 195, 200
Foster, Kenelm, 200
Francesca da Rimini, 89
Franceschetti, Antonio, 194
Francesco di Marco da Prato (merchant), 30
Frederick of Aragon, 23
French romance, 28, 40–45, 76, 86–90, 97, 104, 135, 151
Frescobaldi, Giovanni, 31
Froissart, Jean, 9; *Dit dou bleu Chevalier*, 170; *Paradys d'Amours*, 14
Fusco, Jacobello, 32

Gallus, 51–2
Gamelyn, 78, 80, 194
Geoffrey of Monmouth, 19
Geoffrey of Vinsauf, *Poetria Nova*, 104, 121, 128, 192
Giano, 19
Gibello, 80, 87
Giotto, 18
Giovanna I, Queen of Naples (1343–82), 24
Giovanni da Strada, 28
Goliard verses, 26
Gonzaga, Guido, 27
Gordon, R. K., 74
Gower, John, 6, 53, 201
Gozzi, Maria, 74
Granson, Oton de, 36
Graziolo dei Bambaglioli, *Inferno* commentary, 31
Green, R. F., 195
Guerra degli otto santi, Cantare della, 79, 90
Gui de Warewic, 184
Guido delle Colonne, *Historia destructionis Troiae*, 74, 183
Guillaume de Lorris, 8, 10, 12, 51–2, 62, 68, See also *Roman de la Rose*
Guingamor, 194
Guy de Warwik, Le Rommant de, 184
Guy of Warwick, 46, 61, 150, 187

Haidu, Peter, 200
Hainault, Philippa of, 36
Harley MS 2253, 193
Hauvette, H., 107
Havely, N. R., 115, 120
hendecasyllabics, 75–6

Henry III of England, 29
Henry VII, Emperor, 32
Henryson, Robert, 74
Hoffman, Richard L., 59
Holcot, Robert, 70, 180
Homer, 51–2
Horace, *Ars poetica*, 25, 198
Howard, Donald R., 184
Hymen, 69–70

Ilario, 50, 120
Intelligenza, 12, 13, 22, 40, 172
internal debate, 98–100, 136, 143
inventio, 84
Isidore of Seville, 187; *Cronaca*, 27
Istorietta troiana, 188
Ivo, bishop of Chartres (attributed to), *Liber Sacrificiorum*, 26

Jason, 14, 59
Jauss, H. R., 94, 189, 202
Jean de Meun, 10, 27, 41, 51–4, 62, 68–70, 72, 179. See also *Roman de la Rose*
Jean le Bon, 29
Jehan Acart de Hesdin, *Prise amoreuse*, 34
Jerome, *Contra Jovinianum*, 26
John of Gaunt, 37
John of Wales, 72
Jordan, Robert, 104, 189

Kane, George, 72
Kean, P. M., 8
King Alisaunder, 90
King Horn, 85, 191
Kynde, 136

La Donna del Vergiù, 89–90, 93
Lai le Freine, 87, 190
Langland, William, 61
Latini, Brunetto, 10, 55, 152; *Rettorica*, 59; *Tesoretto*, 10–15, 55, 59, 75, 146, 151, 172, 184; *Trésor*, 10
Léonard, E. G., 28
Lewis, C. S., 2, 3, 9, 49, 72, 149
Liber de dictis antiquorum, 26
Linus, 52
Liombruno, Storia di, 87
Livy, 26, 122
locus amoenus, 13, 143
Lollius, 50, 120
London, 23, 35–8, 149
Loomis, L. H., 190, 191
Lowes, J. L., 179, 186
Lucan, 19, 46–7, 182; *De bello civili*, 47; *Pharsalia*, 51
Ludwig of Bavaria, 23
Lyons, Richard (merchant and financier), 28

Machaut, Guillaume de, 8–10, 22, 134, 136; *Dit de la fonteinne amoreuse*, 170; *Dit dou Vergier*, 14; *Jugement dou Roy de Behaingne*, 14, 200; *Remede de Fortune*, 14, 136